The Expeditions

Letter from the General Editor

The Library of Arabic Literature is a new series offering Arabic editions and English translations of key works of classical and pre-modern Arabic literature, as well as anthologies and thematic readers. Books in the series are edited and translated by distinguished scholars of Arabic and Islamic studies, and are published in parallel-text format with Arabic and English on facing pages. The Library of Arabic Literature includes texts from the pre-Islamic era to the cusp of the modern period, and encompasses a wide range of genres, including poetry, poetics, fiction, religion, philosophy, law, science, history, and historiography.

Supported by a grant from the New York University Abu Dhabi Institute, and established in partnership with NYU Press, the Library of Arabic Literature produces authoritative Arabic editions and modern, lucid English translations, with the goal of introducing the Arabic literary heritage to scholars and students, as well as to a general audience of readers.

Philip F. Kennedy
General Editor, Library of Arabic Literature

كِتَابُ ٱلْمَغَازِي

لأَبِي عُرْوَةَ مَعْمَرِ بْنِ رَاشِدٍ البَصْرِيّ

فِي رِوَايَةِ

أَبِي بَكْرٍ عَبْدِ الرَّزَّاقِ بْنِ هَمَّام الصَّنْعَانِيّ عنه

The Expeditions

An Early Biography of Muḥammad

by

Maʿmar ibn Rāshid

according to the recension of

ʿAbd al-Razzāq al-Ṣanʿānī

Edited and translated by
SEAN W. ANTHONY

Foreword by
M. A. S. ABDEL HALEEM

Dev Publishers & Distributors
New Delhi

Published by
Dev Publishers & Distributors
Second Floor, Prakashdeep,
22, Delhi Medical Association Road,
Darya Ganj, New Delhi – 110 002

www.devbooks.co.in

ISBN 978-93-81406-75-5

Dev Publishers & Distributors, 2017

Printed in India.

For Susu and Suraya,
who love Muḥammad

Table of Contents

Foreword

Scholars of Arabic literature and readers with an interest in Arabic and Islamic civilization are now most fortunate to have available to them the works being published as the Library of Arabic Literature, the first series to attempt a systematic coverage of the Arabic literary heritage. The editors have already shown good judgment in selecting books for the series, and the present volume, *The Expeditions*, an early biography of the Prophet Muḥammad by Maʿmar ibn Rāshid, is no exception.

Maʿmar ibn Rāshid (d. 153/770) was a contemporary of Ibn Isḥāq (d. 151/768), author of the famous *Al-Sīrah al-Nabawiyyah* (*The Prophetic Biography*), also known as *Sīrat rasūl Allāh* (*The Biography of the Messenger of God*), which has come to be widely circulated and is known simply as the *Sīrah*. Alfred Guillaume's English translation of Ibn Isḥāq's *Sīrah* was published more than fifty years ago,[1] so the English translation of another important early text about the life of the Prophet Muḥammad is well overdue. Indeed, there is a real need for more such texts from the early Islamic period to see the light of day.

It should be pointed out that these two works are not the earliest writings on the subject of the Prophet's life. In his discussion of the genres of *maghāzī* and *sīrah*, the Ottoman literary historian Ḥājjī Khalīfah (d. 1067/1657) reports that Ibn Isḥāq compiled his work from preexisting materials, and goes on to identify ʿUrwah ibn al-Zubayr (d. 93/711–12) as the earliest to gather material on the topic.[2] Thus, both Maʿmar ibn Rāshid and Ibn Isḥāq must have taken their information from written sources as well as authenticated oral reports collected by ʿUrwah and others.[3]

The major contribution of Maʿmar ibn Rāshid and Ibn Isḥāq was to bring the material from different sources together in one place. Other early Muslim scholars immediately recognized the value of this activity. This is why we have Ibn Isḥāq's work in a recension by the later Ibn Hishām (d. 212/828 or 218/833), and Maʿmar ibn Rāshid's work in a recension by ʿAbd al-Razzāq al-Ṣanʿānī (d. 211/827). Similarly, written material about the pillars of Islam—including ritual prayer (*ṣalāh*), the giving of alms (*zakāh*), fasting in Ramadan (*ṣawm*), and pilgrimage to Mecca (ḥajj)—cannot be assumed to have appeared for the first time at the end of the first or at the beginning of the second Hijri century. Muslims had been continually engaging in ritual activities, and writing about them, since the time of the Prophet. Nor should it be assumed that hadiths (reports about the Prophet Muḥammad) were only written down when al-Bukhārī (d. 256/870) and the other famous collectors of hadiths of that era produced their great compilations. Nonetheless, the compilation by Maʿmar ibn Rāshid of the present book was significant in its time for preserving the earlier scattered material.

The Arabic edition produced here, carefully edited from the extant manuscripts, as well as the translation into lucid English, have been undertaken by a gifted young scholar. What is more, his detailed introduction contains much useful guidance for the reader. Scholars of early Islam, Arabists, and interested readers will find this volume a welcome addition to the literature available and to their libraries.

Professor M. A. S. Abdel Haleem, OBE
School of Oriental and African Studies, University of London

Acknowledgements

The idea for this translation first came to me a decade ago while reading through the back matter of Michael Cook's excellent monograph *Muḥammad*, published in Oxford University Press's now-defunct "Past Masters" series in 1983. Cook opined that, given the daunting size of the English translation of Ibn Hishām's redaction of the biography of Muḥammad compiled by Ibn Isḥāq, "an annotated translation of Maʿmar ibn Rāshid's account as transmitted by ʿAbd al-Razzāq ibn Hammām would be a welcome addition to the literature."[4] Reading these words as a first-year graduate student some two decades after they had been written, I presumed that the feat had already been accomplished. In fact, it had not.

That same first year of graduate study at the University of Chicago, I would also face the formidable challenges of translating *maghāzī* literature for the first time. I was fortunate enough to do so in nearly ideal conditions: in a class supervised by Fred M. Donner. I recall with fondness convening in Prof. Donner's office in the Oriental Institute. Seated around a large wooden table, my classmates and I pored over every jot and tittle of the text under Donner's tutelage. It was a great place to begin a journey—a journey made all the more amazing by the instruction I would receive at the hands of two of the finest Arabists I have had the pleasure to know, Prof. Wadād al-Qāḍī and Prof. Tahera Qutbuddin. To all three of these mentors, I remain profoundly thankful.

In pursuing this project I have incurred many a debt that, for now, I can only repay with gratitude. I am deeply grateful to Phil Kennedy, James Montgomery, Shawkat Toorawa, and the rest of editorial board of the Library of Arabic Literature (LAL), who were so open to taking my project under their wings and who continued to nurture the project and me as I gradually came to grasp the incredible vision of the series. Chip Rossetti, LAL's managing editor, was a constant guide and ever helpful throughout the project's realization. Rana Mikati lent me her keen eye and saved me from a number of errors in translation. Most of all, my project editor, Joseph Lowry, deserves my deepest gratitude. Continually challenging me and pushing me to better refine the translation, Prof. Lowry saved me from many errors and missteps along the way. If this project is any way successful and its fruits deemed praiseworthy, he surely deserves as much of the credit as I. "As iron sharpens iron does one person's wit sharpen the other's" (Prov. 20:17). Of course, any faults this work contains are mine alone.

I was fortunate to be able to work on this project unimpeded for the 2012–13 academic year thanks to the generous support of a grant from the National Endowment for the Humanities and the willingness of the University of Oregon's History Department to grant me a yearlong leave. That this volume joins the ranks of the many illustrious projects funded by the endowment is an especially great honor. It is my hope that the NEH's support for the flourishing of the humanities, and thus enrichment of all humanity's heritage, will continue to thrive in the decades and centuries to come.

Many less directly involved in the project also made its current form possible. I must thank Feryal Selim for helping me acquire digital scans of the Murad Mulla manuscript from the Süleymaniye Library, as well as my many undergraduate students who allowed me to try out early drafts of this translation in class and who provided me with interesting and often unexpected feedback. An old friend, Craig Howell, provided me with great conversation and excellent insight into how a nonspecialist might read the text.

To my wife and children, I offer my deepest and most heartfelt thanks. You are beyond all else the inspiration behind my strivings and the center from which I draw my strength.

Introduction

The Expeditions (Ar. *Kitāb al-Maghāzī*) by Maʿmar ibn Rāshid (d. 153/770) is an early biography of the Prophet Muḥammad that dates to the second/eighth century and is preserved in the recension of his student ʿAbd al-Razzāq ibn Hammām of Sanaa (d. 211/827). The text is exceptional because, alongside Ibn Hishām's (d. 218/834) redaction of the prophetic biography of Muḥammad ibn Isḥāq (d. 150/767–68),[5] *The Expeditions* is one of the two earliest and most seminal examples of the genre of prophetic biography in Arabic literature to have survived.

Early biographies of the Prophet Muḥammad—and by "early" I mean written within two centuries of his death in 10/632—are an extremely rare commodity. In fact, no surviving biography dates earlier than the second/eighth century. The rarity of such early biographies is sure to pique the curiosity of even a casual observer. The absence of earlier biographical writings about Muḥammad is not due to Muslims' lack of interest in telling the stories of their prophet. At least in part, the dearth of such writings is rooted in the concerns of many of the earliest Muslims that any recording of a book of stories about Muḥammad's life would inevitably divert their energies from, and even risk eclipsing, the status of Islam's sacred scripture, the Qur'an, as the most worthy focus of devotion and scholarship. This paucity of early biographies is also partially the result of the fact that, before the codification of the Qur'an, the Arabic language had not fully emerged as a medium in which written literary works were produced.

For modern historians enthralled by such issues, the attempt to tease out the consequences of this chronological gap between Muḥammad's lifetime and our earliest narrative sources about him can be all-consuming. Debates thus continue in earnest over whether we may know anything at all about the "historical Muḥammad" given the challenges presented by the source material. But what is meant exactly by the "historical Muḥammad"? Modern historians speak of the historical Muḥammad as a type of shorthand for an historical understanding of Muḥammad's life and legacy that is humanistic, secular, and cosmopolitan. This is to say that any talk of a historical Muḥammad is merely an interpretation of his life that is distinct from, but not necessarily incompatible with, either how his faith community imagined him centuries after his death or how rival faith communities viewed him through the lens of their own hostile religious polemic. Yet all modern understandings of Muḥammad inevitably derive from a body of texts written by a faith community, for we have no contemporary witnesses to Muḥammad's prophetic mission, and the earliest testimonies that do survive are penned by outsiders whose depictions and understanding of Islam in its earliest years are sketchy at best and stridently hostile at worst.[6] Hence, to speak of a *historical* Muḥammad is not to speak of the *real* Muḥammad. We recognize that we seek to understand, explain, and reconstruct the life of a man using the tools and methods of modern historical criticism. Whatever form such a project takes, and regardless of the methodology adopted, there is no escaping the basic conundrum facing all historians of early Islam: they must fashion their reconstruction of Muḥammad's biography from the memories and interpretations of the community that revered him as Prophet. In other words, historians concerned with such topics must dare wrestle with angels.[7]

Today, many scholars remain steadfastly optimistic that writing a biography of the historical Muḥammad is feasible and worthwhile,[8] though just as many take a decidedly more pessimistic view. More than a few have dismissed the idea of writing Muḥammad's historical biography as fundamentally impossible.[9] This debate remains intractable and scholarly consensus elusive. It is my pleasure then, and in some ways my great relief, to table this contentious debate and instead present the reader with one of the earliest biographies of Muḥammad ever composed. This relatively straightforward task, although not without formidable challenges, allows one to sidestep the fraught questions surrounding the man behind the tradition and permit a broader audience to encounter the early tradition on its own terms.

Much of this book's contents relate the story one might expect of any telling of Muḥammad's life. A boy born among the denizens of the Hejaz region of Western Arabia is orphaned by the unexpected deaths of first his parents and then his grandfather. As the child grows into a man, omens portend his future greatness, but his adult life initially unfolds as an otherwise prosaic and humble one, not too atypical for an Arabian merchant whose life spanned the late sixth and the early seventh centuries AD. Working for a widowed merchant woman of modest means, he ekes out an existence in her employ, until he eventually weds her and strives to live a modest, honorable life in a manner that earns him the esteem and admiration of his tribe, the Quraysh. The man's life forever changes when one night he encounters an angel atop a mountain on the outskirts of his hometown, Mecca. The angel charges him to live the rest of his days as God's last prophet and the steward and messenger of His final revelation to humankind.

This man proclaims his message to be one with the monotheism first taught by Abraham, the venerable patriarch of the Hebrew Bible and the common ancestor of the Arabs and Jews. Denouncing the cultic practices surrounding Mecca's shrine, the Kaaba, and the dissolute lives of its patron tribe, the Quraysh, as pagan, idolatrous, and morally corrupt, the man soon finds himself at odds with those who profit both economically and politically from the status quo. The Quraysh reckon the man's prophetic message a serious threat to their livelihood and power, and soon the prophet and his earliest followers suffer persecutions and tribulations that take them to the precipice of despair. Yet God at last provides succor to His servants: Two warring tribes, the Aws and the Khazraj, living in a city north of Mecca called Yathrib, invite the man and his people to live in their midst, agreeing to submit to whatever peace the Meccan prophet might bring.

Fleeing persecution, the prophet undertakes his emigration to Yathrib, his Hijrah, where he establishes a new community (*ummah*), united not by tribal affiliation and genealogy but by faith and loyalty to the prophet's message. Yathrib becomes Medina, "the Prophet's city" (*madīnat al-nabī*). The days of persecution now ending, the prophet leads his followers in battle to conquer Arabia and forge a new polity guided by God's hand. These early conquests augur a greater destiny: the spread of his religion far beyond the deserts of Arabia. Within a hundred years of the prophet's death, his community stretches from Spain to the steppes of Central Asia, and the rest, as they say, is history.

Though the above biographical details are widely known, few laypersons recognize that none come to us from the Qur'an. Even if the scripture at times references such events implicitly, it never narrates them. Notwithstanding its inestimable value, the Qur'an offers little material that might allow the modern historian to reconstruct the life of its Messenger, even in its most basic outlines. Moreover, though Muḥammad, as God's Messenger, delivered the Qur'an to his early followers and thence humanity, Muslims did not regard the Qur'an as a record of the Prophet's own words or actions—rather, the Qur'an was solely God's Word, and with the death of His Messenger, the canon of the scripture closed. For detailed narratives of the lives of Muḥammad and his Companions we are wholly dependent on a later tradition external to the Qur'an.

Despite its limited utility in reconstructing the biography of Muḥammad, the sacred corpus known as the Qur'an (Ar. *al-qur'ān*; lit., the "recitation" or "reading") is still very likely to be our earliest and most authentic testimony to Muḥammad's teachings and the beliefs of his earliest followers. The scripture was organized and arranged into a codex (Ar. *muṣḥaf*), not within the lifetime of Muḥammad but under his third successor, or caliph (Ar. *khalīfa*), ʿUthmān ibn ʿAffān (r. 23–35/644–56). ʿUthmān's codex was subsequently refined and reworked under the caliph ʿAbd al-Malik ibn Marwān between 84/703 and 85/704.[10] A parallel, albeit much slower and more fraught, process was undertaken by early Muslims to preserve the prophet's words and deeds, which led to the formation of the second sacred corpus of Islam, known collectively as hadith (Ar. *al-ḥadīth*; lit., "sayings"), which is distinct from the Qur'an and is often referred to as "traditions." Unlike the Qur'an, which Muslims codified in a matter of decades, the hadith canon took centuries to form.[11]

The Expeditions belongs to a subgenre of the hadith known as the *maghāzī* traditions, which narrates specific events from the life of the Prophet Muḥammad and his Companions and whose collection and compilation into a discrete genre of prophetic biography preceded the canonization of hadith considerably.[12] The Arabic word *maghāzī* does not connote "biography" in the modern sense. It is the plural of *maghzāh*, which literally means "a place where a raid/expedition (*ghazwah*) was made." The English title I have adopted, *The Expeditions*, is serviceable as translations go, but may lead an English-speaking audience to ask why these traditions are ostensibly gathered under the rubric of Muḥammad's military campaigns rather than, say, "biography" as such.

As is often the case with translations, the English "expeditions" does not quite do justice to the fullest sense of the Arabic *maghāzī*, for much of what this book contains has little to do with accounts of military expeditions or the glories of martial feats, although there are plenty of those.[13] The word *maghāzī* invokes the discrete locations of key battles and raids conducted by the Prophet and his followers, yet it also invokes a more metaphorical meaning that is not restricted to targets of rapine or scenes of battle and skirmishes. *Maghāzī* are also sites of sacred memory; the sum of all events worthy of recounting. A *maghzāh*, therefore, is also a place where any memorable event transpired and, by extension, the *maghāzī* genre distills all the events and stories of sacred history that left their mark on the collective memory of Muḥammad's community of believers.

The origins of this particular collection of *maghāzī* traditions (for there were many books with the title *Kitāb al-Maghāzī*)[14] begins with a tale of serendipity. As the story goes, Maʿmar ibn Rāshid was a Persian slave from Basra who traveled the lands of Islam trading wares for his Arab masters from the Azd tribe. While traveling through Syria trading and selling, Maʿmar sought out the rich and powerful court of the Marwānids. Seeking this court out required boldness: the Marwānids were the caliphal dynasty that reigned supreme over the Umayyad empire throughout the first half of the second/eighth century. When Maʿmar arrived at the court, it was his good fortune to find the royal family busy making preparations for a grand wedding banquet, and thus eager to buy his wares for the festivities. Though Maʿmar was a mere slave, the noble family treated him generously and spent lavishly on his goods. Somewhat boldly, Maʿmar interjected to pursue a more uncommon sort of remuneration: "I am but a slave," he protested. "Whatever you grant me will merely become my masters' possession. Rather, please speak to this man on my behalf that he might teach me the Prophet's traditions."[15] That "man" of whom Maʿmar spoke was, by most accounts, the greatest Muslim scholar of his generation: Ibn Shihāb al-Zuhrī (d. 124/742). Indeed, al-Zuhrī's stories about Muḥammad and his earliest followers comprise the bulk of the material Maʿmar preserves in this volume.

It is somewhat fitting that this book should have had its inception at a banquet, for the book itself is a banquet of sorts—a feast of sacred memory. This book takes one not only into halls of history but also through the passages of memory. Nostalgia permeates its stories. Sifting through its pages, the flavors of memory wash over the palate: the piquant spice of destiny, the bittersweet flavor of saturnine wisdom, the sweetness of redemption, dashes of humor and adventure, and the all-pervasive aroma of the holy.

The *maghāzī* tradition in general and Maʿmar's *Maghāzī* in particular are therefore not merely rote recitations of events and episodes from Muḥammad's life. They are more potent than that. The *maghāzī* tradition is a cauldron in which the early Muslims, culturally ascendant and masters over a new imperial civilization, mixed their ideals and visions of their model man, Muḥammad, and brewed them with the triumphalism of a victory recently savored. Muslims recorded and compiled these traditions as their newborn community surveyed the wonders of a journey traveled to a destination hardly imagined at its outset.

The origins and composition of *The Expeditions*

The Expeditions is best understood not as a conventionally authored book produced by the efforts of a single person but as an artifact of a series of teacher–pupil relationships between three renowned scholars of the early Islamic period. These scholars are Ibn Shihāb al-Zuhrī (d. 124/742) of Medina, Maʿmar ibn Rāshid (d. 153/770) of Basra, and ʿAbd al-Razzāq ibn Hammām of Sanaa (d. 211/827). The relationship between the latter two scholars in particular produced a number of books that have survived until our day, this volume being merely one.[16] This serial teacher–pupil nexus is of the utmost importance for understanding not only how this book came into being, but also for reading the book and understanding why its structure unfolds the way it does. Simply put, the traditions contained in *The Expeditions* represent, for the most part, the lectures of al-Zuhrī recorded by Maʿmar, which Maʿmar in turn supplemented with materials from his other, more minor teachers when lecturing to his own students. Among these students was ʿAbd al-Razzāq, who committed Maʿmar's lectures to writing and thus preserved the book in the form in which it has survived until today.[17] These methods were, in effect, how most books on topics such as history, law, and religious learning were made in second and third/eighth and ninth centuries, but more on this below.

What this means, of course, is that Maʿmar is not the "author" of this text in the conventional sense, which is not, however, to say that he is not directly responsible for this text. My assignation of authorship to him is not arbitrary; in my estimation he remains the pivotal personality responsible for its content and form, even if speaking of his "authorship" necessarily requires some qualifications. *The Expeditions* actually contains many authorial voices that are not Maʿmar's, including those of his teachers and, more rarely, that of his student ʿAbd al-Razzāq. How does one explain this?

The simplest place to begin is to point out a formal characteristic of early Arabic literary texts that dominates most narrative writing from the time of its emergence in the first half of the second/eighth century. This formal characteristic is the *isnād-khabar* ("chain-report") form, a crucial couplet that forms the building blocks of sacred, historical, and even literary narratives and that gives rise to the distinctively anecdotal character of Islamic historical writing and much of Arabic literature.[18] The word *khabar* and its more sacred counterpart *ḥadīth* convey the sense of "report," "account," or even "saying." (This last meaning is especially true for the word *ḥadīth*, most frequently used to refer to the sayings of the Prophet.) The word *isnād*, on the other hand, refers to a chain of supporting authorities that ostensibly certifies the veracity of the account. Every text utilizing this form begins by citing a chain of successive authorities who passed on the story one to another, and only then proceeds to relate the actual narrative.

In practice, the process works like this: Maʿmar's student ʿAbd al-Razzāq commits to memory and records his teacher's tradition (i.e., a *khabar* as related by him) but ʿAbd al-Razzāq also memorizes the chain of authorities (*isnād*) that

Maʿmar cites before he begins relating his tradition. This chain of authorities presumably goes back to eyewitnesses of the events, although in practice this is not always the case. Such chains are also cumulative. On any subsequent occasion in which ʿAbd al-Razzāq relates the tradition, he will begin by citing Maʿmar as his authority for the account and then continue to list all of Maʿmar's authorities before he relates the text of the account itself. Although citing *isnād*s is an archaic tradition, it is also a living one: Muslims today still relate such traditions with chains of transmission that reach back to the first generation of Muslims.[19]

These narratives are usually fairly short, although a *khabar* can be rather long in the *maghāzī* genre. *Khabar*s tend to remain relatively short, for example, in works concerned with Islamic ritual and law. The important point to keep in mind is that they are self-contained textual units that proliferated among early Muslims before the existence of any book or any similar type of systematic compilation gathered them together—that is, their transmission was initially oral and their reception initially aural. Such narratives were gathered and preserved by the earliest compilers like precious pearls, worthy of appreciation on the merits of their individual beauty and value alone. Yet, like any collector of pearls is wont to do, these precious pearls of narrative were also arranged to make literary necklaces of sorts, which became the first books. These books could be arranged according to diverse interests: legal and ritual topics (*fiqh*), the exegesis of the Qur'an (*tafsīr*), or, as in the present case, stories of the Prophet's life and the experiences of his earliest followers. With this systematic presentation of narrative material, the literary phase of early Islamic historiography begins.[20]

It is difficult to date the beginnings of *maghāzī* literature with precision because the earliest exempla of the genre are lost or are only partially preserved, sometimes in highly redacted forms, in later works. Maʿmar ibn Rāshid's most influential teacher, Ibn Shihāb al-Zuhrī of Medina, is a crucial trailblazer in the composition of *maghāzī* traditions, but the Islamic tradition names other scholars who predate al-Zuhrī. Two of these merit particular mention.

Abān ibn ʿUthmān (d. 101–5/719–23), a son of the third caliph ʿUthmān ibn ʿAffān (r. 23–35/644–55), is reported as being among the first, if not *the* first, to write a book containing "the conduct (*siyar*) of the Prophet and his expeditions (*maghāzī*)."[21] The sole person to relate a detailed story of Abān's writing activities is the Abbasid-era historian al-Zubayr ibn Bakkār (d. 256/870). According to him, Abān's project to compile the story of Muḥammad's life was first undertaken in 82/702 at the behest of the Umayyad prince, and later caliph, Sulaymān ibn ʿAbd al-Malik, who even furnished Abān with ten scribes (*kuttāb*) and all the parchment he required for the project. Sulaymān, however, was incensed when he actually read the fruit of Abān's labors: the text was bereft of tales of Sulaymān and Abān's Umayyad ancestors from Mecca and was instead chock-full of the virtues of Muḥammad's Medinese Companions, the Allies (Ar. *al-anṣār*). How could this be, the prince demanded, when the Allies had betrayed the caliph 'Uthmān, of blessed memory, and Abān's father no less! In al-Zubayr ibn Bakkār's account, Abān retorted that all he had written was true, in spite of whatever culpability they shared in 'Uthmān's assassination in 35/656. Hearing none of it, Sulaymān consulted his father, the caliph 'Abd al-Malik, who ordered the book burned to ashes.[22] This is all one ever hears of Abān's book of *maghāzī*, and scant trace of his writings otherwise remain, if indeed they ever existed.[23]

The situation is more promising for the writings of Abān's contemporary, the prominent scholar of Medina 'Urwah ibn al-Zubayr (d. ca. 94/712–13). Like Abān, 'Urwah was the son of a prominent early Companion of Muḥammad, al-Zubayr ibn al-'Awwām (d. 35/656). Furthermore, his mother was the daughter of the first caliph of Islam, Abū Bakr al-Ṣiddīq, and sister to Muḥammad's favorite wife 'Ā'ishah. Indeed, 'Urwah's maternal aunt 'Ā'ishah often serves as a key authority for 'Urwah's accounts, if one considers his chain of authorities (*isnād*) genuine. The man was extraordinarily well connected and deeply imbedded in the circles of the elite of the early Islamic polity.

Although no work of 'Urwah's has survived per se, his impact on the works surviving from subsequent generations can be better scrutinized and gauged than can Abān ibn 'Uthmān's. Modern scholars who have dedicated themselves to excavating later collections for survivals of 'Urwah's traditions have concluded that the broad outlines of at least seven events from Muḥammad's life, ranging from his first revelation and his Hijrah to Medina to his many battles thereafter, can be detected even if the original wording of 'Urwah's accounts may be lost.[24] Indeed, judging by the citations thereof contained in *The Expeditions*, this corpus of traditions from 'Urwah proved to be seminal for Ma'mar's teacher al-Zuhrī. Several redacted letters attributed to 'Urwah discussing events from Muḥammad's life ostensibly also survive in the work of a later historian, Abū Ja'far al-Ṭabarī (d. 310/923). Curiously though, all the letters are addressed to the Umayyad caliph 'Abd al-Malik ibn Marwān, who is otherwise known for his opposition to such books, preferring instead to promote the study of the Qur'an and Sunnah (i.e., scripture and religious law), as witnessed in the above story of Abān ibn 'Uthmān's efforts to compile such traditions.[25] Despite considerable advances in our knowledge of ʿUrwah and his corpus in recent decades, the fact remains that his corpus is now lost and its exact contours are the object of speculation (albeit well informed). The authenticity of the ʿUrwah corpus is still being vigorously debated.[26]

The author of *The Expeditions*, Maʿmar ibn Rāshid, was born in 96/714 and was active two generations after Abān and ʿUrwah. Maʿmar was a slave-client (Ar. *mawlā*; pl. *mawālī*) of the Ḥuddān clan of the Azd, a powerful Arab tribe that had its base of power in Maʿmar's native Basra as well as Oman. Like many scholars of his generation, Maʿmar was of Persian extraction. However, having lived in the midst of the Islamic-conquest elite all his life, he was deeply entrenched in their culture and had thoroughly assimilated their language and religion, Arabic and Islam, which he claimed as his own. Indeed, his native city of Basra originated not as a Persian city but rather as an Arab military garrison built upon the ruins of an old Persian settlement known as Vaheshtābādh Ardashīr near the Shaṭṭ al-ʿArab river. The early participants in the Islamic conquests constructed their settlement on this site in southern Iraq out of the reed beds of the surrounding marshes in 14/635, soon after they had vanquished the Persian armies of the moribund Sasanid dynasty. Basra continued to function as one of the main hubs of culture for the Islamic-conquest elite throughout Maʿmar's lifetime. Maʿmar served his Azdī masters not as a domestic slave or fieldworker, but as a trader, probably mostly of cloth and similar fineries. Such was the lot of many slaves in the early Islamic period: they were often skilled as traders, artisans, or merchants of some type, and in bondage would continue to practice their livelihood, only with the added necessity of paying levies on their profits to their masters, who in turn granted them access to the wealth, power, and prestige of the new Islamic-conquest elite.

Maʿmar's duties to his Arab masters required such remuneration, but the burden does not seem to have hampered his freedom of movement and association. He began to study and learn the Qur'an and hadith at a tender age as he sought knowledge from the famed scholars of his native Basra, such as Qatādah ibn Diʿāmah (d. 117/735) and al-Ḥasan al-Baṣrī (d. 110/728–29), whose funeral he attended as an adolescent. Indeed, it was his trading that enabled him to journey afar and pursue knowledge and learning beyond the environs of Basra. In time, his trading took him to the Hejaz, the cultural and religious heart of Islamic society in his era, as well as to Syria, the political center of the Umayyad empire, which stretched from Iberia to Central Asia when he first embarked on his studies of *maghāzī* traditions. He spent the final years of his life, likely from 132/750 onward, as a resident of Sanaa in Yemen, where he married and where he would pass away in 153/770.

The preponderance of materials transmitted by Maʿmar in *The Expeditions* derives from his teacher, the Medinese scholar Ibn Shihāb al-Zuhrī. Al-Zuhrī was a master narrator of the *maghāzī* genre and, after his most accomplished student Muḥammad ibn Isḥāq (d. 150/767–78), is the most seminal practitioner of the genre in early Islamic history. Maʿmar first encountered al-Zuhrī in Medina, while trading cloth on behalf of his Azdī masters. There, Maʿmar claims, he stumbled upon an aged man surrounded by a throng of students to whom he was lecturing. Already having cut his scholarly teeth when studying with the scholars of his native Basra, the young and inquisitive Maʿmar decided to sit down and join their ranks.[27] Maʿmar's encounter with al-Zuhrī in Medina impressed him profoundly, although it was likely somewhat brief. In Medina, it seems, his encounters with al-Zuhrī were mostly those of a curious young onlooker. It was not until al-Zuhrī had relocated his scholarly activities to the Umayyad court in Ruṣāfah and begun to serve as a tutor to the sons of the caliph Hishām ibn ʿAbd al-Malik (r. 105–25/723–43) that Maʿmar would once again encounter the aged scholar.

Ibn Shihāb al-Zuhrī was a formidable figure. His origins were at the farthest end of the social spectrum from Maʿmar's servile class: al-Zuhrī was of the innermost circles of the conquest elite. He was not merely an Arab and a Muslim; he was also a descendant of the Zuhrah clan of Mecca's Quraysh, from whose loins the religion of Islam and caliphal polity had sprung. The Quraysh dominated the articulation of Islam and the affairs of its polity from an early date. Although many of al-Zuhrī's students, like Maʿmar, were non-Arab clients of servile origin, al-Zuhrī reputedly preferred, if feasible, to take his knowledge only from the descendants of Muḥammad's early followers from the Quraysh and from those Arabs who gave Muḥammad's early followers shelter in Medina.[28] Indeed, al-Zuhrī attributed his own vast learning to four "oceans" of knowledge (Ar. *buḥūr*) he encountered among the scholars of Quraysh who preceded him: Saʿīd ibn al-Musayyab (d. 94/713), ʿUrwah ibn al-Zubayr (d. 94/712–13), Abū Salamah ibn ʿAbd al-Raḥmān (d. ca. 94/712–13), and ʿUbayd Allāh ibn ʿAbd Allāh ibn ʿUtbah (d. 98/716).[29] Furthermore, al-Zuhrī was deeply entrenched within the Umayyad state apparatus and its elite, and this at a time when many of his fellow scholars looked askance at any association with the state. A contemporary Syrian scholar, Makḥūl (d. ca. 113/731), reportedly once exclaimed, "What a great man al-Zuhrī would have been if only he had not allowed himself to be corrupted by associating with kings!"[30]

The caliph Hishām brought al-Zuhrī from Medina to his court in Ruṣāfah, where the scholar remained for approximately two decades (i.e., nearly the entirety of Hishām's caliphate), only leaving the caliph's court intermittently.[31] Ruṣāfah, located south of the Euphrates, was once a Syrian Byzantine city named Sergiopolis and was renowned as a destination of pilgrimage for Christian Arabic-speaking tribes visiting the shrine of the martyr St. Sergius as well as for its many churches. Hishām renovated the city and revived the settlement as the site of his court, building a mosque and palaces famous for their cisterns.[32] In Ruṣāfah, Hishām compelled al-Zuhrī to begin writing down traditions about the Prophet Muḥammad's life, as well as about other matters. This was likely against the scholar's will, as the recording of hadith in writing remained a controversial issue at the time. Part of Hishām's commission included the employment of state secretaries (*kuttāb*) to record al-Zuhrī's lectures as he related them to the Umayyad princes, producing by some accounts a considerable body of written work.[33]

It was during al-Zuhrī's residence at the caliph's court in Ruṣāfah that Maʿmar journeyed there as a trader hoping to sell his wares. He humbly requested the attendees at a marriage banquet to grant him access to al-Zuhrī and, thus, to the scholar's famed learning. According to his own testimony, Maʿmar took the majority of his learning from al-Zuhrī while he resided in Ruṣāfah, where Maʿmar claims he had al-Zuhrī nearly all to himself.[34] Maʿmar learned al-Zuhrī's traditions via two means: audition (*samāʿ*) and collation via public recitation (*ʿarḍ*)—meaning that once Maʿmar had memorized the traditions he would recite them back to al-Zuhrī for review and correction. The combination of these two features of Maʿmar's studies with al-Zuhrī rendered his transmission of al-Zuhrī's materials highly desirable in the eyes of other scholars.[35] It is likely that Maʿmar remained in Ruṣāfah, or at least Syria, even beyond al-Zuhrī's death in 124/742. He testifies to having witnessed al-Zuhrī's personal stores of notebooks (*dafātir*) being hauled out on beasts of burden for transfer to some unspecified location after the caliph al-Walīd II ibn Yazīd was assassinated in a coup d'état by Yazīd III in Jumada II 126/April 744.[36]

After the coup had toppled Walīd II, Syria descended into a vortex of violence that made life there precarious; even the Umayyad dynasty did not survive the ensuing conflicts that collectively came to be called the Third Civil War (*fitnah*). The denouement of this conflict in 132/750 also saw the ascendance of a new caliphal dynasty, the Abbasids.[37] It was likely this tumultuous series of events that caused Maʿmar to journey far to the south, to Sanaa in Yemen. Scholars of any sort, let alone one of Maʿmar's stature, seem to have been rare in the region at the time, so the locals quickly made arrangements to marry him to a local woman with the hope of tethering him to the city for the long haul.[38]

In Yemen, Maʿmar's most promising and, in due time, most famous pupil was ʿAbd al-Razzāq ibn Hammām al-Ṣanʿānī. Of the twenty-odd years Maʿmar reputedly spent in Yemen until his death in 153/770, his relationship with ʿAbd al-Razzāq spanned the final seven to eight years.[39] The importance of ʿAbd al-Razzāq's role in the preservation of Maʿmar's learning is beyond doubt. This is in part due to the considerable scholarly output of ʿAbd al-Razzāq himself, which included the ten surviving volumes of his own hadith compilation, the monumental *al-Muṣannaf*. However, ʿAbd al-Razzāq was also the first scholar to transmit and present Maʿmar's scholarship in a recognizably "book-like" form.[40]

Early Muslim scholars did not usually compose books in order to display their scholarly prowess. Indeed, to possess such books for any purpose except private use could considerably harm one's scholarly reputation, as it suggested that one's knowledge (Ar. *ʿilm*) was not known by heart, and therefore not truly learned.[41] Knowledge was, in this sense, expected to be embodied by a scholar and only accessible by personally meeting and studying under said scholar. As a general rule, books were for private use, not public dissemination. This attitude toward writing and knowledge, indeed, was the root of al-Zuhrī's alarm when the Umayyad caliph Hishām compelled him to have his knowledge copied into books. Maʿmar, one of al-Zuhrī's closest students at Ruṣāfah, seems to have first seen al-Zuhrī's private collection of notebooks only after they were removed from his teacher's private storage (Ar. *khazāʾin*) after his death, for al-Zuhrī's books were largely irrelevant to the interpersonal process of the transmission of knowledge that Maʿmar enjoyed under his tutelage. Books were no substitute for the authenticating relationship between a scholar and his pupil. Those who had derived their knowledge only from books were scorned. Indeed, when a Damascene scholar who had purchased a book by al-Zuhrī in Damascus began to transmit the material he had found therein, he was denounced as a fraud.[42]

Hence, it was as a compliment to his revered teacher's learning and to his awe-inspiring ability to recall vast stores of hadith from memory at will that ʿAbd al-Razzāq would remark that he never once saw Maʿmar with a book, except for a collection of long narratives (as one finds in *The Expeditions*, for instance), which he would occasionally take out to consult.[43] However, it would be inaccurate to say that written materials had no role to play whatsoever. Teachers could and did bestow private writings on students or close confidants. Such writings, it seems, would fall somewhere between the "lecture notes" used by scholars as an aide-mémoire and the published books produced by later generations. Maʿmar reputedly composed such a tome (Ar. *sifr*) for his fellow Basran scholar Ayyūb al-Sakhtiyānī on one occasion,[44] and for ʿAbd al-Razzāq al-Ṣanʿānī on another.[45] *The Expeditions* may have been one such work preserved in the course of ʿAbd al-Razzāq's indefatigable pursuit of knowledge: what Sebastian Günther has designated as a "literary composition."[46] Simply put, although *The Expeditions* was the product of Maʿmar's lectures to ʿAbd al-Razzāq, the end product was a composition polished enough to be disseminated to others and not restricted to Maʿmar's private use. Hence, although the work was the product of a teacher's lessons and granted to a student to transmit as such, *The Expeditions*, as well as other compositions like it, functioned as a work that conformed to a literary form and was organized according to a topical and well-thought-out presentation of material.

However, such books were not intended to replace the memorization of received knowledge. The practice of memorization was still cultivated with the utmost care. ʿAbd al-Razzāq would fondly recall Maʿmar feeding him the fruit of the myrobalanus plant (Ar. *halīlaj*), presumably to sharpen his memory.[47] Memorization would remain the sine qua non of scholarly mastery for some time to come. Yet even ʿAbd al-Razzāq had considerable resources at his disposal to aid his preservation of vast amounts of hadith, exceeding the capacity of even the most prodigious memory. When he attended lectures of learned men alongside his father and brother, ʿAbd al-Razzāq reputedly brought with him an entourage of stationers (Ar. *warrāqūn*) to record what they had heard via audition.[48]

The preservation of texts such as Maʿmar's *The Expeditions* is admittedly not entirely straightforward, but this is in large part due to the fact that the genres of Arabic prose were still inchoate and evolving. With the exception of scattered papyrus fragments that testify to their material existence,[49] none of the second/eighth-century works of Arabic historical writing survives into modern times, save in later recensions. These recensions themselves are often at least two generations removed from the work's putative author. Hence, the works of the master architect of the *maghāzī* genre, the Medinese scholar Muḥammad ibn Isḥāq (d. 150/767–68), survive, but only in abridged, and perhaps even expurgated, versions of later scholars such as Abū Jaʿfar al-Ṭabarī (d. 310/923), ʿAbd al-Malik ibn Hishām (d. 218/834), and al-ʿUṭāridī (d. 272/886).[50] That Maʿmar's *Expeditions* itself only survives in the larger, multivolume compilation of his student ʿAbd al-Razzāq al-Ṣanʿānī called the *Muṣannaf* is therefore not in the least atypical.

The two works of Maʿmar and Ibn Isḥāq can be fruitfully compared. Compiled at the behest of the Abbasid caliph al-Manṣūr (r. 136–58/754–75),[51] Ibn Isḥāq's *Book of Expeditions* (*Kitāb al-Maghāzī*) is a massive enterprise, a masterpiece of narrative engineering that recounts God's plan for humanity's universal salvation, at the apex of which appears the life of Muḥammad, Islam's prophet.[52] Ibn Isḥāq's work dwarfs Maʿmar's. The Cairo edition of the Arabic text of Ibn Hishām's *redaction* of Ibn Isḥāq's work, *al-Sīrah al-nabawiyyah* (*The Prophetic Life-Story*), runs to over 1,380 pages of printed text. The full version as conceived by Ibn Isḥāq, had it survived, would have been far longer. Originally, the structure of Ibn Isḥāq's *Kitāb al-Maghāzī* appears to have been tripartite: *al-Mubtada'* ("the Genesis," relating pre-Islamic history and that of the Abrahamic prophets from Adam to Jesus), *al-Mabʿath* ("the Call," relating Muḥammad's early life and his prophet career in Mecca), and *al-Maghāzī* ("the Expeditions," relating the events of his prophetic career in Medina until his death). In addition to these three sections, there might have existed a fourth: a *Tārīkh al-khulafā'*, or "History of the Caliphs."[53]

Maʿmar's *Expeditions*, by contrast, is a far more slender, economical volume, even though it covers similar ground. *The Expeditions* is a substantial, though probably not exhaustive, collection of al-Zuhrī's *maghāzī* materials. Most of the major set pieces are present, though there appear to be some glaring omissions, such as the ʿAqabah meetings between Muḥammad and the Medinese tribes prior to the Hijrah.[54] Though some scholars have raised questions about these missing pieces from Maʿmar's *Expeditions*, which for whatever reason ʿAbd al-Razzāq did not transmit, such traditions are likely to be few and far between, if indeed they ever existed.[55] Hence, the extensive "editing" of Ibn Isḥāq's materials that one finds in Ibn Hishām's version of Ibn Isḥāq's text, for instance, is sparsely present, if not entirely absent, from ʿAbd al-Razzāq's recension of Maʿmar's work.

Furthermore, Maʿmar's narrative in *The Expeditions* seems, unlike the grandiose architecture one finds in Ibn Isḥāq's work, to have been compiled without a strong concern for chronology. It does begin with a solid chronological structure: At the outset, we encounter Muḥammad's grandfather, ʿAbd al-Muṭṭalib, fearlessly facing down the war elephant and troops of the Axumite vicegerent Abrahah as they march against Mecca. Soon thereafter we witness the fame and divine favor he earns for his steadfast commitment to God's sacred city and its shrine, the Kaaba, when the location of its sacred well, Zamzam, first discovered by Abraham's son Ishmael, is revealed to him. The narrative marches onward through Muḥammad's birth, youth, adulthood, call to prophecy, and even episodes from his Meccan ministry prior to undertaking the Hijrah to Medina. However, after this stretch, the narrative's wheels appear to fall off and we are suddenly witnessing the treaty of al-Ḥudaybiyah some six years after the Hijrah. Its purposeful march seems to halt and then begin to careen from one episode in Muḥammad's life to the next without a strong interest in chronological order. Still, one must be careful not to overstate the case. The main battles of the Medinese period appear in chronological order, and the stories of Muḥammad's succession, the conquests, and the Great Civil War (*al-fitnah al-kubrā*) appear after the story of the Prophet's death and roughly in chronological succession. As Schoeler observed, chronology is not determinative for the text's structure; Maʿmar's approach is, instead, rather ad hoc.[56] Yet this is not to say that Maʿmar's approach is not also haphazard. The chapter headings, for instance, seem to reflect Maʿmar's division of the work. Although some of these headings appear redundant at first glance, a closer reading suggests that the somewhat redundant chapter headings function as a divider to mark off materials Maʿmar transmits from al-Zuhrī from those he transmits from other authorities, such as Qatādah or ʿUthmān al-Jazarī. One must emphasize that even if the chronological arc of Muḥammad's life does not determine the book's structure, its arc remains implicit within each episode.

In summary, the importance of *The Expeditions* by Maʿmar ibn Rāshid is multifaceted. As an early written work of the second/eighth century, and as one of the earliest exempla of the *maghāzī* genre, Maʿmar's text is a precious artifact of the social and cultural history of a bygone age that witnessed the birth of Arabic as a medium of writerly culture. The text demands the attention of specialist and non-specialist readers alike, due to its intrinsic value as an early source for the lives of Muḥammad and his earliest followers. It is for us moderns an indispensable window onto how early Muslims attempted to articulate a vision of their Prophet and sacred history.

Note on the Text

The English Translation

The two guiding lights of this English translation have been fidelity and readability, and I have sought to balance one against the other. With fidelity to the Arabic text comes the hazard of a rendering so wooden and cold that the translation is alienating or unintelligible. With readability in English comes the hazard of bowdlerization, producing a text so pureed that the hearty textures of its original cultural and historical contexts vanish. My hope is that the reader will find much that is delightful, curious, and surprising in the text but that the idiom of the translation and of the original Arabic will work hand in glove and allow the text to come to life.

Readers uninitiated to the genres of prophetic biography and hadith will likely find some features of the text difficult to adjust to at first, so some words of advice on reading the text are in order. First, the presence of chains of transmission, *isnād*s, between reports may seem disjointed initially. It may be helpful to view them as a snapshot of the context in which the text was being read aloud—an exchange between a teacher and a pupil. The context remains conspicuous thanks to the chains of transmission, which serve almost as a frame story in which a storyteller relates the narratives about Muḥammad and his Companions.

Second, much of the text is not in chronological order, and for this reason the reader should not feel obligated to read the chapters in the order presented by the text. I have included a timeline of events to aid the reader in ascertaining what events happen when. I have also listed these events according to the calculations attributed to al-Zuhrī, Maʿmar's teacher. I have done so for pragmatic reasons, not because I believe they are necessarily the most correct. Indeed, al-Zuhrī's calculations occasionally depart considerably from the standard dates one is likely to find in a textbook. With that being said, and despite Maʿmar's pragmatic approach to chronology, the first chapter remains, in my opinion, the best place to begin. There the reader will find stories of Muḥammad's youth, his growth into manhood, and his call to prophecy.

Finally, the bilingual nature of this text has determined many of the decisions I have made along the way, and I have chosen to see the presence of the Arabic edition as freeing rather constricting in making decisions about translation.

The reader who is bilingual in Arabic and English, or at least aspiring to be, is advised to note the following:

- Chains of transmission, *isnād*s, are set in a smaller font, and I have made explicit the teacher–pupil relationship in the translation where the Arabic merely has *ʿan* ("from"), by translating the preposition as "on the authority of . . ."
- In the Arabic edition, I have retained honorific invocations for the Prophet and his Companions, such as *ṣallā Allāhu ʿalayhi wa-sallam* (God bless him and keep him) and *raḍiya Allāhu ʿanhu* (May God be pleased with him), but I have omitted them in most cases from the English translation.
- I freely replace demonstratives and pronouns with their referents to remove ambiguity and vice versa when English style so dictates.
- Transitional phrases and conjunctions (*fa-*, *thumma*, *ḥattā idhā*, *baynamā*, *lammā*, etc.) lend themselves to multiple translations; thus, I have taken the liberty to translate their sense into a variety of nonliteral English permutations.
- Dense and idiomatic Arabic expressions that literal translations into English would leave abstruse have been unpacked, and I have often departed from the syntax of the Arabic original in order to render the text into more idiomatic English.
- Similarly, the repetitive use of *qāla*/*qālat*, "he/she said," in the text would try an English speaker's patience if translated literally; therefore, I have freely translated the verb as he or she said, replied, answered, declared, etc.
- Many technical terms are directly translated into English, hence "the Sacred Mosque" for *al-masjid al-ḥarām* and "Emigrants" and "Allies" rather than *al-muhājirūn* and *al-anṣār*. Yet I have also adopted the anglicized equivalents of other technical terms given their widespread use in English—e.g., hajj for *ḥajj*, rather than "Pilgrimage," Hijrah for *hijrah* rather than "Emigration," and Shura for *shūrā* rather than "Consultative Assembly"—mostly due to the imprecision of their English equivalents. ("Pilgrimage," for instance, does not allow one to distinguish efficiently between the seasonal and non-seasonal pilgrimages: the *ḥajj* versus the *ʿumrah*.) All such words, likely to be unfamiliar to the nonspecialist reader, can be located in the glossary.
- For quotations from the Qur'an, I cite the translation of M. A. S. Abdel Haleem; however, I have also significantly modified Abdel Haleem's

translation when his rendering is either at odds with or does not sufficiently illuminate the interpretation of the Qur'an suggested by the narrative. Also, there is a minor discrepancy in the manner in which citations of the Qur'an are found in the Arabic edition and the translation that merits the reader's attention. Citations of the Qur'an often appear in the Arabic edition in a truncated form. This citational practice reproduces the manuscript and reflects the cultural context in which the text was produced, a context that assumed a baseline fluency in the Qur'an that is now rare among a modern readership, whether Muslim or non-Muslim. I have thus included qur'anic citations in their entirety in my English translation for the sake of readers lacking an intimate familiarity with the Qur'an.

A note on Arabic names: The forms of names one encounters in Arabic literature can be quite daunting for the uninitiated, but the system is easy to learn with a little time. A typical full name consists of a personal name (*ism*) followed by a genealogy (*nasab*) that starts with one's father and continues back several generations. The *nasab* is recognizable by the words *ibn* and *bint*, which mean "son" and "daughter," respectively. Hence, Maʿmar ibn Rāshid literally means "Maʿmar, the son of Rāshid" and Asmāʾ bint ʿUmays means "Asmāʾ, the daughter of ʿUmays." In spoken address, convention often dictates the use of a *kunyah*, or teknonym, such as Abū ("Father of") or Umm ("Mother of"). This means that although ʿAlī ibn Abī Ṭālib or al-ʿAbbās ibn ʿAbd al-Muṭṭalib are referred to as ʿAlī and al-ʿAbbās in the narrative of the text, in formal direct speech they are referred by their *kunyah*s, Abū l-Ḥasan (Father of al-Ḥasan) and Abū l-Faḍl (Father of al-Faḍl), respectively, unless they are being addressed by an intimate friend.

Other common names are theophoric, meaning that they include a name of God. These names include two parts: the first is *ʿabd*, meaning "slave/servant," and the second the name of God. For example, ʿAbd Allāh means "Servant of God" and ʿAbd al-Raḥmān "Servant of the Merciful." Many names also contain one or more *nisbah*s, names that end in *–ī* for men and *–iyyah* for women. *Nisbah*s are adjectives that refer to a tribe and place of birth or residence; thus, al-Zuhrī is so called because he comes from the tribe of Zuhrah, and ʿAbd al-Razzāq is called al-Sanʿānī because he comes from the city of Sanaa.

The Arabic Edition

The Expeditions survives only in ʿAbd al-Razzāq's redaction and is contained in his *Muṣannaf*. The relevant section of his *Muṣannaf* survives only in a single, partial manuscript: Murad Mulla 604, fols. 66r–99r [م], which dates to 747/1346–47 and is currently held at the Süleymaniye Library in Istanbul, Turkey. Relying on a sole extant manuscript is, of course, far from ideal. Fortunately, many of the initial difficulties were mitigated by the previous efforts of two editors: Ḥabīb al-Raḥmān al-Aʿẓamī, who first edited and compiled the surviving portions of the ʿAbd al-Razzāq's *Muṣannaf*, a project published by al-Maktab al-Islāmī in Beirut in 1972; and an edition of the *The Book of Expeditions* produced by Suhayl Zakkār under the title *al-Maghāzī al-nabawiyyah* and published by Dār al-Fikr in Beirut in 1981. Both editions were significant achievements in their own right, in particular Zakkār's far superior reading of the text, but both also suffer from a number of shortcomings that I have sought to ameliorate in the present edition.

I have aimed to improve upon the previous editions of the text by judiciously taking into account the different transmissions (Ar. *riwāyāt*) of the text, no matter how piecemeal. Even here, however, there are hazards. It is significant that the transmission (*riwāyah*) for the Murad Mulla manuscript of ʿAbd al-Razzāq's *Muṣannaf* in which the sole transcription of Maʿmar's *Kitāb al-Maghāzī* survives is from the Yemeni scholar Abū Yaʿqūb Isḥāq ibn Ibrāhīm al-Dabarī (d. ca. 285–6/898–9). Isḥāq al-Dabarī was a native of Sanaa who seems to have remained in the city throughout his life, establishing a reputation as one of the most important transmitters of ʿAbd al-Razzāq's scholarly corpus. Indeed, of the thirty-three books that survive from the *Muṣannaf* as cobbled together by its modern editor, al-Aʿẓamī, Isḥāq al-Dabarī's transmission preserves 90 percent thereof (i.e., twenty-nine of the work's thirty-three divisions).[57] Quotations and excerpts from other transmissions of Maʿmar's *Maghāzī* via ʿAbd al-Razzāq survive, but only in piecemeal fashion and as small parts of larger, collected works, such as the *Musnad* of ʿAbd al-Razzāq's student Aḥmad ibn Ḥanbal (d. 241/855), and not as an integral book. Isḥāq al-Dabarī, by contrast, transmitted Maʿmar's *Maghāzī* from ʿAbd al-Razzāq both as part of the latter's *Muṣannaf* and as a standalone work.[58]

There are several indications that Isḥāq al-Dabarī was primed to be a key transmitter of the *Muṣannaf* from a tender age. His father, Ibrāhīm ibn ʿAbbād al-Dabarī, was the appointed lector for ʿAbd al-Razzāq's works (*qāriʾ al-dīwān*) late in the scholar's life, and he supervised his son's recording of ʿAbd al-Razzāq's corpus, which his son received via audition (*samāʿ*).[59] The main intent of Ibrāhīm al-Dabarī in requiring his son Isḥāq to hear the corpus of ʿAbd al-Razzāq as early as ten, or by some accounts even seven years of age was likely to ensure the durability of his son's transmission. The most sought-after *isnād*s for a hadith often had—and continue to have—a property called *ʿuluww*, a term roughly meaning "height" or "elevation." There are many reasons an *isnād* with "height" was the ideal for scholars of the hadith. One pragmatic reason was because such an elevated *isnād* covers the largest amount of time with the fewest names of scholars, and therefore is easier to commit to memory. More important, however, an elevated *isnād* contained fewer names between the transmitter (*rāwī*) and the Prophet, and therefore was "nearer" to the Prophet.[60] Having heard ʿAbd al-Razzāq's corpus at such a young age ensured that the *isnād*s from Isḥāq would have this property of *ʿuluww*, and his father's supervision ostensibly assured the accuracy of his transmission.

Most hadith scholars of the subsequent generation indeed recognized Isḥāq al-Dabarī's transmission as thoroughly reliable;[61] however, it is noteworthy that earlier scholars, in particular older students of ʿAbd al-Razzāq, did question the quality of Isḥāq al-Dabarī's transmission. Aḥmad ibn Ḥanbal, for instance, held that because ʿAbd al-Razzāq had lost his eyesight in 200/815–16, subsequent transmissions from him were of a shoddier quality, given that ʿAbd al-Razzāq could no longer personally review and verify the accuracy of his students' written notes.[62] Ibn Ḥanbal's comments may in fact be directed against Isḥāq al-Dabarī's transmission, which he began receiving via audition sometime between 202/817 and 205/821, after ʿAbd al-Razzāq lost his eyesight.[63] Certainly the fact that Ibrāhīm al-Dabarī supervised his son's audition of ʿAbd al-Razzāq's corpus mitigates this criticism to some degree; however, at least one scholar of the following century, Ibn Mufarrij (d. 380/990–91), saw fit to compose an entire book detailing and correcting the errors made by Isḥāq al-Dabarī in his transmission of ʿAbd al-Razzāq's corpus.[64]

The Murad Mulla manuscript upon which I have based my tradition is written in a fine, readable hand, but the text does suffer from the usual array of scribal errors and lacunae that one finds in most manuscripts. As a result, the text in several parts was in need of "reconstruction" inasmuch as I have not regarded the text of the manuscript itself as so "sacred" as to bind me to reproduce slavishly its errors and lacunae. With the exception of a handful of instances, such reconstructions are possible due to the proliferation of texts that directly cite ʿAbd al-Razzāq's transmission (*riwāyah*) of Maʿmar's text. The most important of these are ʿAbd al-Razzāq's *Tafsīr* [تع] (which survives in two manuscript testimonies predating the Murad Mulla manuscript),[65] Aḥmad ibn Ḥanbal's *Musnad* [ح], and al-Ṭabarānī's *Muʿjam al-kabīr* [طـ]. Where the readings in these other texts depart from the manuscript in merely iterative or minor ways, I have favored the Murad Mulla manuscript rather than the citations found in other works.[66]

I have consulted further sources appearing in the critical apparatus to the text that play a more marginal role in establishing the text. Hence, less ideally, I have relied occasionally on citations of traditions found in the *Kitāb al-Maghāzī* from lines of transmission that derive from students of Maʿmar other than ʿAbd al-Razzāq to reconstruct obscure passages. As a means of last resort, I have occasionally drawn upon alternative transmissions of al-Zuhrī's traditions. Difficult passages often had no clear parallel or citation in other sources, and in such cases I leaned upon my own *ijtihād* and corrected the text of the manuscript to the best of my ability to guess the original reading in the hope that, indeed, *kull mujtahid muṣīb*, "every qualified scholar hits the mark." Whether or not I have succeeded, I leave to my colleagues' judgment. The intrepid Arabist concerned with such minutiae will find the indications thereof marked in the critical apparatus to the text.

Given the LAL's focus on readability, I have endeavored to make my editorial decisions as transparent as possible while simultaneously unobtrusive to the casual reader. I have also edited my Arabic text with the underlying assumption that it will be read as a bilingual text alongside the English translation. Thus, cosmetic textual features such as section numbering, paragraphing, font size, standardized orthography, and punctuation have been introduced to facilitate easy cross-referencing between the Arabic edition and English translation.

The following sigla designate the sources referred to throughout the textual apparatus (full bibliographic references to the editions used appear in the bibliography):

[خ] al-Bukhārī, *al-Ṣaḥīḥ*
[بد] al-Bayhaqī, *Dalāʾil al-nubuwwah*
[بس] al-Bayhaqī, *al-Sunan al-kubrā*
[بل] al-Balādhurī, *Ansāb al-ashrāf*
[تط] al-Ṭabarī, *al-Tārīkh*
[تع] ʿAbd al-Razzāq al-Ṣanʿānī, *al-Tafsīr*
[ح] Aḥmad ibn Ḥanbal, *al-Musnad*
[ز] al-Azraqī, *Akhbār Makkah*

[ط] al-Ṭabarānī, *al-Muʿjam al-kabīr*

[عب] Ibn ʿAbd al-Barr, *al-Durar fī ikhtiṣār al-maghāzī wa-l-siyar* or *al-Tamhīd li-mā fī l-Muwaṭṭaʾ min al-maʿānī waʾl-asānīd*

[لش] Hibat Allāh al-Lālakāʾī, *Sharḥ uṣūl iʿtiqād ahl al-sunnah waʾl-jamāʿah*

[م] MS Murad Mulla 604

[ن] Abū Nuʿaym al-Iṣfahānī, *Dalāʾil al-nubuwwah*

Timeline

Dates and events for the life of Muḥammad are fraught with difficulties; therefore, dates are here given according to al-Zuhrī's calculations.

After 558 (?)	The "Elephant Troop" and Abrahah, king of Ḥimyar, march against Mecca to destroy the Kaaba
608 (?)	Muḥammad receives his first revelation atop Mount Ḥirā'
622, Sept.	Muḥammad's Hijrah from Mecca to Medina
624, Mar.	Battle of Badr
624, Sept.–Oct.	Expulsion of the Jewish clan al-Naḍīr from Medina
625, Mar.–Apr.	Battle of Uḥud
627, Feb.–Mar.	Battle of the United Clans/the Trench
628, Feb.–Mar.	Treaty of Ḥudaybiyah
630, 3 Jan.	Muḥammad's Conquest of Mecca
632, 27 May	Muḥammad's Death
644, Nov.	Assassination of the second caliph ʿUmar ibn al-Khaṭṭāb
656, June	Assassination of the third caliph ʿUthmān ibn ʿAffān
656–61	The Great Civil War (*al-fitnah al-kubrā*)
656, Nov.–Dec.	The Battle of the Camel between ʿAlī ibn Abī Ṭālib and ʿĀ'ishah bint Abī Bakr, al-Zubayr ibn al-ʿAwwām, and Ṭalḥah ibn ʿUbayd Allāh
657, July	The Battle of Ṣiffīn between ʿAlī and Muʿāwiyah ibn Abī Sufyān
661, Jan.	Assassination of ʿAlī
661–750	The Umayyad Caliphate
680–92	Second Civil War—the Marwānid Umayyads emerge victorious over their Zubyarid rivals
685–705	Caliphate of ʿAbd al-Malik ibn Marwān
723–43	Caliphate of Hishām ibn ʿAbd al-Malik
742	Ibn Shihāb al-Zuhrī dies
744–50	Third Civil War ensues after the assassination of al-Walīd II, leading to the rise of Abbasid dynasty of caliphs
754–75	Caliphate of Abū Jaʿfar al-Manṣūr
768	Muḥammad ibn Isḥāq dies
770	Maʿmar ibn Rāshid dies
827	ʿAbd al-Razzāq al-Ṣanʿānī dies

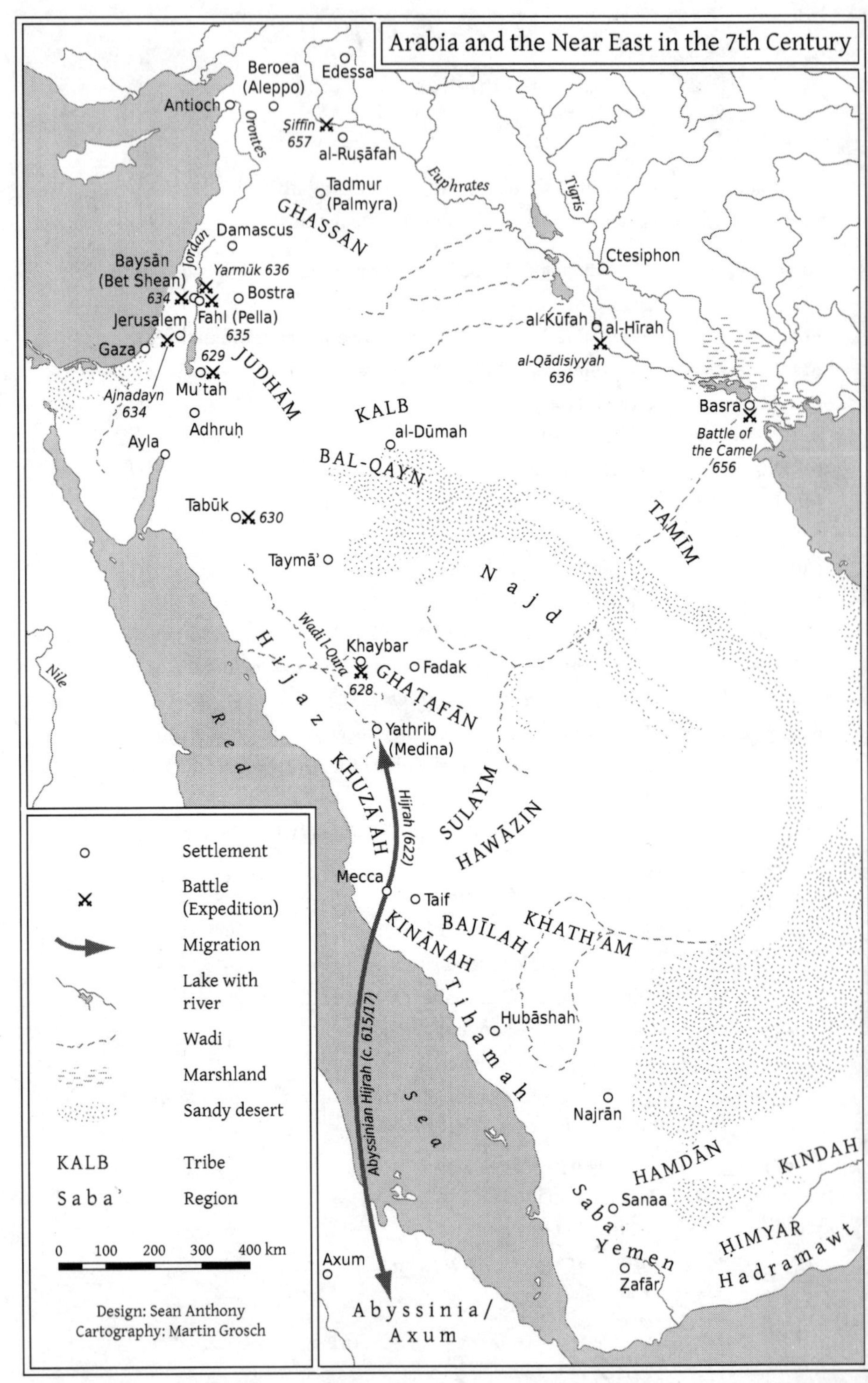
Arabia and the Near East in the 7th Century
Beroea (Aleppo)
Edessa
Antioch
Orontes
Ṣiffīn 657
al-Ruṣāfah
Euphrates
Tigris
Tadmur (Palmyra)
GHASSĀN
Damascus
Jordan
Baysān (Bet Shean)
634
Yarmūk 636
Bostra
Jerusalem
Faḥl (Pella) 635
Gaza
629
JUDHĀM
Ajnadayn 634
Mu'tah
Adhruḥ
Ayla
Ctesiphon
al-Kūfah
al-Ḥīrah
al-Qādisiyyah 636
Basra
Battle of the Camel 656
KALB
al-Dūmah
BAL-QAYN
Tabūk 630
Taymā'
TAMĪM
Najd
Wadi l-Qura
Khaybar
628
Fadak
GHAṬAFĀN
Ḥijaz
Nile
Red Sea
Yathrib (Medina)
KHUZĀ'AH
Hijrah (622)
SULAYM
HAWĀZIN
Mecca
Taif
KINĀNAH
BAJĪLAH
KHATH'AM
Tihamah
Hubāshah
Abyssinian Hijrah (c. 615/17)
Najrān
HAMDĀN
KINDAH
Saba'
Sanaa
Yemen
ḤIMYAR
Hadramawt
Ẓafār
Axum
Abyssinia/Axum
Settlement
Battle (Expedition)
Migration
Lake with river
Wadi
Marshland
Sandy desert
KALB Tribe
Saba' Region
0 100 200 300 400 km
Design: Sean Anthony
Cartography: Martin Grosch

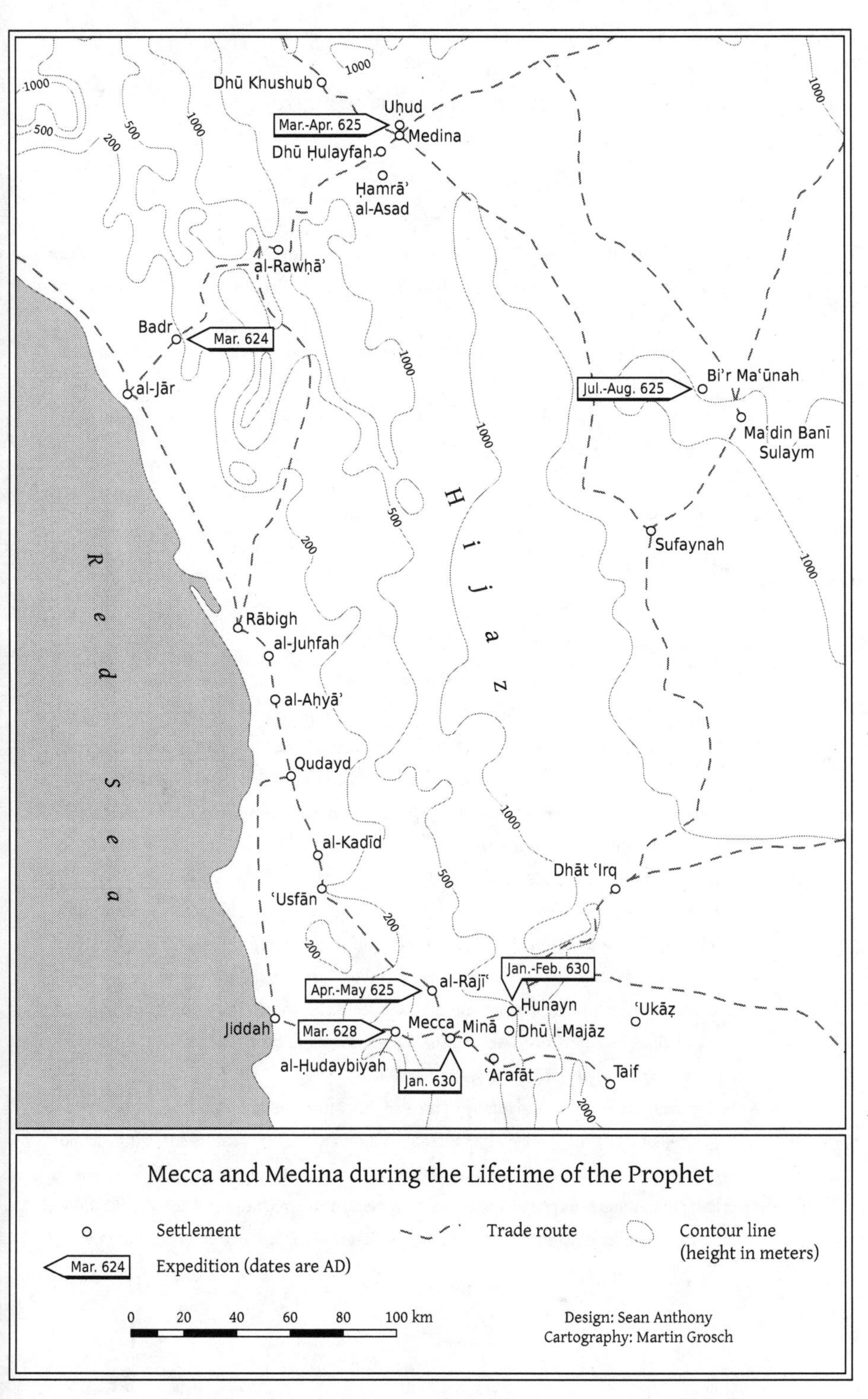

Mecca and Medina during the Lifetime of the Prophet

Notes to the Frontmatter

Foreword

1 Muḥammad Ibn-Isḥāq, 'Abd-al-Malik Ibn-Hishām, and Alfred Guillaume. *The Life of Muhammad: A Translation of [Ibn] Isḥāq's Sīrat rasūl Allāh* (London: Oxford University Press, 1955).

2 Ḥājjī Khalīfah. *Kashf al-ẓunūn 'an asāmī al-kutub wal-funūn*, vol. 2. (Beirut: Dār al-'Ilm, 1994), 604.

3 On 'Urwah ibn al-Zubayr, see Andreas Görke and Gregor Schoeler, *Die altesten Berichte über das Leben Muḥammads* (Princeton: Darwin Press, 2008).

Acknowledgements

4 *Muhammad*, 91.

Introduction

5 The precise title of Ibn Isḥāq's work is not certain, though the most likely candidate is *Kitāb al-Maghāzī*. Ibn Hishām's redaction is usually referred to as *al-Sīrah al-nabawiyyah* (Eng. *The Prophetic Life-Story*), but this title has little to do with Ibn Isḥāq's original work. See Horovitz, *Earliest Biographies*, 80 and n. 93 thereto and Schoeler, *Biography*, 28–29.

6 This is not to say, however, that the earliest testimonies are bereft of historical insight; see Hoyland, "The Earliest Christian Writings on Muḥammad," and Anthony, "Muḥammad, the Keys to Paradise, and the *Doctrina Iacobi*."

7 In the West, scholarship on the historical Muḥammad is inevitably considerably indebted to the tradition of historical Jesus scholarship, a tradition that is now over two centuries old. However, it must be said that historians of early Islam are rarely fluent in the most up-to-date scholarship on the historical Jesus. In the massive literature on the challenges and aims of writing the biography of the historical Jesus, E. P. Sanders' *The Historical Figure of Jesus* remains a classic.

8 Hoyland, "Writing the Biography of the Prophet Muhammad."

9 See Chabbi, "La biographie impossible de Mahomet." In the most recent decade anglophone scholarship has all but abandoned writing traditional, historical biographies in favor of monographs proposing radical new views of Islamic origins. The two most noteworthy monographs on this score are Shoemaker, *The Death of a Prophet*, and Powers,

Muḥammad Is Not the Father of Any of Your Men. Germanophone and francophone scholars, on the other hand, have been considerably more active in writing more traditional, historical biographies during the last decade; e.g., see Tilman Nagel's massive *Mohammed: Leben und Legende* and *Allahs Liebling*, and Hichem Djaït's three-volume history *La vie de Muḥammad* (originally written in Arabic). Although the full impact of the scholarly reception of Djaït's work has yet to be seen, a positive evaluation of Djaït's project can be found in Nicolai Sinai, "Hisham Djait." By contrast, the response to Nagel's biography has been rather tepid; e.g., see Hagan, "The Imagined and Historical Muḥammad," and Schoeler's *Biography*, 11–13 and "Grundsätzliches zu Tilman Nagels Monographie."

10 Donner, *Narratives of Islamic Origins*, 35–63; Neuwirth, *Der Koran als Text der Spätantike*, 235–75; Hamdan, "The Second *Maṣāḥif* Project"; Comerro, *La constitution du muṣḥaf de ʿUthmān*; Sadeghi and Goudarzi, "Ṣanʿāʾ 1 and the Origins of the Qurʾān."

11 An excellent and fluent introduction to hadith as well as the formation of its canon can be found in Brown, *Ḥadīth*; however, Brown's treatment of the earliest phases of hadith transmission and collection is a tad tendentious. For an important corrective, see Reinhart, "Juynbolliana," 436 ff.

12 Cf. Görke, "The Relationship between *Maghāzī* and *Ḥadīth*."

13 The reader may find it surprising that the word jihad (Ar. *al-jihād*) appears only once in the text; see 13.2.

14 Cf. the list of *maghāzī* titles gathered in Sezgin, *Geschichte des arabischen Schrifttums*, 1:887b–888a.

15 Ibn ʿAsākir, *Dimashq*, 59:393.

16 These works include two collections of prophetic traditions, *al-Jāmiʿ* and *Ṣaḥīfat Hammām ibn Munabbih*, and ʿAbd al-Razzāq's exegesis of the Qur'an, *al-Tafsīr*; see *EI3*, "ʿAbd al-Razzāq al-Ṣanʿānī" (H. Motzki).

17 Boekhoff-van der Voort ("The *Kitāb al-maghāzī*," 29–30) recently tabulated the percentage of the materials ʿAbd al-Razzāq derived solely from Maʿmar in the *Kitāb al-Maghāzī* as 93.9 percent; however, her tabulation is somewhat misleading, as she counts ʿAbd al-Razzāq's annotations and glosses of Maʿmar's traditions, which rarely go beyond a sentence or two, as equal to Maʿmar's fully realized narrations, which stretch on for pages. In fact, all of the narratives derive from Maʿmar except for a short narrative about Abū Bakr (24.3) and two longish narrations that ʿAbd al-Razzāq adds to the end of Maʿmar's account of the marriage of Fāṭimah (31.2–31.3).

18 Donner, *Narratives*, 255–70; Robinson, *Islamic Historiography*, 15–17, 92–93.

19 Brown, *Ḥadīth*, 4 f.

20 Donner, *Narratives*, 280 ff.

21 See al-Zubayr ibn Bakkār, *Muwaffaqayyāt,* 332–35.

22 Cf. Horovitz, *Earliest Biographies,* 6–11 and esp. n. 30 thereto. The account of Sulaymān ibn ʿAbd al-Malik is from al-Zubayr ibn Bakkār, *Muwaffaqayyāt,* 332–35. A shorter version appears in Balādhurī, *Ansāb,* 4/2: 490. The dating of these events by al-Zubayr ibn Bakkār may be off by a year or so; see *EI3,* "Abān b. ʿUthmān" (Khalil Athamina).

23 Efforts to locate traces of his work have produced little. His material is often confused with that of another author of a *Kitāb al-Maghāzī,* the early Shiʿite scholar Abān ibn ʿUthmān al-Aḥmar al-Bajalī (d. ca. 200/816), whose work is also lost. Portions of the latter's work seem to be preserved by Amīn al-Dīn al-Ṭabrisī (d. 548/1154) in the portion of his *Iʿlām al-warā* dedicated to the biography of Muḥammad. See Modarressi, *Tradition and Survival,* 130 and Jarrar, "Early Shīʿī Sources."

24 Görke and Schoeler, *Die älteste Berichte,* 258 ff., 289; cf. an English summary in Görke, "Prospects and Limits," 145 f.

25 Balādhurī, *Ansāb,* 4(2):490; Schoeler posits that ʿAbd al-Malik later had a change of heart, but does not speculate why. See Schoeler, *Biography,* 31.

26 Shoemaker ("In Search of ʿUrwa's *Sīra*") provides the most thorough critique of the recent attempts to rediscover ʿUrwah's corpus in later sources; now, cf. the riposte by Görke, Schoeler, and Motzki, "First Century Sources."

27 Ibn ʿAsākir, *Dimashq,* 59:393.

28 Ibn Saʿd, *Ṭabaqāt,* 2(2):135, "*min abnāʾ al-muhājirūn waʾl-anṣār.*"

29 Ibn Abī Khaythamah, *Tārīkh,* 2:127–28; Fasawī, *Maʿrifah,* 1:479.

30 Cited in Lecker, "Biographical Notes," 34. As Lecker demonstrates (ibid., 37–40), al-Zuhrī served as a judge (*qāḍī*) for at least three caliphs, administered the collection of taxes, and was known, moreover, for wearing the clothing of the high-ranking Umayyad soldiery (*al-jund*).

31 Fasawī, *Maʿrifah,* 1:636; cf. Lecker, "Biographical Notes," 32–33 and n. 46 thereto.

32 Guidetti, "Contiguity between Churches and Mosques," 20 ff.

33 Lecker, "Biographical Notes," 25–28; cf. Cook, "The Opponents of the Writing of Tradition," 459–62 and Schoeler, *Oral and Written,* 140–41 on the controversy.

34 Abū Nuʿaym, *Ḥilyah,* 3:363; Ibn ʿAsākir, *Dimashq,* 59:399–400.

35 Ibn Abī Khaythamah, *Tārīkh,* 1:271, 325–26: Ibn ʿAsākir, *Dimashq,* 59:412. On collation in the transmission of knowledge, see Déroche, *Qurʾans of the Umayyads,* 70; Gacek, *Arabic Manuscripts,* 65 ff.; al-Qāḍī, "How 'Sacred' Is the Text of an Arabic Medieval Manuscript," 28 f.; and Mashūkhī, *Anmāṭ al-tawthīq,* 47.

36 Ibn Saʿd, *Ṭabaqāt,* 2(2):136; Fasawī, *Maʿrifah,* 1:479, 637–38; Ibn ʿAsākir, *Dimashq,* 59:400; cf. the discussion in Cook, "The Opponents of the Writing of Tradition,"

459–60. The fate of these writings is unknown, but it is significant that they survived al-Zuhrī's death despite al-Walīd II's antipathy toward al-Zuhrī. The caliph allegedly declared that he would have killed the scholar had he survived to see his caliphate. See Horovitz, *Earliest Biographies*, 58–59. The dislike was apparently mutual. According to one account, al-Zuhrī pleaded with Zayd ibn ʿAlī to delay his revolt against Hishām so that he might openly offer Zayd his support once al-Walīd II had come to power. Zayd, of course, did not follow al-Zuhrī's council and was crucified as a rebel by Hishām in 122/740. See Balādhurī, *Ansāb*, 2:621 and Anthony, *Crucifixion*, 46 ff.

37 Cf. Robinson, "The Violence of the Abbasid Revolution."

38 Ibn ʿAsākir, *Dimashq*, 59:408.

39 Ibn ʿAsākir, *Dimashq*, 36:167, 173 f.; cf. Horovitz, *Earliest Biographies*, 73.

40 This applies not only to the *Kitāb al-Maghāzī* but also to Maʿmar's *al-Jāmiʿ* and, to a lesser extent ʿAbd al-Razzāq's *Tafsīr*, or Qur'an commentary, the bulk of which derives from Maʿmar.

41 See Cook, "The Opponents of the Writing of Tradition"; Kister, "Notes on the Transmission of Ḥadīth"; and Schoeler, *Oral and Written*, 111–41 et passim on this issue.

42 Ibn Ḥajar, *Tahdhīb*, 10:220. Indeed, Muḥammad ibn Isḥāq, Maʿmar's contemporary, courted controversy by merely integrating the books of others into his *Kitāb al-Maghāzī* rather than only including materials from scholars under whom he directly studied. See Schoeler, *Biography*, 26.

43 Ibn ʿAsākir, *Dimashq*, 59:417, *mā ra'aynā li-Maʿmar kitāb ghayr hādhihi l-ṭiwāl fa-innahu yakhrujuhā bi-lā shakk.*

44 Ibn ʿAsākir, *Dimashq*, 59:395, 409.

45 Ibn Abī Khaythamah, *Tārīkh*, 1:324; cf. Cook, "The Opponents of the Writing of Tradition," 469–70 for further material on Maʿmar's ambivalent attitude toward written materials.

46 Günther, "New Results"; cf. the systematic attempt of A. Elad to apply Günther's concept of "literary composition" to early Islamic historiography in Syria in his article "The Beginning of Historical Writing," 121 ff.

47 Ibn ʿAsākir, *Dimashq*, 36:178; according to A. Dietrich, the plant was reputed to confer "a lucid intellect." See *EI2*, "Halīladj."

48 Ibn Abī Khaythamah, *Tārīkh*, 1:330.

49 The first of these is a papyrus fragment held at the Oriental Institute of the University of Chicago, erroneously attributed to Maʿmar ibn Rāshid by Nabia Abbott (*Studies in Arabic Literary Papyri*, 1:65–79), and subsequently correctly identified by M.J. Kister as from the work of the Egyptian scholar and judge (*qāḍī*) Ibn Lahīʿah (d. 175/790). See

Kister, "Notes on the Papyrus Text." A second papyrus, likely dating to the early third/ninth century, is attributed to Wahb ibn Munabbih (d. ca. 101–02/719–20); on which, see Khoury, *Wahb b. Munabbih.*

50 Schoeler, *Biography*, 32–34.

51 On Ibn Isḥāq and the Abbasids, see Horovitz, *Earliest Biographies*, 79–80; Sellheim, "Prophet, Chalif und Geschichte."

52 Sellheim, "Prophet, Chalif und Geschichte," 40 f.; Robinson, *Islamic Historiography*, 135.

53 Horovitz, *Earliest Biographies*, 80–89. Indeed, Nabia Abbot identified a papyrus fragment from Ibn Isḥāq's *Tārīkh al-khulafāʾ*. See Abbott, *Studies in Arabic Literary Papyri*, 1:80–99. Her comments on the text ought to be supplemented by those of Kister, "Notes on an Account of the Shura."

54 For traditions ascribed to al-Zuhrī on the ʿAqabah meetings, see Bayhaqī, *Dalāʾil*, 2:421–23, 454; none of these are Maʿmar traditions, but rather come from Mūsā ibn ʿUqbah. For traditions from Maʿmar on the topic, which however are not related on the authority of al-Zuhrī, see ʿAbd al-Razzāq, *Tafsīr*, 1:129 (ad Q Nisāʾ 4:103); idem, *Muṣannaf*, 6: 4, 6–7. For other narrations attributed to al-Zuhrī more generally but not related by Maʿmar, see ʿAwwājī, *Marwīyāt al-Zuhrī*. Most events listed by ʿAwwājī that Maʿmar does not relate in a narration from al-Zuhrī notably derive either from Ibn Isḥāq or Mūsā ibn ʿUqbah.

55 Maher Jarrar (*Die Prophetenbiographie*, 29) believed ʿAbd al-Razzāq to have included only a portion of Maʿmar's *maghāzī* corpus from Zuhrī, but the evidence he adduces for this assertion is wanting. Of the examples he cites (ibid., 54 n. 158), at least two of them actually *do* appear in the *Kitāb al-Maghāzī*, despite his claims to the contrary (Abū Nuʿaym, *Dalāʾil*, 2:504–5 is 5.1 of this volume; Dhahabī, *Tārīkh*, 6:20–21 is 1.10); and two other traditions appear in ʿAbd al-Razzāq's *Tafsīr* (Abū Nuʿaym, *Dalāʾil*, 1:224 = ʿAbd al-Razzāq, *Tafsīr*, 1:169; Dhahabī, *Tārīkh*, 1:610 = ʿAbd al-Razzāq *Tafsīr*, 1:288–89). The other examples he cites are minor, short traditions that are certainly related to "*maghāzī*" concerns, but are not centerpieces of the *maghāzī* tradition; see Abū Nuʿaym, *Dalāʾil*, 1:272 (how the Hāshim clan came to reside in the piedmont of Abū Ṭālib); Dhahabī, *Tārīkh*, 1:575 (Gabriel announces ʿUmar's conversion), 594 (on Medina's female diviner Faṭīmah), 642 (on the prayers as revealed in Mecca). More substantial omissions from Maʿmar ibn Rāshid's *maghāzī* materials, especially traditions on the reigns of the first four caliphs, can be found throughout *Ansāb al-ashrāf* of al-Balādhurī (d. 279/892). The scholar al-Wāqidī and his scribe Ibn Saʿd are a potential source, too, for further *maghāzī* traditions from Maʿmar; however, Wāqidī is known to play fast and loose with his source material, making the prospect of recovering Maʿmar's authentic material from him slim.

56 Schoeler, *Biography*, 27.

Note on the Text

57 Motzki, "The Author and His Work," 181.

58 Ibn Khayr, *Fahrasah*, 1:153, 289–90; cf. Ibn al-Nadīm, *Fihrist*, 1:296 and 2:94.

59 Ibn Khayr, *Fahrasah*, 1:155.

60 The hadith scholar Abū Bakr Ibn Abī Shaybah (d. 235/849) exhorted his fellow scholars that "seeking elevated *isnād*s is part of religion (*ṭalab al-isnād al-ʿālī min al-dīn*)"; cited in Brown, *Ḥadīth*, 47 ff.

61 Dhahabī, *Tārīkh*, 6:714–15; Ibn Khayr, *Fahrasah*, 1:154 f.

62 Abū Zurʿah, *Tārīkh*, 1:457; Ibn ʿAsākir, *Dimashq*, 36:174. ʿAbd al-Razzāq's fondess for Ibn Ḥanbal as one of his star students was renowned. See Ibn al-Jawzī, *Virtues of the Imam Aḥmad ibn Ḥanbal*, 1: 46–7, 280–81, 424–7.

63 Dhahabī, *Tārīkh*, 6:714; cf. Ibn Ḥajar, *Lisān*, 2:36 f.

64 Ibn Mufarrij's work is no longer extant, to my knowledge, but is said to have been titled *Kitāb Iṣlāḥ al-ḥurūf allatī kāna Isḥāq ibn Ibrāhīm al-Dabarī yuṣaḥḥifuhā fī Muṣannaf ʿAbd al-Razzāq*; see Ibn Khayr, *Fahrasah*, 1:155.

65 Sezgin, *Geschichte des arabischen Schrifttums*, 1:99.

66 Cf. al-Qāḍī, "How 'Sacred' Is the Text of an Arabic Medieval Manuscript?"

كِتَابُ ٱلمَغَازِي

The Expeditions

بسم الله الرحمن الرحيم ١،٠

باب ما جاء في حفر زمزم

عبد الرزّاق عن معمرعن الزهريّ، قال: ١،١

إنّ أوّل ما ذكرمن عبد المطّلب جدّ رسول الله صلّى الله عليه وسلم أنّ قريشاً ١،١،١
خرجت من الحرم فارّةً من أصحاب الفيل وهوغلام شابّ. فقال: والله لا أخرج من
حرم الله أبتغي العزّ[١] في غيره. فجلس عند البيت وأجلت عنه قريش. فقال:

اللّٰهُمَّ إِنَّ المَرءَ يَمنَعُ رَحلَهُ فَامنَع رِحَالَكْ
لَا يَغلُبَنَّ صَلِيبُهُم وَمِحَالُهُم غَدوًا مِحَالَكْ

فلم يزل ثابتاً حتّى أهلك الله تبارك وتعالى الفيل وأصحابه فرجعت قريش وقد عظُم فيهم بصبره وتعظيمه محارمَ الله.

فبينا هو[٢] على ذلك، وُلد له أكبرُ بنيه فأدرك، وهو الحارث بن عبد المطّلب، فأُتي ٢،١،١
عبدُ المطّلب في المنام، فقِيلَ[٣] له: احفر زمزم خبيئة الشيخ الأعظم.

قال: فاستيقظ، فقال: اللّهمّ بيّنْ لي. فأُري في المنام مرةً أخرى: احفر زمزم تكتم بين الفرث والدم في مبحث الغراب في قرية النمل[٤] مستقبلة الأنصاب الحمر.

---

١ ز، بد (كلاهما من رواية عبد الله بن معاذ الصنعاني عن معمرعن الزهري)؛ مم: الغير. ٢ ز، بد؛ مم: هم.
٣ ز، بد؛ مم: قال. ٤ ز، بد ؛ مم: الدم.

In the Name of God, the Merciful, the Compassionate 0.1

The Digging of the Well of Zamzam

ʿAbd al-Razzāq, on the authority of Maʿmar, on the authority of al-Zuhrī, who said: 1.1

The first thing mentioned regarding ʿAbd al-Muṭṭalib, the grandfather of the 1.1.1
Messenger of God, is that when the Quraysh left Mecca's Sacred Precincts[1] fleeing the Elephant Troop[2] he was still a young man, a youth. He said, "By God, I will not forsake the Sacred Precincts of God to seek glory elsewhere!" He sat down next to the Sacred House,[3] even though the Quraysh had abandoned it. Then he declaimed:

> O Lord, a man protects his mount, so protect your mounts.
> Do not allow their cross[4] and stratagem to defeat your stratagem tomorrow.

He remained steadfast in his place until God destroyed the war elephant and its troop. The Quraysh then returned, and ʿAbd al-Muṭṭalib became greatly esteemed among them for his perseverance and reverence for the holy things of God.

In the midst of these events, the eldest of his sons was born to him and 1.1.2
came of age. His name was al-Ḥārith ibn ʿAbd al-Muṭṭalib. By and by, ʿAbd al-Muṭṭalib received a visitation in his sleep,[5] a voice that said to him, "Dig out Zamzam and that which was cached by the most honored shaykh."[6] He awoke and prayed, "O Lord, make this clearer to me!" Then he was granted another vision in his sleep: "Dig Zamzam, hidden between the viscera and blood,[7] where the crow searches, in the anthill, facing the red-stained altars."[8]

ʿAbd al-Muṭṭalib got up and strode over to the Sacred Mosque, where he sat down inside looking for the sacred signs that were hidden from him. At the

قال: فقام عبد المطّلب، فمشى حتّى جلس في المسجد الحرام ينظر ما خُبِئ له من الآيات، فنُحرت بقرة بالحزورة، فأفلتت[١] من جازرها بحشاشة نفسها حتّى غلبها الموت في المسجد في موضع زمزم. فجزرت تلك البقرة في مكانها حتّى احتُمِلَ لحمها. فأقبل غراب يهوي حتّى وقع في الفرث، فبحث في قرية النمل.[٢]

فقام عبد المطّلب يحفر هنالك، فجاءته قريش فقالوا لعبد المطّلب: ما هذا الصنيع؟ لم نكن نُزنّك بالجهل، لِمَ تحفر في مسجدنا؟ فقال عبد المطّلب: إنّي لحافر هذه البئر ومجاهد من صدّني عنها! فطفق يحفر، هو وابنه الحارث، وليس له يومئذ ولد غيره. فيسعى عليهما ناس من قريش فينازعونهما ويقاتلونهما وينهى عنه الناس من قريش لما يعلمون من عتق نسبه وصدقه واجتهاده في دينه يومئذ حتّى إذا أمكن الحفر واشتدّ عليه الأذى نذر إنْ وُفي له بعشرة من الولدان ينحر أحدهم. ثمّ حفر حتّى أدرك سيوفاً دُفنت في زمزم. فلمّا رأت قريش أنّه قد أدرك السيوف، فقالوا لعبد المطّلب: أَحْذِنا ممّا وجدت! فقال عبد المطّلب: بل هذه السيوف لبيت الله.

ثمّ حفر حتّى أنبط الماء، فحفرها في القرار، ثمّ بحرها حتّى لا تُنزف، ثمّ بنى عليها حوضاً. وطفق هو وابنه ينزعان، فيملآن ذلك الحوض، فيشرب منه الحاجّ. فيكسره ناس من حسدة قريش بالليل، ويصلحه عبد المطّلب حين يصبح. فلمّا أكثروا إفساده، دعا عبد المطّلب ربّه، فأُري في المنام. فقيل له: قل: اللّهمّ إني لا أحلُّها لمغتسل ولكن هي لشارب حِلّ وبِلّ. ثمّ كُفيتَهم. فقام عبد المطّلب حين أجفلت[٣] قريش بالمسجد، فنادى بالّذي أُري، ثمّ انصرف. فلم يكن يفسد عليه حوضه أحد من قريش إلّا رُمي بداء في جسده حتّى تركوا له حوضه ذلك وسقايته.

---

١ مم: فأفتلت؛ ز، بد: انفلتت. ٢ ز، بد؛ مم: الدم. ٣ مم؛ ز: احفلت؛ بد: اختلفت.

Ḥazwarah market a cow had been slaughtered, but it broke free with its last gasps and fled from its butcher until death overtook it inside the Mosque where Zamzam lay. The cow was butchered at that spot and its meat carried away. A crow then approached, swooping down to land in the cow's inedible remains, and began searching in the anthill.[9]

ʿAbd al-Muṭṭalib stood and began digging at that very spot. The Quraysh came to him and asked, "What are you doing? We have never taken you for an ignorant man. Why are you digging in our mosque?"[10] ʿAbd al-Muṭṭalib replied, "I am digging this well, and I will defy anyone who prevents me from doing so!" Straightaway he began digging, he and his son al-Ḥārith. In those days, he had no other son besides him. People from the Quraysh would watch them both warily, often even intervening and fighting them. Others from the Quraysh forbade them from doing so because of what they knew of the prestige of ʿAbd al-Muṭṭalib's lineage, his honesty, and his commitment to his religion in those days. Thus it was that, although it was possible for him to dig, he was also subjected to harm and abuse; and so he swore an oath: if ten sons were to be granted to him, he would sacrifice one of them. Continuing to dig, he eventually discovered swords that had been buried in Zamzam.[11] When the Quraysh saw that he had unearthed the swords, they said, "Give us a share of what you have found." "No!" ʿAbd al-Muṭṭalib replied. "These swords belong to God's House."

He dug still more until water sprang forth. Then he dug out the bottom and dredged the well so that it would not run dry. Next he built a basin over the well. Straightaway he and his son began to draw out water and to fill that basin so that pilgrims might drink from it, but some of the Quraysh, full of resentment, would break the basin at night. ʿAbd al-Muṭṭalib would repair it when he awoke, but after they had ruined it several times, ʿAbd al-Muṭṭalib called out to his Lord. Again he was granted a vision in his sleep, and a voice instructed him, "Cry out: 'By God, I will not permit the well to be used by one undertaking ablutions. Rather, it is free to all and a source of refreshment for those seeking to quench their thirst.' Then you will have fulfilled your obligations toward them."[12] ʿAbd al-Muṭṭalib went before the Quraysh while they were disconcerted in the mosque and proclaimed the vision shown to him and then departed. Thereafter, not one of the Quraysh would ruin his basin without being afflicted by some bodily illness, and eventually they left him to tend to his basin and provide water for the pilgrims.

ثمّ تزوّج عبد المطّلب النساء، فولد له عشرة رهط. فقال: اللّهمّ إنّي كنت نذرت لك نحر أحدهم وإنّي أقرع بينهم. فأَصِبْ بذلك من شئتَ. فأقرع بينهم، فصارت القرعة على عبد الله بن عبد المطّلب، وكان أحبّ ولده إليه. فقال: اللّهمّ هو أحبُّ إليك أو مئة من الإبل؟ قال: ثمّ أقرع بينه وبين مئة من الإبل، فصارت القرعة على مئة من الإبل، فنحرها عبد المطّلب مكان عبد الله. ٣،١،١

وكان عبد الله أحسن رجل رُئِي في قريش قطّ، فخرج يوماً على نساء من قريش مجتمعاتٍ. فقالت امرأة منهنّ: يا نساء قريش! أيّتكنّ يتزوّجها هذا الفتى؟ فتَصْطَبُ[1] النور بين عينيه فإنّ بين عينيه نوراً. فتزوّجته[2] آمنة ابنة وهب بن عبد مناف بن زهرة. فجمعها، فالتقت، فحملت برسول الله صلّى الله عليه وسلّم.

ثمّ بعث عبد المطّلب عبد الله بن عبد المطّلب يمتار له تمراً من يثرب، فتوفّي عبد الله بها. وولدت آمنة رسول الله صلّى الله عليه وسلّم. فكان في حجر عبد المطّلب، فاسترضعه امرأة من بني سعد بن بكر. ٤،١،١

فنزلت به الّتي ترضعه سوق عكاظ. فرآه كاهن من الكهّان، فقال: يا أهل عكاظ! اقتلوا هذا الغلام! فإنّ له ملكاً! فراعت به أمّه الّتي ترضعه، فنجاه الله.

ثمّ شبّ عندها حتّى إذا سعى وأخته من الرضاعة تحضنه. فجاءت[3] أخته من أمّه الّتي ترضعه، فقالت: أي أمّتاه! إنّي رأيتُ رهطاً أخذوا أخي آنفاً، فشقّوا بطنه! فقامت أمّه الّتي ترضعه فزعةً حتّى أتته. فإذا هو جالس منتقعاً لونه. لا ترى عنده أحداً.

فارتحلت به حتّى أقدمته على أمّه. فقالت لها: اقبضي عنّي ابنك، فإنّي قد خشيت عليه. فقالت أمّه: لا، والله ما بابني ممّا[4] تخافين. لقد رأيت وهو في بطني أنّه خرج نور منّي أضاءت منه قصور الشام. ولقد ولدته حين ولدته، فخرّ معتمداً على يديه رافعاً رأسه إلى السماء.

---

١ مم: نصطت؛ بد: تصطاد. ٢ مم: فزوجته. ٣ بد؛ مم: فجاءته. ٤ بد؛ ساقطة من مم.

After this, ʿAbd al-Muṭṭalib married several women, and ten sons were born to him, a full troop. "O Lord," he said, "I gave You my oath that I would sacrifice one of them. I shall cast lots for them,[13] so choose in this way whomever You will." He cast lots between them, and the lot fell upon ʿAbd Allāh ibn ʿAbd al-Muṭṭalib, who was the most beloved of all his children, so he said, "O Lord, which is more desirous to You, he or a hundred camels?" He cast lots between his son and a hundred camels, and the lot fell upon the hundred camels. Thus, ʿAbd al-Muṭṭalib sacrificed the camels in ʿAbd Allāh's stead.[14] 1.1.3

Now ʿAbd Allāh was the finest-looking man ever seen among the Quraysh, and one day when he passed by some Qurashī women gathered together, one of the women said, "O ladies of Quraysh! Which of you shall be wedded to this young man?"—and the light between his eyes shimmered, for light shone from between them.[15] Thus it was that Āminah bint Wahb ibn ʿAbd Manāf ibn Zuhrah was wedded to him. He consummated the union and took her maidenhead, whereupon she became pregnant with the Messenger of God.

Later ʿAbd al-Muṭṭalib sent ʿAbd Allāh ibn ʿAbd al-Muṭṭalib to transport dates for him from Yathrib. ʿAbd Allāh ibn ʿAbd al-Muṭṭalib passed away while in Yathrib, and Āminah gave birth to the Messenger of God. He was placed in the custody of ʿAbd al-Muṭṭalib and nursed by a woman from the Saʿd ibn Bakr clan. 1.1.4

On one occasion, his milch-mother[16] brought him to the market of ʿUkāẓ. One of the diviners[17] saw him and said, "O people of ʿUkāẓ!—kill this boy! For he is destined to rule over us!" His milch-mother became frightened for him, but God delivered him.

The Prophet spent his boyhood in her house,[18] and when he began to walk, his milch-sister was charged with looking after him. Once his milch-sister came and cried, "O mother! I just now saw a band of men take my brother and split open his abdomen!"[19] Terrified, his milch-mother rose up and rushed to him; however, he merely sat there, white with fright, and she saw no one else with him.

She then set out with him so that she could present him to his mother. His milch-mother said to her, "Take your son from me, for I am afraid for his sake." "No, by God," said his mother, "there is no reason to be afraid for my son. While he was in my womb, I saw a vision: a light shone forth from me that illuminated the palaces of Syria.[20] I gave birth to him, and right after he was born, he prostrated himself by leaning on his hands and lifting his head toward the heavens."

فافتصلته أمّه وجدّه عبد المطّلب. ثمّ توفّيت أمّه. فيتمّ[1] في حجر جدّه، فكان، وهو غلام، يأتي وسادة جدّه فيجلس عليها، فيُخرِج جدَّه وقد كبِر، فتقول الجارية الّتي تقوده: انزل عن وسادة جدّك! فيقول عبد المطّلب: دعي ابني فإنّه محسن[2] بخير.

٥،١،١ ثمّ توفّي جدّه ورسول الله صلّى الله عليه وسلّم غلامٌ، فكفله أبو طالب وهو أخو عبد المطّلب لأبيه وأمّه. فلمّا ناهز الحلم، ارتحل به أبو طالب تاجرًا قبل الشام. فلمّا نزلا تيماء، رآه حبر من يهود تيماء.[3] فقال لأبي طالب: ما هذا الغلام منك؟

فقال: هو ابن أخي.

قال له: أشفيق أنت عليه؟

قال: نعم.

قال: فوالله لئن قدمت به إلى الشام لا تصل به إلى أهلك أبدًا ليقتلنّه! إنّ هذا عدوّهم!

فرجع أبو طالب من تيماء إلى مكّة.

٦،١،١ فلمّا بلغ رسول الله صلّى الله عليه وسلّم الحلم، أجمرت امرأة الكعبة، فطارت شرارة من مجمرها في ثياب الكعبة، فأحرقتها ووهت. فتشاورت قريش في هدمها وهابوا هدمها. فقال لهم الوليد بن المغيرة: ما تريدون بهدمها، الإصلاح تريدون أم الإساءة؟

فقالوا: بل الإصلاح.

قال: فإنّ الله لا يهلك المصلح.

قالوا: فمن الّذي يعلوها فيهدمها؟

قال الوليد: أنا أعلوها فأهدمها!

فارتقى الوليد بن المغيرة على ظهر البيت ومعه الفأس، فقال: اللّهمّ إنّا لا نريد إلّا الإصلاح! ثمّ هدم، فلمّا رأته قريش قد هدم منها ولم يأتِهم ما خافوا من العذاب،

---

١ بد ؛ مم: فهم. ولعلّ المقصود في مم: فهو.   ٢ مم؛ بد: يحسّ.   ٣ بد؛ مم: تميم.

His mother and grandfather ʿAbd al-Muṭṭalib had him weaned from his milch-mother, and soon thereafter his mother passed away. The Prophet thus became an orphan in the custody of his grandfather. While he was still a boy, he would march up to his grandfather's cushion and sit on it, pushing his grandfather off. His grandfather had grown quite old with age, and the slave girl who looked after ʿAbd al-Muṭṭalib would say, "Get down from your grandfather's cushion!" But ʿAbd al-Muṭṭalib would reply, "Leave my boy be, for it suits the lad."

While the Messenger of God was still a boy, his grandfather also passed 1.1.5
away, and his uncle Abū Ṭālib, the full brother of ʿAbd Allāh, became his guardian. When the Prophet attained puberty, Abū Ṭālib traveled with him to Syria to trade, but when they arrived in the oasis of Taymāʾ a rabbi from the Jews of Taymāʾ saw him. The rabbi said to Abū Ṭālib, "This young man isn't your son, is he?"

"He's my brother's son," Abū Ṭālib replied.

"Do you care for the boy?" asked the rabbi.

"Yes," he said.

"By God," said the rabbi, "if you bring him to Syria, you will never again return him to your people. They will certainly kill him—for this young man is their enemy!"[21]

Abū Ṭālib returned, therefore, from Taymāʾ to Mecca.

When God's Messenger reached puberty, a woman accidentally set fire 1.1.6
to the Kaaba when sparks from the fire she had kindled flew up and onto its covering. The fire burned the Kaaba, and its structure became unstable. The Quraysh deliberated among themselves over whether it should be demolished, but they were too terrified to go through with it. Al-Walīd ibn al-Mughīrah said to them, "What do you want to accomplish by demolishing it? To repair it or to ruin it?"

"Only to repair it," they said.

"God will surely not cause any man to perish who seeks to repair it," al-Walīd said.

Then they asked, "But who will climb it and tear it down?"

"I will be the one to climb," answered al-Walīd.

Al-Walīd ibn al-Mughīrah climbed to the top of the Sacred House, taking an ax with him, and declared, "O Lord, we desire nothing but to undertake a repair." Then he began to tear down the Kaaba. When the Quraysh saw that

هدموا معه حتّى إذا بنوها. فبلغوا موضع الركن. اختصمت[1] قريش في الركن، أيّ القبائل ترفعه؟ حتّى كاد يشجر بينهم. فقالوا: تعالوا نحكّم أوّل من يطلع علينا من هذه السكّة.[2] فاصطلحوا على ذلك، فطلع عليهم رسول الله صلّى الله عليه وسلّم، وهو غلام عليه وِشَاحُ نَمِرَةٍ، فحكّموه فأمر بالركن فوضع في ثوب. ثمّ أمر بسيّد كلّ قبيلة، فأعطاه بناحية الثوب. ثمّ ارتقى ورفعوا إليه الركن، فكان هو يضعه.

٧،١،١ ثم طفق لا يزداد فيهم على[3] السنين إلا رضىً حتى سمّوه الأمين قبل أن ينزل عليه الوحي. ثمّ طفقوا لا ينحرون جزوراً إلّا درأوه[4] فيدعو لهم فيهم.

فلمّا استوى وبلغ أَشُدَّه، وليس له كثير مال، استأجرته خديجة ابنة خويلد إلى سوق حباشة، وهو سوق بتهامة، واستأجرت معه رجلاً آخر من قريش. فقال رسول الله صلّى الله عليه وسلّم وهو يحدّث عنها: ما رأيت من صاحبة أجير خيراً من خديجة. ما كنّا نرجع، أنا وصاحبي، إلّا وجدنا عندها تحفةً من طعام تخبّئه لنا.

قال: فلمّا رجعنا من سوق حباشة، قال رسول الله صلّى الله عليه وسلّم، قلت لصاحبي: انطلق بنا نتحدّث[5] عند خديجة. قال: فجئناها، فبينا نحن عندها، إذ دخلت علينا منتشية من مولّدات قريش. والمنتشية: الناهد الّتي تشتهي الرجل. قالت: أمحمّد هذا؟ والّذي يُحلف به إنْ جاء لخاطباً؟ فقلتُ: كلّا! فلمّا خرجنا، أنا وصاحبي، قال: أمن خطبة خديجة تستحي؟ والله ما من قرشيّة إلّا تراك لها كفواً.

قال: فرجعنا إليها مرةً أخرى، فدخلتْ علينا تلك المنتشية. فقالت: أمحمّد هذا؟ والّذي يُحلف به إن جاء لخاطباً. قال: قلت على حياء: أجل.

قال: فلم تعصنا خديجة ولا أختها. فانطلقتْ إلى أبيها خويلد بن أسد، وهو ثمل من الشراب. فقالت: هذا ابن أخيك محمّد بن عبد الله يخطب خديجة وقد رضيت خديجة. فدعاه، فسأله عن ذلك، فخطب إليه، فأنكحه. قال: فخلّقت خديجة وحلّت عليه حلّة، فدخل رسول الله صلّى الله عليه وسلّم بها.

---

١ بالأصل: اجتمعت؛ والصواب من كتاب الحج في مم. ٢ بالأصل: الشوكة؛ والصواب من كتاب الحج في مم.
٣ مم: عن. ٤ مم: دروه. ٥ زب؛ مم: نحدث.

he had demolished some of it and that the chastisement they feared had not come, they began to work alongside him to demolish it. When they had rebuilt it and reached as far as the cornerstone,[22] the Quraysh quarreled over which tribe would put it back in place, and a fight nearly broke out between them. Then someone said, "Come now, let us choose the first one we see coming down this road," and they agreed upon that. It was the Messenger of God who approached them—he was a boy at the time, wearing a striped sash[23]—so they appointed him for the task. They ordered the cornerstone to be placed inside a cloth. After that, he called for the head of each tribe, and gave each an edge of the cloth. Then he ascended, and they raised the cornerstone aloft for him. Thus it was the Messenger of God who put the cornerstone in place.

As the years passed, he became all the more admired among them, and 1.1.7
eventually they named him "the Trustworthy" (*al-amīn*) before the revelation descended upon him. So it came to be that none would butcher a camel for sale without urging him to invoke God's blessing over it on their behalf.

Once he had grown to his full height and reached manhood—though without attaining any great wealth—Khadījah bint Khuwaylid hired him, sending him to Ḥubāshah, a market in Tihāmah. She also hired alongside him another man from the Quraysh. Speaking of Khadījah, the Messenger of God remarked, "Of all the women who hired servants, I never saw one kinder than Khadījah. We would always return, my companion and I, and find at her home a gift of food she had stored away for us."

The Prophet continued, "When we returned from the Ḥubāshah market, I said to my companion, 'Let's leave, and we'll have a chat at Khadījah's house.' So we went there, and while we were in her home, a *muntashiyah*—one of the slave-born women of the Quraysh—came into the room where we were. A *muntashiyah* is a buxom young woman who desires men. She said, 'Is this Muḥammad? By Him with Whom pacts are made, has he come as a suitor?' And I said, 'Not at all!' Once my companion and I had left, he said, 'Are you too shy to accept Khadījah's proposal? By God, there's not a single Qurashī woman would not consider you her equal!'"

The Prophet continued, "We returned to her another time, and that buxom girl returned to us and asked, 'Is this Muḥammad? By Him with Whom pacts are made, has he come as a suitor?' 'Yes,' I replied bashfully."

The Prophet said, "Khadījah would never act contrary to either our wishes or her sister's,[24] and her sister had gone off to see her father, Khuwaylid

فلمّا أصبح، صحا الشيخ من سكره. فقال: ما هذا الخلوق؟ ما هذه الحلّة؟ قالت أخت خديجة: هذه حلّة كساكها ابن أخيك محمّد بن عبد الله. أنكحته خديجة وقد بنى بها! فأنكر الشيخ، ثمّ سلّم إلى أن صار ذلك واستحيى. وطفقت رجّاز من رجّاز قريش تقول:

لَا تَزهَدِي خَدِيجُ عن مُحَمَّدْ   جِلدٌ يُضِيءُ كَضِيَاءِ الفَرقَدْ

١،١،٨ فلبث رسول الله صلّى الله عليه وسلّم مع خديجة حتّى ولدت له بعض بناته، وكان لها وله القاسم. وقد زعم بعض العلماء أنّها ولدت له غلاماً آخر يُسمّى الطاهر. قال: وقال بعضهم: ما نعلمها ولدت له إلّا القاسم. وولدت له بناته الأربع: زينب وفاطمة ورقيّة وأمّ كلثوم. وطفق رسول الله صلّى الله عليه وسلّم بعدما ولدت له بعض بناته يتحنّث وحُبّب إليه الخلاء.

١،٢ عبد الرزّاق قال: أخبرنا معمر قال: أخبرنا الزهريّ قال: أخبرني عروة عن عائشة، قالت:

١،٢،١ أوّل ما بُدئ به رسول الله صلّى الله عليه وسلّم من الوحي الرؤيا الصادقة[١] فكان لا يرى رؤيا إلّا جاءت مثل فلق الصبح. ثمّ حبّب إليه الخلاء، فكان يأتي حراءً فيتحنّث فيه، وهو التعبّد الليالي ذوات العدد، ويتزوّد لذلك. ثمّ يرجع إلى خديجة، فيتزوّد لذلك، فيرجع إلى خديجة، فيتزوّد[٢] لمثلها.

فحينما جاءه الحقّ، وهو في غار حراء، فجاءه الملك فيه. فقال له: اقرأ! يقول لرسول الله صلّى الله عليه وسلّم: اقرأ! فقال رسول الله صلّى الله عليه وسلّم:

---

١ مم، ن؛ بد: الصالحة.   ٢ ن، بد؛ مم: فيترون.

ibn Asad, who was drunk. She said, 'This is your nephew, Muḥammad ibn 'Abd Allāh, who wishes to become betrothed to Khadījah, and Khadījah has consented.'" Khuwaylid invited the Messenger of God over and asked him about the marriage arrangement. Khuwaylid then betrothed Khadījah to him and gave her to him in marriage. Khadījah was covered in perfume, and the Messenger of God was dressed in a wedding garment. Then the Messenger of God consummated the marriage with Khadījah.

When her father awoke the next morning, the old man had recovered from his drunkenness and said, "What is this perfume? And this wedding garment?" Khadījah's sister replied, "This is the wedding garment in which your nephew Muḥammad ibn 'Abd Allāh has clothed you! You married him to Khadījah, and he's consummated the marriage!" The old man at first denied this but then resigned himself to what had transpired and became ashamed. At that moment some of the *rajaz* poets[25] of Quraysh began to recite:

Do not abstain, O Khadījah, from Muḥammad,
Whose skin glimmers like the light of Pherkad.[26]

The Messenger of God remained with Khadījah, and eventually she bore him several daughters. The two of them also had al-Qāsim. Some scholars claim that she bore him another young boy named al-Ṭāhir. Another scholar said, "We do not know of her giving birth to any boy except al-Qāsim, and she also bore him his four daughters: Zaynab, Fāṭimah, Ruqayyah, and Umm Kulthūm." After she had born him a number of daughters, the Messenger of God also began to practice acts of religious devotion,[27] and he became fond of seclusion. **1.1.8**

'Abd al-Razzāq said: Ma'mar related to us and said: al-Zuhrī related to us and said: 'Urwah related to me that 'Ā'ishah said: **1.2**

The first revelation experienced by the Messenger of God came to him in the form of the "true vision."[28] Not a vision came that did not resemble the breaking of dawn. Afterward, he became fond of seclusion and would go to Mount Ḥirā', where he practiced acts of religious devotion—meaning that he worshipped God for nights on end. He would provision himself for that and then return again and again to Khadījah to reprovision himself for further journeys. **1.2.1**

When the Truth came to him, he was in a cave on Mount Ḥirā', and the angel came to him there. The angel said to him, "Read!" And again the angel commanded the Messenger of God, "Read!" The Messenger of God said,

قلتُ: ما أنا بقارئ! فأخذني، فغطّني حتّى بلغ منّي الجهد. ثمّ أرسلني، فقال: اقرأ. فقلت: ما أنا بقارئ. فأخذني فغطّني الثالثة حتّى بلغ منّي الجهد. ثمّ أرسلني، فقال: ﴿ اقْرَأْ بِاسْمِ رَبِّكَ الَّذِي خَلَقَ ﴾ حتّى بلغ ﴿ مَا لَمْ يَعْلَمْ ﴾.

٢،٢،١ فرجع بها ترجُف بَوادِرُه حتّى دخل على خديجة. فقال: زمّلوني! فزمّلوه حتّى ذهب عنه الروع. فقال لخديجة: ما لي؟ وأخبرها الخبر، فقال: قد خشيت عليّ! فقالت: كلّا! والله لا يخزيك الله أبداً. إنّك لتصل الرحم وتصدق الحديث وتقري الضيف وتعين نوائب الحقّ!

٣،٢،١ ثم انطلقت به خديجة حتّى أتت به ورقة ابن نوفل بن راشد بن عبد العزّى بن قصيّ، وهو ابن عمّ خديجة، أخو أبيها. وكان تنصّر في الجاهليّة وكان يكتب الكتاب العربيّ. فكتب بالعربيّة من الإنجيل ما شاء الله[1] أن يكتب. وكان شيخاً كبيراً قد عمي.

فقالت خديجة: أيْ ابن عمّي! اسمع من ابن أخيك!

فقال ورقة: ابن أخي؟ ما ترى؟ فقال رسول الله صلّى الله عليه وسلّم ما رأى. فقال ورقة: هذا الناموس الّذي أنزل على موسى عليه السلام! يا ليتني فيه جذعاً حين يخرجك قومك!

فقال رسول الله صلّى الله عليه وسلّم: أَوَمخرجيّ هم؟

فقال ورقة: نعم، لم يأتِ أحد بما أتيت به إلّا عودي وأوذي. وإن يدركني يومك، أنصرك نصراً مؤزّراً.

ثم لم ينشب ورقة أن توفّي.

٤،٢،١ وفتر الوحي فترةً حتّى حزن رسول الله صلّى الله عليه وسلّم، فيما بلغنا، حزناً بدا منه أشدّ حزناً[2] غدا منه مراراً كي يتردّى من رؤوس شواهق الجبال. فلمّا ارتقى بذروة جبل، تبدّى له جبريل عليه السلام فقال: يا محمّد! يا رسول الله حقّاً! فيسكن لذلك

---

١ بد: ساقطة من مم. ٢ مم؛ عب: حزناً شديداً.

"I said, 'But I cannot read!' So he took hold of me and crushed me until I could no longer bear it. Then he released me and said, 'Read!' 'I cannot read!' I said. He took me and crushed me a third time, until I could no longer bear it. He again released me and said:

> «Read in the name of your Lord who created: He created man from a clinging form. Read! Your Lord is the Most Bountiful One who taught by means of the pen, who taught man what he did not know.»"[29]

Muḥammad returned with these words,[30] his shoulders trembling, and eventually he reached Khadījah. He said, "Cover me! Cover me!"[31] They covered him in a cloth until the terror had left him. He said to Khadījah, "What's wrong with me?" And he related to her what had transpired. "Are you fearful for my sake?" he said. "Not at all!" Khadījah said. "By God, God will never disgrace you, for you are a man who honors the bonds of kinship and speaks only the truth, who acts hospitably toward guests and aids his kinsmen in their duress."[32] 1.2.2

Khadījah then set off with the Prophet to bring him to Waraqah ibn Nawfal ibn Rāshid ibn 'Abd al-'Uzzā ibn Quṣayy, Khadījah's cousin, the son of her father's brother. He had converted to Christianity during the Age of Ignorance prior to Islam. He was able to write the Arabic script and had written as much of the Gospels in Arabic as God had willed.[33] At the time, he was quite an old shaykh and had gone blind. 1.2.3

Khadījah said to him, "O cousin! Listen to your nephew!"

Waraqah said, "My nephew? What did you see?" When the Messenger of God explained what he had seen, Waraqah declared, "This is the Nomos[34] that God sent down to Moses! If only I could be a strong youth when your people exile you!"

The Messenger of God said, "Will they really exile me?"

Waraqah replied, "Yes, for oppression and persecution await all to whom God has given what He has given you. If I live to see your time come, I will surely aid you to become victorious."

It was not long before Waraqah died.

The revelation ceased for a time so that the Messenger of God became— 1.2.4
as we have been informed—profoundly saddened. One could see that the deepest sadness had fallen upon him. Because of this, he went out in the morning

جأشه وتقرّ نفسه. فرجع، فإذا طالت عليه فترة الوحي، عاد لمثل ذلك. فإذا رقى بذروة جبل تبدّى له جبريل عليه السلام فقال له مثل ذلك.

قال معمر: قال الزهريّ: فأخبرني أبو سلمة بن عبد الرحمن عن جابر بن عبدالله قال: ٣،١

سمعت رسول الله صلّى الله عليه وسلّم، وهو يحدّث عن فترة الوحي. فقال في حديثه: بينا أنا أمشي سمعت صوتاً من السماء ورفعت رأسي. فإذا الذي جاءني بحراء جالساً على كرسيّ بين السماء والأرض، فجئت منه رعباً. ثمّ رجعت، فقلت: زمّلوني، زمّلوني! ودثّروني! فأنزل الله تعالى ﴿ يَأَيُّهَا الْمُدَّثِّرُ ﴾ إلى ﴿ وَالرُّجْزَ فَاهْجُرْ ﴾ قبل أن تفرض الصلاة، وهي الأوثان.

قال معمر: قال الزهريّ: أخبرني عروة:[1] ٤،١

أنّ خديجة توفّيت. فقال رسول الله صلّى الله عليه وسلّم: أُريت في الجنّة بيتاً لخديجة من قصب، لا صخب فيه ولا نصب. وهو قصب من اللؤلؤ.

قال: سئل رسول الله صلّى الله عليه وسلّم عن ورقة بن نوفل، كما بلغنا، فقال: رأيته في المنام عليه ثياب بياض. وقد أظنّ أن لو كان من اهل النار لم أرَ عليه البياض.

قال: ثمّ دعا رسول الله صلّى الله عليه وسلّم إلى الإسلام سرّاً وجهراً وإلى هَجْر[2] الأوثان.

---

١ [عروة] أنا؛ ساقطة من م. ٢ [وإلى هجر] من عب (رواية محمد بن كثير الصنعانيّ عن معمر عن الزهريّ)؛ ساقطة في م.

to the heights of the mountains to cast himself from their peaks several times, but whenever he climbed to the summit of a mountain, Gabriel would appear to him and say, "O Muḥammad! O True Messenger of God!" And so his anxiety would subside, and his soul become steadfast. He returned home, and when the lapse in revelation continued for a long time, he would return to doing as he had done before. Whenever he would climb to a mountain's summit, Gabriel would appear to him again and speak to him as he had before.[35]

Maʿmar said: al-Zuhrī said: Abū Salamah ibn ʿAbd al-Raḥmān related to me on the authority **1.3**
of Jābir ibn ʿAbd Allāh al-Anṣārī, who said:

I heard the Messenger of God speaking about the lapse in revelation. He said, "While I was walking about, I heard a voice from heaven, so I lifted my head. And lo, before me was the one who had come to me at Mount Ḥirāʾ, seated on a throne suspended between heaven and earth. I became absolutely terrified because of him. Later I returned and said, 'Cover me! Cover me!' and 'Wrap me up!' Then God most high revealed:

> «O you wrapped in his cloak, arise and give warning! Proclaim the greatness of your Lord; cleanse yourself; keep away from filth.»"

This was before the prayers had been made obligatory. "Filth" means idols.[36]

Maʿmar said: al-Zuhrī said: **1.4**

ʿUrwa related to me that, when Khadījah passed away, the Messenger of God said, "I received a vision of a house in Paradise for Khadījah made of reeds, in which there is neither clamor nor toil. It is fashioned from reeds of pearl."[37]

When the Messenger of God was asked about Waraqah ibn Nawfal—as was reported to us—he said, "I dreamt of Waraqah and he was wearing a white cloak. I am inclined to think that, were he among the denizens of hellfire, I would not have seen him in white."

Then the Messenger of God began to call the people to Islam secretly and publicly, and for the people to abandon[38] their idols.

قال معمر: وأخبرنا قتادة عن الحسن وغيره، فقال: ٥،١

كان أوّل من آمن به عليّ بن أبي طالب رضي الله عنه، وهو ابن خمس عشرة أو ستّ عشرة.

قال: أخبرني عثمان الجزري عن مقسم عن ابن عبّاس، قال: ٦،١

عليّ أوّل من أسلم.

قال: سألت الزهريّ، فقال: ٧،١

ما علمنا أحداً أسلم قبل زيد بن حارثة.

قال: فاستجاب له من شاء الله من أحداث الرجال وضعفاء الناس حتّى كثر من ٨،١
آمن به. وكفّار قريش منكرين لما يقول، يقولون إذا مرّ عليهم في مجالسهم فيشيرون إليه: إنّ غلام بني عبد المطّلب هذا ليكلَّمُ، زعموا، من السماء!

قال معمر: قال الزهريّ: ٩،١

ولم يتبعه من أشراف قومه غير رجلين، أَبي بكر وعمر رحمهما الله. وكان عمر ١،٩،١
شديداً على رسول الله صلّى الله وسلّم وعلى المؤمنين. فقال النبيّ صلّى الله عليه وسلّم: اللّهمّ أيّد دينك بابن الخطّاب!

فكان أوّل إسلام عمر، بعدما أسلم قبله ناس كثير، أن حُدّث أنّ أخته أمّ جميل ٢،٩،١
ابنة الخطّاب أسلمت وأنّ عندها كتفاً اكتتبتها من القرآن تقرأه سرّاً. وحُدّث أنّها لا تأكل من الميتة الّتي يأكل منها عمر. فدخل عليها، فقال: ما الكتف الّذي ذُكر لي عندك تقرئين فيها ما يقول ابن أبي كبشة؟ يريد رسول الله صلّى الله عليه وسلّم.

Maʿmar said: Qatādah ibn Diʿāmah related to us on the authority of al-Ḥasan al-Baṣrī and others, saying: 1.5

The first to believe in Muḥammad was ʿAlī ibn Abī Ṭālib, who was fifteen or sixteen years old at the time.

Maʿmar said: ʿUthmān al-Jazarī related to me on the authority of Miqsam, citing Ibn ʿAbbās, who said: 1.6

ʿAlī was the first to become Muslim.

Maʿmar said: I asked al-Zuhrī and he said: 1.7

We do not know of anyone who became Muslim before Zayd ibn Ḥārithah.

Maʿmar continued: 1.8

Those whom God willed to do so answered the Prophet's call—namely, the young and the destitute—and eventually the number who believed in him increased greatly, even though the infidel Quraysh rejected what the Prophet preached. They would point to him whenever he passed by them in their assemblies and say, "This boy from the sons of ʿAbd al-Muṭṭalib hears a voice, as they allege, from heaven!"[39]

Maʿmar said: al-Zuhrī said: 1.9

From the notables of the Prophet's tribe, only two men followed him: Abū Bakr and ʿUmar ibn al-Khaṭṭāb. Now ʿUmar used to be a strident opponent of the Messenger of God and the Believers, so the Prophet prayed, "O Lord, support your religion with Ibn al-Khaṭṭāb!" 1.9.1

The beginning of ʿUmar's conversion to Islam—after many had already become Muslims before him—was as follows: ʿUmar was informed that his sister, Umm Jamīl bint al-Khaṭṭāb, had become a Muslim and that she possessed a shoulder blade on which she had written verses from the Qurʾan and from which she read aloud in secret. ʿUmar was also told that she no longer ate of the carrion from which he ate.[40] Thus, he went to her and asked, "What is this shoulder blade that I hear you have in your possession? Are you reading from it the things about which Ibn Abī Kabshah speaks?"—by whom he meant the Messenger of God.[41] "I don't have a shoulder blade," she replied. So ʿUmar 1.9.2

فقالت: ما عندي كتف. فصكّها، أو قال: فضربها، عمر. ثمّ قام فالتمس الكتف في البيت حتّى وجدها. فقال حين وجدها: أمّا إنّي قد حُدّثت أنّك لا تأكلين طعامي الّذي آكل منه! ثمّ ضربها بالكتف فشجّها شجّتين.

ثمّ خرج بالكتف حتّى دعا قارئًا، فقرأ عليه. وكان عمر لا يكتب. فلمّا قُرئت ٣،٩،١
عليه، تحرّك قلبه حين سمع القرآن ووقع في نفسه الإسلام. فلمّا أمسى، انطلق حتّى دنا من رسول الله صلّى الله عليه وسلّم، وهو يصلّي ويجهر بالقراءة. فسمع رسولَ الله صلّى الله عليه وسلّم يقرأ ﴿وَمَا كُنْتَ تَتْلُوا مِنْ قَبْلِهِ مِنْ كِتَٰبٍ وَلَا تَخُطُّهُ بِيَمِينِكَ﴾ حتّى بلغ ﴿الظَّالِمِينَ﴾ وسمعه يقرأها ﴿وَيَقُولُ ٱلَّذِينَ كَفَرُوا لَسْتَ مُرْسَلًا﴾ حتّى بلغ ﴿عِلْمُ ٱلْكِتَٰبِ﴾.

قال: فانتظر عمر رسول الله صلّى الله عليه وسلّم حتّى سلّم من صلاته. ثمّ انطلق رسول الله صلّى الله عليه وسلّم إلى أهله، فأسرع عمر المشي في أثره حين رآه. فقال: انظرني يا محمّد! فقال النبيّ صلّى الله عليه وسلّم: أعوذ بالله منك! فقال عمر: انظرني يا محمّد! يا رسول الله! قال: فانتظره رسول الله صلّى الله عليه وسلّم، فآمن به عمر وصدّقه.

فلمّا أسلم عمر رضي الله عنه، انطلق حتّى دخل على الوليد بن المغيرة.[١] فقال: أي ٤،٩،١
خالي! أشهد أنّي أؤمن بالله و رسوله وأشهد أن لا إله إلّا الله وأنّ محمّدًا عبده و رسوله صلّى الله عليه وسلّم. فأخبرْ بذلك قومك!

فقال الوليد: ابن أختي! تثبّت في أمرك! فأنت على حال تُعْرَف بالناس. يصبح المرء فيها على حال ويمسي على حال.

فقال عمر: والله قد تبيّن لي الأمر، فأخبرْ قومك بإسلامي!

١ في الأصل: خالد بن الوليد بن المغيرة.

beat her—or, al-Zuhrī said, he hit her—and then he began searching for the shoulder blade. When he found the shoulder blade, he struck her with it, splitting her skull open in two places, and said, "And that's for what I have been hearing about you refusing to eat the same food as me!"

After this ʿUmar left, carrying the shoulder blade with him, so that he might summon a reader to read it to him, for ʿUmar was illiterate. When the words were read to him, his heart quickened, and hearing the Qurʾan, Islam settled in his heart. When evening came, he went to see the Messenger of God, who was praying and reciting the Qurʾan in public. ʿUmar heard the Messenger of God recite aloud: 1.9.3

> «You never recited any Scripture before We revealed this one to you; you never wrote one down with your hand. If you had done so, those who follow falsehood might have cause to doubt. But no, this Qurʾan is a revelation that is clear to the hearts of those endowed with knowledge. No one refuses to acknowledge Our revelations but the evildoers.»[42]

He also heard him recite:

> «Those who disbelieve say, "You have not been called as a Messenger." Say, "God is a sufficient witness between me and you: all knowledge of Scripture comes from Him."»[43]

ʿUmar waited for the Messenger of God until he had finished the saying of "Peace!" at the end of the ritual prayer.[44] The Messenger of God set off to see his followers, and ʿUmar walked after him hurriedly when he saw him go. Then ʿUmar said, "Wait for me, Muḥammad!" The Prophet said, "I seek refuge in God from you!" ʿUmar said, "Wait for me, Muḥammad! *O Messenger of God!*" The Messenger of God waited for him, and ʿUmar believed in him and acknowledged the truth of his message.

Once ʿUmar had become a Muslim, he left to visit al-Walīd ibn al-Mughīrah. 1.9.4
He said: "O Uncle! I bear witness that I believe in God and His Messenger, and I testify that there is no god but God and that Muḥammad is His servant and Messenger! So go inform your people of this!"

But al-Walīd said, "My nephew! Remain firm in your stance toward Muḥammad. Your stature among the people is well known. Will a man rise amid his people in the morning in one state and begin the evening in another?"

فقال الوليد: لا أكون أوّل من ذكر ذلك عنك.[١]

فدخل عمر مجالسهم.[٢] فلمّا علم عمر أنّ الوليد لم يذكر شيئاً من شأنه، دخل على جميل بن معمر الجمحيّ. فقال: أخبر أنّي أشهد أن لا إله إلّا الله وأنّ محمّداً عبده ورسوله.

قال: فقام جميل بن معمر يجرّ رداءه من العجلة جرّاً حتّى تتبّع مجالس قريش. فقال: ١،٩،٥
صبأ عمر بن الخطّاب! فلم ترجع إليه قريش شيئاً. وكان عمر سيّد قومه، فهابوا الإنكار عليه. فلمّا رآهم لا ينكرون ذلك عليه، مشى حتّى أتى مجالسهم، أكمل ما كانت، فدخل الحِجْر، فأسند ظهره إلى الكعبة. فقال: يا معشر قريش! أتعلمون أنّي أشهد أن لا إله إلّا الله وأنّ محمّداً عبده ورسوله! فثاروا، فقاتله رجال منهم قتالاً شديداً وضربهم عامّة يومه حتّى تركوه. واستعلن بإسلامه وجعل يغدو عليهم ويروح، يشهد أن لا إله إلّا الله وأنّ محمّداً عبده ورسوله. فتركوه، فلم يؤذوه بعد ثورتهم الأولى. فاشتدّ ذلك على كفّار قريش فعدوا[٣] على كلّ رجل أسلم، فعذّبوا من المسلمين نفراً.

قال معمر: قال الزهريّ: ١،١٠

وذكر ضلال آبائهم الّذين ماتوا كفّاراً، فشقّوا رسولَ الله صلّى الله عليه وسلّم وعادَوه. فلمّا أُسْرِيَ به إلى المسجد الأقصى، أصبح الناس يخبر أنّه قد أسري به. فارتدّ أناس ممّن كان قد صدّقه وآمن به، وفتنوا وكذّبوا به. وسعى رجل من المشركين إلى أبي بكر، فقال: هذا صاحبك يزعم أنّه قد أسري به الليلة إلى بيت المقدس، ثمّ رجع من ليلته!

فقال أبو بكر: أَوَقال ذلك؟

---

١ مم: عندك.   ٢ مم: فاستالناليا؛ القراءة علاه لزكار.   ٣ [فعدوا] أنا: ساقطة من مم.

"By God," retorted ʿUmar, "the matter has become clear to me, so inform your people that I have become Muslim."

"I will not be the first to tell them this about you," said al-Walīd.

ʿUmar then entered the elders' assemblies, and once he ascertained that al-Walīd had not mentioned anything about him, he went to Jamīl ibn Maʿmar al-Jumaḥī and said, "Spread the news: I testify that there is no god but God and that Muḥammad is his servant and Messenger."

Jamīl ibn Maʿmar stood up, hurriedly picking up his cloak, and the assem- 1.9.5
blies of the Quraysh followed him. "ʿUmar ibn al-Khaṭṭāb has abandoned his religion!" declared Jamīl,[45] but the Quraysh said nothing in reply, for ʿUmar was an esteemed leader of his tribe, and they were afraid to denounce him. When ʿUmar saw that they did not denounce him because of what he had done, he headed straightaway to their assemblies,[46] which were as well attended as they had ever been. He then entered the walled enclosure of the Kaaba, pressed his back up against the Kaaba, and cried out, "O company of Quraysh! Do you not know that I testify that there is no god but God and that Muḥammad is his servant and Messenger?" Then they rose up in a fury, and some of their men attacked him fiercely. He spent most of that day fighting them off, and eventually they left him alone. Thus did he seek to announce his acceptance of Islam, walking to and fro in their midst and testifying that there is no god but God and that Muḥammad is His servant and Messenger. Eventually they left him alone, for they had failed to harm him after being incited against him the first time. This greatly distressed the infidels of the Quraysh, so they began persecuting[47] every man who embraced Islam, and even tortured a number of the Muslims.

Maʿmar said: al-Zuhrī said: 1.10

The Messenger of God spoke of the damnation of the ancestors of the Quraysh who had died as infidels, so they caused trouble for the Messenger of God and showed him enmity. When God carried him away by night to al-Aqṣā Mosque, the people began to report that this had transpired. As a result, many of those who had believed and had faith in him apostatized. They lost faith and declared him to be a liar. One of the Pagans strolled over to Abū Bakr and said, "This companion of yours claims to have been carried away this very night to the Jerusalem Temple, and then to have returned in the same night!"

Abū Bakr replied, "He said that, did he?"

"Yes!" they said.

قالوا: نعم!

فقال أبو بكر: فإنّي أشهد إنْ كان قال ذلك لقد صدق.

فقالوا: أتصدّقه بأنّه جاء الشام في ليلة واحدة، ورجع قبل أن يصبح؟

قال أبو بكر: نعم، إنّي أصدّقه بأبعد من ذلك! أصدّقه بخبر السماء بكرةً وعشياً!

فلذلك سمّى أبا بكر بالصدّيق.

١١،١ قال معمر: قال الزهريّ: وأخبرني أنس بن مالك:

أنّ النبيّ صلّى الله عليه وسلّم فُرضت عليه الصلوات ليلة أسري به خمسين، ثمّ نُقِّصت إلى خمس، ثمّ نُودي: يا محمّد! ﴿مَا يُبَدَّلُ ٱلْقَوْلُ لَدَيَّ﴾ وإنّ لك بالخمس خمسين.

١٢،١ قال معمر: قال الزهريّ: أخبرني أبو سلمة عن جابر بن عبد الله، قال:

قال النبيّ صلّى الله عليه وسلّم: قمتُ في الحِجر حين كذّبني قومي، فرُفع لي بيت المقدس حتّى جعلت أنعت لهم.

١٣،١ قال معمر: قال الزهريّ: فأخبرني سعيد بن المسيّب عن أبي هريرة، قال:

قال النبيّ صلّى الله عليه وسلّم حين أسري به: لقيتُ موسى. قال: فنعته: فإذا رجل، حسبتُه قال، مضطرب رَجِل الرأس كأنّه من رجال شنوءة. قال: ولقيتُ عيسى عليه السلام. فنعته، فقال: ربعة أحمر فكأنّما خرج من ديماس. قال: ورأيت إبراهيم وأنا أشبه ولده به.

قال: وأتيتُ بإنائين، في أحدهما لبن وفي الآخر خمر. فقيل لي: خذْ أيّهما شئت. فأخذت اللبن، فشربته. فقيل لي: هديت للفطرة، أو أصبت الفطرة، أما إنّك لو أخذت الخمر، غوت أمّتك.

Abū Bakr responded, "I testify that if he said such a thing then he has spoken the truth!"

They said, "Do you believe that he went to Syria in a single night and returned before the morning came!"

Abū Bakr replied, "Yes, and I'll believe something even more improbable than that! I believe in his report of having been to heaven morning and night!"

For this reason, the Prophet named Abū Bakr al-Ṣiddīq "the one who bears witness to truth."[48]

Maʿmar said: al-Zuhrī said: Anas ibn Mālik informed me: 1.11

The night the Prophet was carried away God made fifty prayers incumbent upon him, but they were decreased to five. Then a voice called out, "O Muḥammad! «My decree cannot be altered»[49] and you have been given five instead of fifty."

Maʿmar said: al-Zuhrī said: Abū Salamah related to me on the authority of Jābir ibn ʿAbd 1.12
Allāh, who said:

The Prophet said, "I stood in the walled enclosure of the Kaaba when my tribe called me a liar. Then the Temple in Jerusalem came to me in a vision so vividly that I was able to describe it to them."

Maʿmar said: al-Zuhrī said: Saʿīd ibn al-Musayyab related to me on the authority of Abū 1.13
Hurayrah, who said:

The Prophet said—after he had been carried away at night—"I met Moses." Then the Prophet described him: "There he was"—I reckon he said—"quite a tall man with curly hair, like the men of the Shanū'ah tribe." Muḥammad also said, "I met Jesus," and he described him saying, "stocky, of ruddy complexion, as though he had just exited from a public bathhouse.[50] I saw Abraham, too; I, of all his descendants, resemble him the most."

The Prophet also said, "Two containers were brought to me; in one was milk and in the other wine. I was given the choice: [51] 'Take whichever you desire.' I took the milk and drank it, and then it was said me, 'You have been guided according to humankind's original faith.'[52] Or, 'You have chosen correctly according to humankind's original faith. If you had chosen the wine, your community would have been led astray.'"

غَزْوَةُ الحُدَيْبِيَةِ

عبد الرزّاق عن معمر قال: أخبرني الزهريّ، قال: أخبرني عروة بن الزبير عن مسور بن مخرمة ومروان بن الحكم. ١،٢
صدّق كلّ واحد منهما صاحبه. قالا:

خرج رسول الله صلّى الله عليه وسلّم زمن الحديبية في بضع عشرة مئة من أصحابه حتّى إذا كانوا بذي الحليفة. قلّد رسول الله صلّى الله عليه وسلّم الهدي وأشعره. وأحرم بالعمرة، وبعث بين يديه عيناً له من خزاعة يخبره عن قريش. وسار رسول الله صلّى الله عليه وسلّم حتّى إذا كانوا بغدير الأشطاط قريباً من عسفان. أتاه عينه الخزاعيّ، فقال: إنّي تركت كعب بن لؤيّ وعامر بن لؤيّ. قد جمعوا لك الأحابيش وجمعوا لك جموعاً وهم مقاتلوك وصادّوك عن البيت.

فقال النبيّ صلّى الله عليه وسلّم: أشيروا عليّ. أترون[١] أن نميل إلى ذراري هؤلاء الّذين أعانوهم، فنصيبهم؟ فإنْ قعدوا، قعدوا موتورين محروبين.[٢] وإن نجوا،[٣] تَكُنْ عنقاً قطعها اللهُ. أم ترون أن نؤمّ البيت، فمن صدّنا قاتلناه. فقالوا: رسول الله أعلم. يا نبيّ الله، إنّما جئنا معتمرين ولم نجئ لقتال أحد، ولكن من حال بيننا وبين البيت قاتلناه. قال النبيّ صلّى الله عليه وسلّم: فروحوا إذاً.

قال معمر: قال الزهريّ: ٢،٢

وكان أبو هريرة يقول: ما رأيتُ أحداً قطّ كان أكثر مشورةً لأصحابه من رسول الله صلّى الله عليه وسلّم.

---

١ ح؛ [أترون] ساقطة من مم؛ وفي ط: أترون لي. ٢ ح، ط؛ مم: موزويين. ٣ ح؛ ط: حاءوا؛ مم: سحو.

The Expedition of Ḥudaybiyah[53]

ʿAbd al-Razzāq, on the authority of Maʿmar, who said: al-Zuhrī related to me, saying: ʿUrwah ibn al-Zubayr related to me from Miswar ibn Makhramah and Marwān ibn al-Ḥakam, each of whom attested to the truth of the other's account. They said: 2.1

The Messenger of God departed from Medina at the time of Ḥudaybiyah, leading a group of his Companions numbering a couple thousand men. When eventually they arrived at Dhū l-Ḥulayfah, the Messenger of God adorned the sacrificial camel with garlands and made an incision on its hump, marking it for sacrifice. He donned the two seamless garments for undertaking the rites of a pilgrimage to Mecca[54] and sent ahead of him one of his spies from the Khuzāʿah tribe to bring him reports concerning the Quraysh. The Messenger of God then marched onward. When he reached the pool of al-Ashṭāṭ, close to ʿUsfān, his Khuzāʿī spy came to him and said, "I just left the Kaʿb ibn Lu'ayy and ʿĀmir ibn Lu'ayy clans; they've gathered some hired troops[55] and several bands of men to oppose you. They're set to battle you and bar you from the Sacred House."

The Prophet said, "Lend me your counsel—do you reckon that we should seize the women and children of those who have aided them in order to capture them? If they stand down, then they do so as defeated men unable to retaliate. If they escape, then their necks will be God's to sever. Or do you reckon that we should head for the Sacred House and battle against anyone who bars us from entering?"

They said, "The Messenger of God knows best, O Prophet of God! We have only come as pilgrims and not to fight anyone. But we are ready to fight whoever stands between us and the Sacred House." "Go forth then," said the Prophet.

Maʿmar said: al-Zuhrī said: 2.2

Abū Hurayrah would say, "I've never seen anyone more inclined to consult his companions than the Messenger of God."

قال الزهريّ في حديث مسور بن مخرمة ومروان: ٣،٢

فراحوا حتّى إذا كانوا ببعض الطريق. قال النبيّ صلّى الله عليه وسلّم: إنّ خالد بن الوليد بالغميم في خيل لقريش طليعةً فخذوا ذات اليمين. فوالله ما شعر بهم خالد إذا هو بقترة الجيش فانطلق. فإذا هو يركض نذيرًا لقريش. وسار النبيّ صلّى الله عليه وسلّم حتّى كانوا بالثنيّة الّتي يهبط عليهم منها بركت به راحلته. فقال الناس: حَلْ! حَلْ! فقالوا: خلأت القصواء، خلأت القصواء! فقال النبيّ صلّى الله عليه وسلّم: ما خلأت القصواء وما ذاك لها بخلق ولكنّها حبسها حابس الفيل. ثمّ قال: والّذي نفسي بيده، لا يسألوني خُطّة يعظّمون فيها حرمات الله إلّا أعطيتهم إيّاها. ثمّ زجرها، فوثبت به. ١،٣،٢

قال: فعدل عنهم[1] حتّى نزل بأقصى الحديبية على ثمد قليل الماء، إنّما يتبرّضه الناس تبرّضاً. فلم يلبثه الناس أن نزحوه. فشُكي إلى رسول الله صلّى الله عليه وسلّم، فانتزع سهماً من كنانته، ثمّ أمرهم أن يجعلوه فيه. قال: فوالله ما زال يجيش لهم بالريّ حتّى صدروا عنه.

فبينا هم كذلك إذ جاء بديل بن ورقاء الخزاعيّ في نفر من قومه من خزاعة، وكانوا عيبة نصح رسول الله صلّى الله عليه وسلّم من أهل تهامة. فقال: إنّي تركت كعب بن لؤيّ وعامر بن لؤيّ نزلوا[2] أعداد مياه الحديبية معهم العُوذ المطافيل وهم مقاتلوك وصادّوك عن البيت. ٢،٣،٢

فقال النبيّ صلّى الله عليه وسلّم: إنّا لم نجئ لقتال أحد ولكنّا جئنا معتمرين. وإنّ قريشاً قد نهكتْهم الحرب وأضرّت بهم. فإنْ شاؤوا مادَدْتُهم مدّةً ويخلّوا بيني وبين الناس. فإن أظهر فإن شاؤوا أن يدخلوا فيما دخل فيه الناس، فعلوا. وإنْ لا، فقد جمّوا وإن أبَوا، فوالّذي نفسي بيده، لأقاتلنّهم على أمري هذا حتّى تنفرد سالفتي! أو لينفذنّ الله[3] أمره!

---

١ ط؛ ح: عنها. ساقطة في مم. ٢ ح، ط: [نزلوا] ساقطة من مم. ٣ ح، ط: [الله] ساقطة من مم.

Al-Zuhrī continued with the story reported by Miswar ibn Makhramah and Marwān: 2.3

They then went forth and, at a certain point on the journey, the Prophet said, "Khālid ibn al-Walīd is at al-Ghamīm with a troop of cavalry from the Quraysh serving as scouts, so take the path to the right." And, by God, not until Khālid came upon the army's dusty trail did he realize they had been there. Then Khālid headed off straightaway, racing to warn the Quraysh. The Prophet marched onward until he reached the mountain pass from which he could descend upon the Quraysh. His she-camel, al-Qaṣwā', knelt down there, and the people said, "*Ḥal, ḥal!*"[56] They also said, "Al-Qaṣwā' has turned defiant; al-Qaṣwā' has turned defiant!" "Al-Qaṣwā' has not turned defiant," the Prophet replied, "for that's not in her nature. Rather, He Who halted the march of the war elephant[57] has caused her to stop." Later he said, "By Him in Whose hands my soul resides, there is no course of action magnifying the sacred things of God that I will not grant them." Then the Prophet spurred on his she-camel, and she rushed forward with him on her back. 2.3.1

He turned away from them and descended to the farthest reaches of Ḥudaybiyah, at a spot overlooking a dried-up puddle containing little water. The people sipped at it little by little, and they had not tarried there long before they drank it all up. Complaints were made to the Messenger of God, so he removed an arrow from his quiver and ordered them to place it in the puddle.

Al-Zuhrī said: By God, it did not cease gushing forth water until they had left.[58]

Meanwhile, Budayl ibn Warqā' al-Khuzā'ī came in a group of his tribesmen from Khuzā'ah who were trusted advisers of the Messenger of God from the people of Tihāmah. Budayl said, "I just left the Ka'b ibn Lu'ayy and 'Āmir ibn Lu'ayy clans. They have encamped among the wells of Ḥudaybiyah—and with them are women and children—and they are ready to battle against you and to bar you from the Sacred House." 2.3.2

The Prophet said, "We have not come to battle against anyone. Rather, we have come as pilgrims. War has exhausted the Quraysh and brought them to ruin. If they wish, I shall grant them a period of respite, but they must leave me and the people alone. If I prevail, and if they wish to join the people in embracing Islam, then they may do so. If not, and if, after having gathered their strength, they refuse, then by Him in Whose hand my soul resides, I will not hesitate to fight against them for the sake of this cause of mine until my neck is severed! Surely God will see His cause through to the end!"

فقال بديل: سأبلغهم ما تقول. فانطلق حتّى أتى قريشاً، فقال: إنّا جئناكم من عند هذا الرجل وسمعناه يقول قولاً. فإنْ شئتم أن نعرضه عليكم، فعلنا. فقال سفهاؤهم: لا حاجة لنا أن تحدّثنا عنه بشيء. وقال ذوو الرأي منهم: هاتِ ما سمعته يقول. قال: سمعته يقول: كذا وكذا. فحدّثهم بما قال النبيّ صلّى الله عليه وسلّم. فقام عروة بن مسعود الثقفيّ، فقال: أي قومي! ألستم بالولد؟

قالوا: بلى!

قال: أو لستُ بالوالد؟

قالوا: بلى!

قال: فهل تتهموني؟

قالوا: لا!

قال: ألستم تعلمون أنّي استنفرتُ أهل عُكاظ؟ فلمّا بلّحوا عليّ، جئتكم بأهلي وولدي ومن أطاعني؟

قالوا: بلى!

قال: فإنّ هذا قد عرض عليكم خُطّة[1] رشد. فاقبلوها ودعوني آتِه.

فقالوا: فأتِه.

فأتاه.

٢،٣،٣ قال: فجعل يكلّم النبيّ صلّى الله عليه وسلّم، فقال رسول الله صلّى الله عليه وسلّم نحوًا من قوله ببديل. فقال عروة عند ذلك: أي محمّد! أرأيت إنْ استأصلتَ قومك؟ هل سمعتَ بأحد[2] من العرب اجتاح أصله قبلك؟ وإنْ تكن الأخرى، فإنّي لا أرى[3] وجوهاً وأرى أشواباً من الناس خليقاً أن يفرّوا عنك.

فقال أبو بكر رحمه الله ورضي عنه: امصُص بَظْرَ اللّات! أنحن نفرّ عنه وندعه؟

فقال: من ذا؟

قال: أبو بكر.

---

١ ح، ط؛ م: خصلة. ٢ ح، ط؛ [بأحد] ساقطة من م. ٣ ح؛ م، ط: : لأرى.

Budayl said, "I will convey your words to them." He then set out until he reached the Quraysh, whereupon he declared, "We have come to you having met this man Muḥammad, and we have heard him put forward a proposal. If you wish for us to present it to you, then we will do so." Their dim-witted men said, "We don't need for you to tell us anything!" But the reasonable ones said, "Tell us what you heard him say." Budayl said, "This is what I heard him say . . ." and so continued to relate to them what he heard the Prophet say.

Then ʿUrwah ibn Masʿūd al-Thaqafī stood up and said, "My people! Are you not like my children?"

"Aye," they said.

He said, "Am I not like your father?"

"Aye," they said.

"Do you," he asked, "hold me in any suspicion?"

"No," they said.

He said, "Do you not know that I called the people of ʿUkāẓ to your aid? When they failed to heed me, did I not come to you with my family, my sons, and whoever else would obey me?"[59]

"Aye," they said.

He said, "This man has offered you an upright course of action, so accept it and allow me to go see him."

"Go to him, then," they said.

So he went.

So ʿUrwah conversed with the Prophet, and the Messenger of God said more 2.3.3
or less what he had said to Budayl. At that point, ʿUrwah said, "O Muḥammad! Have you not considered what will happen if your people come to ruin? Have you ever heard of any other Arab before you who so devastated his people? And if that doesn't come to pass, I see no men of renown here—I see only a motley group of people apt to forsake you."

"Go suck on Allāt's clit!" interjected Abū Bakr. "Are we the sort to forsake him and leave him?"

"Who is that?" demanded ʿUrwah.

"Abū Bakr," the Prophet said.

"By Him in Whose hand my soul resides!" replied ʿUrwah. "Were it not for my respect for you, I would have surely retaliated!"

ʿUrwah resumed his conversation with the Prophet, and as he was speaking to him, he grabbed hold of the Prophet's beard. Now al-Mughīrah ibn Shuʿbah

قال: أما والّذي نفسي بيده، لولا[١] يد لك عندي لم أَجْزِك بها لأجبتُك.

قال: وجعل يكلّم النبيّ صلّى الله عليه وسلّم، فكلّما كلّمه،[٢] أخذ بلحيته، والمغيرة بن شعبة قائم على رأس النبيّ صلّى الله عليه وسلّم ومعه السيف وعليه المِغفَر. فكلّما أهوى عروة يده إلى لحية النبيّ صلّى الله عليه وسلّم، ضرب يده بنعل السيف وقال: أخّر يدك عن لحية رسول الله صلّى الله عليه وسلّم.

فرفع عروة رأسه، فقال: من هذا؟

فقالوا: المغيرة بن شعبة.

فقال: أي غُدَرُ، أولستَ أسعى في غدرتك؟

وكان المغيرة بن شعبة صحب قوماً في الجاهليّة، فقتلهم وأخذ أموالهم. ثمّ جاء فأسلم، فقال رسول الله صلّى الله وسلّم: أمّا الإسلام فأقبل. أمّا المال، فلستُ منه في شيء.[٣]

ثمّ إنّ عروة جعل يرمق صحابة النبيّ صلّى الله عليه وسلّم بعينيه. قال: فوالله ما تنخّم رسول الله صلّى الله عليه وسلّم نخامةً إلّا وقعت في يد رجل منهم. فدلّك بها وجهه وجلده. وإذا أمرهم، ابتدروا أمره. وإذا توضّأ، كادوا يقتتلون على وضوئه. وإذا تكلّموا، خفضوا أصواتهم عنده وما يحدّون إليه النظر[٤] تعظيماً له.

فرجع عروة إلى أصحابه، فقال: أي قوم! والله لقد وفدت على الملوك ووفدت[٥] على قيصر وكسرى والنجاشيّ. والله إنْ رأيت ملكاً قطّ يعظّمه أصحابه ما يعظّم أصحاب محمّد صلّى الله عليه وسلّم محمّداً. والله إنْ تنخّم نخامةً إلّا وقعت في كفّ رجل منهم، فدلّك بها وجهه وجلده. وإذا أمرهم، ابتدروا أمره. وإذا توضّأ، كادوا يقتتلون على وضوئه. وإذا تكلّموا، خفضوا أصواتهم عنده وما يحدّون إليه النظر تعظيماً له. وإنّه قد عرض عليكم خطّة رشد، فاقبلوها. فقال رجل من كنانة: دعوني آتِه. فقالوا: ائتِه.

فلمّا أشرف على النبيّ صلّى الله عليه وسلّم وأصحابه، قال رسول الله صلّى الله عليه ٤،٣،٢
وسلّم: هذا فلان، وهو من قوم يعظّمون البُدْن، فابعثوها له. فبعثوها له واستقبله القوم

---

١ ح، ط؛ م: ألا. ٢ بخ: تكلم كلمة. ٣ ط؛ [في شيء] ساقطة من م. ٤ ط؛ [النظر] ساقطة من م. ٥ ط؛ م: رفدت.

was standing right next to the Prophet, armed with a sword and wearing a helmet. Whenever ʿUrwah would reach out his hand to grasp the Prophet's beard, al-Mughīrah would hit his hand with the hilt of the sword and exclaim, "Remove your hand from the beard of God's Messenger!"

ʿUrwah lifted his head and asked, "Who's this?"

"Al-Mughīrah ibn Shuʿbah," they answered.

"What a scoundrel!" ʿUrwah exclaimed. "Why, you've been most keen to pursue your treachery!"

Now, while a disbeliever, al-Mughīrah ibn Shuʿbah had entered into the company of a clan whose members he later murdered and robbed of their wealth.[60] Afterward he came to Medina and became a Muslim. The Messenger of God said, "As for your submission to God, I accept it. As for the property you stole, I have no part in that."

Then ʿUrwah began to look around at the companions of the Prophet, staring at them wide-eyed. "By God," he said, "when the Messenger of God hawks up his phlegm, one of these men catches it in his hand and smears it on his face and skin. And when he commands them to do something, they hasten to accomplish his orders. And when he performs his ablutions, they nearly kill themselves over the ablution water. Whenever they speak, they lower their voices before him, and out of deference to him, they never look him in the eye."

ʿUrwah returned to his companions and said, "O people! By God, I have been sent as an emissary to kings, sent as an emissary to Caesar, Khosroes, and the Negus![61] By God, I have never seen a king whose companions so revered him as the companions of Muḥammad revere Muḥammad. By God, if he were to hawk up phlegm, then it would be caught in the palm of one of his companions, who would smear it on his face and his skin! If he commands them to do something, they hasten to accomplish his orders. Whenever he performs his ablutions, they nearly kill themselves over the ablution water. Whenever they speak, they lower their voices before him, and out of deference to him, they never look him in the eye. Indeed, he has presented you with an upright course of action, so accept it." A man from the Kinānah tribe said, "Permit me to go to him." "By all means," they said, "go to him."

When the man from Kinānah saw the Prophet and his companions from 2.3.4
a distance, the Messenger of God said, "This is so-and-so; he's from a tribe that greatly reveres sacrificial camels. Send them out to him." They sent the camels out to him, and the people headed toward him crying out the pilgrims'

يلبّون. فلمّا رأى ذلك، قال: سبحان الله، ما ينبغي لهؤلاء أن يصدّوا عن البيت. قال: فلمّا رجع إلى أصحابه، قال: رأيتُ البُدْن قد قلّدت وأشعرت، فما أرى أن يُصدّوا عن البيت. فقال رجل منهم يقال له مِكْرَز بن حفص: دعوني آته. قالوا: ائته. فلمّا أشرف عليهم، قال النبيّ صلّى الله عليه وسلّم: هذا مكرز، وهو رجل فاجر. فجعل يكلّم النبيّ صلّى الله عليه وسلّم. فبينا هو يكلّمه، إذ جاءه سهيل بن عمرو.

قال معمر: فأخبرني أيّوب عن عكرمة: ٢،٣،٥

أنه لمّا جاء سهيل قال النبيّ صلّى الله عليه وسلّم: إنّه قد سهُل لكم من أمركم.

قال معمر: قال الزهريّ في حديثه: ٢،٣،٦

فجاء سهيل بن عمرو، فقال: هاتِ! اكتب بيننا وبينكم كتابًا. فدعا النبيّ صلّى الله عليه وسلّم الكاتب.[١]

فقال النبيّ: اكتب: بسم الله الرحمن الرحيم.

فقال سهيل: أمّا الرحمن، فوالله ما أدري من هو. ولكن اكتب: باسمك اللّهمّ، كما كنت تكتب.

فقال المسلمون: والله لا يكتبها إلّا بسم الله الرحمن الرحيم!

فقال النبيّ صلّى الله عليه وسلّم: اكتب: باسمك اللّهمّ. ثمّ قال: هذا ما فاصل[٢] عليه محمّد رسول الله.

فقال سهيل: والله لو كنّا نعلم أنّك رسول الله، ما صددناك عن البيت ولا قاتلناك! ولكن اكتب: محمّد بن عبد الله.

فقال النبيّ صلّى الله عليه وسلّم: والله إنّي لرسول الله وإنْ كذّبتموني، اكتب: محمّد بن عبد الله.

قال الزهريّ: وذلك لقوله: لا يسألوني خطّةً يعظّمون فيها حرمة الله إلّا أعطيتهم إيّاها.

فقال النبيّ صلّى الله عليه وسلّم: على أن تخلّوا بيننا وبين البيت، فنطوف به.

---

١ بخ، ط:[فقال هاتِ اكتب بيننا وبينكم كتابًا فدعا النبيّ صلى الله عليه وسلّم الكاتب] ساقطة من م. ٢ م؛ بخ: قاضى.

invocations: "Here we are, O Lord!"[62] Once he saw that, he exclaimed, "Glory be to God! It is not proper for these people to be turned away from the Sacred House."

When he returned to his people, he said, "I saw that the sacrificial camels had been garlanded and marked for sacrifice, so I do not think these people should be turned away from the Sacred House." One of their men, Mikraz ibn Ḥafṣ, said, "Allow me to go to him." "Go to him," they said. When he could see them from a distance, the Prophet said, "This is Mikraz; he's a dissolute man." Mikraz began speaking to the Prophet, and while he was speaking, Suhayl ibn ʿAmr came to see the Prophet.

Maʿmar said: Ayyūb informed me on the authority of ʿIkrimah: 2.3.5

When Suhayl came, the Prophet said, "Your cause has just become easier for you."[63]

Maʿmar said: al-Zuhrī continued with his narration: 2.3.6

Suhayl ibn ʿAmr came and said, "Let's do this and be done with it! Write an agreement between us and yourselves."

The Prophet called for the scribe and said, "Write: *In the name of God, the Merciful and the Compassionate.*"[64]

Suhayl said, "As for 'the Merciful,' by God, I know not who he is. Rather, write: *In your name, O Lord*, as you used to write."[65]

The Muslims said, "By God, don't write anything except for *In the name of God, the Merciful and the Compassionate*!"

"Write: *In your name, O Lord*," ordered the Prophet, and then he said, "*This is what Muḥammad the Messenger of God negotiated.*"

"By God," Suhayl objected, "if we had recognized you as being the Messenger of God, then we would neither have barred you from the Sacred House nor fought against you! Rather, write: *Muḥammad ibn ʿAbd Allāh.*"

"By God, I am indeed the Messenger of God," replied the Prophet, "but if you disbelieve, write: *Muḥammad ibn ʿAbd Allāh.*"

Al-Zuhrī added: And that was due to the Prophet's declaration, "I will grant them any course of action that magnifies the sanctity of God."

The Prophet said, "Let it be stipulated that you grant us access to the Sacred House, so that we may circumambulate it."

"We can't have the Arabs saying that we gave in under pressure; rather, that pilgrimage can wait until next year," replied Suhayl. So it was written. Then Suhayl continued, "And let it be stipulated that none of our men may

فقال سهيل: لا تحدّث العرب أنّا أُخذنا ضغطةً، ولكن ذلك العام المقبل. فكتب، فقال سهيل: على أنّه لا يأتيك منّا رجل وإن كان على دينك إلّا رددتَه إلينا.

فقال المسلمون: سبحان الله! كيف يردّ إلى المشركين وقد جاء مسلماً؟

فبينا هم كذلك، إذ جاء أبو جندل بن سهيل بن عمرو يرسف في قيوده، وقد خرج من أسفل مكّة حتّى رمى بنفسه بين أظهر المسلمين. فقال سهيل: هذا يا محمّد! أوّل من أقاضيك عليه أن تردّه إليّ.

فقال النبيّ صلّى الله عليه وسلّم: إنّا لم نقضِ الكتاب بعد.

قال: فوالله إذاً لم أصالحك على شيء أبداً.[١]

فقال النبيّ صلّى الله عليه وسلّم: فأَجِزه لي.

فقال: ما أنا بمجيزه لك.

قال: بلى قد أجزناه لك!

فقال أبو جندل: أي معشر المسلمين! أردّ إلى المشركين وقد جئت مسلماً؟ ألا ترون ما قد لقيت؟ وكان قد عُذّب عذاباً شديداً في الله.

٧،٣،٢ فقال عمر بن الخطّاب: والله، ما شككتُ منذ أسلمت إلّا يومئذ. قال: فأتيت النبيّ صلّى الله عليه وسلّم، فقلتُ: ألستَ نبيّ الله حقّاً؟

قال: بلى.

قلت: ألسنا على الحقّ وعدوّنا على الباطل؟

قال: بلى.

قلت: فلِمَ نعطي الدنيّة في ديننا؟

فقال: إنّي رسول الله ولست أعصيه، وهو ناصري.

قلت: أولست كنت تحدّثنا أنّا سنأتي البيت، فنطوف به؟

قال: بلى، فأخبرتُك أنّك تأتيه العام؟

قلت: لا.

١ بج، ط: [إليّ فقال النبيّ صلى الله عليه وسلّم إنّا لم نقض الكتاب بعد قال فوالله إذاً لم أصالحك على شيء أبداً] ساقطة من مم.

come to you, even if they have accepted your religion, without you returning them to us."

"Glory be to God!" said the Muslims, "How can a person be sent back to the Pagans when he has come to Medina seeking protection as a Muslim?"[66]

At that very moment, Abū Jandal ibn Suhayl ibn ʿAmr[67] came forward shackled in his bonds. He had fled from the lowlands of Mecca and thrown himself before the Muslims. Suhayl then exclaimed, "This one, O Muḥammad, is the first one I'll charge you to return to me!"

"We have not yet finished the written agreement," replied the Prophet.

"By God, then, I will never draw up a treaty with you," retorted Suhayl.

"Hand him over to me," the Prophet demanded.

"I will not release him to you!" Suhayl declared.

"In that case," the Prophet said, "we have released him to you!"

Abū Jandal then cried out, "O Muslims! Shall I be sent back to the Pagans after I have come to you as a Muslim? Do you not see how I have been treated?" Indeed, Abū Jandal had been severely tortured for his belief in God.

ʿUmar ibn al-Khaṭṭāb said, "By God, until that day, I had never once had 2.3.7
doubts since becoming Muslim, so I went to the Prophet and asked:

"'Are you not truly God's prophet?'

"'Yes,' he said.

"'Are we not in the right and our enemies in the wrong?'

"'Yes,' he said.

"'Then why,' I asked, 'do we wrap our religion in disgrace?'

"'I am indeed the Messenger of God,' he said, 'and I do not disobey Him. He is the one who grants me victory.'

"'Did you not tell us that we would come to the Sacred House and circumambulate it?'

"'Yes,' he said, 'but did I inform you that you would come to it this year?'

"'No,' I said.

"He said, 'But you will indeed go to it and circle around it.'"

ʿUmar said, "Then I came to Abū Bakr and asked,

"'O Abū Bakr! Is this not truly the prophet of God?'

"'Yes,' he said.

"I asked, 'And are we not on the side of truth and our enemies on the side of error?'

"'Yes,' he said.

قال: فإنّك آتيه ومطوّف به.

قال: فأتيتُ أبا بكر، فقلتُ: يا أبا بكر! أليس هذا نبيّ الله حقّاً؟

قال: بلى.

قلتُ: ألسنا على الحقّ وعدوّنا على الباطل؟

قال: بلى.

قلتُ: فلِمَ نعطي الدنية في ديننا إذاً؟

قال: أيّها الرجل! إنّه رسول الله وليس يعصي ربّه وهو ناصره. فاستمسك بغَرْزِه حتّى تموت. فوالله إنّا[1] لعلى الحقّ.

قلت: أوليس كان يحدّثنا أنّا سنأتي البيت ونطوف به؟

قال: فأخبرك أنه سيأتيه العام؟

قلت: لا.

قال: فإنّك آتيه ومطوّف به.

قال الزهريّ: قال عمر: فعملت لذلك أعمالاً.

٨،٣،٢ قال: فلمّا فرغ من قضيّة الكتاب، قال رسول الله صلّى الله عليه وسلّم لأصحابه: قوموا، فانحروا، ثمّ احلقوا. قال: فوالله ما قام منهم رجل حتّى قال ذلك ثلاث مرّات. قال: فلمّا لم يقم منهم أحد، قام فدخل على أمّ سلمة، فذكر لها ما لقي من الناس. فقالت أمّ سلمة: يا نبيّ الله! أتحبّ ذلك؟ اخرج، ثمّ لا تكلّم أحداً منهم حتّى تنحر بدنك وتدعو حالقك، فيحلقك. فقام فخرج فلم يكلّم أحداً منهم حتّى فعل ذلك. نحر بدنه ودعا حالقه فحلقه. فلمّا رأوا ذلك، قاموا فنحروا وجعل بعضهم يحلق بعضاً حتّى كاد يقتل بعضهم بعضاً غمّاً.

٩،٣،٢ ثم جاءه نسوة مؤمنات، فأنزل الله ﴿يَأَيُّهَا الَّذِينَ آمَنُوا إِذَا جَاءَكُمُ الْمُؤْمِنَاتُ مُهَاجِرَاتٍ﴾ حتّى بلغ ﴿بِعِصَمِ الْكَوَافِرِ﴾. فطلّق عمر يومئذ امرأتين كانتا في الشرك، فتزوّج إحدَهما معاوية بن أبي سفيان والأخرى صفوان بن أميّة.

---

١ مم؛ ط، بخ: إنه.

"'Then why,' I asked, 'do we wrap our religion in disgrace?'

"He replied, 'Listen, man! He is indeed the Messenger of God! He does not disobey his Lord, and He is the one who grants him victory. So hold tightly to his saddle until you die. By God, we are on the side of truth!'

"I asked, 'And has he not told us that we will come to the Sacred House and circumambulate it?'

"'Did he inform you that you would come to it this year?' Abū Bakr asked.

"'No,' I said.

"'But,' he said, 'you will indeed come to it and circle around it.'"

Al-Zuhrī said: 'Umar said, "Because of my doubts, I performed several good deeds in expiation."

When he had finished with the matter of the written agreement, the Messenger of God said to his companions, "Rise up and make your sacrifices, and then shave your heads," but not a single man from among them stood up, even after the Prophet had said that three times. When not one of them had risen, he stood up and went to see Umm Salamah. When he told her how the people had responded to him, Umm Salamah said, "O Prophet of God! If you don't like that, then go back out, but don't say anything to them until you have sacrificed your camel and called for your barber to shave your head." So he got up, went out, uttered not a word to any of them, and did just that: he sacrificed his camel and called for his barber, who shaved his head. When his followers saw this, they stood up, sacrificed their camels, and each began shaving the head of the other, nearly killing each other out of remorse. 2.3.8

Afterward, believing women came to the Prophet, and God revealed: 2.3.9

> «You who believe! Test the believing women who come to you as emigrants—God knows best about their faith—and if you are sure of their belief, do not send them back to the disbelievers: they are not lawful wives for them. Give the disbelievers whatever bride gifts they have paid—if you choose to marry them, there is no blame on you once you have paid their bride gifts—and do not yourselves hold on to marriage ties with the unbelieving women.»[68]

And on that very day 'Umar ibn al-Khaṭṭāb divorced two women who had remained polytheists. One of them was subsequently married to Mu'āwiyah ibn Abī Sufyān and the other to Ṣafwān ibn Umayyah.

ثم رجع النبيّ صلّى الله عليه وسلّم إلى المدينة، فجاءه أبو بصير، رجل من قريش ١٠،٣،٢
وهو مسلم، فأرسلوا في طلبه رجلين. فقالوا: العهد الّذي جعلتَ لنا. فدفعه إلى
الرجلين، فخرجا حتّى إذا بلغا به ذا الحليفة. فنزلوا يأكلون من تمر لهم.

فقال أبو بصير لأحد الرجلين: والله إنّي لأرى سيفك هذا، يا فلان، جيّداً!

فاستلّه الآخر، فقال: أجل، والله إنّه لجيّد. لقد جرّبت به، ثمّ جرّبت.

فقال أبو بصير: أرِني أنظر إليه؟

فأمكنه منه، فضربه به حتّى برد. وفرّ الآخر حتّى أتى المدينة. فدخل المسجد يعدو.[١] فقال رسول الله صلّى الله عليه وسلّم حين رآه: لقد رأى هذا ذعراً. فلمّا انتهى إلى النبيّ صلّى الله عليه وسلّم، قال: قُتل والله صاحبي، وإنّي لمقتول.

فجاء أبو بصير، فقال: يا نبيّ الله! قد والله أوفى الله ذمّتك. قد رددتَني إليهم، ثمّ أنجاني الله منهم.

فقال النبيّ صلّى الله عليه وسلّم: ويل أمّه! مِسْعَرَ حَرْبٍ لو كان له[٢] أحد!

فلمّا سمع ذلك، عرف أنّه سيردّه إليهم فخرج حتّى أتى سِيفَ البحر. قال: وينفلت منهم أبو جندل بن سهيل فلحق بأبي بصير حتّى اجتمعت منهم عصابة.

قال: فوالله ما يسمعون بعيرٍ خرجت لقريش إلى الشام إلّا اعترضوا لهم،[٣] فقتلوهم ١١،٣،٢
وأخذوا أموالهم. فأرسلت قريش إلى النبيّ صلّى الله عليه وسلّم تناشده بالله والرحم
إلّا أرسل إليهم فمن أتاه، فهو آمن. فأرسل النبيّ صلّى الله عليه وسلّم إليهم.

---

١ بخ، ط؛ مم: يعدُ. ٢ بخ، ط؛ مم: لها. ٣ مم؛ بخ، ط: لها.

Later, the Prophet returned to Medina, where Abū Baṣīr, a Qurashī man who became Muslim, came to him. The Meccans sent two men in his pursuit, and they demanded, "Honor the agreement that you made with us." So the Prophet handed Abū Baṣīr over to the two men. The two men departed, and in time they brought Abū Baṣīr to Dhū l-Ḥulayfah, where they made their camp and ate some dates they had with them. 2.3.10

Abū Baṣīr said to one of the two men, "By God, I see this sword of yours is quite fine!"

The other unsheathed it and said, "Yes, by God, it is indeed quite fine. I've wielded it in battle many times over."

"Do you think," asked Abū Baṣīr, "that I could have a look at it?"

The man handed it to him, and Abū Baṣīr struck him down, leaving him stone-cold dead. The other man fled and eventually reached Medina. He sprinted into the mosque, and when the Messenger of God saw him, he said, "This man has seen something terrifying!" When he reached the Prophet, he said, "My companion, by God, he's been killed! And I'm as good as dead!"

Abū Baṣīr arrived and said, "O Prophet of God, God has honored your end of the bargain. You returned me to them, but God delivered me from them."

The Prophet said, "Woe to your mother! He would set the fires of war ablaze if he had supporters!"

When Abū Baṣīr heard those words, he knew that the Prophet would return him to the Quraysh, so he left Medina and made for the coast. Abū Jandal ibn Suhayl also escaped from the Quraysh; they joined forces and formed a band of marauders.[69]

By God, whenever these men heard that a Qurashī caravan was on its way to Syria, they would attack it, kill the men, and take their possessions. The Quraysh sent a message to the Prophet, invoking God and their bonds of kinship, stating that, if the Prophet were to send a message to those men, then whoever would come to him would be safe. So the Prophet sent a message to them, and God revealed: 2.3.11

> «In the valley of Mecca it was He who held their hands back from you and your hands back from them after He gave you the advantage over them—God sees all that you do. They were the ones who disbelieved, who barred you from the Sacred Mosque, and who prevented the offering from reaching its place of sacrifice. If there had not been among them, unknown to you, believing men and

فأنزل الله ﴿هُوَ الَّذِي كَفَّ أَيْدِيَهُمْ عَنكُمْ وَأَيْدِيَكُمْ عَنْهُم﴾ حتّى بلغ ﴿حَمِيَّةَ الْجَاهِلِيَّةِ﴾. وكانت حميّتهم أنّهم لم يقرّوا أنّه نبيّ الله ولم يقرّوا بسم الله الرحمن الرحيم وحالوا بينه وبين البيت.

عبد الرزّاق عن عكرمة بن عمّار قال: أخبرنا أبو زميل سماك الحنفي أنّه سمع ابن عبّاس يقول: ٤،٢

كاتب الكتّاب يوم الحديبية عليّ بن أبي طالب.

عبد الرزّاق قال:[١] أخبرنا معمر، قال: ٥،٢

سألت عنه الزهريّ فضحك وقال: هو عليّ بن أبي طالب. ولو سألت عنه هؤلاء لقالوا: عثمان، يعني بني أميّة.

عبد الرزّاق عن معمر عن الزهريّ، قال: ٦،٢

كان هرقل حزّاءً ينظر في النجوم. فأصبح يوماً وقد أنكر أهل مجلسه هيئته. فقالوا: ما شأنك؟

فقال: نظرت في النجوم الليلة فرأيتُ ملك الختان قد ظهر.

قالوا: فلا يشقّ ذلك عليك، فإنما يختتن اليهود. فابعث إلى مدائنك، فاقتل كلّ يهوديّ.

قال الزهريّ: وكتب إلى نظير له حزّاء أيضاً نظر في النجوم. فكتب إليه بمثل قوله. قال: ورفع إليه مَلِك بصرى رجلاً من العرب يخبره عن النبيّ صلّى الله عليه وسلّم. فقال: انظروا أمختتن هو؟ قالوا: فنظروا، فإذا هو مختتن. فقالوا: هذا ملك الختان قد ظهر.

---

١ كذا في م.

women whom you would have trampled underfoot, inadvertently incurring guilt on their account—God brings whoever he will into his mercy—if the believers had been clearly separated, We would have inflicted a painful punishment on the disbelievers. While the disbelievers had fury in their hearts—the fury of ignorance . . .»[70]

Their "fury" means that they neither affirmed that he was the Prophet of God nor used the words *In the name of God, the Merciful and the Compassionate*, and that they stood between him and the Sacred House.

ʿAbd al-Razzāq, on the authority of ʿIkrimah ibn ʿAmmār, who said: Abū Zamīl Simāk al-Ḥanafī informed us that he heard Ibn ʿAbbās say: **2.4**

The scribe who wrote down the pact on the day of Ḥudaybiyah was ʿAlī ibn Abī Ṭālib.

ʿAbd al-Razzāq said: Maʿmar reported to us: **2.5**

I asked al-Zuhrī about this, and he laughed and said, "The scribe was ʿAlī ibn Abī Ṭālib, but were you to ask them"—by whom he meant the Umayyads—"they would say it was ʿUthmān." [71]

ʿAbd al-Razzāq, on the authority oMaʿmar, on the authority of al-Zuhrī who said: [72] **2.6**

Heraclius was a seer[73] who would look into the stars. One morning when he awoke, the people of his court saw something amiss in his appearance. So they asked him, "What troubles you?"

"I looked into the stars last night," he said, "and I saw that the king of the circumcised[74] has appeared."

"Do not let this trouble you," they said, "for only the Jews are circumcised. Dispatch an order to your cities to have every Jew killed."

Al-Zuhrī said: Heraclius wrote to one of his fellow seers, who also looked into the stars, and he wrote back to him with the like of what Heraclius had told his court. Later, the ruler of Bostra sent him an Arab man to inform Heraclius about this Prophet, so Heraclius said, "Find out whether he is circumcised!" His courtiers answered, "They have looked, and lo, he is circumcised." "Truly," they said, "the king of the circumcised has appeared."

عبد الرزّاق عن معمر عن الزهريّ قال: أخبرني عبيد الله ابن عبد الله بن عتبة بن مسعود عن ابن عبّاس، قال: ٧،٢
حدّثني أبو سفيان من فيه إلى فيّ، قال:

انطلقتُ في المدّة الّتي كانت بيننا وبين رسول الله صلّى الله عليه وسلّم. قال: فبينا ١،٧،٢
أنا بالشام، إذ جيء بكتاب من رسول الله صلّى الله عليه وسلّم إلى هرقل. قال: وكان دحية الكلبيّ جاء به، فدفعه إلى عظيم بصرى. فدفعه عظيم بصرى إلى هرقل. فقال هرقل: أهاهنا أحد من قوم هذا الرجل الّذي يزعم أنّه نبيّ؟ قالوا: نعم.

قال: فدُعيتُ في نفر من قريش، فدخلنا على هرقل، فجلسنا إليه. فقال: أيّكم أقرب نسباً من هذا الرجل الّذي يزعم أنّه نبيّ؟

قال أبو سفيان: فقلت: أنا. فأجلسوني بين يديه، وأجلسوا أصحابي خلفي. ثمّ دعا بترجمانه. فقال:

قل لهم: إنّي سائل[1] هذا عن هذا الرجل الّذي يزعم أنّه نبيّ. فإنْ كذب فكذّبوه.

قال أبو سفيان: وأَيْمُ الله لولا أن يؤثَر[2] عليّ الكذب لكذبت.

ثم قال لترجمانه: سله، كيف حسبه فيكم؟

قال: قلت: هو فينا ذو حسب.

قال: فهل كان من آبائه ملك؟

قال: قلت: لا.

قال: فهل تتهمونه بالكذب قبل أن يقوله؟

قال: قلت: لا.

قال: فمن اتّبعه، أشرافكم أم ضعفاؤكم؟

قلت: بل ضعفاؤنا.

قال: هل يزيدون أم ينقصون؟

قال: قلت: لا، بل يزيدون.

قال: هل يرتدّ أحد عن دينه بعد أن يدخل فيه سخطةً له؟

---

١ ط؛ مم: مسائل.   ٢ ط؛ مم: يؤثر الله.

ʿAbd al-Razzāq, on the authority of Maʿmar, on the authority al-Zuhrī who said: ʿUbayd Allāh ibn ʿAbd Allāh ibn ʿUtbah ibn Masʿūd related to me from Ibn ʿAbbās, who said: Abū Sufyān reported to me straight from his lips to mine: 2.7

Abū Sufyān said: I went on a journey during the respite from the fighting between us and the Messenger of God, and while I was in Syria, a missive from the Messenger of God was delivered to Heraclius. It was Diḥyah al-Kalbī who carried and delivered it to the governor of Bostra, who in turn delivered the letter to Heraclius. Heraclius said, "Is there in Arabia anyone who claims he is a prophet from this man's people?" "Yes," his attendees answered. 2.7.1

Abū Sufyān continued: I was summoned along with several of the Quraysh, so we entered Heraclius' court and sat down with him. He asked, "Which of you is the closest relative of this man who claims he is a prophet?"

"I am," I said, so they sat me down in front of him and sat my companions behind me. Then he called for his translator and said,

"Say to them: 'I am going to ask this one here about the man who claims he is a prophet. If he lies, then the others are to expose him as a liar.'"

(Abū Sufyān admitted: I swear by God, if it were not for the risk of earning a reputation as a liar, then I would have lied!)

Then Heraclius said to his translator, "Ask him, 'How is he esteemed among you?'"

"He is well esteemed among us," I said.

"Was there a king among his ancestors?" he asked.

"No," I said.

"Did any of you accuse him of mendacity before he said this?" he asked.

"No," I said.

"And who follows him," he asked, "the powerful or the powerless?"

"Just the powerless," I said.

He asked, "Do their numbers decrease rather than increase?"

"No," I said, "they are increasing."

He asked, "Does anyone who has entered his religion apostatize from it out of any displeasure with him?"

"No," I said.

"Have you fought against him?" he asked.

"Yes," I said.

"How did your battles against him fare?" he asked.

قلت: لا.

قال: فهل قاتلتموه؟

قلت: نعم.

قال: كيف يكون قتالكم إيّاه؟

قال: قلت: يكون الحرب بيننا وبينه سجالاً. يصيب منّا ونصيب منه.

قال: فهل هو يغدر؟

قلت: لا، نحن منه في هدنة لا ندري ما هو صانع فيها.

قال: فوالله ما أمكنني من كلمة أُدخل فيها غير هذه.

قال: فهل قال هذا القول أحد قبله؟

قلت: لا.

قال لترجمانه: قل له: إنّي سألتكم عن حسبه، فقلتَ إنّه فينا ذو حسب. وكذلك ٢،٧،٢ الرسل تُبعث في أحساب قومها. وسألتك هل كان في آبائه ملك، فزعمت أن لا. فقلت: فلو كان في آبائه ملك،[١] قلت رجل يطلب ملك آبائه. وسألتك عن أتباعه، أضعفاؤهم أم أشدّاؤهم؟[٢] قال: فقلتَ: بل ضعفاؤهم وهم أتباع الرسل. وسألتك: هل كنتم تتهمونه بالكذب قبل أن يقول ما قال؟ فزعمت أن لا. فقد عرفت أنّه لم يكُن ليَدَع الكذب على الناس، ثمّ يذهب فيكذب على الله! وسألتك هل يرتدّ أحد منهم عن دينه بعد أن يدخل فيه سخطةً[٣] له؟ فزعمتَ أن لا. وكذلك الإيمان إذا خالط بشاشة القلوب. وسألتك: هل يزيدون أم ينقصون؟ فزعمت أنّهم يزيدون. وكذلك الإيمان لا يزال إلى أن يتمّ. وسألتك هل قاتلتموه؟ فزعمت أنّكم[٤] قاتلتموه، فيكون الحرب بينكم وبينه سِجالاً، ينال منكم وتنالون منه. وكذلك الرسل تبتلى. ثمّ يكون لهم العاقبة. وسألتك هل يغدر؟ فزعمت أنّه لا يغدر[٥] وكذلك الرسل لا يغدر. وسألتك هل

١ ط؛[فزعمت أن لا فقلت فلوكان في آبائه ملك] ساقطة من م. ٢ م؛ ط: أشرافهم. ٣ م؛ ط: سخطاً. ٤ ط؛ م: أنك.

٥ ط؛[وكذلك الرسل تبتلي ثمّ يكون لهم العاقبة وسألتك هل يغدر فزعمت أنه لا يغدر] ساقطة من م.

"The war between us and them has been a stalemate," I said. "A number of ours have fallen, and a number of theirs have fallen."

"Does he commit any treachery?" he asked.

"No," I said, "we are at an armistice with him. We don't know what he's planning to do at this time."

Abū Sufyan said: By God, Heraclius did not permit me to say another word about the subject.

"Has anyone else made this claim before him?" he asked.

"No," I said.

Heraclius then said to his translator, "Say to him, 'I asked all of you about 2.7.2
how this prophet is esteemed, and you said, "He is well esteemed among us." And so are all prophets God has sent esteemed among their people. I asked you if there was a king among his ancestors, and you claimed there was not. I said that if there had been a king among his ancestors, then I would have said he is a man seeking the kingdom of his forefathers. I asked you about his followers "Are they the powerless among them or the strong?" You said the powerless among them, and the powerless are indeed the followers of prophets. I asked you, "Did you accuse him of mendacity before saying what he said?" And you claimed not. Then I knew that he would not eschew lying to the people and then go and lie against God. I asked you, "Has any one of them apostatized from his religion after entering it due to displeasure with him?" You claimed not, and so it is with true faith, when it gladdens hearts. I asked you, "Are they increasing in number or decreasing?" You claimed that they were increasing in number, and so it is with true faith—it does not cease to grow until it is complete. And I asked you, "Have you fought against him?" You claimed that you had fought against him, and that the war between you has been a stalemate. Sometimes he gains the upper hand and sometimes you gain the upper hand. And so it is that the prophets are tested. Afterward, to them belongs the final outcome. And I asked you, "Does he act treacherously?" And you claimed that he does not act treacherously. And so it is—the prophets do not act treacherously. I also asked you, "Has anyone made this claim before him?" And you claimed not. So I say, "If this claim was made by someone before, then I would have said he is a man following a claim said before him." What does he command of you all?'"

I said, "He commands us to pray, to pay alms, to act virtuously, and to honor the bonds of kinship."

قال أحد هذا القول قبله؟ فزعمت أن لا. فقلت: لوكان قال[1] هذا القول أحد قبله، قلت رجل ائتمّ بقول قيل قبله. قال: بِمَ يأمركم؟

قلتُ: يأمرنا بالصلاة والزكاة والعفاف والصلة.

قال: إن يكُ ما تقوله حقًّا، فإنه نبيّ. وإنّي كنت أعلم أنه لخارج ولم أكُن أظنّه منكم. ولوكنت أعلم أنّي أَخلُص إليه لأحببتُ لقاءَه. ولوكنت عنده لغسلت عن[2] قدميه وليبلغنّ ملكه ما تحت قدميّ.

٣،٧،٢ قال: ثمّ دعا بكتاب رسول الله صلّى الله عليه وسلّم، فقرأه، فإذا فيه:

بِسْمِ اللهِ الرَّحْمٰنِ الرَّحِيْمِ، مِنْ مُحَمَّدٍ رَسُوْلِ اللهِ إِلىٰ هِرَقْلَ عَظِيْمِ الرُّوْمِ. سَلامٌ عَلىٰ مَنِ اتَّبَعَ الهُدى. أَمَّا بَعْدُ، فَإِنِّي أَدْعُوكَ بِدعايَةِ الإِسْلامِ. أَسْلِمْ تَسْلَمْ، وأَسلِمْ يُؤْتِكَ اللهُ أَجرَكَ مرَّتَيْنِ. وإنْ تولَّيْتَ، فإنّ عَلَيْكَ إِثْمُ الأَرِيْسِيْن. و ﴿ يَٰٓأَهۡلَ ٱلۡكِتَٰبِ تَعَالَوۡاْ إِلَىٰ كَلِمَةٖ سَوَآءِۭ بَيۡنَنَا وَبَيۡنَكُمۡ أَلَّا نَعۡبُدَ إِلَّا ٱللَّهَ ﴾ إلى قوله ﴿ فَٱشۡهَدُواْ بِأَنَّا مُسۡلِمُونَ ﴾.

فلمّا فرغ من قراءة الكتاب، ارتفعت الأصوات عنده وكثر اللغط. وأمر بنا، فأُخرجنا.

قال: فقلت لأصحابي حين خرجنا: لقد أَمِرَ أمرُ ابن أبي كبشة حتّى أدخل اللهُ عليّ الإسلام.

٤،٧،٢ قال الزهريّ: فدعا هرقل عظماء الروم، فجمعهم في دار له. فقال: يا معشر الروم! هل لكم إلى الفلاح والرشد آخر الأبد وأن يثبت لكم ملككم؟ قال: فحاصوا حيصة حمر الوحش إلى الأبواب، فوجدوها قد غُلّقت. قال: فدعاهم، فقال: إنّي اختبرتُ شدّتكم على دينكم، فقد رأيتُ منكم الّذي أحببتُ. فسجدوا له و رضوا عنه.

١ ط؛[قال] ساقطة من م. ٢ ظ وبد؛ [عن] ساقطة من م.

"If what you say is true," he said, "then he is a prophet, and I have indeed come to know that he has appeared. I did not suspect that he would be one of you Arabs. Had I known that I could reach him, then it would have delighted me to encounter him; and had I found myself in his company, then I would have washed his feet. His dominion will stretch to the very earth beneath my feet."[75]

Abū Sufyān said: Then he called for the letter of the Messenger of God and read it. Its contents were as follows: 2.7.3

> In the name of God, the Merciful, the Compassionate. From Muḥammad the Messenger of God to Heraclius the Emperor of Rome. Peace upon those who follow guidance. Now to the heart of the matter: I summon you with the summons of Islam. Submit and be saved. Submit, and God will reward you twice over. But if you turn away, then you will fall prey to the sin of the wicked tenants.[76] «People of the Book! Come to common terms between us and you, that we shall worship none but God and shall ascribe no partner to Him, nor shall we take others beside God as lords. If they turn away, say, "So bear witness that we are Muslims."»[77]

When he had finished reading the letter, many voices were raised around him and there arose a great clamor. He then ordered that we be shown out of the hall.

Abū Sufyān added: I said to my companions when we left, "This affair of Ibn Abī Kabshah has grown to such proportions that God may even cause me to embrace Islam!"

Al-Zuhrī said: Heraclius summoned the dignitaries of Rome and gathered them together in one of his residences. Then he said, "Romans! Do all of you wish to have felicity and guidance until the end of time and to secure your dominion for yourselves? Then give your allegiance to this prophet!" Then the dignitaries hurriedly fled to the doors like wild asses, but found that they had been locked. Then he summoned them back and said, "I have tested your dedication to your religion, and I am pleased with what I have seen from you." Then they bowed low before him and voiced their satisfaction with him. 2.7.4

وَقعَةُ بَدر

عبد الرزّاق عن معمر عن الزهريّ في قوله ﴿إِن تَسْتَفْتِحُوا فَقَدْ جَاءَكُمُ الْفَتْحُ﴾، قال: ١،٣

استفتح أبو جهل بن هشام، فقال: اللّهمّ أيّنا كان أفجر لك وأقطع للرحم، فأَحِنْهُ اليوم، يعني محمّداً ونفسه، فقتله الله يوم بدر كافراً إلى النار.

عبد الرزّاق عن معمر عن الزهريّ في حديثه عن عروة بن الزبير قال: ٢،٣

أُمر رسول الله صلّى الله عليه وسلّم بعدُ بالقتال في آيٍ من القرآن، فكان أوّل مشهد شهده رسول الله صلّى الله عليه وسلّم بدراً. وكان رأس المشركين يومئذ عتبة بن عبد شمس فالتقوا ببدر يوم الجمعة لسبع أو ستّ عشرة ليلةً مضت من رمضان. وأصحاب رسول الله صلّى الله عليه وسلّم ثلاث مئة وبضع عشرة رجلاً والمشركون بين الألف والتسع مئة. وكان ذلك يوم الفرقان وهزم الله يومئذ المشركين فقتل منهم زيادة على سبعين مُهَج وأسر منهم مثل ذلك.

قال الزهريّ: ولم يشهد بدراً إلّا قرشيّ أو أنصاريّ أو حليف لأحد الفريقَين.

عبد الرزّاق عن معمر قال: أخبرني أيّوب عن عكرمة: ٣،٣

١،٣،٣ أنّ أبا سفيان أقبل من الشام في عير لقريش، وخرج المشركون مُغَوِّثين لعيرهم. وخرج النبيّ صلّى الله عليه وسلّم يريد أبا سفيان وأصحابه، فأرسل رسول الله صلّى

The Incident at Badr[78]

ʿAbd al-Razzāq, on the authority of Maʿmar, on the authority of al-Zuhrī, who said concerning God's decree, «Disbelievers, if you were seeking a divine decision, now you have witnessed one»:[79] 3.1

Abū Jahl ibn Hishām sought a divine decision, praying, "O Lord, make known which of us"—by whom he meant Muḥammad and himself—"is more insolent against you and guiltiest of severing the bonds of kinship! May you cause him to perish this day!" Indeed, God killed Abū Jahl on the day of Badr as an infidel doomed to the fires of Hell.

ʿAbd al-Razzāq, on the authority of Maʿmar, on the authority of al-Zuhrī narrating from ʿUrwah ibn al-Zubayr, who said: 3.2

The Messenger of God received the command to wage war soon thereafter in several verses of the Qur'an.[80] The first battle that the Messenger of God witnessed was at Badr, and on that day, the leader of the Pagans was ʿUtbah ibn Rabīʿah ibn ʿAbd Shams. They met at Badr on Friday after the seventeenth, or the sixteenth, night of Ramadan had passed.[81] The companions of the Messenger of God numbered over 310 men, and the Pagans numbered between 900 and 1,000. That was "the day of manifest redemption,"[82] for God defeated the Pagans on that day. More than seventy souls from their ranks were killed and a similar number taken captive.

Al-Zuhrī said: There was no one who witnessed Badr who was not either a Qurashī, an Ally, or a confederate of one of the two factions.

ʿAbd al-Razzāq, on the authority of Maʿmar who said: Ayyūb reported to me on the authority of ʿIkrimah that: 3.3

Abū Sufyān had drawn near to Medina in a caravan of the Quraysh returning from Syria, and the Pagans marched out to provide support for their caravan because the Prophet had set out in pursuit of Abū Sufyān and his troop. The Messenger of God sent two men as spies to discover at which well Abū Sufyān had stopped. The two went out to search for him and ascertained his 3.3.1

الله عليه وسلّم رجلين من أصحابه عيناً طليعةً ينظران بأيّ ماء هو. فانطلقا حتّى إذا علما عِلْمَه وخبُرا[1] خبره، جاءا سريعين، فأخبرا النبيّ صلّى الله عليه وسلّم.

٢،٣،٣ وجاء أبو سفيان حتّى نزل على الماء الّذي كان به الرجلان، فقال لأهل الماء: هل أحسستم أحداً من أهل يثرب؟

قالوا: لا.[2]

قال: فهل مرّ بكم أحدٌ؟

قالوا: ما رأينا إلّا رجلين من أهل كذا وكذا.

قال أبو سفيان: فأين كان مناخهما؟

فدلّوه عليه، فانطلق حتّى أتى بعرًا لهما ففتّه. فإذا فيه النوى، فقال: أنّى لبني فلان هذا النوى؟ هذي نواضح أهل يثرب. فترك الطريق وأخذ سِيف البحر.

٣،٣،٣ وجاء الرجلان فأخبرا النبيّ صلّى الله عليه وسلّم خبره. فقال: أيّكم أخذ هذه الطريق؟

قال أبو بكر رحمه الله: أنا، هو بماء كذا وكذا ونحن بماء كذا وكذا. فيرتحل فينزل بماء كذا وكذا وننزل بماء كذا وكذا، ثمّ ينزل بماء كذا وكذا وننزل بماء كذا وكذا. ثمّ نلتقي بماء كذا وكذا كأنّا فرسا رهانٍ.

٤،٣،٣ فسار النبيّ صلّى الله عليه وسلّم حتّى نزل بدراً. فوجد على ماء بدر بعض رقيق قريش ممّن خرج يغيث أبا سفيان، فأخذهم أصحابه فجعلوا يسألونهم. فإذا صدقوهم، ضربوهم. وإذا كذبوهم، تركوهم. فمرّ بهم النبيّ صلّى الله عليه وسلّم وهم يفعلون ذلك، فقال النبيّ صلّى الله عليه وسلّم: إن صدقوكم، ضربتموهم، وإذا كذبوكم، تركتموهم!؟ ثمّ دعا واحداً منهم، فقال: من يطعم القوم؟ قال: فلان وفلان. فعدّ رجلاً يطعمهم، كلّ رجل منهم يوماً. قال: فكم يُنحر لهم؟ قال: عشراً من الجزور. فقال النبيّ صلّى الله عليه وسلّم: الجزور بمئة وهم بين الألف والتسع مئة.

٥،٣،٣ قال: فلمّا جاء المشركون وصافّوهم، وكان النبيّ صلّى الله عليه وسلّم قد استشار قبل

١ تع؛ مم: أخبرا. ٢ [قالوا: لا] من تع؛ وساقطة من مم.

whereabouts and what he was up to; then they quickly returned to report back to the Messenger of God.

Abū Sufyan proceeded as far as the well where the two men had been and alighted there. He asked the people near the well, "Have you noticed anyone from Yathrib?" 3.3.2

"No," they answered.

Then he asked, "Has anyone at all passed by you?"

"We've seen no one," they answered, "except for two men from such-and-such place."

"And where did the two men make camp?"

They led him to the place, and he walked about until he came upon their feces, which he crumbled apart. There in the feces he found the pits of dates, whereupon he asked, "Aren't these the dates that come from such-and-such clan? These are the watering holes of the people of Yathrib!" He then left the desert route and went along the coast.

The two spies returned and reported to the Prophet the news about Abū Sufyān. The Prophet then asked, "Who among you has taken this route?" 3.3.3

"I have," Abū Bakr answered. "He is at such-and-such well, and now we are at such-and-such well. Soon he will travel on and make camp at such-and-such well, and we will make camp at such-and-such well. Next he will make camp at such-and-such well, and we will make camp at such-and-such well. Then at last we will meet at such-and-such well, like two thoroughbreds eager for contest."

The Prophet marched onward until he made camp at Badr. At Badr's well, he found some slaves belonging to the Quraysh who had gone out to give support to Abū Sufyān. His companions captured them and began interrogating them. Whenever the slaves would tell them the truth, they beat them, but if the slaves lied to them, they desisted. The Prophet passed by them while they were doing this, and said, "If they tell you the truth, you beat them, but if they lie to you, you don't?"[83] Then he summoned one of the slaves and asked, "Who is it that feeds the tribe?" "So-and-so and so-and-so," he replied and so recounted all those men responsible for feeding them daily. The Prophet asked, "How many cattle are slaughtered for them?" "Ten camels," he answered. Then the Prophet said, "A slaughtered camel feeds one hundred men, so they must number between nine hundred and a thousand." 3.3.4

When the Pagans had come and arrayed themselves for battle against the Muslims, the Prophet had already consulted with his Companions on how they 3.3.5

ذلك في قتالهم. فقام[1] أبو بكر يشير عليه، فأجلسه النبيّ صلّى الله عليه وسلّم. ثمّ استشار، فقام عمر يشير عليه، فأجلسه النبيّ صلّى الله عليه وسلّم. ثمّ استشارهم. فقام سعد بن عبادة، فقال: يا نبيّ الله! لكأنّك تعرض بنا اليوم لتعلم ما في نفوسنا. والّذي نفسي بيده، لو ضربتَ أكبادها حتّى تبلغ[2] برك الغماد من ذي يمن لكنّا معك. فوطّن رسول الله صلّى الله عليه وسلّم أصحابه على الصبر والقتال، وسُرّ بذلك منهم.

٦،٣،٣ فلمّا التقوا، سار في قريش عتبة بن رِبيعة، وقال: أيْ قومي! أطيعوني اليوم[3] ولا تقاتلوا محمّداً صلّى الله عليه وسلّم وأصحابه! فإنّكم إنْ قاتلتموهم، لم يزل بينكم إحنة ما بقيتم وفساد. لا يزال الرجل منكم ينظر إلى قاتل أخيه وإلى قاتل ابن عمّه. فإن يكن ملكاً، أكلتم في ملك أخيكم. وإن يكُ نبياً، فأنتم أسعد الناس به. فإن يكُ كاذباً، كفتكموه ذؤبان العرب. فأبَوا أن يسمعوا مقالته، وأبَوا أن يطيعوه. فقال: أنشدكم الله في هذه الوجوه الّتي كأنّها المصابيح أن تجعلوها أنداداً لهذه الوجوه الّتي كأنّها عيون الحيات.

فقال أبو جهل: لقد ملأتَ سحرك رعباً. ثمّ سار في قريش، ثمّ قال: إنّ عتبة بن ربيعة إنما يشير عليكم بهذا لأنّ ابنه مع محمّد صلّى الله عليه وسلّم ومحمّداً صلّى الله عليه وسلّم ابن عمّه. فهو يكره أن يُقتل ابنه وابن عمّه.

فغضب عتبة بن ربيعة، فقال: أي مُصَفِّر استه! ستعلم أيّنا أجبن والأم[4] وأفشل لقومه اليوم. ثمّ نزل ونزل معه أخوه شيبة بن رِبيعة وابنه الوليد بن عتبة. فقالوا: أَبرِزْ إلينا أكفاءَنا.[5] فثار الناس من بني الخزرج، فأجلسهم النبيّ صلّى الله عليه وسلّم. فقام عليّ وحمزة وعبيدة بن الحارث بن المطّلب[6] بن عبد مناف، فاختلف كلّ رجل منهم وقرنه ضربتين. فقتل كلّ واحد منهم صاحبه. وأعان حمزة علياً على صاحبه، فقتله. وقُطعت رجل عبيدة، فمات بعد ذلك.

١ مم: قال. ٢ [تبلغ] من تع؛ وساقطة من مم. ٣ [اليوم] من تع؛ وساقطة من مم. ٤ مم: ألم. ٥ مم: أكفئنا.
٦ مم: عبد المطّلب.

ought to conduct the battle. Abū Bakr stood and gave the Prophet his counsel, and the Prophet asked him to sit down. Then the Prophet again sought counsel, so ʿUmar stood and gave the Prophet his counsel, and the Prophet asked him to sit down. Once again the Prophet sought counsel from his companions. Saʿd ibn ʿUbādah stood and spoke: "O Prophet of God! It is as though you have examined us today to learn what is in our hearts. By the One in whose hands my soul resides, were you to strike at their hearts until you reach Birk al-Ghimād of Dhū Yaman[84] we would still be alongside you!" Thereupon the Messenger of God urged his companions to be resolute and prepare for battle, and he was pleased with their readiness.

When the armies met, ʿUtbah ibn Rabīʿah marched out before the Quraysh and said, "Listen, my tribe! Heed my request and do not go out to battle against Muḥammad and his companions! Verily, if you fight against them, you will find only ruin and an intractable feud that you will not survive. Your men will still look to destroy his brother's killer and his cousin's killer. If he be a king, then you will feast in the kingdom of your brother; and if he be a prophet, then by him you will become the most blessed of people. If he be a liar, then it suffices for you to leave him to the Arab *diebs*,[85] for they refuse to listen to his words and refuse to obey him." Then he continued, "I implore you, by God, to follow these instructions like a lantern's light! Follow them as a fitting substitute for instructions that lure you like serpents' eyes!" 3.3.6

Abū Jahl replied, "You've filled your mouth with cowards' prattle!" Then he marched out before the Quraysh and said, "Indeed, ʿUtbah ibn Rabīʿah has only given you this counsel because his son fights with Muḥammad, and Muḥammad is his paternal cousin. He is loath to battle lest his son or cousin be slain."

ʿUtbah ibn Rabīʿah became furious and retorted, "You yellow asshole! Today you'll see just who's the most spineless, sordid craven among his tribe!" Then he descended to the battlefield, and with him came his brother Shaybah ibn Rabīʿah and his son al-Walīd ibn ʿUtbah. They cried out, "Bring us your challengers!" A number of the Khazraj clan rose up, but the Prophet ordered them to sit back down. Then ʿAlī, Ḥamzah, and ʿUbaydah ibn al-Ḥārith ibn al-Muṭṭalib ibn ʿAbd Manāf stood up.[86] Each man and his opponent exchanged two blows, and each slew his rival. Ḥamzah aided ʿAlī against his opponent and slew him. ʿUbaydah's leg was severed, and he died not long after that.

وكان أوّل قتيل قُتل من المسلمين مهجع مولى عمر.[1] ثمّ انزل الله نصره وهزم ٧،٣،٣
عدوّه. وقُتل أبو جهل بن هشام. فأخبر النبيّ صلّى الله عليه وسلّم، فقال: أفعلتم؟
قالوا: نعم، يا نبيّ الله! فسُرّ بذلك وقال: إنّ عهدي به في ركبتيه حوراء.[2] فاذهبوا،
فانظروا هل ترون ذلك؟ قال: فنظروا، فرأوه.

قال: وأُسر يومئذ ناس من قريش. ثمّ أمر النبيّ صلّى الله عليه وسلّم بالقتلى. فجرّوا ٨،٣،٣
حتّى ألقوا في قليب. ثمّ أشرف عليهم رسول الله صلّى الله عليه وسلّم، فقال: أي
عتبة بن ربيعة! أي أميّة بن خلف! فجعل يسمّيهم بأسمائهم رجلاً رجلاً. هل وجدتم
ما وعد ربّكم حقًّا؟ قالوا: يا نبيّ الله! ويسمعون ما تقول؟ فقال النبيّ صلّى الله عليه
وسلّم: ما أنتم بأعلم بما أقول منهم، أي إنّهم قد رأوا أعمالهم.

قال معمر: وسمعت هشام بن عروة يحدّث: ٤،٣

أنّ النبيّ صلّى الله عليه وسلّم بعث يومئذ زيد بن حارثة بشيرًا يبشّر أهل المدينة، فجعل ناس لا يصدّقونه ويقولون:[3] والله ما رجع هذا إلّا فارًّا. وجعل يخبرهم بالأسارى ويخبرهم بمن قُتل، فلم يصدّقوه حتّى جيء بالأسارى مقرنين في قدّ. ثمّ فاداهم النبيّ صلّى الله عليه وسلّم.

١ مم: مهجع بن مولى عمر. ٢ مم: حور. ٣ [ويقولون] من تع؛ ساقطة من مم.

The first of the slain on the Muslims' side was Mihjaʿ, a slave-client of ʿUmar. Then God sent down His victory and defeated the enemy. Abū Jahl ibn Hishām was slain. When this was reported to the Prophet, he said, "Was this your deed?" "Yes, O Prophet of God," they replied. He was pleased and said, "I recall that he had a pale scar across his knees. Go back and see whether it's there." They went to look and it was. 3.3.7

On that day a number of the Quraysh were taken captive. The Prophet commanded that bodies of the slain be brought over and dumped into an old well. Then the Messenger of God cast his gaze over the dead and said, "O ʿUtbah ibn Rabīʿah! O Umayyah ibn Khalaf!"—and he began calling out their names one by one—"Have you now found your Lord's warning to be true?" His companions asked, "O Prophet of God, do they hear what you say?" The Prophet replied, "You are no more knowledgeable of what I say than they"—meaning that they had seen the consequence of their deeds.[87] 3.3.8

Maʿmar said: I heard Hishām ibn ʿUrwah report: 3.4

On that day, the Prophet sent Zayd ibn Ḥārithah to announce the good news to the inhabitants of Medina. Some people refused to accept the truth of his report and said, "By God, this man has only returned because he's fleeing!" Zayd started to tell them about the captives and those who had been slain, but they did not believe him until the captives were brought bound and tied. Later, the Prophet ransomed the captives.

مَنْ أَسَرَهُ النبيّ صلّى الله عليه وسلّم مِن أَهْلِ بَدْرٍ

أخبرنا عبد الرزّاق قال: أخبرنا معمر عن قتادة وعثمان الجزريّ قالا: ١،٤

فادى رسول الله صلّى الله عليه وسلّم أسارى بدر وكان فداء كلّ رجل منهم أربعة آلاف. وقُتل عقبة بن أبي معيط قبل الفداء وقام عليه عليّ بن أبي طالب فقتله. فقال: يا محمّد! فمن للصبية؟! قال: النار!

عبد الرزّاق عن معمر قال: أخبرني عثمان الجزريّ عن مقسم قال: ٢،٤

لمّا أُسر العبّاس في الأُسارى يوم بدر، سمع رسول الله صلّى الله عليه وسلّم أنينه وهو في الوثاق. جعل النبيّ صلّى الله عليه وسلّم لا ينام تلك الليلة ولا يأخذه نوم. ففطن له رجل من الأنصار، فقال: يا رسول الله! إنّك لتؤرّق منذ الليلة.

فقال: العبّاس، أوجعه الوثاق فذلك أَرَّقَني.

فقال: أفلا أذهب فأُرخي عنه شيئاً؟

قال: إنْ شئت فعلت ذلك من قِبَل نفسك.

فانطلق الأنصاريّ فأرخى عن وثاقه. فسكن وهدأ، فنام رسول الله صلّى الله عليه وسلّم.

The Combatants Whom the Prophet Took Captive at Badr

ʿAbd al-Razzāq related to us: Maʿmar related to us on the authority of Qatādah and ʿUthmān al-Jazarī, both of whom said: **4.1**

The Messenger of God ransomed the captives from Badr, and the ransom for each man was four thousand dirhams. ʿUqbah ibn Abī Muʿayṭ was killed before being ransomed. ʿAlī ibn Abī Ṭālib attacked and killed him. Before he died, ʿUqbah said, "O Muḥammad! Who will look after my children?" "Hellfire!" he answered.

ʿAbd al-Razzāq, on the authority of Maʿmar, who said: ʿUthmān al-Jazarī related to me on the authority of Miqsam, who said: **4.2**

When al-ʿAbbās was taken among the captives at the Battle of Badr, the Messenger of God heard him sobbing in his fetters. That night the Prophet could not sleep, nor would slumber overtake him. One of the Allies noticed this and said, "O Messenger of God, you've been kept awake the entire night!"

"It's al-ʿAbbās," replied the Prophet. "The fetters hurt him, and that is what kept me awake."

"Shall I go and slacken his bonds a bit?" asked the man from the Allies.

"Do so if you like," the Prophet answered, "but only on your own account."

The Ally set off and loosened the bonds of al-ʿAbbās. He became composed and quiet, and the Messenger of God slept.

وَقعَةُ هُذَيل بالرَّجِيع (وَالرَّجِيع مَوْضِعٌ)

١.٥ عبد الرزّاق عن معمر عن الزهريّ عن عمرو بن أبي سفيان الثقفيّ عن أبي هريرة، قال:

١.١.٥ بعث رسول الله صلّى الله عليه وسلّم سريّةً عيناً له، وأمّر عليهم عاصم بن ثابت، وهو جدّ عاصم بن عمر، فانطلق حتّى إذا كانوا ببعض الطريق بين عسفان ومكّة نزولاً. فذُكروا لحيّ من هذيل يقال لهم بنو لحيان، فتبعوهم بقريب من مئة رجل رامٍ حتّى رأوا آثارهم حتّى نزلوا منزلاً يرونه.[١] فوجدوا فيه نوى تمر يرونه[٢] من تمر المدينة. فقالوا: هذا من تمر يثرب، فاتّبعوا آثارهم حتّى لحقوهم. فلمّا أحسّهم عاصم بن ثابت وأصحابه لجأوا إلى فدفد. وجاء القوم، فأحاطوا بهم. فقالوا: لكم العهد والميثاق. إنْ نزلتم إلينا، لا نقتل منكم رجلاً. فقال عاصم بن ثابت: أمّا أنا فلا أنزل في ذمّة كافر. اللّهمّ أخبرْ عنّا رسولك!

٢.١.٥ قال: فقاتلوهم حتّى قتلوا عاصماً في سبعة نفر، وبقي خبيب بن عديّ وزيد بن دثنّة ورجل آخر. فأعطوهم العهد والميثاق إن نزلوا إليهم. فنزلوا إليهم. فلمّا استمكنوا منهم، حلّوا أوتار قسيّهم، فربطوهم بها. فقال الرجل الثالث الّذي كان معهما: هذا أوّل الغدر. فأبى أن يصحبهم. فجرّوه، فأبى أن يتّبعهم. وقال: لي في هؤلاء أُسوة. فضربوا عنقه. وانطلقوا بخبيب بن عدي وزيد بن دثنّة حتّى باعوهما بمكّة.

٣.١.٥ فاشترى خبيباً بنو الحارث بن عامر بن نوفل وكان هو[٣] قتل الحارث يوم بدر. فمكث عندهم أسيرًا حتّى إذا[٤] أجمعوا على قتله. استعار موسى من[٥] إحدى بنات الحارث ليستحدّ بها، فأعارته. قالت: فغفلتُ عن صبيٍّ لي. فدرج إليه حتّى أتاه. قالت: فأخذه فوضعه على فخذه. فلمّا رأيتُه، فزعتُ فزعًا عرفه فيّ، والموسى بيده.

---

١ مم؛ بخ: حتّى أتوا منزلا نزلوه. ٢ مم؛ بخ: تزوده. ٣ [هو] من بخ؛ ساقطة من مم. ٤ [إذا] من بخ؛ ساقطة من مم.
٥ [من] من بخ؛ ساقطة من مم.

The Incident Involving the Hudhayl Tribe at al-Rajīʿ [88]

ʿAbd al-Razzāq, on the authority of Maʿmar, on the authority of al-Zuhrī, on the authority of ʿAmr ibn Abī Sufyān al-Thaqafī, on the authority of Abū Hurayrah, who said: 5.1

The Messenger of God dispatched a scouting expedition and appointed over them as commander ʿĀṣim ibn Thābit, who is also the grandfather of ʿĀṣim ibn ʿUmar. They set out and eventually made camp along the route between ʿUsfān and Mecca. Word of their whereabouts reached a clan of the Hudhayl tribe called the Liḥyān, and the Liḥyān pursued them with around a hundred archers. Once they had caught sight of their tracks, they alighted at a campsite they spotted. There they found date pits that they recognized as being from Yathrib. "This is a date from Yathrib!" they exclaimed and followed their tracks until they caught up with them. When ʿĀṣim ibn Thābit and his companions caught sight of them, they fled to a patch of high ground in the desert waste. The Liḥyānīs came and surrounded them, saying, "If you surrender to us, you'll have our oath and pledge that not one of your men will be killed." ʿĀṣim ibn Thābit replied, "As for me, I'll never surrender to the protection of an infidel! O Lord, inform your Messenger of our plight!" 5.1.1

The Liḥyānīs fought them and eventually succeeded in killing ʿĀṣim and six others. Khubayb ibn ʿAdī, Zayd ibn Dathinnah, and another man survived, and the Liḥyānīs offered them their oath and pledge of safety if they surrendered. Thus they surrendered. When the Liḥyānīs had seized them, they unfastened their bowstrings and used them to tie the men up. The third man alongside Khubayb and Zayd said, "This is only the first act of treachery." He refused to accompany his captors, so they dragged him. He still refused to follow them, saying, "My lot is with the slain." So they beheaded him and set off with Khubayb ibn ʿAdī and Zayd ibn Dathinnah, whom they sold as slaves in Mecca. 5.1.2

The sons of al-Ḥārith ibn ʿĀmir ibn Nawfal purchased Khubayb because he had killed their father al-Ḥārith at the Battle of Badr. He remained with them as a captive until they had all agreed to kill him. While captive, Khubayb asked to borrow a razor from one of al-Ḥārith's daughters for trimming his pubic hair,[89] and she loaned him one. She said, "I had lost track of one of my boys, 5.1.3

قال: أتخشين أن أقتله؟ ما كنت لأن أفعل إن شاء الله. قال: فكانت تقول: ما رأيتُ أسيرًا خيرًا من خبيب. لقد رأيته يأكل من قطف عنب، وما بمكّة يومئذ ثمرة وإنّه لموثق في الحديد. وما كان إلّا رزق رزقه الله إيّاه.

٤،١،٥ ثمّ خرجوا به من الحرم ليقتلوه. فقال: دعوني أصلّي ركعتين. فصلّى ركعتين. ثمّ قال: لولا أن تروا أنّ ما بي جزع من الموت، لزدتُ. فكان أوّل من سنّ الركعتين عند القتل هو. ثمّ قال: اللّهمّ أحصِهم عددًا! قال:

وَلَسْتُ أُبَالِي حِينَ أُقْتَلُ مُسْلِمًا   عَلَى أَيِّ شَقٍّ كَانَ لله مَصْرَعِي
وَذلِكَ فِي ذَاتِ الإِلهِ وَإِنْ يَشَأْ   يُبَارِكْ عَلَى أَوْصَالِ شِلْوٍ مُمَزَّعِ

ثمّ قام إليه عقبة بن الحارث فقتله.

٥،١،٥ قال: وبعث قريش إلى عاصم ليؤتوا بشيء من جسده يعرفونه، وكان قتل عظيمًا من عظمائهم. فبعث الله مثل الظلّة من الدبر فحمته من رسلهم، فلم يقدروا على شيء منه.

٢،٥ عبد الرزّاق عن معمر عن عثمان الجزريّ عن مقسم مولى ابن عبّاس. قال معمر: وحدّثني الزهريّ ببعضه. قال:

١،٢،٥ إنّ ابن أبي معيط وأبيّ بن خلف الجمحيّ التقيا فقال عقبة بن أبي معيط لأبيّ بن خلف، وكانا خليلَين في الجاهليّة وكان أبيّ بن خلف أتى النبيّ صلّى الله عليه وسلّم فعرض عليه الإسلام. فلمّا سمع ذلك عقبة، قال: لا أرضى عنك حتّى تأتي محمّدًا فتتفل في وجهه وتشتمه وتكذّبه. قال: فلم يسلّطه الله على ذلك.

٢،٢،٥ فلمّا كان يوم بدر أُسر عقبة بن أبي معيط في الأسارى، فأمر النبيّ صلّى الله عليه وسلّم عليّ بن أبي طالب أن يقتله. فقال عقبة: يا محمّد! من بين هؤلاء أُقتل؟ قال: نعم.

who tiptoed his way around to Khubayb. He lifted the boy up and placed him on his lap. When I saw him with the razor in his hand, I had quite a fright, which he noticed. 'Are you afraid I'll kill him?' he asked. 'I would never do such a thing, God willing!'" She continued, "I never saw a captive as virtuous as Khubayb. Indeed, I saw him eating from a bunch of grapes, even though in that season there was no fruit in Mecca and he was still shackled in irons. It was nothing less than a gift of sustenance granted him by God."

Afterward, the sons of al-Ḥārith took Khubayb out of the Sacred Precincts to kill him.[90] Khubayb said, "Allow me to do two prostrations' worth of prayers," which he did.[91] Then he said, "I'll pray no more, for otherwise you'll suspect I fear death." Thus Khubayb was the first to establish the precedent of undertaking two prostrations' worth of prayers before facing execution. He said, "O Lord! Reckon well my killers' number!"[92] and recited: 5.1.4

'Tis no concern to be killed a Muslim;
whatever the cause, 'twas for God I struggled.
'Tis for God to decide, if He wills;
He blesses a body's limbs even if mangled.

Then ʿUqbah ibn al-Ḥārith went over to him and slew him.

The Quraysh sent their messengers to obtain a piece of ʿĀṣim ibn ʿUqbah's corpse and thus confirm his death—for ʿĀṣim had killed one of their greatest men—but God sent a swarm of bees as thick as a cloud to protect ʿĀṣim's corpse from their messengers, and they were unable to acquire any part of his body. 5.1.5

ʿAbd al-Razzāq, on the authority of Maʿmar, on the authority of ʿUthmān al-Jazarī, on the authority of Miqsam, the slave-client of Ibn ʿAbbās. Maʿmar said: and al-Zuhrī also related to me part of the narration: 5.2

ʿUqbah ibn Abī Muʿayṭ and Ubayy ibn Khalaf al-Jumaḥī once met together. The two were close friends during the Era of Ignorance, and Ubayy ibn Khalaf had just been with the Prophet, who had encouraged him to become a Muslim. When ʿUqbah heard about this, he said to Ubayy, "I won't be able to stand the sight of you until you go to Muḥammad, spit in his face, curse him, and denounce him as a liar!" But God would not permit him to do such a thing. 5.2.1

At the battle of Badr, ʿUqbah ibn Abī Muʿayṭ was among the captives. The Prophet ordered ʿAlī ibn Abī Ṭālib to kill him, and ʿUqbah cried out, "O Muḥammad! Am I alone to be killed of all these people?" 5.2.2

قال: لِمَ؟

قال: بكفرك وفجورك وعتوّك على الله ورسوله.

قال معمر: وقال مقسم: ٣،٥

فبلغنا، والله اعلم، أنه قال: فمن للصبية؟ قال: النار! قال: فقام إليه عليّ بن أبي طالب فضرب عنقه.

وأمّا أبيّ بن خلف، فقال: والله لأقتلنّ محمّداً. فبلغ ذلك رسول الله صلّى الله عليه وسلّم، فقال: بل أنا أقتله، إن شاء الله. قال: فانطلق رجل ممّن سمع ذلك من النبيّ صلّى الله عليه وسلّم إلى أبيّ بن خلف، فقال: إنه لمّا قيل لمحمّد صلّى الله عليه وسلّم ما قلتَ. قال: بل أنا أقتله إن شاء الله. فأفزعه ذلك وقال: أنشدك بالله، أ سمعتَه يقول ذلك؟ قال: نعم. فوقعت في نفسه لأنّهم لم يسمعوا رسول الله صلّى الله عليه وسلّم يقول قولاً إلّا كان حقّاً. فلمّا كان يوم أحد، خرج أبيّ بن خلف مع المشركين فجعل يلتمس غفلةَ النبيّ صلّى الله عليه وسلّم ليحمل عليه، فيحُول رجلٌ من المسلمين بينه وبين النبيّ صلّى الله عليه وسلّم. فلمّا رأى ذلك رسولُ لله صلّى الله عليه وسلّم، قال لأصحابه: خَلّوا عنه. فأخذ الحربة فجندله[1] بها، يقول: رماه بها، فتقع في ترقوته تحت تَسْبِغَة البيضة وفوق الدرع. فلم يخرج منه كبير[2] دم واحتقن الدم في جوفه. فجعل يخور كما يخور الثور. فأقبل أصحابه حتّى احتملوه وهو يخور. وقالوا: ما هذا؟ فوالله ما بك إلّا خدش. فقال: والله لو لم يصبني إلّا بريقه لقتلني.[3] أليس قد قال: أنا أقتله إن شاء الله؟ والله لوكان الّذي بي بأهل ذي المجاز[4] لقتلهم. قال: فما لبث إلّا يوماً أو نحو ذلك حتّى مات إلى النار. فأنزل الله فيه ﴿وَيَوْمَ يَعَضُّ ٱلظَّالِمُ عَلَىٰ يَدَيْهِ﴾ إلى قوله ﴿ٱلشَّيْطَانُ لِلْإِنسَانِ خَذُولًا﴾.

---

١ أنا. مم: جزله؛ تع: رجله. ٢ مم؛ تع: كثير. ٣ تع؛ مم: إلا ليقتلني. ٤ أنا. وفي مم: المجاز؛ تع: أهل الحجاز.

"Yes," answered the Prophet.

"Why?" he asked.

The Prophet replied, "For your disbelief, your depravity, and your insolence toward God and his Messenger!"

Maʿmar said: Miqsam said: 5.3

It was reported to us—though God knows best—that ʿUqbah said: "But who will watch over my children?" And the Prophet replied, "Hellfire!" So ʿAlī ibn Abī Ṭālib walked over to ʿUqbah and beheaded him.

As for Ubayy ibn Khalaf, he said, "By God, I will kill Muḥammad!" Word of this reached the Messenger of God, and he said, "Rather, I shall kill him, God willing." A man who overheard the Prophet say this set out to find Ubayy ibn Khalaf. He said to Ubayy, "Indeed, when Muḥammad was told what you said, he replied, 'Rather, I will kill him, God willing.'" That terrified Ubayy, who said, "I abjure you, by God! Did you really hear him say that?" "Yes," the man replied, and the words pierced Ubayy's heart, because no one had ever heard the Messenger of God speak a word that was not true. At the battle of Uḥud, Ubayy ibn Khalaf marched out with the Pagans, and he began to search for the Prophet to catch him unawares and attack him. A Muslim man barred the way between him and the Prophet, but when the Messenger of God saw this, he said to his companions, "Leave him to me!" The Prophet grabbed his lance and knocked Ubayy to ground—or he speared him with it, he said—and the lance lodged in his collar, right beneath the gorget of his helm and above his chainmail. There was not a lot of blood from the wound, because the blood filled his gut. He began bellowing like a bull, and his companions came forward and carried him away still bellowing. "What is this?" they said. "By God, you've merely been grazed!" Ubayy replied, "By God, he'd have killed me even if he had only hit me with his spittle! Did he not say, 'I will kill him, God willing'? By God, were he to have struck the people at the market of Dhū l-Majāz with its like, he would have slain them all!"

Ubayy survived but a day, or nearly that, before he died, destined for Hell. Concerning him, God revealed:

> «On that Day the evildoer will bite his own hand and say, "If only I had taken the same path as the Messenger. Woe is me! If only I had not taken so-and-so as a friend— he led me away from the Revelation after it reached me; Satan has always betrayed humankind."»[93]

وَقعَةُ بَنِي النَّضِير

عبد الرزّاق عن معمر عن الزهريّ في حديثه عن عروة: ١،٦

ثمّ كانت غزوة بني النضير، وهم طائفةٌ من اليهود، على رأس ستّة أشهر من وقعة بدر. وكانت منازلُهم ونخلُهم بناحية من المدينة، فحاصرهم رسول الله صلّى الله عليه وسلّم حتّى نزلوا على الجلاء وعلى أنّ لهم ما أقلّت الإبل من الأمتعة والأموال إلا الحلْقة، يعني السلاح. فأنزل الله فيهم ﴿سَبَّحَ لِلَّهِ مَا فِي ٱلسَّمَٰوَٰتِ وَمَا فِي ٱلْأَرْضِ وَهُوَ ٱلْعَزِيزُ ٱلْحَكِيمُ ☆ هُوَ ٱلَّذِي أَخْرَجَ ٱلَّذِينَ كَفَرُواْ مِنْ أَهْلِ ٱلْكِتَٰبِ مِن دِيَٰرِهِمْ لِأَوَّلِ ٱلْحَشْرِ﴾. فقاتلهم النبيّ صلّى الله عليه وسلّم حتّى صالحهم على الجلاء. فأجلاهم إلى الشام، فكانوا من سبطٍ لم يصِبهم جلاءٌ فيما خلا وكان الله قد كتب عليهم الجلاء. لولا ذلك ليُعذِّبهم في الدنيا بالقتل والسباء. وأمّا قوله: ﴿لِأَوَّلِ ٱلْحَشْرِ﴾، فكان جلاؤهم ذلك أوّل حشرٍ في الدنيا إلى الشام.

عبد الرزّاق عن معمر عن الزهريّ قال: وأخبرني عبد الله بن عبد الرحمن بن كعب بن مالك عن رجلٍ من أصحاب النبيّ صلّى الله عليه وسلّم: ٢،٦

أنّ كفّار قريش كتبوا إلى عبد الله بن أُبَيّ ابن سلول، ومن كان يعبد الأوثان من الأوس والخزرج، ورسول الله صلّى الله عليه وسلّم يومئذٍ بالمدينة قبل وقعة بدر، يقولون: إنّكم آويتم صاحبنا وإنّكم أكثر أهل المدينة عدداً، وإنّا نُقسم بالله لتقتلُنَّهُ أو لتُخرِجُنَّهُ أو لنستعينُنَّ عليكم العرب، ثمّ لنسيرُنَّ إليكم بأجمعنا حتّى نقتل مقاتلتكم ونستبيح نساءكم. ١،٢،٦

The Incident Concerning the Clan of al-Naḍīr[94]

6.1 ʿAbd al-Razzāq, on the authority of Maʿmar, on the authority of al-Zuhrī, according to his narration from ʿUrwah:

Then there transpired the raid on the clan of al-Naḍīr, a faction of Jews, six months after the incident at Badr.[95] Their homes and date palms were located on the outskirts of Medina. The Messenger of God besieged them until they surrendered and entered exile, agreeing to take with them only what wealth and effects their camels could carry, minus any arms, meaning weaponry. Concerning them, God revealed:

> «Everything in the heavens and earth glorifies God; He is the Almighty, the Wise. It was He who drove from their homes those of the People of the Book who broke faith at the first banishment...»[96]

The Prophet fought against them until they sued for peace and accepted exile. He exiled them to Syria, even though they were from a tribe that had not once been exiled in ages past. Yet God decreed exile as their punishment, and if it were not so, they would have been chastised with death and captivity in this world. As for God's word «the first banishment», this means that their exile was the first time in this earthly life that Jews were banished to Syria.[97]

6.2 ʿAbd al-Razzāq, on the authority of Maʿmar, on the authority of al-Zuhrī, who said: ʿAbd al-Raḥmān ibn ʿAbd Allāh ibn Kaʿb ibn Mālik reported to me on the authority of one of the Prophet's companions that:

6.2.1 The infidel Quraysh wrote to ʿAbd Allāh ibn Ubayy ibn Salūl and also to those members of the Aws and Khazraj tribes who were idolaters. This occurred while the Messenger of God resided in Medina but before the incident at Badr. The infidel Quraysh said, "You have given shelter to our tribesman, and you remain the more numerous of Medina's inhabitants. We swear by God that you had better either kill him or expel him, or else we will rally the Arabs to help us and march against you in our full numbers, slaying your warriors and ravishing your women!"

فلمّا بلغ ذلك ابن أُبَيّ ومن معه من عبدة الأوثان، تراسلوا، فاجتمعوا وأرسلوا وأجمعوا لقتال النبيّ صلّى الله عليه وسلّم وأصحابه. فلمّا بلغ ذلك النبيّ صلّى الله عليه وسلّم، لقيهم في جماعة. فقال: لقد بلغ وعيدُ قريش منكم المبالغ. ما كانت لتكيدكم بأكثر ممّا تريدون أن تكيدوا به أنفسكم. فأنتم هؤلاء تريدون أن تقتلوا أبناءكم وإخوانكم. فلمّا سمعوا ذلك من النبيّ صلّى الله عليه وسلّم، تفرّقوا. فبلغ ذلك كفّار قريش.

وكانت وقعة بدر فكتبت كفّار قريش بعد وقعة بدر إلى اليهود: أنّكم أهل الحلقة ٢،٢،٦
والحصون وأنّكم لتقاتلُنّ صاحبنا أو لنفعلنّ كذا وكذا. ولا يحول بيننا وبين خَدَم نسائكم شيء،[1] وهو الخلاخل. فلمّا بلغ كتابُهم اليهود، أجمعت بنو النضير بالغدر. فأرسلت إلى النبيّ صلّى الله عليه وسلّم: أُخرج إلينا في ثلاثين رجلاً من أصحابك ولنخرج في ثلاثين حبرًا حتّى نلتقي في مكان كذا، نصَف بيننا وبينكم فيسمعوا منك. فإن صدّقوك وآمنوا بك، آمنّا كلُّنا.

فخرج النبيّ صلّى الله عليه وسلّم في ثلاثين من أصحابه وخرج إليه ثلاثون حبرًا من اليهود حتّى إذا برزوا في براز من الأرض. قال بعض اليهود لبعضٍ: كيف تخلصون إليه، ومعه ثلاثون رجلاً من أصحابه، كلّهم يحبّ أن يموت قبله. فأرسلوا إليه: كيف تفهم ونفهم ونحن ستّون رجلاً؟ أُخرج في ثلاثة من أصحابك. ويخرج إليك ثلاثة من علمائنا، فليسمعوا منك. فإن آمنوا بك، آمنّا كلّنا وصدّقناك.

فخرج النبيّ في ثلاثة نفر من أصحابه، واشتملوا على الخناجر وأرادوا الفتك برسول الله صلّى الله عليه وسلّم. فأرسلت امرأةٌ ناصحةٌ من بني النضير إلى بني أخيها،

١ [شيء] من بد؛ ساقطة من م.

When word of this reached Ibn Ubayy and the idolaters who were with them, they exchanged messages and convened. They then dispatched a message to the Quraysh, agreeing to murder the Prophet and his Companions. When the Prophet caught wind of this, he and a band of his men confronted them, saying, "The threats of the Quraysh have certainly wreaked havoc upon you. They didn't beguile you nearly as much as you wish to beguile yourselves. You are the ones who seek to kill your own sons and brothers." When they heard the words the Prophet had spoken, they dispersed and went their separate ways, and word of these matters reached the infidel Quraysh.

Subsequently, the battle of Badr transpired. It was after the events at Badr **6.2.2**
that the infidel Quraysh wrote the Jews as follows: "Indeed, you are a well-armed and well-fortified people, so you had better kill our tribesman, or else we will surely take action and nothing will stand between us and the attendants of your womenfolk"—by "the attendents of your womenfolk" they meant their golden anklets.[98] When their letter reached the Jews, the clan of al-Naḍīr chose treachery. Then they sent a message to the Prophet, saying, "Come out to meet us with thirty of your companions, and we will come forth with thirty rabbis. We can meet at such-and-such place, halfway between you and us, and listen to what you have to say. If the rabbis believe in the truth of what you say and believe in you, then we shall all believe."

The Prophet then set out, taking thirty of his companions with him. Thirty of the Jews' rabbis also came out to meet him, and eventually they had all gathered at an open expanse of earth. The Jews began to say to one another, "How will we be able to reach Muḥammad when he has thirty of his companions at his side—each of them more willing than the next to lay down his life for him?" So they sent him this message: "How can we understand what's being said if we number altogether sixty men? Come forward with only three of your companions, and three of our scholars will set out to meet with you so that they can listen to what you have to say. And if they believe in your message, we too will believe, all of us, and testify to the truth of your message."

The Prophet then set out with only three of his companions. The Jews had brought daggers and concealed them, for they wanted to assassinate God's Messenger. However, an honest Jewess from al-Naḍīr sent word to her nephews—for her brother was one of the Muslim Allies—and she informed her brother about the plans of al-Naḍīr to betray the Messenger of God. Quickly

وهو رجل مسلم من الأنصار، فأخبرته خبرَ ما أرادت بنو النضير من الغدر برسول الله صلّى الله عليه وسلّم. فأقبل أخوها سريعاً حتّى أدرك النبيّ صلّى الله عليه وسلّم. فسارّه بخبرهم قبل أن يصل النبيّ صلّى الله عليه وسلّم إليهم.

فرجع النبيّ صلّى الله عليه وسلّم. فلمّا كان من الغد، غدا عليهم رسولُ الله صلّى الله عليهم وسلم بالكتائب، فحاصرهم. وقال لهم: إنّكم لا تأمنون عندي إلا بعهدٍ تعاهدوني عليه. فأبَوا أن يعطوه عهداً، فقاتلهم يومهم ذلك، هو والمسلمون. ثمّ غدا الغد على بني قريظة بالخيل والكتائب وترك بني النضير ودعاهم إلى أن يعاهدوه. فعاهدوه، فانصرف عنهم، وغدا إلى بني النضير بالكتائب. فقاتلهم حتّى نزلوا على الجلاء وعلى أنّ لهم ما أقلّت الإبل إلّا الحلقة. والحلقة: السلاح. فجاءت[1] بنو النضير واحتملوا ما أقلّت الإبل من أمتعتهم وأبواب بيوتهم وخشبها. فكانوا يخرّبون بيوتهم فيهدمونها فيحملون ما وافقهم من خشبها.

وكان جلاؤهم ذلك أوّل حشر الناس إلى الشام. وكان بنو النضير من سبط ٣،٢،٦
من أسباط بني إسرائيل. لم يصِبهم جلاءٌ منذ كتب الله على بني إسرائيل الجلاء.
فلذلك أجلاهم رسول الله صلّى الله عليه وسلّم. فلولا ما كتب الله عليهم من الجلاء
لعذّبهم في الدنيا كما عُذّبت بنو قريظة. فأنزل الله ﴿سَبَّحَ لِلَّهِ مَا فِي ٱلسَّمَٰوَٰتِ وَمَا فِي ٱلْأَرْضِ
وَهُوَ ٱلْعَزِيزُ ٱلْحَكِيمُ﴾ حتّى بلغ ﴿وَٱللَّهُ عَلَىٰ كُلِّ شَيْءٍ قَدِيرٌ﴾. وكانت نخل بني النضير
لرسول الله صلّى الله عليه وسلّم خاصّةً، فأعطاه اللهُ إيّاها وخصّه بها. فقال

[1] مم؛ بد: فجلت.

her brother set off, and when he reached the Prophet he disclosed their secret plans before the Prophet had reached the Naḍīr clan.

The Prophet turned back and then came to the Naḍīr clan the next morning with several arrays of armed men and besieged them. He said to them, "Unless you enter into a pact with me, you'll have no guarantee of protection." They refused to agree to a pact with the Prophet, so he and the Muslims fought against them that very day. The following morning, the Prophet went to the Qurayẓah clan with cavalry and several arrays of armed men, leaving the Naḍīr clan behind.[99] He summoned the Qurayẓah clan to make a pact with him, and so they did. The Prophet then turned away from the Qurayẓah clan and headed back to the Naḍīr clan with his armed men. He fought them and eventually they surrendered, agreeing to be exiled and to take with them only what their camels could carry, minus any arms—meaning weapons. The clan of al-Naḍīr left Medina carrying only as many of their effects as their camels could bear. These included even the doors of their homes and the wooden beams, for they had taken apart their houses and dismantled them to carry away all the wood they could salvage.

Their exile was the first time a people had been banished to Syria. The clan **6.2.3**
of al-Naḍīr was descended from one of the original tribes of the Israelites, and they had not suffered exile since God had decreed exile on the Children of Israel.[100] This is the reason that the Messenger of God exiled them, for if God had not decreed exile against them, then He would have chastised them in this world, as was the fate of the Qurayẓah clan.[101] Thus, God revealed:

> «Everything in the heavens and earth glorifies God; He is the Almighty, the Wise. It was He who drove those People of the Book from their homes at the first banishment—you believers never thought they would go, and they themselves thought their fortifications would protect them against God. God came upon them from where they least expected and put panic into their hearts: their homes were destroyed by their own hands and the hands of the believers. Learn from all this, those of you with insight! If God had not decreed exile for them, He would have chastised them in this world. In the Hereafter, they will have the chastisement of Hellfire, because they set themselves against God and his Messenger: God is stern in punishment toward anyone who sets himself against Him. Whatever you believers may have done to their

﴿مَا أَفَاءَ اللهُ عَلَىٰ رَسُولِهِ مِنْهُمْ فَمَا أَوْجَفْتُمْ عَلَيْهِ مِنْ خَيْلٍ وَلَا رِكَابٍ﴾ يقول: بغير قتال.
قال: فأعطى النبيّ صلّى الله عليه وسلّم أكثرها للمهاجرين وقسمها بينهم وقسم منها[1] لرجلين من الأنصار كانا ذوي حاجةٍ. لم يقسم لرجلٍ من الأنصار غيرهما، وبقي منها صدقة رسول الله صلّى الله عليه وسلّم الّتي في أيدي[2] بني فاطمة.

عبد الرزّاق عن معمر قال: أخبرني من سمع عكرمة يقول: ٣،٦

مكث النبيّ صلّى الله عليه وسلّم بمكّة خمس عشرة سنة منها أربعٌ أو خمسٌ يدعو إلى الإسلام سرًّا ، وهو خائفٌ، حتّى بعث الله على الرجال الّذين أنزل فيهم ﴿إِنَّا كَفَيْنَاكَ ٱلْمُسْتَهْزِئِينَ﴾ ﴿الّذين جعلوا ٱلقرآنَ عِضِين﴾ . والعِضين بلسان قريش: السحر، يقال للساحرة: عاضية.[3] فأمر بعداوتهم، فقال: ﴿ٱصْدَعْ بِمَا تُؤْمَرُ وَأَعْرِضْ عَنِ ٱلْمُشْرِكِينَ﴾ .

ثمّ أمر بالخروج إلى المدينة، فقدم في ثمان ليال خلون من شهر ربيع الأوّل. ثمّ كانت وقعة بدر. ففيهم أنزل الله ﴿وَإِذْ يَعِدُكُمُ ٱللهُ إِحْدَى ٱلطَّائِفَتَيْنِ﴾ وفيهم نزلت ﴿سَيُهْزَمُ ٱلْجَمْعُ﴾ . وفيهم نزلت ﴿حَتَّىٰ إِذَا أَخَذْنَا مُتْرَفِيهِم بِٱلْعَذَابِ﴾ . وفيهم نزلت ﴿لِيَقْطَعَ طَرَفًا مِّنَ ٱلَّذِينَ كَفَرُوا﴾ . وفيهم نزلت ﴿لَيْسَ لَكَ مِنَ ٱلْأَمْرِ شَيْءٌ﴾ .

---

١ [وقسّم منها] مند؛ ساقطة من مم. ٢ د؛ مم: في يد. ٣ كذا في مم؛ وفي تع: العاضهة.

> palm trees—cutting them down or leaving them standing on their roots—was done by God's leave, so that he might disgrace those who defied Him. God turned their possessions over to His Messenger as spoils; spoils that you believers did not even have to spur on your horses or camels to acquire. God gives authority to His messengers over whomever He will: God has power over all things.»[102]

The date palms of the Naḍīr clan became the reserve of the Messenger of God, for God had given them to him and favored him thereby.[103] Thus He addressed the believers: «God turned their possessions over to His Messenger as spoils; spoils that you believers did not even have to spur on your horses or camels to acquire»,[104] meaning that it was accomplished without killing.

The Prophet gave most of the spoils to the Emigrants. He divided the spoils between them and also portioned out some to two men from the Allies who were in need, but no other Ally besides those two received any portion thereof. The remainder of the spoils was set aside as the charitable trust of God's Messenger, now in the hands of his daughter Fāṭimah's descendants.

ʿAbd al-Razzāq, on the authority of Maʿmar, who said: someone who heard ʿIkrimah informed me, saying: **6.3**

The Prophet remained in Mecca for fifteen years.[105] For four or five of those years, he summoned people to Islam in secret—for he feared for his safety—until God sent His word against those men concerning whom He revealed, «We are enough for you against all those who ridicule your message» and «Those who make out the Qur'an to be sorcery, *ʿiḍīn*»[106]—in the language of the Quraysh the word *ʿiḍīn* means "sorcery," and thus a "sorcerer" is called a *ʿāḍiyah*. God then issued the command to oppose them and decreed, «So proclaim openly what you have been commanded and ignore the idolaters.»[107]

Afterward, God issued the command for them to leave for Medina. The Prophet arrived on the ninth of the month of Rabīʿ I.[108] Then the incident at Badr occurred, concerning which God revealed: «Remember how God promised you believers that one of the groups would fall to you»,[109] and concerning which he revealed: «Their forces will be routed.»[110] He also revealed concerning them: «When we bring our punishment on those corrupted with wealth»;[111] and also: «And in order to cut off the flanks of the disbelievers' army», as well as: «The matter is not for you, Prophet, to decide.»[112] God sought to defeat the army, but the Messenger of God sought the caravan.[113]

أراد الله القوم وأراد رسول الله صلّى الله عليه وسلّم العير. وفيهم نزلت ﴿أَلَمْ تَرَ إِلَى ٱلَّذِينَ بَدَّلُوا نِعْمَتَ ٱللَّهِ كُفْرًا﴾ الآية. وفيهم نزلت ﴿أَلَمْ تَرَ إِلَى ٱلَّذِينَ خَرَجُوا مِن دِيَٰرِهِمْ﴾ الآية. وفيهم نزلت ﴿قَدْ كَانَ لَكُمْ ءَايَةٌ فِي فِئَتَيْنِ ٱلْتَقَتَا﴾، في شأن العير ﴿وَٱلرَّكْبُ أَسْفَلَ مِنكُمْ﴾، أخذوا أسفل الوادي.

هذا كلّه في أهل بدر. وكانت قبل بدر بشهرين سريّة، يوم قتل الحضرميّ. ثمّ كانت أُحُد، ثمّ يومُ الأحزاب بعد أُحد بسنتَين، ثمّ كانت الحديبية وهو يوم الشجرة. فصالحهم النبيّ صلّى الله عليه وسلّم على أن يعتمر في عام قابل في هذا الشهر. ففيها نزلت ﴿ٱلشَّهْرُ ٱلْحَرَامُ بِٱلشَّهْرِ ٱلْحَرَامِ﴾، فشهر عام الأوّل بشهر العام الثاني،[1] فكانت ﴿ٱلْحُرُمَٰتُ قِصَاصٌ﴾. ثمّ كانت الفتح بعد العمرة، ففيها نزلت ﴿حَتَّىٰٓ إِذَا فَتَحْنَا عَلَيْهِم بَابًا ذَا عَذَابٍ شَدِيدٍ إِذَا هُمْ فِيهِ مُبْلِسُونَ﴾، وذلك أن نبيّ الله صلّى الله عليه وسلّم غزاهم ولم يكونوا أعدّوا له أُهبَةَ القتال. ولقد قُتل من قريش أربعة رهط ومن حلفائهم من بني بكر خمسين أو زيادة. وفيهم نُزلت لمّا دخلوا في دين الله ﴿هُوَ ٱلَّذِيٓ أَنشَأَ لَكُمُ ٱلسَّمْعَ وَٱلْأَبْصَٰرَ﴾. ثمّ خرج إلى حنين بعد عشرين ليلة، ثمّ إلى الطائف، ثمّ رجع إلى المدينة، ثمّ أمّر أبا بكر على الحجّ، ثمّ حجّ رسولُ الله صلّى الله عليه وسلّم العام المقبل، ثمّ ودّع الناس، ثمّ رجع. فتوفي في ليلتين خلتا من شهر ربيع. ولمّا رجع أبو بكر من الحجّ، غزا رسول الله صلّى الله عليه وسلّم تبوكًا.[2]

١ [الثاني] أنا. ٢ كذا في م.

Concerning them, God revealed: «Do you not see those who, in exchange for God's favor, offer only ingratitude?»,[114] and He revealed: «Consider those people who abandoned their homes . . .»[115] Also, He revealed concerning them: «You have already seen a sign in the two armies that met in battle.»[116] On the matter of the caravan, He revealed: «the caravan was below you»[117] because they had entered the lowest part of the valley.

All of these verses relate to the combatants at Badr. Two months before Badr, there was a raid—it was the day on which al-Ḥaḍramī was slain.[118] Then there was the battle of Uḥud, then the Battle of the United Clans took place two years after Uḥud. Then there was al-Ḥudaybiyah—the Day of the Tree—when the Prophet agreed to a treaty stipulating that he would undertake a lesser pilgrimage on the same month of the following year. On this matter, God revealed: «A sacred month for a sacred month,» that is, the month in the first year was exchanged for that of the second year and «violation of sanctity calls for fair retribution.»[119] The conquest of Mecca followed the lesser pilgrimage, concerning which God revealed: «Until We open a gate to severe torment for them—then they will be plunged into despair.»[120] That is because the Prophet raided them, but they had sufficiently prepared for battle. Of the Quraysh, four persons were killed and of their allies from the Bakr clan, at least fifty or more. Once they embraced God's religion, He revealed concerning them: «It is God who endowed you with hearing and sight.»[121] Then, twenty nights later, the Prophet set off for Ḥunayn, then went to Taif, and finally returned to Medina, whence he ordered Abū Bakr to lead the hajj. The Prophet undertook the hajj himself the following year, after which he delivered his farewell sermon. He returned to Medina, where he passed away on the third day of the month of Rabīʿ I.[122] Also, when Abū Bakr had returned from the hajj, the Messenger of God raided Tabūk.[123]

وَقعةُ أُحُد

عبد الرزّاق عن معمر عن الزهريّ في حديثه عن عروة، قال: ١،٧

كانت وقعة أُحُد في شوّال على رأس ستّة أشهر من وقعة بني النضير.

قال الزهريّ عن عروة في قوله ﴿وَعَصَيْتُم مِّن بَعْدِ مَا أَرَاكُم مَّا تُحِبُّونَ﴾: ٢،٧

إنّ النبيّ صلّى الله عليه وسلّم قال يوم أُحُد حين غزا أبو سفيان وكفّار قريش: ١،٢،٧
إنّي رأيتُ كأنّي لبست درعاً حصينةً فأوّلتُها المدينة. فاجلسوا في ضيعتكم وقاتلوا من ورائها. وكاني المدينة قد شبّكت[1] بالبنيان فهي كالحصن. فقال رجلٌ ممّن لم يشهد بدراً: يا رسول الله! اخرج بنا إليهم فلنقاتلهم. فقال عبد الله بن أبيّ ابن سلول: نعم، والله يا نبيّ الله! ما رأيت إنّا والله ما نزل بنا عدوّ قطّ فخرجنا إليه، فأصاب فينا. ولا تنأنا[2] في المدينة وقاتلنا من ورائها إلّا هزمنا عدوَّنا.

فكلّمه أناس من المسلمين. فقالوا: بلى، يا رسول الله! اُخرج بنا إليهم. فدعا بلأمته فلبسها. ثمّ قال: ما أظنّ الصرعى إلّا ستكثر منكم ومنهم. إنّي أرى في النوم بَقَراً[3] منحورةً. فأقول بَقَرٌ والله بخير. فقال رجلٌ: يا رسول الله! بأَبي أنت وأمّي! فاجلس بنا. فقال: إنّه لا ينبغي لنبيّ إذا لبس لأْمَتَه أن يضعها حتّى يلقى البأس. فهل من رجل يدلّنا الطريق على القوم من كثب؟ فانطلقت به الأَدِلاّءُ بين يديه حتّى إذا كان بالشَوْط[4] من الجبّانة. انخزل عبد الله بن أبيّ بثلث الجيش، أو قريب من ثلث الجيش. فانطلق النبيّ صلّى الله عليه وسلّم حتّى لقوهم بأُحُد وصافّوهم. وقد كان النبيّ صلّى الله عليه وسلّم عهد إلى أصحابه إن هم هزموهم أن لا يدخلوا لهم عسكرًا ولا يتّبعوهم.

---

١ مم؛ تع: فرشت. ٢ مم: تنينا؛ تع: ثبتنا. ٣ [بَقَرًا] في تع؛ ساقطة من مم. ٤ تع؛ مم: بالواسط.

The Incident at Uḥud[124]

ʿAbd al-Razzāq, on the authority of Maʿmar, on the authority of al-Zuhrī who, in his narration from ʿUrwah, said: 7.1

The incident at Uḥud was in the month of Shawwal, six months after the incident involving the clan of al-Naḍīr.[125]

Al-Zuhrī, on the authority of ʿUrwah, said concerning God's decree «you disobeyed once He had brought you within sight of your goal»:[126] 7.2

On the day of the Battle of Uḥud, when Abū Sufyān and the infidel Quraysh attacked, the Prophet said, "I had a vision that I donned an impenetrable coat of armor, which I surmise must be Medina. Remain, therefore, in your stately houses and fight from within their walls." Now Medina was a maze of buildings, making it like a fortress. One of the men who had not fought at Badr said, "O Messenger of God! March us out to them so that we may engage them in battle!" ʿAbd Allāh ibn Ubayy ibn Salūl said, "I agree, by God, O Prophet of God! Truly I don't see it so. I swear by God that no enemy has ever visited defeat upon us when we have met them in open battle unless some evil had befallen us. Nor have we ever remained in Medina and fought from behind its walls without meeting defeat at the hands of our enemies." 7.2.1

A number of other Muslims spoke to him, saying, "We agree, O Messenger of God! March us out against them." So the Prophet called for his armor. When he had donned it, he said, "I suspect the number of the fallen will be great on both sides. While asleep, I had a vision of a slaughtered animal—a cow, I'd say. By God, this omen is a boon."[127] A man replied, "O Messenger of God, I would sacrifice the life of my mother and father for you! Please remain here with us." He continued, "It does not behoove a prophet, once he has donned his armor, to remove it until he has faced the trial. Are there men nearby who might lead the way to the enemy?" The guides then set off and led him to al-Shawṭ of al-Jabbānah. ʿAbd Allāh ibn Ubayy remained behind with fully a third of the army, or nearly a third.[128] The Prophet continued onward and eventually encountered the Meccans at Uḥud, where the Muslims

فلمّا التقوا، هزموا وعصَوا النبيّ صلّى الله عليه وسلّم، وتنازعوا واختلفوا. ثمّ صرفهم الله عنهم ليبتليهم كما قال الله. وأقبل المشركون وعلى خيلهم خالد بن الوليد بن المغيرة، فقَتَلَ من المسلمين سبعين رجلاً، وأصابتهم جراح شديدة. وكُسرت رباعيّة رسول الله صلّى الله عليه وسلّم ووُثِئَ وجهُه حتّى صاح الشيطان بأعلى صوته: قُتل محمّد!

قال كعب بن مالك: ٣،٧

فكنت أوّل من عرف النبيّ صلّى الله عليه وسلّم. عرفتُ عينيه من وراء المغفر. فناديتُ بصوتي الأعلى: هذا رسول الله صلّى الله عليه وسلّم! فأشار إليّ أن اسكت. وكفّ اللهُ المشركين والنبيّ صلّى الله عليه وسلّم وأصحابه وقوف. فنادى أبو سفيان بعدما مُثّل ببعض أصحاب رسول الله صلّى الله عليه وسلّم، وجُدِعوا، ومنهم من بُقر بطنُه. فقال: أبو سفيان: إنّكم ستجدون في قتلاكم بعض المثل. فإن ذلك، لم يكن عن ذوي رأينا ولا سادتنا. ثمّ قال أبو سفيان: اعلُ هبل. فقال عمر بن الخطّاب: اللهُ أعلى وأجلّ. فقال: أنعمتَ عيناً،[١] قتلى بقتلى بدر. فقال عمر: لا يستوي القتلى، قتلانا في الجنّة وقتلاكم في النار. فقال أبو سفيان: لقد خِبْنا إذاً. ثمّ انصرفوا راجعين. وندب النبيّ صلّى الله عليه وسلّم أصحابه في طلبهم يومئذٍ عبد الله بن مسعود. وذلك حين قال الله ﴿ٱلَّذِينَ قَالَ لَهُمُ ٱلنَّاسُ إِنَّ ٱلنَّاسَ قَدْ جَمَعُوا۟ لَكُمْ فَٱخْشَوْهُمْ فَزَادَهُمْ إِيمَٰنًا وَقَالُوا۟ حَسْبُنَا ٱللَّهُ وَنِعْمَ ٱلْوَكِيلُ﴾ .

١ مم؛ تع: أنعمت فعالِ عنها.

arrayed themselves in battle ranks to face them. The Prophet had sworn to his companions that, if the Meccans were to defeat them, no army would capture or pursue them. When the two forces met, the Meccans defeated them. The Muslims disobeyed the Prophet, and they fought and quarreled among themselves. Thus God removed his favor from them to try them—as God had decreed. The Pagans charged, with Khālid ibn al-Walīd ibn al-Mughīrah leading their cavalry, and seventy men from the Muslim side were slain and many severely wounded. One of the Messenger of God's teeth[129] was broken, and his face was bruised, prompting Satan to cry out in his loudest voice, "Muḥammad has been slain!"

Kaʿb ibn Mālik said: 7.3

I was the first to find the Prophet. I recognized his eyes through his coif of chainmail, so I cried out as loud as I could, "This is the Messenger of God!" but he signaled for me to be quiet. God soon caused the Pagans to relent, and the Prophet and his companions ceased fighting. Then Abū Sufyān cried out to them, for the corpses of a number of the slain among the Prophet's companions had been mutilated—their limbs had been severed from their corpses, and one of them had had his chest rent.[130] Abū Sufyān called out, "You are certain to find among your slain some whose corpses have been mutilated. That was not done with the consent either of our men of esteemed judgment or of our nobles. May Hubal be exalted!" "*God* is most exalted and most glorious!" retorted ʿUmar, but Abū Sufyān persisted: "What a wondrous deed you have wrought—the slain a recompense for the slain of Badr!" Again ʿUmar retorted, "The slain are not equal! Our slain are in Paradise, but your slain are in Hellfire!" "Then surely our hope is for naught," Abū Sufyān responded, and then they withdrew and returned to Mecca.

The Prophet assigned a group of his companions to pursue the Meccans, and eventually they reached the area near Ḥamrāʾ al-Asad. Among those who pursued the Meccans that day was ʿAbd Allāh ibn Masʿūd. That was at the time God decreed:

> «Those whose faith only increased when people said, "Fear your enemy: they have amassed a great army against you," and who replied, "God is enough for us: He is the best protector."»[131]

٤،٧ عبد الرزّاق عن معمر عن الزهريّ في حديثه:

فلمّا دخل رسول الله صلّى الله عليه وسلّم المسجد، دعا المسلمين لطلب الكفّار، فاستجابوا. فطلبوهم عامّة يومهم. ثمّ رجع بهم رسول الله صلّى الله عليه وسلّم. فأنزل الله ﴿ٱلَّذِينَ ٱسۡتَجَابُواْ لِلَّهِ وَٱلرَّسُولِ مِنۢ بَعۡدِ مَآ أَصَابَهُمُ ٱلۡقَرۡحُ﴾ الآية.

٥،٧ ولقد أخبرنا عبد الرزّاق أنّ وجه رسول الله صلّى الله عليه وسلّم ضُرب يومئذٍ بالسيف سبعين ضربةً، وقاه الله شرّها كلّها.

ʿAbd al-Razzāq, on the authority of Maʿmar, on the authority of al-Zuhrī according to his 7.4
narrative:

When the Messenger of God entered the mosque, he enjoined the Muslims to pursue the infidels. They heeded his summons and pursued them for most of the day. Afterward the Messenger of God returned with them to Medina, and God revealed: «Those who responded to God and the Messenger after they suffered defeat»[132]

ʿAbd al-Razzāq had related to us[133] that, though the Messenger of God's face 7.5
was struck with seventy blows of the sword on that day, God prevented every single blow from harming him.

وَقْعَةُ ٱلأَحْزَابِ وَبَنِي قُرَيْظَةَ

١،٨ عبد الرزّاق عن معمر عن الزهريّ:[١]

١،١،٨ ثمّ كانت وقعة الأحزاب بعد وقعة أُحُد بسنتين، وذلك يومُ الخندق، ورسول الله صلّى الله عليه وسلّم جانب المدينة، ورأس المشركين يومئذٍ أبو سفيان. فحاصروا[٢] رسولَ الله صلّى الله عليه وسلّم وأصحابه بضع عشرة ليلةً حتّى خلص إلى كلّ امرئٍ منهم الكرب وحتّى قال النبيّ صلّى الله عليه وسلّم، كما أخبرني ابن المسيّب: اللّهمّ إنّي أنشدك عهدك ووعدك، اللّهمّ إنّك إن تشاء أن لا تُعبد.

٢،١،٨ فبينا هم[٣] على ذلك، أرسل النبيّ صلّى الله عليه وسلّم إلى عيينة بن حصن بن بدر الفزاريّ، وهو يومئذ رأس المشركين من غطفان وهو مع أبي سفيان: أرأيتَ إن جعلتُ لك ثلث تمر الأنصار، أترجع بمن معك من غطفان وتخذّل بين الأحزاب؟ فأرسل إليه عيينة: إن جعلتَ لي الشّطر فعلتُ. فأرسل إلى سعد بن معاذ، وهو سيّد الأوس، وإلى سعد بن عبادة، وهو سيّد الخزرج. فقال لهما: إنّ عيينة بن حصن قد سألني نصف تمركما على أن ينصرف بمن معه من غطفان ويخذّل بين الأحزاب. وإنّي قد أعطيتُه الثلث، فأبى إلّا الشطر. فماذا تريان؟ قالا: يا رسول الله! إن كنتَ أُمِرتَ بشيء، فامضِ لأمر الله. فقال رسول الله صلّى الله عليه وسلّم: لو كنتُ أُمِرتُ بشيء لم أستأمركما، ولكن هذا رأيي أَعرضه عليكما. قالا: فإنّا لا نرى أن نعطيه إلّا السيف. قال: فنعم إذاً.

١ [عن معمر عن الزهريّ] في تع؛ ساقطة من مم. ٢ تع؛ مم: حاصرا. ٣ تع؛ مم: فبلناهم.

The Incident Involving the United Clans and the Qurayẓah Clan[134]

'Abd al-Razzāq, on the authority of Ma'mar, on the authority of al-Zuhrī: 8.1

The incident involving the United Clans, which is the Battle of the Trench, took place two years after the incident at Uḥud.[135] The Messenger of God had taken command over the Medinese side, and that day Abū Sufyān led the Pagans. They besieged the Messenger of God and his companions for over ten days until despair overtook every Medinese, at which point the Prophet—according to what Ibn al-Musayyab reported to me—said, "O Lord! I implore You to stay true to Your pledge and covenant—unless, O Lord, You truly do not wish to be worshipped!" 8.1.1

While they were swept up in these events, the Prophet sent a message to 'Uyaynah ibn Ḥiṣn ibn Badr al-Fazārī, who in those days was the leader of the Pagans of the Ghaṭafān tribe and on the side of Abū Sufyān. "If I were to offer you a third of the Allies' harvest, would you return, along with all those who are with you from Ghaṭafān, and dissuade the united clans from fighting?" 'Uyaynah sent back a message to him, responding, "If you hand half of the harvest over to me, I shall do so." The Prophet then sent a message to Sa'd ibn Mu'ādh, who was the chieftain of the Aws, and also to Sa'd ibn 'Ubādah, who was the chieftain of the Khazraj. He said to them, "'Uyaynah ibn Ḥiṣn has demanded half of your harvest as a condition for withdrawing with his allies from Ghaṭafān and dissuading the united clans from fighting. I had already offered him a third, but he refused to accept anything but half the harvest. How do you two see the matter?" "O Messenger of God!" the two replied. "If you have been commanded by God to do a thing, then let God's decree be fulfilled!" The Messenger of God retorted, "Had I been commanded by God to do a thing, then I wouldn't have sought your consent. Rather, this is my own opinion I present to you." They replied, "Indeed, then, our view is that we shall grant him nothing but the sword." And the Prophet answered, "So then, the matter is settled." 8.1.2

قال معمر: فأخبرني ابن أبي نجيح: ٢،٨

أنّهما قالا له: والله يا رسول الله! لقدكان يَمُرُّ في الجاهليّة يَجُرُّ سُرمه في عام السَنَة حول المدينة. ما يُطيق أن يدخلَها.[١] أفالآن حين جاء الله بالإسلام نعطيهم ذلك؟ قال النبيّ صلّى الله عليه وسلّم: فنعم إذاً.

قال الزهريّ في حديثه عن ابن المسيّب: ٣،٨

فبينا هم كذلك، إذ جاءهم نعيم بن مسعود الأشجعيّ، وكان يأمنه الفريقان، كان ١،٣،٨ موادعاً لهما. فقال: إنّي كنتُ عند عيينة وأبي سفيان إذ جاءهم رسول بني قريظة أن اثبتوا، فإنّا سنُخالف المسلمين إلى بيضتهم. قال النبيّ صلّى الله عليه وسلّم: فلعلّنا أمرناهم بذلك. وكان نعيم رجلاً لا يكتم الحديث، فقام بكلمة النبيّ صلّى الله عليه وسلّم. فجاءه عمر فقال: يا رسول الله، إن كان هذا الأمر من الله، فامضِه. وإن كان رأياً منك، فإنّ شأن قريش وبني قريظة أَهْوَنُ من أن يكون لأحد عليك فيه مقالٌ. فقال النبيّ صلّى الله عليه وسلّم: عليَّ الرجل. رُدُّوه! فردُّوه. فقال: انظر الّذي ذكرنا لك فلا تذكره لأحدٍ، فإنّما أغرا به.

فانطلق حتّى أتى عيينة وأبا سفيان، فقال: هل سمعتم من محمّد يقول قولاً إلّا كان حقّاً؟ قالا: لا. قال: فإنّي لمّا ذكرت له شأن قريظة. قال: فلعلّنا أمرناهم بذلك. قال أبو سفيان: سنعلم ذلك إن كان مكرًا. فأرسل إلى بني قريظة أنّكم قد أمرتمونا أن نثبت وأنّكم ستخالفون المسلمين إلى بيضتهم، فأعطونا بذلك رهينةً. فقالوا إنّها قد دخلت ليلة[٢] السبت وإنّا لا نقضي في السبت شيئاً. فقال أبو سفيان: إنّكم في مكر من بني قريظة، فارتحلوا. وأرسل الله عليهم الريح وقذف في قلوبهم الرعب. فأطفأت نيرانُهم، وقُطعت أرسان خيولهم، وانطلقوا منهزمين من غير قتال.

---

١ [يمر في الجاهلية يجر سرمه في عام السنة حول المدينة. ما يطيق أن يدخلها.] من تع؛ ساقطة من م. ٢ تع؛ م: عليلة.

Ma'mar said: Ibn Abī Najīḥ reported to me that: 8.2

The two said to him, "We swear by God, O Messenger of God, that in the Age of Ignorance 'Uyaynah ibn Ḥiṣn would come by Medina in a year of drought dragging his sorry ass around here. He couldn't gain entrance then, so now, after having been honored by Islam, are we to just hand over the harvest to him?"

Al-Zuhrī, continuing his report from Ibn al-Musayyab, said: 8.3

Meanwhile, Nu'aym ibn Mas'ūd al-Ashja'ī came to them. His safety had been 8.3.1
guaranteed by both factions, and he was party to a nonaggression pact with both. Nu'aym said, "I was in the company of 'Uyaynah and Abū Sufyān when the messenger of the Qurayẓah tribe came to them, saying, 'Be resolute, for we will take the Muslims unawares from their own safe haven.'" The Prophet replied, "Perhaps we ordered them to do that." Nu'aym was not the type of man to keep secrets, so he divulged what the Prophet had said. Then 'Umar came to the Prophet and said, "O Messenger of God, if this be God's decree, then let it come to pass, but if it be merely your opinion, then consider this: The matter of the Quraysh and the Qurayẓah clan is too perilous to just take one person's advice on the matter!" The Prophet replied, "Let me handle the man. Bring him back." They brought Nu'aym back to the Prophet, who said to him, "Consider carefully what we have said to you, but do not mention it to anyone." However, the Prophet was merely spurring Nu'aym on.

Nu'aym then departed, and when he came to 'Uyaynah and Abū Sufyān, he asked them, "Have you ever heard Muḥammad say anything that wasn't true?" "No," they answered, and he continued, "Indeed, when I myself mentioned the affair of the Qurayẓah clan to him, he said, 'Perhaps we ordered them to do that.'" Abū Sufyān responded, "We must know for sure whether this is a ploy." So he sent a message to the Qurayẓah clan: "You have ordered us to remain resolute, claiming that you will take the Muslims unawares from their safe haven. Give us, then, a guarantee of that." They replied, "The night of the Sabbath has come upon us, and we do not attend to any affair on the Sabbath." Abū Sufyān exclaimed, "You all have been duped by the Qurayẓah's gambit. Now ride off!" God then sent the tempest against them. Casting fear into their hearts, he extinguished the blaze of their fires and broke the halter of their steeds. Thus they fled, vanquished without battle.

قال: فذلك حين يقول: ﴿وَكَفَى ٱللَّهُ ٱلْمُؤْمِنِينَ ٱلْقِتَالَ وَكَانَ ٱللَّهُ قَوِيًّا عَزِيزًا﴾.

٢،٣،٨ قال: فندب النبيّ صلّى الله عليه وسلّم أصحابه في طلبهم، فطلبوهم حتّى بلغوا حمراء الأسد. قال: فرجعوا. قال: فوضع النبيّ صلّى الله عليه وسلّم لأمته، واغتسل واستجمر. فنادى النبيَّ صلّى الله عليه وسلّم جبريلُ: عذيرَكَ مِن محاربٍ، ألا أراك قد وضعت اللأمة ولم نضعها نحن بعد؟ فقام النبيّ صلّى الله عليه وسلّم فَزِعًا، فقال لأصحابه: عزمتُ عليكم ألّا تصلّوا العصر حتّى تأتوا بني قريظة. فغربت الشمس قبل أن يأتوها، فقالت طائفةٌ من المسلمين: إنّ النبيّ صلّى الله عليه وسلّم لم يُرِدْ أن تدعوا الصلاة. فصلّوا. فقالت طائفةٌ: إنّا لَفي عزيمة رسول الله صلّى الله عليه وسلّم، وما علينا من بأس. فصلّت طائفةٌ إيمانًا واحتسابًا وتركت طائفةٌ إيمانًا واحتسابًا.[1] قال: فلم يعنّف النبيّ صلّى الله عليه وسلّم واحدًا من الفريقَين.

٣،٣،٨ وخرج النبيّ صلّى الله عليه وسلّم فمرّ بمجالس بينه وبين بني قريظة. فقال: هل مرّ بكم من أحد؟ فقال: نعم، مرّ علينا دحية الكلبيّ على بغلة شهباء تحته قطيفة ديباج. فقال النبيّ صلّى الله عليه وسلّم: ليس ذلك، ولكنّه جبريل أُرسل إلى بني قريظة ليزلزل حصونهم ويقذفَ في قلوبهم الرعب. فحاصرهم أصحاب النبيّ صلّى الله عليه وسلّم. فلمّا انتهى أصحاب النبيّ صلّى الله عليه وسلّم أمر أصحابه[2] أن يستروه بجَحَفهم لِيَقُوه الحجارة حتّى يسمع كلامهم. ففعلوا، فناداهم: يا إخوة القردة والخنازير! فقالوا: يا أبا القاسم! ما كنتَ فاحشًا! فدعاهم إلى الإسلام قبل أن يقاتلهم. فأبوا أن يجيبوه إلى الإسلام. فقاتلهم رسول الله صلّى الله عليه وسلّم ومن معه من المسلمين حتّى نزلوا على حُكْم سعد بن معاذ. وأبوا أن ينزلوا على حكم النبيّ صلّى الله عليه وسلّم، فنزلوا على داء. فأقبلوا بهم، وسعد بن معاذ أَسِيرًا على أتان، حتّى انتهوا إلى رسول الله صلّى الله عليه وسلّم. فأخذتْ قريظة تُذكّر بحلفهم. وطفق سعد بن معاذ ينفلت إلى رسول الله صلّى الله عليه وسلّم مستأمرًا، ينتظره فيما يريد أن يحكم به. فيجيب له رسول الله

١ [وتركت طائفةٌ إيمانًا واحتسابًا] من تع؛ ساقطة في م. ٢ [أمر أصحابه] من تع؛ ساقطة في م.

That is when God decreed: «God spared the believers from fighting. He is strong and mighty.»[136]

The Prophet dispatched his companions to pursue them, and they pursued them as far as Ḥamrāʾ al-Asad, after which they returned to Medina. The Prophet then removed his armor, performed his ablutions, and perfumed himself.[137] But Gabriel called out to Muḥammad, "Who has excused you from battle? Did I not just see you remove your armor? We angels have yet to remove ours!" Anxiously, the Prophet stood up and said to his companions, "I bid you not to pray the late-afternoon prayer until we get to the Qurayẓah clan." The sun had set before they were able to reach them,[138] so a group of the Muslims said, "The Prophet would not want you to neglect the prayer," and they prayed. Another group of the Muslims said, "We are following the bidding of God's Messenger, so nothing ill will befall us." Thus one group prayed, full of faith and seeking God's reward, and the other neglected the prayer, also full of faith and seeking God's reward. The Prophet, accordingly, did not deal harshly with either group. 8.3.2

The Prophet set out and passed by some of the places that lay between him and the Qurayẓah clan where the people would assemble to meet. "Has anyone passed by you?" he asked. "Yes," said one of them, "Diḥyah al-Kalbī passed by riding on a gray she-mule, seated atop a velvet brocade." The Prophet replied, "That wasn't he. Rather, it was Gabriel, who has been sent to the Qurayẓah clan to cause their fortresses to quake and cast terror into their hearts." The Prophet then laid siege to the Qurayẓah clan, and when the Prophet's companions arrived, he ordered them to cover him with their shield, lest he be pelted by rocks, so that he could hear what the Qurayẓah had to say. Then the Prophet cried out, "You brethren of monkeys and pigs!"[139] They replied, "You didn't used to be so obscene, Abū l-Qāsim!" The Prophet called on them to embrace Islam before waging battle against them, but they refused to answer his call. Then God's Messenger and those Muslims who were with him fought the Qurayẓah until they agreed to surrender to the judgment of Saʿd ibn Muʿādh, for they had refused to surrender to the judgment of God's Messenger. Thus they surrendered themselves over to a woeful end. The Muslims brought forward the Qurayẓah clan while Saʿd ibn Muʿādh was bound like a captive atop a jenny ass.[140] Eventually they reached God's Messenger, whereupon the Qurayẓah started to remind those present of the pact made with their tribe. Saʿd ibn Muʿādh started to look to God's Messenger, hoping for a 8.3.3

صلّى الله عليه وسلّم يريد أن يقول: أتقرّ بما أنا حاكم. وطفق رسول الله صلّى الله عليه وسلّم يقول بقول: نعم. قال سعد: فإنّي أحكم بأن يُقتل مقاتلتهم وتُقسم أموالهم وتُسبى ذراريهم. فقال النبيّ صلّى الله عليه وسلّم: أصاب الحكم.

قال: وكان حييّ بن أخطب استجاش المشركين على رسول الله صلّى الله عليه وسلّم، فجاء إلى بني قريظة، فاستفتح عليهم ليلاً. فقال سيّدهم: إنّ هذا رجل مشؤوم، فلا يشامنّكم حييّ. فناداهم: يا بني قريظة! ألا تستجيبوني؟[١] ألا تلحقوني؟ ألا تضيفوني؟ فإنّي جائعٌ مقرورٌ.[٢] فقالت بنو قريظة: والله لنفتحنّ له. فلم يزالوا حتّى فتحوا له. فلمّا دخل معهم، أطمعهم.[٣] قال: يا بني قريظة! جئتكم في عزّ الدهر. جئتكم في عارضٍ بَرَدٍ لا يقوم لسبيله شيءٌ. فقال له سيّدهم: أتَعِدُنا عارضاً برداً ينكشف عنّا، وتدعنا عند بحر دائم لا يفارقنا. إنّما تعدنا الغرور. ٤،٣،٨

قال: فواثقهم وعاهدهم لئن انفضّت جموع الأحزاب أن يجيء حتّى يدخل معهم أُطمهم. فأطاعوه حينئذ بالغدر بالنبيّ صلّى الله عليه وسلّم والمسلمين. فلمّا فضّ الله جموع الأحزاب، انطلق حتّى إذا كان بالروحاء. ذكر العهد والميثاق الذي أعطاهم، فرجع حتّى دخل معهم. فلمّا أقبلت بنو قريظة أُتي به مكتوفاً بقدٍ.[٤] فقال حييّ للنبيّ صلّى الله عليه وسلّم: أمّا واللهِ ما لُمتُ نفسي في عداوتك، ولكنّه من يخذل الله، يُخذل. فأمر به النبيّ صلّى الله عليه وسلّم، فضُربت عنقه.

١ تع؛ مم: تستجيبوا. ٢ تع؛ مم: مغروز. ٣ تع؛ مم: فلما دخلوا عليهم أطمهم. ٤ أنا، وفي مم: مكتوبًا بقاذ؛ تع: فلما قتلت بنو قريظة أتى ملبوبًا إلى النبيّ.

command from him and trying to discern what the Prophet wished his judgment to be. The Messenger of God answered him, as though wishing Saʿd to say, "Will you confirm whatever judgement I give?" Just as the Prophet began to answer "Yes," Saʿd decreed, "Indeed, I rule that your fighting men are to be killed, your possessions plundered, and your women and children taken as captives." The Prophet then decreed, "The judgment is just."

Ḥuyayy ibn Akhṭab had been mustering the Pagans into an army against the 8.3.4
Messenger of God. He went to the Qurayẓah clan at night, asking them to allow him to enter their quarters. But the chief of their clan said, "This man's coming is ominous. Do not allow Ḥuyayy to bring calamity to you." Then Ḥuyayy cried out to them, "O Sons of Qurayẓah! Will you not answer me? Will you not come out to meet me? Will you not admit me as your guest? I am hungry and cold!" The Qurayẓah clan said, "By God, we must open our doors to him." Soon they opened their doors to him, and when he entered he beguiled them. Ḥuyayy exclaimed, "Sons of Qurayẓah, I have come to you in the nick of time! I come to you with a mighty hailstorm, and nothing can stand in its way!" Their chieftain replied to him, "Can you promise that this hailstorm will spare us; that you will leave us next to a calm ocean and not abandon us? On the contrary, all you promise is folly."

Ḥuyayy gave his word to the Qurayẓah clan and made a covenant with them to the effect that if the groups of the united clans dispersed, he would return to join them in their stronghold. When they followed him, they did so in perfidy against the Prophet and the Muslims. Once God had dispersed those who had amassed from the united tribes, Ḥuyayy fled as far as al-Rawḥāʾ. He remembered the pact and covenant he had given them, and he returned to join them in their stronghold. When the Qurayẓah clan were brought forth to be executed, Ḥuyayy also was brought forth, his hands tied with a single leather strap. Ḥuyayy addressed the Prophet: "I swear by God that I do not reproach myself for having opposed you, but he who forsakes God shall himself be forsaken!"[141] The Prophet issued the command to execute him, and his head was severed from his neck.

وقعة خيبر

عبد الرزّاق عن معمر عن الزهريّ قال: ١٠٩

لمّا انصرف رسول الله صلّى الله عليه وسلّم حتّى أتى المدينة، فغزا خيبر من الحديبية. فأنزل الله عليه ﴿وَعَدَكُمُ ٱللَّهُ مَغَانِمَ كَثِيرَةً تَأْخُذُونَهَا فَعَجَّلَ لَكُمْ هَٰذِهِۦ﴾ إلى ﴿وَيَهْدِيَكُمْ صِرَٰطًا مُّسْتَقِيمًا﴾. فلمّا فتحت خيبر، جعلها لمن غزا معه الحديبية وبايع تحت الشجرة، ممّن كان غائباً أو شاهداً، من أجل أنّ الله كان وعدهم إيّاها، وخمّس رسول الله صلّى الله عليه وسلّم خيبر. ثمّ قسم سائرها مغانم بين من شهدها من المسلمين ومن غاب من أهل الحديبية. ولم يكن لرسول الله صلّى الله عليه وسلّم ولا لأصحابه عُمّال يعملون خيبر ولا يزرعونها.

قال الزهريّ: فأخبرني سعيد بن المسيّب: ٢٠٩

أنّ رسول الله صلّى الله عليه وسلّم دعا يهود خيبر، وكانوا خرجوا على أن يسيروا منها، فدفع إليهم خيبر على أن يعملوها على النصف، فيؤدّونه إلى رسول الله صلّى الله عليه وسلّم وإلى أصحابه. وقال لهم رسول الله صلّى الله عليه وسلّم: أقرّكم على ذلك ما أقرّكم الله.[١] فكان رسول الله صلّى الله عليه وسلّم يبعث إليهم عبد الله بن رواحة الأنصاريّ، فيخرص عليهم النخل حين يطيب أوّل شيء من تمرها قبل أن يؤكل منه شيء، ثمّ يخيّر اليهود: أيأخذونها بذلك الخرص أم يدفعونها بذلك الخرص؟

١ [الله] ساقطة من م؛ كذا في التمهيد لابن عبد البر في رواية عن معمر.

The Incident at Khaybar[142]

'Abd al-Razzāq, on the authority of Maʿmar, on the authority of al-Zuhrī, who said: 9.1

When God's Messenger turned away from al-Ḥudaybiyah to return to Medina, he undertook the raid against Khaybar. Concerning this, God revealed:

> «He has promised you many future gains: He has hastened this gain for you. He has held back the hands of hostile people from you as a sign for the faithful and He will guide you to a straight path.»[143]

When the Prophet conquered Khaybar, he gave its spoils to those who had undertaken the expedition to al-Ḥudaybiyah with him and those who had given the oath of fealty under the tree,[144] whether they had personally witnessed the triumph over Khaybar or had been absent, for God had promised it to them. The Messenger of God took the fifth portion from Khaybar, which was his right,[145] and then divided the rest as spoils among those Muslims who had witnessed the triumph in Khaybar and the rest of the people of al-Ḥudaybiyah who had not. However, neither God's Messenger nor his companions had anyone able to manage Khaybar or cultivate its lands.

Al-Zuhrī said: Saʿīd ibn al-Musayyab related to me that: 9.2

The Messenger of God summoned the Jews of Khaybar, who had been forced to abandon the oasis and had left, and he handed the settlement back over to them on the condition that they would administer its lands and deliver half its produce to God's Messenger and his companions. The Messenger of God said to them, "The decision I have given you accords with what God has decided." God's Messenger used to send the Ally ʿAbd Allāh ibn Rawāḥah to them, and he would appraise the yield of the date palms for them when their first fruits would begin to show signs of ripening and before anything had been eaten. Then he would give the Jews the choice of whether to accept their share on the basis of that appraisal or dispute it.

قال الزهريّ: ثمّ اعتمر رسول الله صلّى الله عليه وسلّم في ذي القعدة من المدّة الّتي ٣.٩
كانت بينه وبين قريش، وخلّوها لرسول الله صلّى الله عليه وسلّم، وخلّفوا حويطب
ابن عبد العزّى القرشيّ ثمّ العدويّ. وأمروا إذا طاف رسول الله صلّى الله عليه وسلّم
ثلاثًا أن يأتيه فيأمره أن يرتحل. وكان رسول الله صلّى الله عليه وسلّم صالحهم على
أن يمكث ثلاثًا يطوف بالبيت، فأتى رسول الله صلّى الله عليه وسلّم حويطب بعد
ثلاث، فكلّمه في الرحيل، فارتحل رسول الله صلّى الله عليه وسلّم قافلًا إلى المدينة.
ثمّ غزا رسول الله صلّى الله عليه وسلّم الفتح، فتح مكّة.

قال الزهريّ: فأخبرني عبيد الله بن عبد الله بن عتبة عن ابن عبّاس: ٤.٩

أنّ النبيّ صلّى الله عليه وسلّم خرج في شهر رمضان من المدينة معه عشرة آلاف من المسلمين. وذلك على رأس ثمان سنين ونصف من مقدمه المدينة. فسار بمن معه من المسلمين إلى مكّة، يصوم ويصومون، حتّى بلغ الكديد، وهو ما بين عسفان وقديد، فأفطر وأفطر المسلمون معه، فلم يصوموا من بقية رمضان شيئًا.

قال الزهريّ: فكان الفطر آخر الأمرين، وإنّما يؤخذ من أمر رسول الله صلّى الله عليه وسلّم الآخر فالآخر.

قال: ففتح رسول الله صلّى الله عليه وسلّم مكّة ليلة ثلاث عشرة خلت من رمضان.

Al-Zuhrī said: After these events, the Messenger of God undertook a minor-pilgrimage in the month of Dhū l-Qadah,[146] while the armistice between him and the Quraysh was still in effect. The Quraysh left Mecca to God's Messenger and appointed Ḥuwayṭib ibn ʿAbd al-ʿUzzā al-Qurashī al-ʿAdawī as their deputy. They stipulated that, if the Messenger of God were to circle around the Kaaba for more than three days, Ḥuwayṭib would approach him and order him to leave.[147] Such was the pact God's Messenger had concluded with the Quraysh: that he would abide for three days circling around the Sacred House. Ḥuwayṭib approached God's Messenger after the three days had passed and discussed the matter of the departure with him. The Messenger of God then departed in his caravan, heading for Medina. Afterward, the Messenger of God undertook the Expedition of the Triumph; that is, the triumph over Mecca. 9.3

Al-Zuhrī said: ʿUbayd Allāh ibn ʿAbd Allāh ibn ʿUtbah reported to me, on the authority of Ibn ʿAbbās: 9.4

The Prophet left Medina during the month of Ramadan alongside ten thousand Muslims—this was just after eight and a half years had passed since his arrival in Medina. He marched with the Muslims to Mecca. He fasted and they fasted until they had reached al-Kadīd, a water source that lies between ʿUsfān and Qudayd. There he broke his fast, as did the Muslims who were with him, and they did not fast for the remainder of Ramadan.

Al-Zuhrī commented: Ceasing the fast was the latter of the two commands; hence, one should observe the later command of the Messenger of God and leave aside the prior.

He continued: The Messenger of God's triumph over Mecca was achieved on the night of the thirteenth of Ramadan.[148]

غزوة الفتح

عبد الرزّاق عن معمر عن عثمان الجزريّ — قال معمر: وكان يقال لعثمان الجزري المشاهد — عن مقسم مولى ابن عبّاس، قال: ١،١٠

لمّا كانت المدّة الّتي كانت بين رسول الله صلّى الله عليه وسلّم وبين قريش زمن الحديبية، وكانت سنتين، ذكر أنّها كانت حربٌ بين بني بكر، وهم حلفاء قريش، وبين خُزاعة، وهم حلفاء رسول الله صلّى الله عليه وسلّم. فأعانت قريش حلفاءها على خزاعة. فبلغ ذلك رسول الله صلّى الله عليه وسلّم، فقال: والّذي نفسي بيده لأمنعنّهم ممّا أمنع منه نفسي وأهل بيتي! وأخذ في الجهاز[١] إليهم. فبلغ ذلك قريشاً، فقالوا لأبي سفيان: ما تصنع؟ وهذه الجيوش تُجهّز إلينا. انطلقْ فجدِّد بيننا وبين محمّد كتاباً. وذلك مقدمه من الشام. ١،١،١٠

فخرج أبو سفيان حتّى قدم المدينة، فكلّمَ رسولَ الله صلّى الله عليه وسلّم، فقال: هلمّ فلنجدّدْ بيننا وبينك كتاباً. فقال النبيّ: فنحن على أمرنا الّذي كان، وهل أحدثتم من حدث؟ فقال أبو سفيان: لا. فقال النبيّ صلّى الله عليه وسلّم: فنحن على أمرنا الّذي كان بيننا. فجاء عليّ بن أبي طالب، فقال: هل لك على أن تَسُودَ العرب وتَمُنَّ على قومك، فتجيرهم وتجدّد لهم كتاباً؟ فقال: ما كنتُ لأفتات على رسول الله صلّى الله عليه وسلّم بأمر. ثمّ دخل على فاطمة، فقال: هل لكِ أن تكوني خير سخلةٍ في العرب، أن تجيري بين الناس؟ فقد أجارت أختُكِ على رسول الله صلّى الله عليه وسلّم زوجها أبا العاص بن الربيع، فلم يغيّر ذلك. فقالت فاطمة: ما كنتُ لأفتات على رسول الله صلّى الله عليه وسلّم بأمر. ثمّ قال ذلك للحسن والحسين. أجيرا ٢،١،١٠

---

١ مم: الجهاد.

The Expedition of the Triumph[149]

ʿAbd al-Razzāq, on the authority of Maʿmar, on the authority of ʿUthmān al-Jazarī—Maʿmar commented that ʿUthmān al-Jazarī was also known as "the eyewitness" (*al-mushāhid*)—on the authority of Miqsam, the slave-client of Ibn ʿAbbas, who said: 10.1

During the two-year period of the Messenger of God's truce with the Quraysh at al-Ḥudaybiyah, it is said that there was a war between the Bakr clan, allied with the Quraysh, and the Khuzāʿah clan, allied with God's Messenger. Now, the Quraysh provided aid to their allies against Khuzāʿah, and when word of this reached the Messenger of God, he said, "By Him in Whose hands my soul resides, I will surely deny them what I and my household have been denied!" He then began making preparations for war against the Quraysh. Word of this reached the Quraysh, and they said to Abū Sufyān, "What are you going to do? These armies are preparing to march against us! Leave now and renew the treaty between us and Muḥammad!" That was during his return from Syria.[150] 10.1.1

Abū Sufyān proceeded onward and eventually came to Medina. Addressing God's Messenger, he said, "Come now, let's renew the treaty between you and us." But the Prophet replied, "We're still bound by the agreement from before. Have you Quraysh committed any infraction?" "No," answered Abū Sufyān, so the Prophet continued, "Then we will continue to observe that agreement." ʿAlī ibn Abī Ṭālib came, and Abū Sufyān said, "Wouldn't you like to be lord over the Arabs and, in a gracious gesture toward your tribe, grant them sanctuary and renew the treaty with them?" ʿAlī replied, "Far be it from me to act contrary to God's Messenger in a matter." Then Abū Sufyān went in to see Fāṭimah and said, "Wouldn't you like to be finest lamb of the Arabs and offer sanctuary among your people? Indeed, your sister protected her husband, Abū al-ʿĀṣ ibn al-Rabīʿ, from God's Messenger, and that was not overruled." Fāṭimah replied, "Far be it from me to act contrary to God's Messenger in a matter." Then he said the same to al-Ḥasan and al-Ḥusayn: "Grant sanctuary among the people—just say, 'Yes'!" But they said nothing. Looking to their 10.1.2

بين الناس، قولا: نعم. فلم يقولا شيئًا ونظرا إلى أمّهما وقالا: نقول ما قالت أمّنا. فلم ينجح من واحد منهم بما طلب.

فخرج حتّى قدم على قريش، فقالوا: ماذا جئت به؟ قال: جئتكم من عند قوم قلوبهم ١٠،١،٣
على قلب واحد. والله ما تركت منهم صغيرًا ولا كبيرًا ولا أنثى ولا ذكرًا إلّا كلّمته. فلم أنجح منهم شيئًا. قالوا: ما صنعت شيئًا، ارجع. فرجع.

وخرج رسول الله صلّى الله عليه وسلّم يريد قريشًا حتّى إذا كان ببعض الطريق. ١٠،١،٤
قال رسول الله صلّى الله عليه وسلّم لناس من الأنصار: انظروا أبا سفيان، فإنّكم ستجدونه. فنظروه فوجدوه. فلمّا دخل العسكر جعل المسلمون يجأونه ويُسرعون إليه. فنادى: يا محمّد، إنّي لمقتول! فأمُر بي إلى العبّاس! وكان العبّاس له خِدْنًا وصديقًا في الجاهليّة. فأمر به النبيّ صلّى الله عليه وسلّم إلى العبّاس، فبات عنده.

فلمّا كان عند صلاة الصبح، وأذّن المؤذّن، تحرّك الناس، فظنّ أنّهم يريدونه. قال: يا عبّاس! ما شأن الناس؟

قال: تحرّكوا للمنادي للصلاة.

قال: فكلّ هؤلاء إنّما تحرّكوا لمنادي محمّد صلّى الله عليه وسلّم؟

قال: نعم.

قال: فقام العبّاس للصلاة وقام معه. فلمّا فرغوا، قال: يا عبّاس! ما يصنع محمّد شيئًا إلّا صنعوا مثله؟

قال: نعم، ولو أمرهم أن يتركوا الطعام والشراب حتّى يموتوا جوعًا لفعلوا. وإنّي لأراهم سيُهلكون قومَك غدًا.

قال: يا عبّاس، فادخل بنا عليه!

فدخل إلى النبيّ صلّى الله عليه وسلّم، وهو في قبّة من أدم وعمر بن الخطّاب خلف القبّة. فجعل النبيّ صلّى الله عليه وسلّم يعرض عليه الإسلام. فقال أبو سفيان: كيف أصنع بالعزّى؟

فقال عمر من خلف القبّة: تخرأ عليها!

mother, they said, "We stand by what our mother says." Thus Abū Sufyān gained nothing he sought from any of them.

Abū Sufyān left and eventually came back to the Quraysh, who asked, "What have you brought?" He answered, "I've come to you from a people of one mind and one heart. By God, whether young or old, male or female, I left none of them be until I had spoken with them, but I gained nothing from them." "You've done nothing! Go back!" they exclaimed, so Abū Sufyān headed back. **10.1.3**

The Messenger of God set out from Medina heading for the Quraysh. **10.1.4** When he had reached a certain point along the way, he said to a group of the Allies, "Search for Abū Sufyān, and you will find him." They searched for him, and indeed they found him. When Abū Sufyān entered the encampment, the Muslims rushed forward to strike him, but he cried out, "Muḥammad! I am already a dead man! Order them to hand me to al-ʿAbbās!" For indeed, al-ʿAbbās had been his comrade and friend during the Age of Ignorance. So the Prophet commanded that he be handed over to al-ʿAbbās, and Abū Sufyān spent the night with him.

When the time for the morning prayer arrived, the muezzin gave the call to prayer and the people began to stir. Abū Sufyān thought that they were coming after him and said, "ʿAbbās, what are these people doing?"

"They've merely begun to stir and answer the crier's call to prayer," he answered.

"All the people are stirring just because of Muḥammad's crier?"

"Yes," answered al-ʿAbbās.

Then al-ʿAbbās stood up for the prayer, and Abū Sufyān stood alongside him. When they had finished, he asked, "ʿAbbās, whenever Muḥammad does something, do they do likewise?"

"Yes," he answered, "and if he were to command them to go hungry and thirsty until they died of starvation, they would do it. Indeed, I believe they will destroy your people tomorrow."

Abū Sufyān pleaded, "Take us to see him!"

He went in to see the Prophet, who was under a domed canopy of leather. Now ʿUmar ibn al-Khaṭṭāb was behind the canopy, and as the Prophet began to explain Islam to him, Abū Sufyān said, "What shall I do with al-ʿUzzā?"

"Take a shit on her!" ʿUmar exclaimed from behind the canopy.

فقال: وأبيك إنّك لفاحش! إنّي لم آتِك، يا ابن الخطّاب! إنمّا جئت لابن عمي وإيّاه أُكلّم.

قال: فقال العبّاس: يا رسول الله! إنّ أبا سفيان رجل من أشراف قومنا وذوي أسنانهم، وأنا أحبّ أن تجعل له شيئًا يُعرف ذلك له.

فقال النبيّ صلّى الله عليه وسلّم: من دخل دار أبي سفيان فهو آمن.

قال: فقال أبو سفيان: أَداري؟ أَداري؟

فقال النبيّ صلّى الله عليه وسلّم: نعم، ومن وضع سلاحه فهو آمن. ومن أغلق عليه بابه فهو آمن.

فانطلق مع العبّاس حتّى إذا كان ببعض الطريق. فخاف منه العبّاس بعض الغدر، فجلّسه على أكَمة حتّى مرت به الجنود.

١٠،١،٥ قال: فمرّت به كبكبة، فقال: من هؤلاء، يا عبّاس؟

فقال: هذا الزبير بن العوّام على المجنّبة اليمنى.

قال: ثمّ مرّت كبكبة أخرى، فقال: من هؤلاء، يا عبّاس؟

قال: هم قضاعة وعليهم أبو عبيدة بن الجرّاح.

قال: ثمّ مرّت به كبكبة أخرى، فقال: من هؤلاء، يا عبّاس؟

قال: هذا خالد بن الوليد على المجنّبة اليسرى.

قال: ثمّ مرّت به قوم يمشون في الحديد، فقال: من هؤلاء، يا عبّاس، الّتي كأنّها حرّة سوداء؟

قال: هذه الأنصار، عندها الموت الأحمر. فيهم رسول الله صلّى الله عليه وسلّم والأنصار حوله.

فقال أبو سفيان: سِرْ، يا عبّاس! فلم أرَ كاليوم صباح قوم في ديارهم!

١٠،١،٦ قال: ثمّ انطلق، فلمّا أشرف على مكّة، نادى وكان شعار قريش: يا آل غالب! أَسْلِمُوا تَسْلَموا!

"And on your father, you vulgar man!" Abū Sufyān retorted. "I did not come to you, Ibn al-Khaṭṭāb; rather, I came to my cousin, and it is he whom I address!"

"O Messenger of God!" al-ʿAbbās interjected. "Indeed, Abū Sufyān is one of the notables of our tribe, one of its elders. It would please me if you were to grant him something in recognition of his status."

The Prophet then decreed, "Whoever enters the house of Abū Sufyān is safe."

Abū Sufyān replied, "My house? My house!"

"Yes," answered the Prophet, "and whoever lays down his weapons is safe; and whoever locks the door to his house is safe."

Abū Sufyān left with al-ʿAbbās, and while they were going down the road, al-ʿAbbās feared that Abū Sufyān might still commit some act of treachery, so he sat him down on a mound of earth until the armies had passed.

A troop of fighting men passed by, and Abū Sufyān asked, "Who are these 10.1.5
men, ʿAbbās?"

"That is al-Zubayr ibn al-ʿAwwām commanding the right flank," al-ʿAbbās answered.

Another troop passed by, and Abū Sufyān asked, "Who are these men, ʿAbbās?"

"They are the Quḍāʿah tribe," he answered, "and it is Abū ʿUbaydah ibn al-Jarrāḥ who leads them."

Yet another troop passed by, and Abū Sufyān asked, "Who are these men, ʿAbbās?"

"That is Khālid ibn al-Walīd commanding the left flank," he answered.

Then there passed by him a company of men marching in iron armor, and he asked, "Who are these men, ʿAbbās, who are like blackened lava strewn across the desert?"

"These are the Allies," he answered, "and they march with the Red Death.[151] In their midst is God's Messenger, and the Allies surround him."

Abū Sufyān exclaimed, "March on, ʿAbbās, for never before today have I seen a people so ready for war and so arrayed in their tribes!"[152]

Abu Sufyān left after that, and when he could look out over Mecca, he cried 10.1.6
out using the war cry of the Quraysh, "O Victorious People! Surrender as Muslims, that you may be saved!"

His wife Hind then came out to join him, but grabbing hold of his beard, cried out, "O Victorious People! Kill the old fool! He's abandoned his religion!"

فلقيته امرأته هند فأخذت بلحيته وفقالت: يا آل غالب! اقتلوا الشيخ الأحمق! فإنّه قد صبأ!

فقال: والّذي نفسي بيده لتسلمنّ أو ليضربنّ عنقُكِ.

١٠،١،٧ قال: فلمّا أشرف النبيّ صلّى الله عليه وسلّم على مكّة، كفّ الناس أن يدخلوها حتّى يأتيه رسول العبّاس. فأبطأ عليه، فقال النبيّ صلّى الله عليه وسلّم: لعلّهم يصنعون بالعبّاس ما صنعت ثقيف بعروة بن مسعود. فوالله إذاً لا أستبقي منهم أحداً.

قال: ثمّ جاءه رسول العبّاس، فدخل رسول الله صلّى الله عليه وسلّم، فأمر أصحابه بالكفّ. فقال: كفّوا السلاح إلّا خزاعة عن بكرساعةً. ثمّ أمرهم فكفّوا. فأمّن الناسَ كلّهم إلّا ابن أبي سرح وابن خطل ومقيس الكنانيّ وامرأةً أخرى. ثمّ قال النبيّ صلّى الله عليه وسلّم: إنّي لم أحرّم مكّة ولكن حرّمها اللهُ. وإنّها لم تحلّل لأحد قبلي ولا تحلّ لأحد بعدي إلى يوم القيامة. وإنّما أحلّها الله في ساعة من نهار.

قال: ثمّ جاءه عثمان بن عفّان بابن أبي سرح، فقال: بايعه، يا رسول الله! فأعرض عنه، ثمّ جاء من ناحية أخرى. فأعرض عنه، ثمّ جاءه أيضاً، فقال: بايعه، يا رسول الله! فقال رسول الله صلّى الله عليه وسلّم: لقد أعرضتُ عنه، وإنّي لأظنّ بعضكم سيقتله. فقال رجل من الأنصار: فهلاّ أومضت إليّ، يا رسول الله؟ قال: إنّ النبيّ لا يومض. وكأنّه رآه غدراً.

١٠،١،٨ قال الزهريّ: فبعث رسول الله صلّى الله عليه وسلّم خالد بن الوليد. فقاتل بمن معه صفوف قريش بأسفل مكّة حتّى هزمهم الله. ثمّ أمر رسول الله صلّى الله عليه وسلّم فرفع عنهم. فدخلوا في الدين، فأنزل الله ﴿إِذَا جَاءَ نَصْرُ اللَّهِ وَالْفَتْحُ﴾ حتّى ختمها.

Abū Sufyān replied, "I swear by the One in Whose hand my soul resides, you will be a Muslim or have your head severed from your neck!"

When the Prophet was able to look out over Mecca, he commanded that none should enter it until al-ʿAbbās's envoy had returned to him.[153] When the wait became long, the Prophet said, "Perhaps they have done to al-ʿAbbās what the Thaqīf tribe did to ʿUrwah ibn Masʿūd.[154] If such be the case, I swear by God, not one of them will be spared." 10.1.7

Soon thereafter, al-ʿAbbās's envoy arrived, and the Messenger of God entered Mecca, ordering his companions not to attack. They kept their weapons undrawn, save for the Khūzaʿah clan, who fought against the Bakr clan for a brief time,[155] but then he commanded them to desist, so they did so. The Prophet gave all the people sanctuary except for Ibn Abī Sarḥ, Ibn Khaṭal, Miqyas al-Kinānī, and a woman.[156] Later the Prophet said, "It is not I who has made Mecca sacred; rather, it is God who sanctified it. Its conquest has been permitted to no man before me, and will not be permitted to any man after me until the Day of Resurrection; and God has only made its conquest licit to me for a single hour before the dawn."

Afterward ʿUthmān ibn ʿAffān came to the Prophet, pleading on behalf of Ibn Abī Sarḥ. "Spare him!" he said, but the Prophet turned from him. ʿUthmān came to him from the other side, saying, "Spare him, O Messenger of God!" The Messenger of God said, "I had turned away from him, suspecting that one of you would kill him." One of the Allies' men said, "Did I not see you wink at me, O Messenger of God?" "The Prophet does not wink," he replied, as though he regarded him as guilty of betrayal.

Al-Zuhrī said: The Messenger of God sent Khālid ibn al-Walīd out to battle 10.1.8
and, with the Muslims by his side, he fought several ranks of the Quraysh in the lower plains of Mecca until God brought them low. The Messenger of God issued the command, and he relented in his attack against them. Thus they embraced the true religion, and God revealed:

> «When God's help comes and the Triumph, when you see people embracing God's faith in crowds, celebrate the praise of your Lord and ask His forgiveness: He is always ready to accept repentance.»[157]

قال معمر: قال الزهريّ: ٢،١٠

ثمّ رجع رسول الله صلّى الله عليه وسلّم بمن معه من قريش، وهي كنانة، ومن أسلم يوم الفتح قبل حنين. وحنين وادٍ في قُبُل الطائف ذو مياه وبه من المشركين يومئذ عجزهوازن ومعهم ثقيف. ورأس المشركين يومئذ مالك بن عوف النصريّ. فاقتتلوا بحنين. فنصر اللهُ نبيّه صلّى الله عليه وسلّم والمسلمين وكان يوماً شديداً على الناس. فأنزل الله ﴿لَقَدْ نَصَرَكُمُ اللهُ فِي مَوَاطِنَ كَثِيرَةٍ وَيَوْمَ حُنَيْنٍ﴾ الآية.

قال معمر: قال الزهريّ: ٣،١٠

وكان رسول الله صلّى الله عليه وسلّم يتألّفهم، فلذلك بعث خالد بن الوليد يومئذ.

عبد الرزّاق عن مالك بن أنس عن ابن شهاب: ٤،١٠

أنّ رسول الله صلّى الله عليه وسلّم دخل مكّة يوم الفتح وعليه المغفر.

Maʿmar said: al-Zuhrī said: 10.2

Afterward the Messenger of God, alongside those Quraysh who went with him—that is, the Kinānah clan—and those who had embraced Islam on the Day of Triumph, returned to Medina before the events at Ḥunayn. Ḥunayn is a wadi lying in the direction of Taif, and has many sources of water. There on the day of the battle were the Pagans from the rear of the Hawāzin tribe,[158] and the Thaqīf tribe was also with them. The leader of the Pagans that day was Mālik ibn ʿAwf al-Naṣrī. They fought a battle at Ḥunayn, and God gave the victory to His Prophet and the Muslims. It was a trying day for the people, so God revealed:

> «God has helped you on many battlefields, even on the day of the Battle of Ḥunayn. You were well pleased with your large numbers, but they were of no use to you: the earth seemed to close in on you despite its spaciousness, and you turned tail and fled.»[159]

Maʿmar said: al-Zuhrī said: 10.3

The Prophet had already begun to cause their hearts to turn;[160] that is the reason he sent Khālid ibn al-Walīd out to battle on that day.

ʿAbd al-Razzāq, on the authority of Mālik ibn Anas, on the authority of Ibn Shihāb: 10.4

When the Messenger of God entered Mecca on the Day of Triumph, he wore a coat of mail.[161]

وَقعَةُ حُنَين

عبد الرزّاق عن معمرعن الزهريّ، قال: أخبرني كثير بن العبّاس بن عبد المطّلب عن أبيه العبّاس، قال: ١،١١

شهدتُ مع رسول الله صلّى الله عليه وسلّم يوم حنين. قال: فلقد رأيتُ النبيّ صلّى الله عليه وسلّم وما معه إلّا أنا وأبو سفيان بن الحارث بن عبد المطّلب. فلزِمْنا رسولُ الله صلّى الله عليه وسلّم، فلم نفارقْه. وهو على بغلة شهباء—وربّما قال معمر: بيضاء— أهداها له فروة بن نفاثة الجذاميّ. قال: فلمّا التقى المسلمون والكفّار، ولّى المسلمون مُدبِرين. وطفق رسول الله صلّى الله عليه وسلّم يركض بغلته نحو الكفّار.

قال العبّاس: وأنا آخذ بلجام بغلة رسول الله صلّى الله عليه وسلّم أَكُفّها، وهو لا يألو ما أسرع نحو المشركين، وأبو سفيان بن الحارث آخذ بغرز رسول الله صلّى الله عليه وسلّم. فقال: يا عبّاس، نادِ أصحاب السَّمُرة! قال: وكنتُ رجلاً صيتاً، فناديتُ بأعلى صوتي: أين أصحاب السمرة؟ قال: فوالله لكأن عطفتَهم حين سمعوا صوتي عَطفة البقر على أولادها، يقولون: يا لبيك! يا لبيك! يا لبيك! وأقبل المسلمون، فاقتتلوا، هم والكفّار. فنادت الأنصار، يقولون: يا معشر الأنصار! ثمّ قصر الداعون على بني الحارث بن الخزرج، فنادوا: يا بني الحارث بن الخزرج! قال: فنظر رسول الله صلّى الله عليه وسلّم، وهو على بغلته كالمتطاول عليها، إلى قتالهم. فقال رسول الله صلّى الله عليه وسلّم: هذا حين حمي الوطيس! قال: ثمّ أخذ رسول الله صلّى الله عليه وسلّم حصيّات، فرمى بهنّ وجوه الكفّار. ثمّ قال: انهزموا وربّ الكعبة! قال: فذهبتُ أنظر، فإذا القتال على هيئته فيما أرى. قال: فوالله ما هو إلّا أن رماهم رسول الله صلّى الله عليه وسلّم بحصياته، فما زلت أرى حدّهم كليلاً. فأمرهم مدبراً حتّى هزمهم

The Incident at Ḥunayn

ʿAbd al-Razzāq, on the authority of Maʿmar, on the authority of al-Zuhrī, who said: Kathīr ibn al-ʿAbbās ibn ʿAbd al-Muṭṭalib reported to me on the authority of his father, al-ʿAbbās, who said: **11.1**

I witnessed the battle of Ḥunayn alongside the Messenger of God. Indeed, I saw the Prophet himself, for the only ones with him were Abū Sufyān ibn al-Ḥārith ibn ʿAbd al-Muṭṭalib and I. We stayed close to the Messenger of God and never left his side. He was mounted on a gray she-mule—or perhaps, Maʿmar said, a white one—which Farwah ibn Nufāthah al-Judhāmī had given him as a gift. When the Muslims and infidels met in battle, the Muslims turned in retreat, but then the Prophet started to lead a charge with his mule in the direction of the infidels.

Al-ʿAbbās said: I was the one holding fast to the reins of the Messenger of God's she-mule, trying to turn her away, and Abū Sufyān held fast to his leather stirrup,[162] but nothing could stop the Prophet from rushing toward the Pagans. Then the Prophet said, "ʿAbbās! Cry out to the companions of the acacia tree!"[163] Now I was a man with a booming voice, and I cried out as loudly as I could, "Where are the companions of the acacia tree?" By God, I let loose a long bellow like a cow for her calves, and when they heard my voice, they cried out, "At your command! At your command! *At your command!*" And when the Muslims drew near, they fought fiercely, they and the infidels. The Allies cried out, saying, "O company of Allies!" Then the men giving the summons singled out the al-Ḥārith ibn al-Khazraj clan and cried out, "O sons of al-Ḥārith ibn al-Khazraj!" God's Messenger, standing high in the saddle on his she-mule, surveyed the battle and said, "Now the furnace[164] is ablaze!" Then God's Messenger grabbed a handful of small stones and cast them into the faces of infidels, whereupon he said, "By the Lord of the Kaaba, they have been vanquished!" I went to look and lo, the battle had been decided, at least as far as I could tell, and by God, it was decided when the Messenger of God cast the small stones against them. I can still see them at the limits of their endurance, when the Prophet ordered the Muslims to withdraw so that God

اللّه تعالى. قال: وكأنّي أنظر إلى النبيّ صلّى اللّه عليه وسلّم يركض خلفهم على بغلة له.

٢،١١ قال الزهريّ: وكان عبد الرحمن بن أزهر يحدّث:

أنّ خالد بن الوليد بن المغيرة يومئذ كان على الخيل، خيل رسول اللّه.

فقال ابن أزهر: فلقد رأيتُ رسول اللّه صلّى اللّه عليه وسلّم، بعدما هزم اللّه الكفّار ورجع المسلمون إلى رحالهم، يمشي في المسلمين ويقول: من يدلّني على رحل خالد بن الوليد؟ فمشيتُ — أو قال: فسعيتُ — بين يديه وأنا غلامٌ محتلمٌ، أقول: من يدلّ على رحل خالد؟ حتّى دُلِلنا عليه. فإذا خالد مستند إلى مؤخّرة رحله، فأتاه رسول اللّه صلّى اللّه عليه وسلّم، فنظر إلى جرحه.

٣،١١ قال الزهريّ: أخبرني سعيد بن المسيّب:

أنّ النبيّ صلّى اللّه عليه وسلّم سبى يومئذ ستّة آلاف سَبْيٍ من إمرأة وغلام، فجعل عليهم رسول اللّه صلّى اللّه عليه وسلّم أبا سفيان بن حرب.

٤،١١ قال الزهريّ: فأخبرني عروة بن الزبير، قال:

لمّا رجعت هوازن إلى رسول اللّه صلّى اللّه عليه وسلّم، قالوا: أنت أبرّ الناس وأوصلُهم، وقد سُبِيَ موالينا ونساؤنا وأُخِذَت أموالُنا. فقال رسول اللّه صلّى اللّه عليه وسلّم، إنّي كنت استأنيت بكم ومعي من ترون. وأحبُّ القولِ إليّ أصدقُه. فاختاروا إحدى الطائفتين: إمّا المال وإمّا السَبْيَ؟ فقالوا: يا رسول اللّه! أمّا إذا خيّرتَنا بين المال وبين الحسب فإنّا نختار الحسب. أو قالوا: ما كنّا نعدل بالحسب شيئاً. فاختاروا نساءهم وأبناءهم. فقام رسول اللّه صلّى اللّه عليه وسلّم وخطب في المسلمين، فأثنى على اللّه بما هو أهله. ثمّ قال:

أمّا بعد، فإنّ إخوانكم هؤلاء قد جاءوا مسلمين، أومستسلمين، وإنّا قد خيّرناهم بين الذراري والأموال. فلم يعدلوا بالأحساب، فإنّي قد رأيتُ أن تردّوا لهم أبناءهم

Most High would vanquish the infidels. It is as if I can still see the Prophet riding behind them on that she-mule of his.

Al-Zuhrī said: ʿAbd al-Raḥmān ibn Azhar reported that: **11.2**

Khālid ibn al-Walīd ibn al-Mughīrah led the cavalry, the cavalry of God's Messenger, that day.

Ibn Azhar said: After God had vanquished the infidels and the Muslims returned to their mounts, I saw the Prophet walking among the Muslims saying, "Who will show me the way to Khālid ibn al-Walīd's mount? So I walked,"—or, he said, I strode—"in front of the Prophet, and at the time I was a young man who had just reached maturity, saying, 'Who will show the way to Khālid's mount?' And eventually we were shown the way to him. There Khālid stood leaning against the rear of his mount, and the Messenger of God went to him and tended to his wound."

Al-Zuhrī said: Saʿīd ibn al-Musayyab reported to me that: **11.3**

On that day the Prophet took six thousand women and children captive, whom the Messenger of God then handed over to Abū Sufyān ibn Ḥarb.

Al-Zuhrī said: ʿUrwah ibn al-Zubayr reported to me, saying: **11.4**

When the Hawāzin came back before the Messenger of God, they said, "You are the most upright and faithful in honoring bonds of kinship, but our women and those in our care have been taken captive, and our wealth seized." The Messenger of God replied, "I patiently bided my time for you, and with me are those you see. To me, the most preferable speech is the most honest. So choose one of the two, either the property or the captives." "O Messenger of God!" they replied. "As far as we are concerned, if you force us to choose between property and honor, we shall choose honor." Or they said, "We esteem honor above all else." Thus they chose their women and children.

Then the Prophet rose to address the Muslims. He first glorified God, as is His due, and then proceeded to say: "As for the matter at hand, these men, your brethren, have come as Muslims"—or "having surrendered ourselves (*mustaslimīn*)"—"and we have given them a choice between their offspring and their property. They regarded nothing as equal to their honor; thus, I have

ونساءهم. فمن أحبّ منكم أن يطيّب ذلك، فليفعل. ومن أحبّ أن يكتب علينا حصته من ذلك حتّى نعطيه من بعض ما يفيئه الله علينا، فليفعل.

فقال المسلمون: طيّبنا ذلك لرسول الله صلّى الله عليه وسلّم. قال: إنّي لا أدري من أذن في ذلك ممّن لم يأذن، فامُروا عرفاءَكم، فليرفعوا ذلك إلينا. فلمّا رفعت العرفاءُ إلى رسول الله صلّى الله عليه وسلّم أنّ الناس قد سلموا ذلك وأذنوا فيه. ردّ رسول الله صلّى الله عليه وسلّم إلى هوازن نساءهم وأبناءهم، وخيّر رسول الله صلّى الله عليه وسلّم نساءً كان أعطاهنّ رجالاً من قريش بين أن يَلْبَثْنَ عند من هنّ[١] عنده وبين أن يرجعن إلى أهلهنّ.

قال الزهريّ: ٥،١١

فبلغني أنّ امرأةً منهم كانت تحت عبد الرحمن بن عوف، فخيّرت، فاختارت أن ترجع إلى أهلها وتركت عبد الرحمن، وكان مُعجَباً بها، وأخرى عند صفوان بن أميّة فاختارت أهلها.

قال الزهريّ: فأخبرني سعيد بن المسيّب، قال: ٦،١١

قسم رسول الله صلّى الله عليه وسلّم ما قسم بين المسلمين. ثمّ اعتمر من الجعرانة بعدما قفل من غزوة حنين، ثمّ انطلق إلى المدينة، ثمّ أمّر أبا بكر على تلك الحجّة.

قال معمر عن الزهريّ، قال: أخبرني ابن كعب بن مالك، قال: ٧،١١

جاء ملاعب الأسنّة إلى النبيّ صلّى الله عليه وسلّم بهديّة، فعرض عليه الإسلام. فأبى أن يُسلم. فقال النبيّ صلّى الله عليه وسلّم: إنّي لا أَقبل هديّة مشرك. قال: فابعث إلى أهل نجد من شئت، فأنا لهم جارٌ. فبعث إليهم نفراً فيهم[٢] المنذر بن عمرو، وهو الذي كان يقال له[٣] أَعْنَقَ لِيمُوت، وفيهم عامر بن فهيرة. فاستجاش عليهم عامر

١ [هنّ] أنا؛ ساقطة في م. ٢ [فيهم] من ط؛ ساقطة من م. ٣ [له] من ط؛ ساقطة من م.

seen it fit for you to return their women and children to them. Whoever wishes to act so magnanimously, let him do so; and whoever wishes to demand compensation for his share so that we may give him a portion of what God has granted us as spoils, let him do so."

The Muslims answered God's Messenger: "The judgment is good!" The Prophet then said, "I do not know who has permitted that and who has not, so command your leaders to convey this information to us." Once the leaders had informed the Messenger of God that the people had acquiesced to the agreement and permitted it, God's Messenger returned the women and children to the Hawāzin clan. God's Messenger also granted to the women whom he had given to several Qurashī men the choice between remaining in the household of those men and returning to their families.

Al-Zuhrī said: **11.5**

I was told that one of the women was in the care of ʿAbd al-Raḥmān ibn ʿAwf, and when she was presented with the choice, she chose to return to her family. She left ʿAbd al-Raḥmān, even though he was smitten with her. Another woman was in the household of Ṣafwān ibn Umayyah, and she also chose her family.

Al-Zuhrī said: Saʿīd ibn al-Musayyab reported me, saying: **11.6**

The Messenger of God determined the portion of the spoils due to the Muslims, and then he undertook a minor-pilgrimage from al-Jiʿrānah after he left in a caravan from Ḥunayn. After that, he departed for Medina and appointed Abū Bakr to oversee the hajj that year.

Maʿmar said, on the authority of al-Zuhrī, who said: Kaʿb ibn Mālik reported to me, saying: **11.7**

The man called Mulāʿib al-Asinnah, "Lover of Spears," came to the Prophet bearing a gift. The Prophet explained Islam to him, but he refused to become a Muslim. The Prophet said, "I cannot accept the gift of a pagan." The man replied, "Then send whomever you wish to the inhabitants of Najd, and I shall guarantee their safety." So the Prophet sent a group. Al-Mundhir ibn ʿAmr, who was called Aʿnaqa Liyamūt, "He who Hastens toward Death," was among them and so was ʿĀmir ibn Fuhayrah. ʿĀmir ibn al-Ṭufayl attempted to muster an army from the ʿĀmir clan to fight against the Muslims, but they refused to

بن الطفيل بني عامر. فأبَوا أن يطيعوه، وأبَوا أن يُخفروا ملاعب الأسنّة. قال: فاستجاش عليهم بني سليم. فأطاعوه، فاتّبعوهم بقريب من مئة رجل رامٍ. فأدركوا بئر معونة، فقتلوهم إلّا عمرو بن أميّة الضمريّ، فأرسلوه.

قال الزهريّ: فأخبرني عروة بن الزبير: ٨،١١

أنّه لمّا رجع إلى النبيّ صلّى الله عليه وسلّم، قال له النبيّ صلّى الله عليه وسلّم: أَمِنَ بينهم؟

قال الزهريّ: وبلغني أنّهم لمّا دفنوا، التمسوا جسدَ عامر بن فهيرة. فلم يقدروا عليه. فيرَون أنّ الملائكة دفنته.

عبد الرزّاق عن معمر، قال: أخبرنا ثمامة بن عبد الله بن أنس عن أَنس بن مالك: ٩،١١

أنّ حرام بن ملحان، وهو خال أنس، طُعِنَ يومئذ. فتلقّى دمَه بكفّه، ثمّ نضحه على رأسه ووجهه. وقال: فُزْتُ وربّ الكعبة.

قال معمر: وأخبرني عاصم أن أنس بن مالك، قال: ١٠،١١

ما رأيتُ رسول الله صلّى الله عليه وسلّم وجد على شيء قطّ ما وجد على أصحاب بئر معونة، أصحاب سريّة المنذر بن عمرو، فمكث شهراً يدعو على الّذين أصابوهم في قنوت الصلاة الغداة. يدعو على رعل وذكوان وعصيّة ولحيان، وهم من بني سليم.

heed him and refused to violate the pact of Mulāʿib al-Asinnah. So ʿĀmir ibn al-Ṭufayl sought to muster an army from the Sulaym clan, and they heeded his call and pursued the Muslims with nearly a hundred archers. They caught up with the Muslims at Biʾr Maʿūnah, where they slew them all save ʿAmr ibn Umayyah al-Ḍamrī, whom they allowed to flee.

Al-Zuhrī said: ʿUrwah ibn al-Zubayr reported to me that: 11.8

When ʿAmr returned to the Prophet, the Prophet said to him, "Did no one else survive?"

Al-Zuhrī added: It is reported that, when the slain were given burials, they searched for the corpse of ʿĀmir ibn Fuhayrah but could not find it. Thus, they believed the angels had buried him.

ʿAbd al-Razzāq, on the authority of Maʿmar, who said: Thumāmah ibn ʿAbd Allāh ibn Anas 11.9
reported to us, on the authority of Anas ibn Mālik, that:

Ḥarām ibn Milḥān—who is the maternal uncle of Anas—was stabbed that day, and gathering blood in the palm of his hand, he smeared it all over his head and face, crying out, "Victory is mine, by the Lord of the Kaaba!"

Maʿmar said: ʿĀṣim reported to me that Anas ibn Mālik said: 11.10

I never saw God's Messenger hold a grudge as deeply as the one he held against the perpetrators of Biʾr Maʿūnah, those who slew al-Mundhir ibn ʿAmr's expedition party. For a month during the invocations preceding the early morning prayer,[165] he cursed those who slew them: the Riʿl, Dhakwān, ʿUṣayyah, and Liḥyān clans—all from the Sulaym tribe.

مَنْ هَاجَرَ إِلَى ٱلْحَبَشَةِ

عبد الرزّاق عن معمر عن الزهريّ في حديثه عن عروة، قال: ١،١٢

فلمّا كثُر المسلمون وظهر الإيمانُ، فتحدّث به المشركون من كفّار قريش بمن آمن من قبائلهم، يعذّبونهم ويسجنونهم، وأرادوا فتنتَهم عن دينهم.

قال: فبلغنا أنّ رسول الله صلّى الله عليه وسلّم قال للّذين آمنوا به: تفرّقوا في الأرض. قالوا: فأين نذهب، يا رسول الله؟ قال: هاهنا. وأشار بيده إلى أرض الحبشة. وكانت أَحبّ الأرض إلى رسول الله صلّى الله عليه وسلّم أن[1] يهاجر قِبَلها. فهاجر ناسٌ ذَوُو عددٍ، منهم من هاجر بأهله ومنهم من هاجر بنفسه، حتّى قدموا أرض الحبشة.

٢،١٢ قال الزهريّ: فخرج في الهجرة جعفر بن أبي طالب بامرأته أسماء بنت عميس الخثعميّة. وعثمان بن عفّان، رحمه الله، بامرأته رقيّة ابنة رسول الله صلّى الله عليه وسلّم.[2] وخرج فيها خالد بن سعيد بن العاص بامرأته أميمة ابنة خلف. وخرج فيها أبو سلمة بامرأته أمّ سلمة ابنة أبي أميمة بن المغيرة. ورجال من قريش خرجوا بنسائهم. وولد بها عبد الله بن جعفر. وولدت بها أمة ابنة خالد بن سعيد، أمّ عمرو بن الزبير وخالد بن الزبير. وولد بها الحارث بن حاطب في ناس من قريش ولدوا بها.

قال الزهريّ: وأخبرني عروة بن الزبير أنّ عائشة قالت: ٣،١٢

١،٣،١٢ لم أعقِل أبواي قطّ إلّا وهما يدينان الدين، ولم يَمرر علينا يومٌ إلّا يأتينا فيه رسولُ الله صلّى الله عليه وسلّم طَرَفَي النهار بكرةً وعشيةً. فلمّا ابتُلِيَ المسلمون، خرج أبو

---

١ [أن] أنا؛ وساقطة من مم. ٢ مم: أميمة ابنة خلف.

Those Who Emigrated to Abyssinia

ʿAbd al-Razzāq, on the authority of Maʿmar, on the authority of al-Zuhrī, narrating a report from ʿUrwah: 12.1

When the Muslims increased in number and the faith became manifest, the Pagans from the infidel Quraysh began to deliberate on the matter of what to do with the members of their own tribes who believed, torturing them and even imprisoning them,[166] for they desired to force them to abandon their religion.

He said: We were told that the Messenger of God said to those who had faith in him, "Seek out another land," but they asked, "O Messenger of God! Where shall we go?" "There," he said, and with his hand pointed toward Abyssinia. It was the land that the Messenger of God preferred above all others for their emigration. People thus emigrated in great numbers, some emigrating with their families and others by themselves, and they eventually arrived in Abyssinia.

Al-Zuhrī said: Jaʿfar ibn Abī Ṭālib emigrated with his wife, Asmāʾ bint 12.2
ʿUmays al-Khathʿamiyyah, and so did ʿUthmān ibn ʿAffān with his wife Ruqayyah, the daughter of God's Messenger. Khālid ibn Saʿīd ibn al-ʿĀṣ also left with his wife, Umaymah, the daughter of Khalaf, as did Abū Salamah with his wife, Umm Salamah, the daughter of Abū Umaymah ibn al-Mughīrah. Several Qurashī men left with their women. ʿAbd Allāh ibn Jaʿfar was born in Abyssinia. Born there too was the slave girl of Khālid ibn Saʿīd's daughter, the mother of ʿAmr ibn al-Zubayr and Khālid ibn al-Zubayr. Among the people of the Quraysh born there was also al-Ḥārith ibn Ḥāṭib.

Al-Zuhrī said: ʿUrwah ibn al-Zubayr reported to me that ʿĀʾishah said: 12.3

There's not a moment I can recall that my parents did not practice the true 12.3.1
religion, and not a day would pass that the Messenger of God didn't visit us twice per day, in the morning and in the evening.[167] When the persecution of the Muslims began, Abū Bakr left Mecca to emigrate to Abyssinia. When he reached Birk al-Ghimād, Ibn al-Dughunnah, the chief of the Qārah tribe, met him and asked, "Where are you headed, Abū Bakr?" Abū Bakr replied,

بكر رضي الله عنه مهاجرًا قِبَل أرض الحبشة حتّى إذا بلغ برك الغماد لقيه ابن الدغنة، وهو سيّد القارة. فقال ابن الدغنة: أين تريد، يا أبا بكر؟ فقال أبو بكر: أخرجني قومي. فأريد أن أسيح في الأرض وأعبد ربي. فقال ابن الدغنة: مثلُكَ، يا أبا بكر، لا يُخرَج ولا يَخرج! إنّك تكسب المعدوم، وتصل الرحم، وتحمل الكلَّ، وتقري الضيف، وتعين على نوائب الحقّ. فأنا لك جارٌ. فارجع، فاعبد ربّك ببلدك.

فارتحل ابن الدغنة، ورجع مع أبي بكر. فطاف ابن الدغنة في كفّار قريش، فقال: إنّ أبا بكر خرج ولا يُخرَج مثله. أتُخرِجون رجلًا يكسب المعدوم، ويصل الرحم، ويحمل الكلّ، ويقري الضيف، ويعين على نوائب الحقّ؟! فأنفذت قريش جوار ابن الدغنة، وأمّنوا أبا بكر. وقالوا لابن الدغنة: مُرْ أبا بكر، فليعبد ربّه في داره وليصلِّ فيها ما شاء، ولا يؤذينا ولا يستعلن بالصلاة والقراءة في غير داره. ففعل.

ثم بدا لأبي بكر، فبنى مسجدًا بفِناء داره. فكان يصلّي فيه ويقرأ. فيتقصّف عليه ٢،٣،١٢
نساءُ المشركين وأبناؤهم، يَعجبون منه وينظرون إليه. وكان أبو بكر رجلًا بكّاءً، لا يملك دمعه حين يقرأ القرآن.

فأفزع ذلك أشراف قريش، فأرسلوا إلى ابن الدغنة. فقدم عليهم، فقال: إنّما أجرْنا أبا بكر على أن يعبد الله في داره. وإنّه قد جاوز ذلك، وبنى مسجدًا بفناء داره، وأعلن الصلاة والقراءة. وإنّا قد خشينا أن يفتن نساءنا وأبناءنا. فأتِه، فمُرْهُ. فإن أحبَّ أن يقتصر على أن يعبد الله في داره فعل وإن أبى إلّا أن يُعلن ذلك، فاسألْهُ أن يَرُدّ عليك ذمّتك. فإنّا قد كرهنا خفرك، ولسنا مقرّين لأبي بكر بالاستعلان.

قالت عائشة: فاتى ابن الدغنة أبا بكر، فقال: يا أبا بكر! قد علمتَ الّذي عقدتُ ٣،٣،١٢
لك. إمّا أن تقتصر على ذلك، وإمّا أن ترجع إليّ ذمّتي. فإنّي لا أُحبّ أن تسمع العرب أنّي أُخفرتُ في عهد رجلٍ عقدت له. فقال أبو بكر: فإنّي أَرُدّ إليك جوارك وأرضى بجوار الله ورسوله.

"My tribe has exiled me, so I intend to journey throughout the land and worship my Lord." Ibn al-Dughunnah replied, "O Abū Bakr! A man such as you should not be exiled—indeed, you succeed where others fail; you cultivate the bonds of kinship and bear all things; you act hospitably toward guests and aid your kinsmen in times of distress. I will act as your protector, so return to your tribe and worship your Lord in your homeland."

Ibn al-Dughunnah embarked on the return journey to Mecca alongside Abū Bakr, and later Ibn al-Dughunnah made his rounds among the infidel Quraysh, saying, "Indeed, Abū Bakr has been exiled, but no one should exile a man such as him! Will you exile a man who finds success where others fail, who cultivates the bonds of kinship and bears all, who acts hospitably toward guests and aids his kinsmen in times of distress?" Thus the Quraysh recognized the protection of Ibn al-Dughunnah and granted Abū Bakr safe haven. They said to Ibn al-Dughunnah, "Order Abū Bakr to worship his Lord in his home and to pray there as he wishes, but also order him neither to trouble us nor to seek to make his prayers and scripture reading known anywhere outside his home," and Ibn al-Dughunnah did so.

After these events, it occurred to Abū Bakr to build a mosque in the inner 12.3.2
courtyard of his home. There he used to pray and recite the Qur'an, but the Pagans' women and children would stumble over one another to see him, and watched amazed. For indeed, Abū Bakr was a man much given to weeping, and he could not restrain his tears when reciting the Qur'an.

These matters frightened the notables of the Quraysh, so they sent a message to Ibn al-Dughunnah. When Ibn al-Dughunnah arrived, they said, "We consented to provide Abū Bakr with a safe haven on the condition that he worship God in his house, but he has transgressed that condition by building a mosque in the inner courtyard of his house, and thus brought attention to all his praying and scripture reading. Indeed, we fear that he is beguiling our women and children, so go to him and order him as follows: If he will be content with going no further than worshipping God in his home, then he may do so; if he refuses to avoid bringing attention to this, then ask him to relieve you of your pact. For we have come to loathe your protection, and will not consent to allow Abū Bakr to bring attention to his faith."

'Ā'ishah said: Ibn al-Dughunnah then came to Abū Bakr and said, "Abū 12.3.3
Bakr, you know the conditions on which I swore an oath to you: either choose not to go beyond their stipulations, or else relieve me of my pact. Indeed,

ورسول الله صلّى الله عليه وسلّم يومئذ بمكّة. فقال رسول الله صلّى الله عليه وسلّم للمسلمين: إنّي قد رأيتُ دار هجرتكم. إنّي أرِيتُ داراً سبخةً ذات نخل بين اللابتين. وهما الحرّتان.

فهاجر من هاجر قِبَل المدينة حين ذكر رسول الله صلّى الله عليه وسلّم ذلك. ورجع إلى المدينة بعض من كان هاجر إلى أرض الحبشة من المسلمين. وتجهّز أبو بكر رضي الله عنه مهاجراً، فقال رسول الله صلّى الله عليه وسلّم: على رِسلك، فإنّي أرجو أن يؤذن لي. فقال أبو بكر: أترجو ذلك، يا نبيّ الله؟ قال: نعم. فحبس أبو بكر نفسه على رسول الله صلّى الله عليه وسلّم لصُحبته، وعلف أبو بكر راحلتين كانتا عنده وَرَقُ السَمُرِ أربعة أشهر.

قال الزهريّ: قال عروة: فقالت عائشة: ٤،١٢

فبينا نحن يوماً جلوساً في بيتنا في نحر الظهيرة. قال قائلٌ لأبي بكر: هذا رسول ١،٤،١٢
الله صلّى الله عليه وسلّم مُقْبِلاً مقنّعاً رأسه، في ساعة لم يكن يأتينا فيها. فقال أبو بكر: فداء له أبي وأمّي، إن جاء به في هذه الساعة لأمر.[١] قالت: فجاء رسول الله صلّى الله عليه وسلّم، فاستأذن. فأذن له، فدخل، فقال النبيّ صلّى الله عليه وسلّم لأبي بكر أخرج من عندك.[٢]

فقال أبو بكر: إنّما هم أهلك، بأبي أنت يا رسول الله!

فقال النبيّ صلّى الله عليه وسلّم: فإنّه قد أذن لي في الخروج.

فقال أبو بكر: فالصحابة، بأبي أنت يا رسول الله!

فقال النبيّ صلّى الله عليه وسلّم: نعم.

فقال أبو بكر: فخُذ، بأبي أنت يا رسول الله وأمّي، إحدى راحلتَيّ هاتَين!

فقال رسول الله صلّى الله عليه وسلّم: بالثمن.

---

١ مم، ح؛ ن: إلا أمرٌ؛ بخ: إلا الأمر. ٢ [فقال النبيّ صلّى الله عليه وسلّم لأبي بكر أخرج من عندك] ح، بخ، ن؛ ساقطة من مم.

I do not wish for the Arabs to hear that I violated an undertaking that I have granted to any man." Abū Bakr replied, "In that case I relieve you of your oath of protection. I shall be content with the protection of God and His Messenger."

That day the Messenger of God was in Mecca, and he said to the Muslims, "Truly I have seen the land of your emigration; indeed, I have been granted a vision of a marshy land full of date palms between the two black fields"—meaning the two fields of lava rock.[168]

Then those who emigrated to Medina undertook their Hijrah when the Prophet spoke of it, and many of those Muslims who had emigrated to Abyssinia returned to Medina. Abū Bakr made provisions to emigrate, but the Messenger of God said, "Not so fast. It would please me if you waited for my command." Abū Bakr replied, "Would that truly please you, O Prophet of God?" "Yes," he answered, so Abū Bakr held himself back for the sake of God's Messenger in order to accompany him. Abū Bakr also began feeding two of his mounts acacia leaves and went on doing so for the next four months.

Al-Zuhrī said: ʿUrwah said: ʿĀʾishah continued: **12.4**

One day while we were sitting in our house at the height of midday, some- **12.4.1**
one said to Abū Bakr, "That's the Messenger of God approaching, wearing a veil around his head!"—and this was an hour at which he was not accustomed to visit us. "My mother's and father's lives for his!" exclaimed Abū Bakr. "There is a reason that he has come at this hour."

The Messenger of God arrived, sought permission to enter, and permission was granted. When he entered, the Prophet said to Abū Bakr, "Leave your home."

"My father's life for yours, O Messenger of God!" Abū Bakr replied. "They too are your people."

"I have been granted permission to depart," answered the Prophet.

"My father's life for yours, O Messenger of God," Abū Bakr continued. "And your Companions as well?"

"Yes," the Prophet answered.

"My father's and mother's lives for yours, O Messenger of God! Take one of these two mounts of mine."

"Only for its cost," he replied.

قالت عائشة: فجهّزناهما أحثّ الجهاز، فصنعنا لهما سُفرةً في جِراب. فقطعت أسماء بنت أبي بكرمن نطاقها، فأوكت به الجراب. فلذلك كانت تُسمّى ذات النطاقين. ثمّ لحق رسول الله صلّى الله عليه وسلّم وأبو بكر بغارٍ في جبل، يقال له ثور. فمكثا فيه ثلاث ليال. ٢،٤،١٢

قال معمر: وأخبرني عثمان الجزريّ أن مقسماً مولى ابن عبّاس أخبره في قوله ﴿وَإِذْ يَمْكُرُ بِكَ ٱلَّذِينَ كَفَرُوا لِيُثْبِتُوكَ﴾. ٥،١٢
قال:

تشاورت قريش بمكّة، فقال بعضهم: إذا أصبح، فأثبتوه بالوثاق، يريدون النبيّ صلّى الله عليه وسلّم. وقال بعضهم: بل اقتلوه. وقال بعضهم: أن أخرجوه. فأطلع الله نبيّه على ذلك. فبات عليٌّ[1] على فراش النبيّ صلّى الله عليه وسلّم تلك الليلة. وخرج النبيّ صلّى الله عليه وسلّم حتّى لحق بالغار. وبات المشركون يحرسون علياً، يحسبون أنّه النبيّ صلّى الله عليه وسلّم. فلمّا أصبحوا، ثاروا إليه. فلمّا رأوا علياً، ردّ الله مكرهم. فقالوا: أين صاحبك هذا؟ قال: لا أدري. فاقتصّوا أثره. فلمّا بلغوا الجبل، اختلط عليهم الأمر، فصعدوا الجبل. فمرّوا بالغار، فرأوا على بابه نسج العنكبوت. فقالوا: لو دخل هاهنا، لم يكن ينسج العنكبوت على بابه. فمكث فيه ثلاثاً.

قال معمر: قال قتادة: ٦،١٢

دخلوا في دار الندوة يأتمرون بالنبيّ صلّى الله عليه وسلّم، فقالوا: لا يدخل معكم أحدٌ ليس منكم. فدخل معهم الشيطان في صورة شيخ من أهل نجد، فقال بعضهم: ليس عليك من هذا عينٌ، هذا رجلٌ من أهل نجد. ١،٦،١٢

قال: فتشاوروا، فقال رجلٌ منهم: أرى أن تُركبوه بعيراً ثمّ تُخرجوه.

---

١ [عليّ] ح، ط؛ ساقطة في مم.

ʿĀʾishah said: We gathered provisions and prepared them for the travelers as fast as we could, putting the supplies in a leather bag. My sister Asmāʾ bint Abī Bakr cut off a piece of her leather belt to fasten the leather bag closed. For this reason was Asmāʾ called Dhāt al-Niṭāqayn, "The Woman with Two Leather Belts."[169] Then Abū Bakr and the Messenger of God took shelter in a cave on a mountain called Thawr. The two remained there for three nights. 12.4.2

Maʿmar said: ʿUthmān al-Jazarī reported to me that Miqsam, the slave-client of Ibn ʿAbbās, reported to him concerning God's decree: «Remember when the disbelievers plotted to take you captive,»[170] saying: 12.5

The Quraysh convened an assembly to consult one another in Mecca. One of them said, "When he awakes, let's bind him in shackles"—by whom they meant the Prophet. Another said, "Rather, let's murder him!" And another said, "Let's cast him out!" But God informed his Prophet of all of this. ʿAlī passed that night sleeping in the Prophet's bed, and the Prophet left to take shelter in the cave. The Pagans spent the night keeping guard over ʿAli, thinking he was the Prophet. When they awoke the next morning, they went to attack him but saw it was ʿAlī, and thus did God foil their plot. The Quraysh demanded, "Where is your companion?" "I do not know," replied ʿAlī, so they began to follow the Prophet's tracks. When they reached the mountain, they lost the trail. They ascended the mountain and came upon the cave, but saw a spiderweb at its mouth. Thus they said, "If he had entered here, then there would be no spiderweb at the mouth of the cave." The Prophet remained inside the cave for three nights.[171]

Maʿmar said: Qatādah said: 12.6

The Quraysh entered the Assembly House to plot against the Prophet and said, "Let no one enter with you who isn't one of you," but Satan entered in the guise of an old man from Najd. Someone said, "You don't need to be wary of this one—this is merely a man from Najd." 12.6.1

Thus, they convened their assembly to consult one another. One of their men said, "I think we should mount him on a camel and then cast him out."

"That's a horrible idea!" Satan objected. "This man has already spread his corruption among you, even though he's in your midst! How much more will

فقال الشيطان: بئسَ ما رأى هذا! هو هذا قد كان يُفسد ما بينكم وهو بين أَظهُركم. فكيف إذا أخرجتموه فأفسد الناس؟ ثمّ حملهم على ذلك يقاتلوكم!

فقالوا: نِعم ما رأى هذا الشيخ. فقال قائلٌ آخر: فإنّي أرى أن تجعلوه في بيت، وفتُطَيِّنُوا عليه بابه، وتدعوه فيه حتّى يموت.

فقال الشيطان: بئس ما رأى هذا! أَفترى قومه يتركونه فيه أبدًا؟ لا بدّ أن يغضبوا له فيخرجوه.

فقال أبو جهل: أرى أن تخرجوا من كل قبيلة رجلاً. ثمّ يأْخذوا أسيافهم، فيضربونه ضربةً واحدةً. فلا يُدرَى مَن قتله فتدُونه.

فقال الشيطان: نِعم ما رأى هذا!

فأطلع الله نبيّه صلّى الله عليه وسلّم على ذلك، فخرج هو وأبو بكر إلى غار من ١٢،٦،٢
الجبل يقال له ثَوْر. ونام عليٌّ على فراش النبيّ صلّى الله عليه وسلّم، وباتوا يحرسونه يحسبون أنّه النبيّ صلّى الله عليه وسلّم. فلمّا أصبحوا، قام عليٌّ لصلاة الصبح بادروا إليه. فإذا هم بعليّ فقالوا: أين صاحبك؟ قال: لا أدري. فاقتصّوا أثره حتّى بلغوا الغار. ثمّ رجعوا فمكث فيه هو وأبو بكر ثلاث ليال.

قال معمر: قال الزهريّ في حديثه عن عروة: ١٢،٧

فمكثا فيه ثلاث ليال يبيت عندهما عبد الله بن أبي بكر، وهو غلامٌ شابٌّ لَقِنٌ[1] ثَقِفٌ، فيخرج[2] من عندهما سَحَرًا فيصبح عند قريش بمكّة كبائتٍ. فلا يسمع أمرًا يُكادانِ به إلّا وعاه حتّى يأتيهما بخبر ذلك حين يختلط الظلام. ويرعى عليهما عامر بن فهيرة مولى أبي بكر مِنْحَةً من غنم، فيُريحها عليهما حين تذهب ساعة من الليل.[3] فيبيتان في رِسلها حتّى ينعق بها[4] عامر بن فهيرة بغلس، يفعل ذلك كلّ ليلة من الليالي الثلاث. واستأجر رسول الله وأبو بكر رجلاً من بني الدئل، من بني عبد ابن عديّ، هاديًا خرّيتًا — والخرّيت: الماهر بالهداية — قد غمس يمينَ حلفٍ في آل العاص بن

١ بخ؛ مم: من. ٢ مم؛ بخ: يرحل. ٣ مم؛ بخ: العشاء. ٤ بخ؛ مم: بهما.

he corrupt other people if you exile him? Then, once he has them on his side, they will make war with you!"

"This old man has spoken well," they said. Someone then spoke out, "I think you should shut him up in a chamber, seal the door so he cannot escape, and leave him there until he dies!"

"That's a horrible idea!" cried Satan. "Do you imagine that his people would ever leave him to die there? Certainly they would become furious and remove him."

Abū Jahl then spoke out: "I think you should put forward a single man from each tribe, each of whom will then take his sword and strike him with one fell swoop. That way no one will know who killed him, and you'll be rid of him!"

"Now that's an excellent idea!" replied Satan.

But God apprised his Prophet of all these goings-on, so he and Abū Bakr **12.6.2**
left for a cave on the mountain called Thawr. ʿAlī slept in the Prophet's bed, and the Quraysh kept watch over him all night long thinking that he was the Prophet. When they awoke in the morning, ʿAlī arose for the morning prayer. They rushed in after him, but they were surprised to find that it was ʿAlī, and asked, "Where is your kinsman?" "I don't know," ʿAlī replied. So they followed the Prophet's tracks until they reached the cave. Afterward they returned, but the Prophet and Abū Bakr remained there for three nights.

Maʿmar said: al-Zuhrī said in his narrative from ʿUrwah: **12.7**

The two remained in the cave for three nights. Abū Bakr's son ʿAbd Allāh, a sharp and clever young man, spent the night with them and would leave them just before daybreak and wake up in the morning among the Quraysh in Mecca, as though he had passed the night there. Not a plot was hatched to entrap them without him uncovering it and bringing word of the plot back to them before dark. ʿĀmir ibn Fuhayrah, the slave-client of Abū Bakr, would herd a flock of sheep for them, leading the flock back from pasture once the first hour of the night had passed. Thus the two would spend the evening in the ease of the flock's nourishment until ʿĀmir ibn Fuhayrah would call to the flock in the deep of night. He did so each of the three nights. The Messenger of God also hired a man from the Diʾl clan of the ʿAbd ibn ʿAdī tribe as a guide and a *khirrīt*—by *khirrīt* he means a skilled guide—who was bound by alliance to the

وائل، وهو على دين كفّار قريش. فأمّناه، فدفعا إليه راحلتيهما، وواعداه غار ثور بعد ثلاث. فأتى غارهما براحلتيهما صبيحة ليال ثلاث. فارتحلا، وانطلق معهما عامر بن فهيرة، مولى أبي بكر، والدليل الدئليّ. فأخذ بهم طريق أذاخر، وهو طريق الساحل.

قال معمر: قال الزهريّ: فأخبرني عبد الرحمن بن مالك المدلجيّ، وهو ابن أخي سراقة بن جعشم، أنّ أباه أخبره ٨،١٢
أنّه سمع سراقة يقول:

جاءتنا رُسُلُ كفّار قريش يجعلون في رسول الله صلّى الله عليه وسلّم وأبي بكر ١،٨،١٢
دية كلّ واحد منهما، لمن قتلهما أو أسرهما. قال: فبينا أنا جالس في مجلس من مجالس قومي من بني مدلج، أقبل رجل منهم حتّى قال علينا. فقال: يا سراقة! إنّي رأيتُ آنفاً أسودةً بالساحل. أراها محمّداً وأصحابه.

قال سراقة: فعرفت أنّهم هم، فقلتُ: إنّهم ليسوا بهم، ولكنّك رأيتَ فلاناً وفلاناً انطلقوا بُغاةً.

قال: ثمّ ما لبثتُ في المجلس إلّا ساعةً حتّى قمتُ. فدخلتُ بيتي، فأمرتُ جاريتي أن تخرج لي فرسي، وهي من وراء أكمة تحسبها عليّ. وأخذتُ رمحي، فخرجتُ به من ظهر البيت، فخططتُ بزُجّي الأرض. وخفضتُ عالية الرمح حتّى أتيتُ فرسي. فركبتُها، فرفعتُها تُقرّب بي حتّى رأيتُ أسودتهم حتّى إذا[1] دنوت منهم. حيث يسمعون الصوت، عثرتْ بي فرسي. فخررتُ عنها فقمت فأهويت بيدي إلى كنانتي. فاستخرجتُ منها، أي الأزلام، فاستقسمتُ بها: أضُرّهم أم لا؟ فرفعتُها تُقرّب بي أيضاً حتّى إذا دنوت، سمعت قراءة رسول الله صلّى الله عليه وسلّم. وهو لا يلتفت وأبو بكر يُكثر الالتفات. ساختْ يدا فرسي في الأرض حتّى بلغت الركبتين. فخررتُ عنها، فزجرتها، فنهضتُ، فلم تكد تخرج يداها. فلمّا استوت قائمةً إذا لأثر يديها عُثانٌ ساطعٌ في السماء مثل الدخان.

---

١ [إذا] ح: ساقطة من م.

people of al-ʿĀṣ ibn Wāʾil and was even an adherent of the religion of the infidel Quraysh. The two of them swore an oath to protect him and entrusted him with their two mounts, having agreed to meet at the Thawr cave after three nights; he came to their cave the day after the third night. They left on their mounts, and ʿĀmir ibn Fuhayrah, the slave-client of Abū Bakr, and the Diʾlī guide departed with them. He took them via the Adhākhir path, which is the path running along the coast.

Maʿmar said: al-Zuhrī said: ʿAbd al-Raḥmān ibn Mālik al-Mudlijī, the nephew of Surāqah ibn Juʿshum, reported to me that his father reported to him that he heard Surāqah say: **12.8**

Messengers from the infidel Quraysh came to us offering a bounty for God's **12.8.1**
Messenger and Abū Bakr,[172] or for either one of them, to whoever either killed them or took them captive. While I sat in a meeting of my clan of the Mudlij tribe, a man approached and addressed us, saying, "Surāqah, I've just seen the faint outlines of people traveling along the coast. I reckon they're Muḥammad and his companions."

Surāqah said: I knew it was them, but I said, "That's certainly not them; rather, you've seen so-and-so and so-and-so who set out in search of something or other."

Surāqah continued: I remained at the meeting for a short time and then left to return home, where I ordered my servant girl to bring out my mare for me. She could sense I was up to something. I took my spear and went behind my house, where I made markings on the ground with the iron butt of my spear. Keeping the tip of my spear low, I went to my mare and mounted her, and then spurred her to gallop off at a brisk pace so that I might see the distant outline of Muḥammad and his companion. Eventually I drew near enough to them that they were within earshot. My mare stumbled, and I fell from the saddle. I stood up and reached back to my quiver, pulling divining arrows[173] from it. I then cast lots: Should I seek to harm them or not? Again I spurred my steed to gallop off at brisk pace and eventually I drew near enough to hear the Messenger of God reciting the Qurʾan. He did not turn to look about, but Abū Bakr did so constantly. Just then the forelegs of my steed sank into the ground up to her knees, and I was again thrown from the saddle. I scolded her and stood back up. Hardly had she pulled her forelegs out and straightened up when, all of a sudden, fumes, *ʿuthān*, billowing up to the sky like smoke, rose from the imprint made by her forelegs.

قال معمر لأبي عمرو بن العلاء: ما العُثان؟ فسكت ساعةً، ثمّ قال: هو الدخان ٢،٨،١٢
من غير نار.

قال معمر: قال الزهريّ في حديثه: ٣،٨،١٢

فاستقسمت بالأزلام، فخرج الذي أكره: لا أضرّهم. فناديتُهما بالأمان. فوقفا وركبت فرسي حتّى جئتهم. وقد وقع في نفسي حين لقيت منهم ما لقيت من الحبس عنهم، أنّه سيظهر أمرُ رسول الله صلّى الله عليه وسلّم. فقلت له: إنّ قومك جعلوا فيك الدية. فأخبرتُهم من أخبار سفري وما يريد الناس بهم، وعرضتُ عليهم الزاد والمتاع. فلم يرزءوني شيئًا، ولم يسألوني إلّا أن أخفِ عنّا. فسألتُه أن يكتب لي كتابَ موادعة آمن به. فأمر عامر بن فهيرة فكتب لي في[1] رقعة من أدم. ثمّ مضى.

قال معمر: قال الزهريّ: وأخبرني عروة بن الزبير ٩،١٢

أنّه لقي الزبير وركبًا من المسلمين، كانوا تجّارًا لمدينة بالشام قافلين إلى مكّة، ١،٩،١٢
فعرضوا للنبيّ صلّى الله عليه وسلّم وأبي بكر ثياب بياض. يقال: كَسَوْهم أعطوهم.

وسمع المسلمون بالمدينة بمخرج رسول الله صلّى الله عليه وسلّم، فكانوا يغدون ٢،٩،١٢
كلّ غداة إلى الحرّة، فينتظرونه حتّى يؤذيهم حرّ الظهيرة. فانقلبوا يومًا بعدما أطالوا انتظاره. فلمّا انتهوا إلى بيوتهم، أوفى رجلٌ من يهود أطمًا من آطامهم لأمرٍ ينظر إليه. فبصر برسول الله صلّى الله عليه وسلّم وأصحابه مبيّضين، يزول بهم السراب. فلم يتناهى اليهوديّ أن نادى بأعلى صوته: يا معشر العرب، هذا جدّكم الّذي تنتظرونه. فثار المسلمون إلى السلاح، فلَقُوا رسول الله صلّى الله عليه وسلّم حتّى أتوه بظاهر الحرّة. فعدل بهم رسول الله صلّى الله عليه وسلّم ذات اليمين حتّى نزل في بني عمرو بن عوف. وذلك يوم الاثنين من شهر ربيع الأوّل. فقام أبو بكر[2] يذكّر الناس، وجلس رسول الله صلّى الله عليه وسلّم صامتًا. وطفق من جاء من الأنصار، ممّن لم يكن رأى رسول الله صلّى الله عليه وسلّم يحسبه أبا بكر، حتّى أصابت رسول الله

---

١ [في] ح؛ ساقطة في م.　٢ بخ في رواية غير معمر عن الزهري؛ م: قام رسول الله.

Maʿmar asked Abū ʿAmr ibn al-ʿAlāʾ, "What does *ʿuthān* mean?" He remained silent for a time, then said, "Smoke without flame." 12.8.2

Maʿmar said: al-Zuhrī continued his narration, saying: 12.8.3

I cast lots using the divining arrows, and they landed on what I most feared: "Do not seek to harm them." So I called out to them, assuring them I meant no harm. They stood up, and I rode my steed over to them. Because I had met with so many obstacles while trying to reach them, I knew in my heart that God's Messenger would be victorious, so I said to him, "Your tribe has offered a bounty in exchange for your life," and I went on to tell them the story of my journey and what certain people sought to do to them. I offered them provisions and other effects, but they took nothing from me, asking only that I conceal their whereabouts. I asked them to write a letter of safe conduct for me by which I might be protected. He ordered ʿĀmir ibn Fuhayrah to write it out for me on a strip of leather, which he did, and after that he went on his way.

Maʿmar said: al-Zuhrī said: ʿUrwah ibn al-Zubayr informed me that: 12.9

The Prophet encountered al-Zubayr and a number of Muslims riding their camels heading toward Mecca—for they had been traveling in Syria as a caravan of merchants for Medina—and they presented the Prophet and Abū Bakr with white garments. It is said that they wrapped them in the garments they had given them. 12.9.1

The Muslims in Medina heard word of the Messenger of God's departure, so they would head out to the lava fields early in the morning to wait for him until they could no longer bear the midday heat. One day they turned back after having waited a long time for him. After they had returned to their homes, a Jewish man looked down from one of the Jews' towering fortresses,[174] hoping to catch sight of something, but he saw instead God's Messenger and his companions clothed in white and hazy in the desert mirage. The Jew immediately cried out in his loudest voice, "O company of Arabs! This is the good fortune you've been expecting!" The Muslims rushed to grab their weapons and went to meet the Messenger of God. Eventually they came to the outer rim of the lava field. He turned off the path, veered to the right, and camped among the ʿAmr ibn ʿAwf clan. That was on Monday in the month of Rabiʿ I.[175] Abū Bakr began to address the people, but the Messenger of God sat and remained quiet. Some of the Allies who came had never seen the Messenger of God, so at first they thought that Abū Bakr was he. Eventually, though, the sun shone 12.9.2

صلّى الله عليه وسلّم الشمسُ. فأقبل أبو بكر حتّى ظلّل عليه بردائه، فعرف الناسُ رسولَ الله صلّى الله عليه وسلّم عند ذلك. فلبث رسول الله صلّى الله عليه وسلّم في بني عمرو بن عوف بضع عشرة ليلةً، وابتنى المسجد الّذي أُسِسَ على التقوى، وصلّى فيه.

٣،٩،١٢ ثمّ ركب رسول الله صلّى الله عليه وسلّم راحلته، فسار، ومشى الناس، حتّى بركت به عند مسجد الرسول صلّى الله عليه وسلّم بالمدينة، وهو يصلّي فيه يومئذ رجال من المسلمين. وكان مربداً للتمر لسهل وسهيل غلامَين يتيمَين أخوَين في حجر أبي أمامة أَسعد بن زرارة من بني النجّار. فقال رسول الله صلّى الله عليه وسلّم حين بركت به راحلته: هذا المنزل، إنْ شاء الله. ثمّ دعا رسول الله صلّى الله عليه وسلّم الغلامين. فساومهما بالمربد ليتّخذه مسجداً. فقالا: بل نهبه لك، يا رسول الله! فأبى النبيّ صلّى الله عليه وسلّم أن يَقبله هبةً حتّى ابتاعه منهما. وبناه مسجداً وطفق رسول الله صلّى الله عليه وسلّم ينقل معهم اللبن في ثيابه. وهو يقول:

هٰذَا الْحِمَالُ لَا حِمَالَ خَيْبَرْ   هٰذَا أَبَرُّ رَبَّنَا وَأَطْهَرْ

ويقول:

اَللّٰهُمَّ[١] إِنَّ الأَجْرَ أَجْرُ الآخِرَةْ   فَارْحَمِ الأَنْصَارَ وَالْمُهَاجِرَةْ

يتمثّل رسول الله صلّى الله عليه وسلّم بشعر رجلٍ من المسلمين لم يُسمَّ لي. ولم يبلغني في الأحاديث أنّ رسول الله صلّى الله عليه وسلّم تمثّل ببيت قطّ من شعر تامّ غير هؤلاء الأبيات. ولكن كان يرجزهم لبناء المسجد.

٤،٩،١٢ فلمّا قاتل رسول الله صلّى الله عليه وسلّم كفّار قريش، حالت الحرب بين مهاجرة أرض الحبشة وبين القدوم على رسول الله صلّى الله عليه وسلّم حتّى لقوه بالمدينة زمن الخندق. فكانت أسماء بنت عميس تُحدّث أنّ عمر بن الخطّاب كان يعيّرهم بالمكث

١ [اللّهمّ] لخ في رواية غير معمر عن الزهري؛ ساقطة من م.

down on the Messenger of God, and Abū Bakr drew near to shade him with his mantle. At that moment, the people recognized the Messenger of God. God's Messenger stayed with the ʿAmr ibn ʿAwf clan for more than ten nights, and then he built the mosque established on piety[176] and prayed therein.

After that, the Messenger of God mounted his riding camel and marched 12.9.3
forward, and the people also walked alongside him, until his mount kneeled at the location of the Messenger's mosque in Medina. That same day he and several of the Muslim men prayed there. That place was an expanse of land used for drying dates and belonged to Sahl and Suhayl, two orphan brothers in the care of Abū Umāmah Asʿad ibn Zurārah of the Najjār clan. When his riding camel kneeled there, the Messenger of God said, "This is the place, God willing." Later, he summoned the two boys and bargained over the price for using the plot for a mosque. They said, "O Messenger of God, we wish to grant it to you as a gift," but the Prophet refused to accept it as a gift and insisted on purchasing it from them. The Prophet then built the mosque—straightaway he began to carry the sunbaked bricks with the coat of his garment alongside the other Muslims, reciting:

This very load, not the load of Khaybar,[177]
our Lord, is most righteous and pure.

He also recited:

O Lord, the reward is the Hereafter,
so show Your mercy to the Allies and Emigrants.

The Messenger of God thus repeated the poetry of a Muslim man whose name I do not know, nor have I heard in the reports about the Prophet that the Messenger of God ever repeated a single complete verse of poetry except for these verses. His intent in doing so was to encourage them to build the mosque.[178]

When the Messenger of God waged war against the infidel Quraysh, the war 12.9.4
prevented those who had emigrated to Abyssinia from coming to the Messenger of God, but eventually they were able to join him in Medina from the time of the Battle of Trench onward. Asmā' bint ʿUmays reported that ʿUmar ibn al-Khaṭṭāb used to reproach them for remaining in Abyssinia, but when they brought this to the attention of God's Messenger—Asmā' claimed—the Messenger of God replied, "You are not as he says." The first verse of the Qur'ān to be revealed concerning the waging of war was:

في أرض الحبشة. فذكر ذلك، زعمت أسماءُ، لرسول الله صلّى الله عليه وسلّم.
فقال رسول الله صلّى الله عليه وسلّم: لستم كذلك. وكان أوّل آية أُنزلت في القتال،
﴿أُذِنَ لِلَّذِينَ يُقَٰتَلُونَ بِأَنَّهُمْ ظُلِمُوا۟ وَإِنَّ ٱللَّهَ عَلَىٰ نَصْرِهِمْ لَقَدِيرٌ﴾ .

«Those who have been attacked are permitted to take up arms because they have been wronged—God has the power to help them.»[179]

حَدِيثُ الثَّلَاثَةِ ٱلَّذِينَ خُلِّفُوا

١،١٣ عبد الرزّاق عن معمر عن الزهريّ، قال: أخبرني ابنُ[١] كعب بن مالك عن أبيه، قال:

٢،١٣ لم أتخلّف عن النبيّ صلّى الله عليه وسلّم في غزاة غزاها حتّى كانت غزوة تبوك إلّا بدراً. ولم يعاتب النبيّ صلّى الله عليه وسلّم أحداً تخلّف عن بدر. إنّما خرج يريد العِير، فخرجت قريش مُغَوِّثِين لعيرهم. فالتقوا عن غير موعد، كما قال اللهُ. ولعمري، إنّ أشرفَ مشاهد رسول الله صلّى الله عليه وسلّم في الناس لبدرٌ. وما أُحِبُّ أنّي كنتُ شهدتها مكان بيعتي ليلة العقبة حيث تواثقنا على الإسلام. ثمّ لم أتخلّف بعدُ عن النبيّ صلّى الله عليه وسلّم في غزاة غزاها حتّى كانت غزوة تبوك، وهي آخر غزوة غزاها.

٣،١٣ وآذن النبيّ صلّى الله عليه وسلّم الناس بالرحيل، وأراد أن يتأهّبوا أُهْبَةَ غزوهم. وذلك حين طاب الظلال، وطابت الثمار، وكان قلّ ما أراد غزوةً إلّا وارى خبرها.[٢] وكان يقول: الحربُ خدعة. فأراد النبيّ صلّى الله عليه وسلّم في غزوة تبوك أن يتأهّب الناس أهبةً، وأنا أيسر ما كنت. قد جمعت راحلتيّ،[٣] وأنا أقدرُ شيء في نفسي على الجهاد وخفّة الحاذ، وأنا في ذلك أصغو إلى الظلال، وطيب الثمار. فلم أزل كذلك حتّى قام النبيّ صلّى الله عليه وسلّم غادياً بالغداة. وذلك يوم الخميس، وكان يحبّ أن يخرج يوم الخميس.[٤] فأصبح غادياً، فقلتُ، أنطلق غداً إلى السوق، فأشتري جَهازي. ثمّ ألحق بهم،[٥] فانطلقت إلى السوق من الغد، فعسُر عليّ بعض شأني أيضاً. فرجعتُ،[٦] فقلت: أرجع غداً إن شاء الله.[٧] فلم أزل كذلك حتّى التبس بي الذنب. وتخلّفت عن رسول الله صلّى الله عليه وسلّم، فجعلت أمشي في الأسواق وأطوفُ بالمدينة. فيَحْزُنُني أنّي لا أرى أحداً تخلّف إلّا رجلاً مغموصاً عليه في النفاق.

١ [ابن] ط؛ ح، تر: عبد الرحمن بن؛ ساقطة من مم. ٢ مم، ط؛ ح: غيرها. ٣ مم؛ ح، ط: راحلتين.
٤ [وكان يحبّ أن يخرج يوم الخميس] ح، ط؛ ساقطة من مم. ٥ [فرجعت] ح، ط؛ مم: ألحقهم. ٦ ح، ط؛ ساقطة من مم.
٧ هنا في ح: فألحق بهم فعسر عليّ بعض شأني أيضاً؛ وكلها ساقطة من مم، ط.

The Story of the Three Who Remained Behind

ʿAbd al-Razzāq, on the authority of Maʿmar, on the authority of al-Zuhrī, who said: the son of Kaʿb ibn Mālik reported to me from his father, who said: 13.1

With the exception of the Battle of Badr, I never failed to accompany the Prophet on an expedition that he undertook until the Tabūk expedition. The Prophet had not censured anyone who failed to accompany him at Badr because he set out only to find the caravan. When the Quraysh set out to come to the rescue of the caravan, they met in battle without having planned to do so previously, as God decreed.[180] By my life, though Badr be the most esteemed of the Prophet's battles in the people's eyes, I would never wish to have witnessed it in exchange for my oath of fealty the night of al-ʿAqabah when we pledged our faith in Islam. After that, I never once failed to accompany the Prophet in an expedition undertaken by him until the Tabūk expedition—and that was the last expedition he would ever undertake. 13.2

The Prophet had given the people permission to set out for battle, for he wanted them to equip themselves for the expedition. This was at the time of year when the shade had become pleasant and the fruit had ripened. Seldom would the Prophet set out for an expedition without concealing the news. As he used to say, "War is guile." The Prophet wanted the people to equip themselves for battle. At that time I had become wealthier than I had ever been before, and I even owned two mounts. I was easily capable of participating in the jihad and was free of cares, so I went to rest in the shade under the ripened fruit. I remained thus until the Prophet set out early in the morning—that was on a Thursday, for he preferred to set out on a Thursday, waking up to head out early in the morning. I said, "I'll leave for the market tomorrow and buy my supplies, then I'll catch up with them." I left for the market the next day, but I encountered some difficulties and went back. "Tomorrow I'll return, God willing," I said, and I remained in this mindset until sin ensnared me and I failed to accompany the Messenger of God. I took to walking through the markets and strolling about Medina, and it pained me that the only man I saw who had remained behind was one despised as a hypocrite. There wasn't a 13.3

وكان ليس أحدٌ تخلّف إلّا رأى أنّ ذلك يخفى له، وكان الناس كثيرًا لا يجمعهم ديوان، وكان جميع من تخلّف عن النبيّ صلّى الله عليه وسلّم بضعة وثمانين رجلاً، ولم يذكُرني النبيّ صلّى الله عليه وسلّم حتّى بلغ تبوكًا. قال: ما فعل كعب بن مالك؟ فقال رجلٌ من قومي: خلّفه يا رسول الله بُرداه والنظر في عطفيه. فقال معاذ بن جبل: بئس ما قلت! ما نعلم عليه إلّا خيرًا.[١] قال: فبينا هم كذلك، إذا هم برجل يزول به السراب، فقال النبيّ صلّى الله عليه وسلّم: كن أبا خيثمة. فإذا هو أبو خيثمة.

٤،١٣ قال: فلمّا قضى النبيّ صلّى الله عليه وسلّم غزوة تبوك، وقفل ودنا من المدينة، جعلت أنظر بماذا أخرج من سخط النبيّ صلّى الله عليه والنبيّ، وأستعين على ذلك بكلّ ذي رأي من أهلي حتّى إذا قيل: النبيّ صلّى الله عليه وسلّم مُصبّحكم غدًا بالغداة. زاح عنّي الباطل وعرفتُ أنّي لا أنجو إلّا بالصدق.

فدخل النبيّ صلّى الله عليه وسلّم ضحىً، فصلّى في المسجد ركعتين. وكان إذا جاء من سفر فعل ذلك، دخل المسجد فصلّى فيه ركعتين. ثمّ جلس، فجعل يأتيه من تخلّف، فيحلفون له ويعتذرون إليه. فيستغفر لهم، ويقبل علانيتهم ويَكِلُ سرائرهم إلى الله. فدخلت المسجد، فإذا هو جالسٌ.

فلمّا رآني تبسّم تَبَسُّمَ المغضب. فجئتُ، فجلستُ بين يديه، فقال: ألم تكن ابتعت ظهرك؟

فقلتُ: بلى، يا نبيّ الله!

قال: فما خلّفك؟

فقلت: والله، لو بين يديّ[٢] أحدٍ غيرك من الناس جلست، لخرجت من سخطه عليّ بعذرٍ. لقد أوتيتُ جَدَلاً، ولقد علمتُ، يا نبيّ الله، أنّي إن أخبرتك اليوم بقول تجد عليّ فيه وهو حقٌّ. فإنّي أرجو فيه عفو الله. وإن حدّثتك اليوم حديثًا ترضى عنه فيه، وهو كذب، أوشك أن يطلعك الله عليه. والله، يا نبيّ الله، ما كنتُ قطّ أيسر، ولا أخفّ حاذًا منّي حيث تخلّفت عنك.

---

١ ح؛ مم، ط: ما نعلم إلا خيرًا. ٢ [يدي] ح؛ ط: أيدي؛ ساقطة من م.

single man who remained behind who did not imagine that he could conceal it from the Prophet, for the people were numerous, and he did not enroll them in a military register.[181] Those who failed to accompany the Prophet numbered over eighty men. The Prophet didn't remember me until he had reached Tabūk, but once he arrived at Tabūk, he asked, "What is Kaʿb ibn Mālik up to?" A man from my tribe answered, "O Messenger of God, he's probably fallen behind tending to his clothes and preening himself!" "That's a horrible thing to say," Muʿādh ibn Jabal interjected. "O Prophet of God, by God, we know only good things of him." While this was going on, they caught a glimpse of a man obscured by the desert mirage. "It's Abū Khaythamah," declared the Prophet, and indeed it was he.

When the Prophet had completed the Tabūk expedition and his caravan 13.4
came near Medina, I began to ponder how I might escape the displeasure of the Prophet, and I sought the aid of some men of wise counsel from my people. Eventually word spread that the Prophet would be arriving early the next morning. All falsehood then left me, and I realized that I would only find salvation by speaking the truth.

The Prophet entered Medina the following day and prayed two prostrations in the mosque, as was his custom upon returning from a journey. After entering the mosque and praying the two prostrations, he sat to hold audience. All those who had remained behind went to him swearing oaths and making excuses before him. He sought divine forgiveness on their behalf and accepted their public confessions, leaving the truth of their affairs to God. I entered the mosque, and there he was sitting in audience.

When he saw me, he smiled the smile of an angry man. I came to him, and when I sat before him, he said, "Did you not purchase your mount?"

"Dear Prophet of God, indeed I did," I answered.

"Then what caused you to remain behind?" he asked.

"By God," I answered, "if I sat before any other man, then I would have attempted to escape his displeasure by offering an excuse—indeed, I am an excellent disputant—but I know, O Prophet of God, that if I tell you something that is true but that makes you angry with me, then I might still hold out hope for God's mercy. Were I to tell you a story merely to placate you, though it be a lie, it is all but certain that God would reveal it to you. I swear by God, O Prophet of God, that I have never been wealthier or more lightly burdened by life than when I failed to accompany you."

قال: أمّا هذا، فقد صدقكم الحديث. قم حتّى يقضي الله فيك.

فقمتُ، فثار بي على أثري أناس من قومي يؤنّبونّي. فقالوا: والله ما نعلمك أذنَبْت ذنباً قطّ قبل هذا. فهلاّ اعتذرت إلى نبيّ الله صلّى الله عليه وسلّم بعذر رضي عنك فيه. وكان استغفار رسول الله صلّى الله عليه وسلّم سيأتي من وراء ذنبك. ولم تَقِف نفسك[1] موقفاً لا تدري ما يُقضى لك فيه.

فلم يؤنّبوني حتّى هممت أن أرجع، فأُكذّب نفسي. فقلتُ: هل قال هذا القول أحدٌ غيري؟

قالوا: نعم، قاله هلال بن أميّة ومرارة بن رِبيعة. فذكروا رجلين صالحين قد شهدا بدراً. لي فيهما أسوةٌ.

فقلت: لا والله لا أرجع إليه في هذا أبداً ولا أُكذّب نفسي.

قال: ونهى النبيّ صلّى الله عليه وسلّم الناس عن كلامنا، أيّها الثلاثة. قال: فجعلت ٥،١٣ أخرج إلى السوق، فلا يكلّمني أحدٌ، وتنكّرلنا الناس حتّى ما هم بالّذي نعرف. وتنكّرت لنا الحيطان حتّى ما هي بالحيطان الّتي تعرف لنا. وتنكّرت لنا الأرض حتّى ما هي بالأرض الّتي نعرف. وكنت أقوى الناس،[2] فكنت أخرج في السوق. فآتي المسجد فأدخل. فآتي النبيّ صلّى الله عليه وسلّم فأسلّم عليه، فأقول: هل حرّك شفتيه بالسلام. فإذا قمتُ أصلّي إلى سارية، فأقبلتُ قِبَل صلاتي. نظر إليّ بمؤخّرعينيه وإذا نظرتُ إليه أعرض عنّي.

قال: واستكان صاحباي، فجعلا يبكيان الليل والنهار، لا يُطّلعان رؤوسهما. ٦،١٣ فبينا أنا أطوف في السوق، إذا رجل نصرانيّ جاء بطعام له يبيعه، يقول: من يدلّني على كعب بن مالك؟ قال: فطفق الناس يشيرون له إليّ. فأتاني، وأتاني بصحيفة من مالك غسّان. فإذا فيها:

أمّا بعد، فإنه بلغني أنّ صاحبك قد جفاك وأقصاك، ولستَ بدار مضيعة ولا هوان. فالحق بنا نواسك.

---

١ [نفسك] ح، ط: ساقطة من م. ٢ م؛ ح: أصحابي؛ يخ: وأما أنا فكنت أشب القوم وأجلدهم.

"As for what you've said," he replied, "your speech is true, but stand up and leave now until God gives his judgment concerning you."

I stood up, and several people from my tribe rose and followed, reproaching me. They said, "By God, we've never known you to commit such a sin before this! Why couldn't you offer an excuse acceptable to God's Prophet, so that the Messenger of God would seek forgiveness on your behalf despite your sin? Why have you put yourself in a position in which you have no idea what judgment might be issued against you?"

They continued their reproaches until I pondered returning and renouncing what I had said, but instead I asked, "Did anyone else say what I said?"

"Yes," they answered, "Hilāl ibn Umayyah and Murārah ibn Rabīʿah said the same." They named two upright men who had witnessed Badr; two exemplary men whose conduct I could follow.

"No," I said to myself, "I will not go back to the Prophet to speak of the matter again, nor will I renounce what I've said."

The Prophet then forbade the people to speak to us, all three of us. I set 13.5
out for the market, and not a soul spoke to me. As the people spurned us they became strangers to us—even the walls and earth spurned us and became foreign to us. Now, I was the strongest of three and would go about the market and enter the mosque. Approaching the Prophet, I would offer greetings of peace, wondering, "Did his lips just murmur 'Peace'?" When I stood to undertake my prayers next to a column of the mosque, I faced in the direction of my prayer; the Prophet watched me from the corner of his eye, but I if I looked toward him, he turned away from me.

My two companions had been plunged deep into misery; weeping night 13.6
and day, they never raised their heads. While I was making rounds in the market, there arrived a Christian man who had come to sell some food, saying, "Who will show me the way to Kaʿb ibn Mālik?" Straightaway the people pointed him in my direction. When he had come to me, he brought with him a scroll from the King of Ghassān, which read,

> Now, word has reached me that your master has dealt harshly with you and repudiated you. You need not take your shelter in a house of loss or ignominy. Come, join us and we will meet your every need.

قال: فقلت: هذا أيضاً من البلاء والشرّ. فسجرت بها التنّور، فأحرقتها فيه.

٧،١٣ فلمّا مضت أربعون ليلة، إذا رسول من النبيّ صلّى الله عليه وسلّم قد أتاني، فقال: اعتزل امرأتك.

فقلت: أطلّقها؟

قال: لا، ولكن لا تقربْها.

قال: فجاءت امرأة هلال بن أميّة، فقالت: يا نبيّ الله! إنّ هلال بن أميّة شيخ كبير ضعيف. فهل تأذن لي أن أخدمه؟

قال: نعم، ولكن لا يقربْكِ.

قالت: يا نبيّ الله! والله، ما به من حركة لشيء، ما زال مُكِبّاً يبكي الليل والنهار، منذ كان من أمره ما كان.

٨،١٣ قال كعبٌ: فلمّا طال عليَّ البلاءُ، اقتحمت على أبي قتادة حائطه، وهو ابن عمي. فسلّمت عليه، فلم يردّ عليَّ. فقلت: أنشدك الله، يا أبا قتادة![1] أتعلم أنّي أحبّ الله ورسوله؟ فسكت، ثمّ قلتُ: أنشدك الله، يا أبا قتادة! أتعلم أنّي أحبّ الله ورسوله؟ فسكت، ثمّ قلتُ: أنشدك الله، يا أبا قتادة! أتعلم أنّي أحبّ الله ورسوله؟ قال: الله ورسوله أعلم. قال: فلم أملك نفسي أن بكيت، ثمّ اقتحمت الحائط خارجاً حتّى إذا مضت خمسون ليلةً من حين نهى النبيّ صلّى الله عليه وسلّم عن كلامنا. صلّيتُ على ظهر بيت لنا صلاة الفجر. ثمّ جلست، وأنا في المنزلة الّتي قال الله ﴿وَضَاقَتْ عَلَيْهِمُ ٱلْأَرْضُ بِمَا رَحُبَتْ وَضَاقَتْ عَلَيْهِمْ أَنفُسُهُمْ﴾ إذ سمعت نداءً من ذِروة سَلْع أن: أبْشِرْ، يا كعب بن مالك! فخررت ساجداً وعرفتُ أنّ الله قد جاءنا بالفرج. ثمّ جاء رجلٌ يركض على فرس يبشّرني. فكان الصوتُ أسرع من فرسه، فأعطيته ثوبيَّ بشارةً ولبستُ ثوبين آخرين.

٩،١٣ قال: وكانت توبتنا نزلت على النبيّ صلّى الله عليه وسلّم ثلث الليل، فقالت أمّ سلمة: يا نبيّ الله، ألا نبشّر كعب بن مالك؟ قال: إذاً يحطمكم الناس ويمنعونكم النوم سائر

١ [حائطه وهو ابن عمي. فسلمت عليه فلم يرد علي فقلت أنشدك الله يا أبا قتادة] ح، ط: ساقطة من م.

I thought, "This evil is yet another trial visited upon me." I then stoked a hearth and burnt the scroll therein.

Forty nights had passed when a messenger from the Prophet came to me 13.7
and said, "Withdraw from your wife."

"Shall I divorce her?" I asked.

"No," he answered, "but do not approach her."

The wife of Hilāl ibn Umayyah came before the Prophet and said, "O Prophet of God! Verily, Hilāl ibn Umayyah is a feeble old man. Will you permit me to serve him?"

"Yes," the Prophet consented, "but he shall not approach you."

"Prophet of God," she replied, "I swear by God that he can hardly move. Since this affair has begun, he's been curled up in a ball, weeping night and day!"

Kaʿb said: When my tribulations became too much to bear, I scaled the wall 13.8
of my cousin, Abū Qatādah. I greeted him with peace, but he did not reply. I said, "I abjure you by God, Abū Qatādah! Don't you know that I love God and His Messenger?" He remained quiet, so I said again, "I abjure you by God, Abū Qatādah! Don't you know that I love God and His Messenger?" Still he remained quiet, so I said again, "I abjure you by God, Abū Qatādah! Don't you know that I love God and His Messenger?" He replied, "God and His Messenger know best." I couldn't hold back my tears, so I scaled his wall to leave. When fifty nights had passed since the Prophet had forbade everyone from speaking to us, I prayed the dawn prayer on the roof of our house. I was sitting in the state that God has described, «when the earth, for all its spaciousness, closed in around them, and when their very souls closed in around them»,[182] when I heard a cry from atop Salʿ mountain: "Good tidings, Kaʿb ibn Mālik!" I fell down prostrate, knowing that God had granted us respite. Soon thereafter, a man came riding on a steed to bring me the good tidings—the man's voice was swifter than his steed. I gave him my two garments as a reward for the good tidings, and donned two others.

God revealed to the Prophet that He had accepted our repentence in the 13.9
final third of the night,[183] and Umm Salamah said, "Dear Prophet of God, shall you not convey the tidings to Kaʿb ibn Mālik?" He replied, "Then the people will crowd in on all of you and prevent you from sleeping for the rest of the night." Umm Salamah had been kindly toward me and greatly saddened over my affair.

الليلة. قال: وكانت أمّ سلمة محسنة[1] في شأني تحزن بأمري.

فانطلقت إلى النبيّ صلّى الله عليه وسلّم: فإذا هو جالسٌ في المسجد، وحوله المسلمون، وهو يستنير كاستنارة القمر. وكان إذا سُرَّ بالأمر استنار. فجئتُ، فجلستُ بين يديه، فقال: أبشِرْ، يا كعب بن مالك، بخير يومٍ أتى عليك منذ ولدتْكَ أمّك.

قال: قلت: يا نبيّ الله، أمرٌ من عند الله، أم من عندك؟

قال: بل من عند الله. ثمّ تلا عليهم ﴿لَقَدْ تَابَ ٱللَّهُ عَلَى ٱلنَّبِيِّ وَٱلْمُهَٰجِرِينَ وَٱلْأَنصَارِ﴾ حتّى بلغ ﴿ٱلتَّوَّابُ ٱلرَّحِيمُ﴾. قال: وفينا أنزلت أيضاً ﴿ٱتَّقُواْ ٱللَّهَ وَكُونُواْ مَعَ ٱلصَّٰدِقِينَ﴾.

قال: قلت: يا نبيّ الله، إن من توبتي إذاً ألّا أحدّث إلّا صدقاً، وأن أنخلع من مالي كلّه صدقةً إلى الله وإلى رسوله.

فقال: أمسك عليك بعض ما لَكَ. فهو خيرٌ لك.

فقلت: إنّي أمسك سهمي الّذي بخيبر.

قال: فما أنعم الله عليّ نعمةً بعد الإسلام أعظم في نفسي من صدقي رسول الله صلّى ١٠،١٣
الله عليه وسلّم حين صدقتُه أنا وصاحباي، إلّا أن نكون[2] كذّبناه فهلكنا كما هلكوا، وإنّي لأرجو أن لا[3] يكون الله عزّ وجلّ ابتلى أحداً في الصدق مثل الّذي ابتلاني، ما تعمّدت لكذبة بعد، وإنّي لأرجو أن يحفظني الله فيما بقي.

قال الزهريّ: فهذا ما انتهى إلينا من حديث كعب بن مالك.

---

١ مم، ط؛ ح: محسنة محتسبة. ٢ مم؛ ح، ط: أن لا نكون. ٣ [لا] ح، ط؛ ساقطة من مم.

I then set off to see the Prophet—there, sitting in the mosque surrounded by the Muslims, he shone as brightly as the shining moon, as he did whenever something had delighted him. I drew closer and sat before him. He said, "Good tidings, Kaʿb ibn Mālik! You've seen no better day since the day your mother gave you birth!"

"Dear Prophet of God," I replied, "is such a decree from God, or from you?"

"From God," he answered, and then he recited to them:

> «God has turned to the Prophet, and the Emigrants and the Allies who followed him in the hour of adversity when hearts almost wavered: He has turned to them; He is most kind and merciful to them. And to the three men who stayed behind: when the earth, for all its spaciousness, closed in around them, when their very souls closed in around them, when they realized that the only refuge from God was with Him, He turned to them in mercy in order for them to return. God is the Ever Relenting, the Most Merciful.»[184]

God also revealed concerning us: «Be mindful of God: stand with those who are true.»[185]

Then I said, "O Prophet of God, with my repentance I swear that I won't utter a word lest it be true and that I surrender my wealth in its entirety as alms over to God and His Messenger."

"Hold on to a portion of wealth for yourself," he replied, "for it is better for you."

"Then I will keep my lot in Khaybar," I answered.

Not since I had embraced Islam had God shown my soul such magnificient grace as when I spoke to God's Messenger, both I and my comrades; otherwise, we would have deceived him and fallen into perdition as did those who had been damned.[186] Verily, it is my hope that God never again try a soul in regard to speaking the truth as He had tried me then. Never again was I inclined to lie, and I hope that God shall preserve me thus for the rest of my days. **13.10**

Al-Zuhrī said: Here ends as much of the story of Kaʿb ibn Mālik as has reached us.

مَنْ تَخَلَّفَ عَنِ ٱلنَّبِيِّ صلّى اللهُ عليه وسلّم في غَزْوَةِ تَبُوك

١،١٤ عبد الرزّاق عن معمر، قال: أخبرني قتادة وعليّ بن زيد بن جدعان أنّهما سمعا سعيد بن المسيّب يقول: حدّثني سعد بن أبي وقاص:

أنّ رسول الله صلّى الله عليه وسلّم لمّا خرج إلى تبوك، استخلف علينا إلى المدينة عليّ بن أبي طالب، فقال: يا رسول الله، ماكنت أحبّ أن تخرج وجهاً إلّا وأنا معك. فقال: أما ترضى أن تكون منّي بمنزلة هارون من موسى، غير أنّه لا نبيّ بعدي؟

٢،١٤ قال معمر: فأخبرني الزهريّ، قال:

كان أبو لبابة ممّن تخلّف عن رسول الله صلّى الله عليه وسلّم في غزوة تبوك، فربط نفسه بسارية. ثمّ قال: والله لا أحلّ نفسي منها ولا أذوق طعاماً ولا شراباً حتّى أموت أو يتوب الله عليّ. فمكث سبعة أيام لا يذوق فيها طعاماً ولا شراباً حتّى كان يخرّ مغشياً عليه. قال: ثمّ تاب الله عليه، فقيل له: قد تِيبَ عليك، يا أبا لبابة.

فقال: والله لا أحلّ نفسي حتّى يكون رسول الله صلّى الله عليه وسلّم يحلّني بيده.

قال: فجاء النبيّ صلّى الله عليه وسلّم، فحلّه بيده. ثمّ قال أبو لبابة: يا رسول الله، إنّ من توبتي أن أهجر دار قومي الّتي أصبتُ فيها الذنبُ وأن أنخلع من مالي كله صدقةً إلى الله وإلى رسوله.

قال: يجزيك الثلث، يا أبا لبابة.

٣،١٤ عبد الرزّاق عن معمر، قال: أخبرني الزهريّ، قال: أخبرني ابن كعب بن مالك، قال:

Those Who Failed to Accompany the Prophet on the Tabūk Expedition

ʿAbd al-Razzāq, on the authority of Maʿmar, who said: Qatādah and ʿAlī ibn Zayd ibn Judʿān related to me that they both heard Saʿīd ibn al-Musayyab say: Saʿd ibn Abī Waqqāṣ reported to me that: 14.1

When the Messenger of God had set off for Tabūk, he appointed ʿAlī ibn Abī Ṭālib over us as his vicegerent.[187] ʿAlī said, "O Messenger of God! I do not wish for you to set off in any direction without me at your side." But the Prophet replied, "Are you not content to be as near to me as Aaron was to Moses, except that there shall be no prophet after me?"

Maʿmar said: al-Zuhrī reported to me: 14.2

Abū Lubābah was among those who failed to accompany the Prophet on the Tabūk expedition. Later he tied himself to a pillar of the mosque and said, "By God, I won't untie myself or taste food or drink until either I die or God accepts my repentance." He remained there seven days, tasting neither food nor drink, until he collapsed to the ground unconscious. God then accepted his repentance, and he was told, "God has accepted your repentance, Abū Lubābah."

"By God," he replied, "I will not untie myself unless the Messenger of God unties me with his own hands!"

So the Prophet came to untie him with his own hands. After this, Abū Lubābah said, "O Messenger of God! With my repentance I swear to forsake my tribe's abode where I committed sin and to surrender my wealth in its entirety as alms to God and His Messenger!"

"A third of it will suffice, Abū Lubābah," replied the Prophet.

ʿAbd al-Razzāq, on the authority of Maʿmar, who said: al-Zuhrī reported to me, saying: the son of Kaʿb ibn Mālik reported to me: 14.3

أوّل أمرعتب على أبي لُبابة أنّه كان بينه وبين يتيم عَذْق. فاختصما إلى النبيّ صلّى الله عليه وسلّم، فقضى به النبيّ صلّى الله عليه وسلّم لأبي لبابة. فبكى اليتيم، فقال النبيّ صلّى الله عليه وسلّم: دَعْهُ له. فأبى. قال: فأَعطِه إيّاه ولك مثله في الجنّة. فأبى، فانطلق ابن الدحداحة، فقال لأبي لبابة: بِعْني هذا العذق بحديقتين. قال: نعم. ثمّ انطلق إلى النبيّ صلّى الله عليه وسلّم، فقال: يا رسول الله، أَرأيتَ إن أعطيتُ هذا اليتيم هذا العذق، أَلي مثلُهُ في الجنّة؟ قال: نعم. فأعطاه إيّاه. قال: فكان النبيّ صلّى الله عليه وسلّم يقول: كم من عذق مُذلَّل لابن الدحداحة في الجنّة.

قال: وأشار إلى بني قريظة حين نزلوا على حكم سعد، فأشار إلى حلقه الذبح وتخلّف عن النبيّ صلّى الله عليه وسلّم في غزوة تبوك. ثمّ تاب الله عليه بعد ذلك.

The first matter for which Abū Lubābah had been censured related to a dispute between him and an orphan over a date palm. They brought their dispute before the Prophet, and he ruled that the tree belonged to Abū Lubābah; but the orphan wept, so the Prophet said, "Hand the tree over to him." Abū Lubābah refused, so the Prophet said, "Give it to him and you shall have its like in Paradise." Yet still he refused. Ibn al-Daḥdāḥah went to speak with Abū Lubābah: "Would you sell this date palm in exchange for two gardens." "Yes," he agreed. Ibn al-Daḥdāḥah then left to go see the Prophet and said, "Messenger of God, do you think, if I give this orphan this date palm, that I shall have its like in Paradise?" "Yes," replied the Prophet, so Ibn al-Daḥdāḥah gave the orphan the tree. Thus the Prophet used to say, "How many fruit-bearing palms await Ibn al-Daḥdāḥah in Paradise!"[188]

Abū Lubābah also gestured toward the Qurayẓah clan when they were handed over to the judgment of Saʿd. That is, he gestured toward his neck, meaning they would be slaughtered. He also failed to accompany the Prophet on the Tabūk expedition, but later God accepted his repentance.

حَدِيثُ ٱلأَوْسِ وَٱلخَزْرَجِ

عبد الرزّاق عن معمر عن الزهريّ عن عبد الرحمن بن كعب بن مالك، قال: ١،١٥

إنّ ممّا صنع الله لنبيّه أنّ هذَين الحيّين من الأنصار، الأوس والخزرج، كانا ٢،١٥
يتصاولان في الإسلام كتصاول الفحلين. لا تصنع الأوس شيئاً إلّا قالت الخزرج: والله لا تذهبون به أبداً فضلاً علينا في الإسلام. فإذا صنعت الخزرج شيئاً قالت الأوس مثل ذلك.

فلمّا أصابت الأوس كعب بن الأشرف، قالت الخزرج: والله لا ننتهي حتّى نجزئ ٣،١٥
عن رسول الله صلّى الله عليه وسلّم مثل الّذي أجزءوا عنه! فتذاكروا أوزن رجل من اليهود. فاستأذنوا النبيّ صلّى الله عليه وسلّم في قتله، وهو سلّام بن أبي الحقيق الأعور أبو رافع بخيبر. فأذن لهم في قتله وقال: لا تقتلوا وليداً ولا امرأةً. فخرج إليه رهطٌ فيهم عبد الله بن عتيك، وكان أمير القوم أحد بني سلمة، وعبد الله بن أنيس ومسعود بن سنان وأبو قتادة وخزاعيّ بن أسود، رجل من أَسلم حليفٌ لهم، ورجلٌ آخر يقال له فلان بن سلمة.

فخرجوا حتّى جاءوا خيبر. فلمّا دخلوا البلد، عمدوا إلى كلّ بيت منها، فغلّقوا من ٤،١٥
خارجه على أهله. ثمّ أسندوا إليه في مشربة له في عَجَلَةٍ من نخل. فأسندوا فيها حتّى ضربوا عليه بابه، فخرجت إليهم امرأته، فقالت: ممّن أنتم؟

فقالوا: نفر من العرب أردنا المِيرة.

فقالت: هذا الرجل. فادخلوا عليه.

فلمّا دخلوا عليه، أغلقوا عليهم وعليهما الباب. ثمّ ابتدروه بأسيافهم. قال قائلُهم: والله ما دلّني عليه إلّا بياضه على الفراش في سواد الليل، كأنّه قِبْطِيّة مُلْقاة. قال: وصاحي بنا امرأته. قال: فيرفع الرجل منّا السيف ليضربها به، ثمّ يذكر نهي

The Story of the Aws and the Khazraj[189]

ʿAbd al-Razzāq, on the authority of Maʿmar, on the authority of al-Zuhrī, on the authority of ʿAbd al-Raḥmān ibn Kaʿb ibn Mālik, who said: 15.1

One of the graces God bestowed on his Prophet was these two tribes of the Allies, the Aws and the Khazraj. They vied to best one another in Islam like two rival stallions. The Aws would not achieve some feat without the Khazraj saying, "By God, you will never surpass us in bringing glory to Islam!" And if it was the Khazraj who achieved the feat, the Aws would say the same. 15.2

When the Aws murdered Kaʿb ibn al-Ashraf,[190] the Khazraj said, "By God, we shall not rest until we have gained satisfaction for God's Messenger as have they!" Thus, they met among themselves to decide on the most influential of the Jews' leaders and then sought the Messenger of God's permission to kill him—and that man was Sallām ibn Abī l-Ḥuqayq al-Aʿwar Abū Rāfiʿ of Khaybar. The Prophet granted them permission to kill him, but he stipulated, "Kill neither child nor woman!" A band then set out; among them was ʿAbd Allāh ibn ʿAtīk—a member of the Salamah clan and the leader of the troop—ʿAbd Allāh ibn Unays, Masʿūd ibn Sinān, Abū Qatādah, Khuzāʿī ibn Aswad, a man from Aslam and a confederate of theirs, and another man called So-and-so ibn Salamah. 15.3

They set out and eventually arrived at Khaybar. Once they had entered the territory, they passed by each home and locked the owners in from the outside. They then made their way to Ibn Abī l-Ḥuqayq, who was in the upper chamber of his house, reachable only by stairs carved from the trunk of a date palm. The men climbed up the palm trunk to knock on his door. His wife came out and said, "Where do you come from?" 15.4

"We are merely Bedouin seeking provisions," they answered.

"This is the man you seek," she replied, "so please enter."

Once inside, they locked the door behind them and rushed at him with their swords. One of them recalled, "By God, in the darkness of the night nothing guided my sword but the whiteness of his pallor on the bed, like an Egyptian shawl cast on the ground!" His wife then screamed at us, and one of our men lifted his sword to strike her, but then he recalled the Prophet's

النبيّ صلّى الله عليه وسلّم. قال: لولا ذلك فرغنا منها بليل. قال: وتحامل عبد الله بن أنيس بسيفه في بطنه حتّى أنفذه. فجعل يقول بطني بطني ثلاثًا. ثمّ خرجنا وعبد الله بن عتيك[١] وكان سيّء البصر. فوقع من فوق العجلة، فوُثِيَتْ رجله وَثْيًا منكرًا.

قال: فنزلنا فاحتملناه فانطلقنا به معنا حتّى انتهينا إلى منهر عين من تلك العيون. ٥،١٥
فمكثنا فيه. قال: وأوقدوا النيران، وأشعلوها في السعف وجعلوا يلتمسون ويشتدّون. وأخفى الله عليهم مكاننا. قال: ثمّ رجعوا.

قال: فقال بعض أصحابنا: أنذهب فلا ندري أمات عدوّ الله أم لا؟ قال: فخرج ٦،١٥
رجل منّا حتّى حشر في الناس، فدخل معهم، فوجد امرأته مُكِبّةً وفي يدها المصباح، وحوله رجال يهود. فقال قائلٌ منهم: أمّا والله لقد سمعتُ صوت ابن عتيك. ثمّ أكذبت نفسي، فقلتُ: وأنّى ابن عتيك بهذه البلاد؟ فقالت شيئًا، ثمّ رفعت رأسَها، فقالت: فاظَ وإلٰه يهود! تقول: مات. قال: فما سمعتُ كلمةً كانت ألذّ منها إلى نفسي. قال: ثمّ خرجتُ، فأخبرتُ أصحابي أنّه قد مات. فاحتملنا صاحبنا، فجئنا إلى رسول الله صلّى الله عليه وسلّم، فأخبرناه بذلك.

قال: وجاءوه يوم الجمعة، والنبيّ صلّى الله عليه وسلّم يومئذ على المنبر يخطب. فلمّا رآهم قال: أفلحت الوجوه.

١ [فجعل يقول بطني ثلاثا ثمّ خرجنا وعبد الله بن عتيك]عب؛ ساقطة من م.

prohibition. "If it were not for that," he said, "we would have finished her off that night." ʿAbd Allāh ibn Unays put his weight behind his sword, stabbing Ibn Abī l-Ḥuqayq in the stomach until it had gone clear through. Ibn Abī l-Ḥuqayq began to cry out, "My stomach! *My stomach!*" three times. Then we left, but ʿAbd Allāh ibn ʿAtīk was poor of sight and stumbled at the top of the stairs and severely injured his foot.

We carried him down the stairs and took him with us as far as one of those 15.5
water canals and stayed there. The Jews of Khaybar then stoked their fires and, after lighting palm branches, began searching for us intently; but God concealed our location from them, and after a while they returned to their homes.

One of our companions said, "How can we leave when we do not know 15.6
whether or not God's foe has truly died?" So one of our men set out to blend in among the crowds. He entered Ibn Abī l-Ḥuqayq's house along with them and found his wife bent over with a lantern in her hand and surrounded by Jewish men. One of the Jews said, "By God, I heard the voice of Ibn ʿAtīk! But I told myself it couldn't be true, saying, 'How could Ibn ʿAtīk be here in these lands?'" Then the wife said something. She raised her head and cried out, "He's gone,[191] by the God of the Jews!"—meaning he had died. I had never heard a word more delightful to my soul! Then I departed and informed my companions that he had indeed died. We carried our companion, and eventually we came to the Messenger of God and informed him of the news.

Al-Zuhrī said: They came on a Friday, and that day the Prophet was preaching from the pulpit. Once he saw them, he cried out, "They have prospered!"

حَدِيثُ الإِفْكِ

١،١٦ عبد الرزّاق عن معمر عن الزهريّ، قال: أخبرني سعيد بن المسيّب وعروة بن الزبير وعلقمة بن وقّاص وعبيد الله بن عبد الله بن عتبة بن مسعود عن حديث عائشة زوج النبيّ صلّى الله عليه وسلّم حين قال لها أهل الإفك ما قالوا، قال:

١،١،١٦ فبرّأها الله، كلّهم حدّثني بطائفةٍ من حديثها، وبعضهم كان أوعى لحديثها من بعضهم وأثبت له اقتصاصاً. وقد وعيتُ عن كلّ واحد منهم الحديث الّذي حدّثني وبعض حديثهم يُصدّق بعضاً. ذكروا أنّ عائشة زوج النبيّ صلّى الله عليه وسلّم، قالت: كان رسول الله صلّى الله عليه وسلّم، إذا أراد أن يخرج سفراً، أقرع بين نسائه فأيّتهن خرج سهمُها خرج بها رسول الله صلّى الله عليه وسلّم معه.

٢،١،١٦ قالت عائشة: فأقرع بيننا في غزاةٍ غزاها، فخرج فيها سهمي. فخرجتُ مع رسول الله صلّى الله عليه وسلّم، وذلك بعد ما أنزل الله علينا الحجاب. وأنا أُحمل في هودجي وأُنزل فيه. فسرنا حتّى إذا فرغ رسول الله صلّى الله عليه وسلّم من غزوه قفل ودنونا من المدينة، آذن ليلةً بالرحيل. فقمتُ حين آذنوا بالرحيل، فمشيتُ حتّى جاوزتُ الجيش. فلمّا قضيتُ شأني، أقبلتُ إلى رحلي. فلمستُ صدري،[١] فإذا عِقْدٌ لي من جزع ظفار قد انقطع. فرجعتُ[٢] فالتمست عِقدي، فحبسني ابتغاؤه. أقبل الرهط الّذين كانوا يرحلون بي، فحملوا الهودج فرحلوه على بعيري الّذي كنتُ أركب، وهم يحسبون أنّي فيه.

٣،١،١٦ قالت:[٣] وكانت النساء إذ ذاك خِفافاً، لم يهبلن ولم يغشهنّ اللحمُ. إنّما يأكلن العُلقة من الطعام. فلم يستنكر القوم ثقل الهودج حين رحلوا ورفعوه. وكنتُ جاريةً

---

١ [فلمست صدري] ح؛ ط: فلمست نحري؛ ساقطة من م. ٢ [فرجعت] ح، ط؛ ساقطة من م. ٣ ح، ط؛ م: قال.

The Story of the Slander

'Abd al-Razzāq, on the authority of Ma'mar, on the authority of al-Zuhrī, who said: Sa'īd ibn al-Musayyab, 'Urwah ibn al-Zubayr, 'Alqamah ibn Waqqāṣ, and 'Ubayd Allāh ibn 'Abd Allāh ibn 'Utbah ibn Mas'ūd all related to me the story of 'Ā'ishah, the Prophet's wife, when the slanderers spoke against her as they did. Al-Zuhrī said: 16.1

God proved her innocence. Each of my sources related to me a portion of her story, some of them being more knowledgeable of her story than the others or more reliable narrators. I committed what I heard of her story from them to memory, and each version confirmed the veracity of the others. They recalled that 'Ā'ishah, the Prophet's wife, said: Whenever the Messenger of God wished to depart on a journey, he would cast lots between his wives. When a certain wife's arrow turned up, he would take her with him. 16.1.1

'Ā'ishah said: He cast lots between us for one of his expeditions. My arrow turned up, so I set out with the Messenger of God. Now that was after God had revealed his decree for us women concerning the veil,[192] so I was lifted up in my howdah and placed atop a camel. We marched out, and eventually the Messenger of God completed his expedition. Returning home, once we had come close to Medina he announced that we would travel through the night. When they made the announcement, I got up and walked away from the army. After I had attended to my personal needs, I headed back to my camel, but when I felt my chest, I realized my necklace—the one fashioned from the beads of Ẓafār—had fallen from my neck. I returned and searched for my necklace, and it was the effort to track it down that delayed me. The troop that I had been with set off to continue the journey. They picked up my howdah and saddled it on the camel I had been riding, thinking I was still in it. 16.1.2

'Ā'ishah said: Women used to be slender things—they didn't grow plump, and meat never stuck to their bones. We only ate tiny morsels of food. The men didn't notice the weight of the howdah when they lifted it up and saddled it—I was only a young maiden then. They prodded the camel on and marched off with it. I found my necklace after the army had marched off, and when I arrived at their encampments, neither hide nor hair of them was to be found. 16.1.3

حديثة السن. فبعثوا الجمل وساروا به، ووجدتُ عقدي بعدما استمرّ الجيش. فجئتُ منازلهم، وليس بها داعٍ ولا مجيبٌ. فتيمّمتُ منزلي الّذي كنتُ فيه وظننتُ أنّ القوم سيفقدوني، فيرجعون إليّ. فبينا أنا جالسةٌ في منزل، غلبتني عيناي. فنمتُ حتّى أصبحتُ. وكان صفوان بن المعطّل السلميّ ثمّ الذكوانيّ، قد عرّس من وراء الجيش. فادّلج، فأصبح عندي، فرأى سواد إنسان نائم. فأتاني، فعرفني حين رآني. وقد كان رآني قبل أن يُضرب عليّ الحجاب. فما استيقظتُ إلّا باسترجاعه حين عرفني، فخمّرتُ وجهي بجلبابي. ووالله ما كلّمني كلمةً ولا سمعتُ منه كلمةً[١] غير استرجاعه حتّى أناخ راحلته. فوطئ على يدها، فركبتُها، فانطلق يقود بي الراحلة حتّى أتينا الجيش بعدما نزلوا موغرين في نحر الظهيرة.

٤،١،١٦ فهلك من هلك في شأني، وكان الّذي تولّى كِبْره عبد الله بن أبيّ بن سلول. فقدمت المدينة، فاشتكيت حين قدمتها شهراً، والناس يخوضون في قول أهل الإفك. ولا أشعر بشيءٍ من ذلك وهو يريبني في وجعي أنّي لا أعرف من رسول الله صلّى الله عليه وسلّم اللطف الّذي كنتُ أرى من حين أشتكي. إنّما يدخل رسول الله صلّى الله عليه وسلّم، فيسلّم ويقول: كيف تيكم؟

فذلك يُريبني ولا أشعر بالشرّ[٢] حتّى خرجت بعدما نَقِهْتُ. وخرجتْ معي أمّ مسطح قبل المناصع، وهو متبرّزنا، وكنّا لا نخرج إلّا ليلاً إلى ليلٍ، وذلك قبل أن نتّخذ الكُنُف قريباً من بيوتنا، وأمرنا أمر العرب الأوّل في التنزّه، وكنّا نتأذى بالكنف أن نتّخذها عند بيوتنا.[٣] فانطلقتُ أنا وأمّ مسطح، وهي ابنة أبي رهم بن عبد المطّلب بن عبد مناف، وأمّها ريطة بنت صخر بن عامر، خالةُ أبي بكر الصدّيق، وابنهما مسطح بن أثاثة ابن عبّاد بن المطّلب بن عبد مناف. فأقبلتُ أنا وابنة أبي رهم قِبَل بيتي حين فرغنا من شأننا، فعثرتْ أمّ مسطح في مِرطها، قالت: تَعِس مسطح!

---

١ [ولا سمعت منه كلمة] ح؛ ساقطة من م، ط. ٢ [بالشر] ح، ط؛ ساقطة من م. ٣ [وأمرنا أمر العرب الأول في التنزه، وكنا نتأذى بالكنف أن نتخذ عند بيوتنا] ح، ط؛ ساقطة من م.

I figured that the men would notice I was lost and return for me. While I was at the campsite, my eyes grew heavy, and I fell asleep. I did not wake until the following morning. Ṣafwān ibn al-Muʿaṭṭal al-Sulamī al-Dhakwānī had passed the night behind the army and set out again before daybreak. He arrived near to where I lay in the early morning, first seeing the dark outlines of a person asleep. When he came closer, he recognized me the moment he saw me, for he had seen me before I had been made to don the veil. I only awoke when I heard him exclaim, "We are God's, and to Him we shall return!" once he recognized me. I then veiled my face with my outer garment. I swear by God, he neither spoke to me nor did I hear him say a single word except, "We are God's, and to him we shall return!" Eventually he made his camel kneel down onto its fore-legs, and I mounted her. He then departed, leading his riding camel with me on it until we reached the army after they had made camp to seek respite from the heat of the midday sun.

It was then that those who brought about their own damnation damned themselves on my account. The man who bore responsibility for the most egregious misdeed was ʿAbd Allāh ibn Ubayy ibn Salūl. I arrived in Medina, and once I arrived, I fell ill for a whole month, and all the while the people were drowning in the gossip of my accusers. Yet I perceived none of it, even though the Prophet did give me reason to be suspicious during my illness. The Messenger of God had always treated me graciously when I had taken ill before, but this time the Messenger of God would merely visit to bid me greetings of peace and ask, "How are you feeling?" **16.1.4**

That gave me reason to be suspicious, but still I perceived no evil until I left the house after I had recovered. I went out with Umm Misṭaḥ toward al-Manāṣiʿ, the place where we women relieved ourselves. We only used to go out there in the evenings, and that was before we started using enclosures closer to our homes. Our custom used to be the same as the Bedouin of old, going out somewhere alone, and it made us cross when we had to start using the enclosures near our houses. So I went out with Umm Misṭaḥ. She was the daughter of Abū Ruhm ibn ʿAbd al-Muṭṭalib ibn ʿAbd Manāf; and her mother was Rīṭah bint Ṣakhr ibn ʿĀmir, Abū Bakr al-Ṣiddīq's maternal aunt; and her son was Misṭaḥ ibn Uthāthah ibn ʿAbbād ibn al-Muṭṭalib ibn ʿAbd Manāf. Abū Ruhm's daughter and I turned back home once we had relieved ourselves, and Umm Misṭaḥ tripped over her robe. "Damn you, Misṭaḥ!" she yelled.

فقلت لها: بئس ما قلتِ! أتسُبّين رجلاً شهد بدراً؟

قالت: أي هنتاه! أوَلم تسمعي ما قال؟

قالت: قلتُ: وماذا قال؟

٥،١،١٦ قالت: فأخبرتني بقولِ أهل الإفك، فازددتُ مرضاً إلى مرضي. فلمّا رجعتُ إلى بيتي، دخل عليّ رسولُ الله صلّى الله عليه وسلّم، فسلَّم. ثمّ قال: كيف تيكم؟ قلتُ: أتأذنُ لي أن آتي أبوَيّ؟

قالت: وأنا حينئذ أريد أن[١] أتيقّن الخبر من قِبَلهما. فأذن لي رسول الله صلّى الله عليه وسلّم فجئتُ أبوَيّ. فقلتُ لأمّي: يا أمّه، ما يتحدّث الناس؟

فقالت: أي بنيّة، هوّني عليك! فوالله لقلّما كانت امرأة قطّ وضيئةً عند رجل يُحبّها ولها ضرائر إلّا أكثرن عليها.

قلتُ: سبحان الله! أوَقد تحدّث الناس بهذا؟

قالت: نعم.

قالت: فبكيتُ تلك الليلة لا يرقأ لي دمع، ولا أكتحل بنوم. ثمّ أصبحتُ أبكي. ودعا رسول الله صلّى الله عليه وسلم عليّ بن أبي طالب وأسامة بن زيد حين استلبث الوحي، يستشيرهما في فراق أهله.

٦،١،١٦ قالت: فأمّا أسامة، فأشار على رسول الله صلّى الله عليه وسلّم بالّذي يعلم من براءة أهله وبالّذي يعلم في نفسه من الوُدّ لهم. فقال: يا رسول الله، هم أهلُك ولا نعلم إلّا خيراً. وأمّا عليّ، فقال: لم يضيّق الله عليك، والنساءُ سواها كثير. وإن تسأل الجارية، تَصْدُقك. قالت: فدعا رسول الله صلّى الله عليه وسلّم بريرة، فقال: أيْ بريرة، هل رأيتِ من شيء يُريبكِ من أمر عائشة؟ فقالت له بريرة: والّذي بعثك بالحقّ، إن رأيتُ عليها أمراً قطّ أغمصه عليها أكثر من أنها جارية حديثة السنّ. تنام عن عجين أهلها، فتأتي الداجن، فتأكله.

١ [أن] ح، ط؛ ساقطة من م.

"That's a horrible thing to say!" I said. "Will you curse a man who witnessed Badr?"

"Silly girl!" she replied. "Haven't you heard what he's said?"

"And what has he said?" I asked.

She then related to me what my slanderers were saying. Thus I added malady to my illness.[193] When I had returned to my home, I went to see the Messenger of God. "How are you feeling?" he asked. I said, "Will you permit me to go to my parents' house?" 16.1.5

At that moment, I wanted to confirm the report with them. The Messenger of God gave me permission, and I went to my parents. I said to my mother, "Dear mother, what do the people say?"

"My dear daughter," she replied, "don't you worry. By God, it seldom happens that a woman so bedazzles a man in love with her that his other wives do not constantly find fault with her."

"Glory be to God," I exclaimed, "are the people really saying such things!"

"Yes," she answered.

I cried that night until I had no more tears, and sleep's antimony did not once touch my eyes. I spent the next morning weeping, too. The Messenger of God then summoned ʿAlī ibn Abī Ṭālib and Usāmah ibn Zayd, for revelations had ceased coming to him for some time, to seek counsel from them as to whether he should divorce his wife.[194]

As for Usāmah, he knew the Prophet's household to be innocent of the charges and also that the Prophet loved his household with all his heart, so he advised God's Messenger accordingly, saying, "O Mesenger of God, they are your family, and we know nothing but good of them." As for ʿAlī, he said, "God does not wish for you to be distraught. There are many women besides her. If you ask her maiden, she will speak to you truthfully." The Messenger of God then summoned Barīrah and asked, "Barīrah, have you ever seen anything that would cause you to suspect ill of ʿĀʾishah?" Barīrah addressed him, "By the Lord who called you to proclaim the Truth, I've never witnessed any ill behavior that would cast any doubt upon her other than the fact that she is a young maiden who will nod off to sleep next to the family's dough, leaving the goats and sheep to eat it!" 16.1.6

The Messenger of God stood to address the people, seeking to justify taking action against ʿAbd Allāh ibn Ubayy ibn Salūl. From the pulpit he said, "O assembly of Muslims! Who will give me cause to act against this man who 16.1.7

قالت: فقام رسول الله صلّى الله عليه وسلّم، فاستعذر من عبد الله بن أبيّ بن ٧،١،١٦
سلول. قالت: فقال رسول الله صلّى الله عليه وسلّم، وهو على المنبر: يا معشر المسلمين! من يعذرني من رجل؟ قد بلغ أذاه في أهل بيتي. فوالله ما علمتُ على أهل بيتي إلّا خيرًا. ولقد ذكروا رجلًا ما علمتُ عليه إلّا خيرًا. وما كان يدخل على أهلي إلّا معي.

فقام سعد بن معاذ الأنصاريّ، فقال: أعذرك منه، يا رسول الله. إن كان من الأوس ضربنا عنقه، وإن كان من إخواننا من الخزرج أمرتنا ففعلنا أمرك.

قال: فقام سعد بن عبادة، وهو سيّد الخزرج وكان رجلًا صالحًا، ولكنّه حملته الجاهليّة. فقال لسعد بن معاذ: لعَمر الله! لا تقتلنه ولا تقدر على قتله!

فقام أسيد بن حضير، وهو ابن عمّ سعد بن معاذ، فقال لسعد بن عبادة: كذبتَ لعمر الله! لنقتلنّه! فإنّك منافق تجادل عن المنافقين!

قالت: فثار الحيّان الأوس والخزرج حتّى همّوا أن يقتتلوا. ورسول الله صلّى الله عليه وسلّم قائمٌ على المنبر، فلم يزل يخفّضهم حتّى سكتوا. وسكت النبيّ.

قالت: ومكثتُ يومي ذلك، لا يرقأ لي دمعٌ ولا أكتحل بنومٍ. وأبوايّ يظنّان أنّ ٨،١،١٦
البكاء فالق كبدي. قالت: فبينا هما جالسان عندي، وأنا أبكي، استأذنت عليّ امرأةٌ. فأذنتُ لها، فجلست تبكي معي. فبينما نحن على ذلك، دخل علينا رسول الله صلّى الله عليه وسلّم، ثمّ جلس. قالت: ولم يجلس عندي منذ ما قيل، وقد لبث شهرًا لا يُوحَى إليه. قالت: فتشهّد رسول الله صلّى الله عليه وسلّم حين جلس. ثمّ قال: أمّا بعد، يا عائشة، فإنّه قد بلغني عنكِ كذا وكذا. فإن كنتِ بريئةً، فسيبرّئكِ اللهُ. وإن كنتِ ألممتِ بذنبٍ، فاستغفري الله وتوبي إليه. فإنّ العبد، إذا اعترف بذنبه ثمّ تاب، تاب الله عليه. قالت: فلمّا قضى رسولُ الله صلّى الله عليه وسلّم مقالته، قلص دمعي حتّى ما أحسّ منه قطرةً. فقلتُ لأبي: أجبْ عنّي رسول الله صلّى الله عليه وسلّم فيما قال. فقال: والله ما أدري ما أقول لرسول الله صلّى الله عليه وسلّم. فقلتُ لأمّي: أجيبي

has brought such pain to my household? By God, I know of nothing but good from my household. They have mentioned a man of whom I also know of nothing but good. Never has he sought to enter the company of my household save by my side."

Saʿd ibn Muʿādh the Ally then stood up and said, "I will take action against him on your behalf, O Messenger of God! If the man be of the Aws clan, then we will strike off his head! And if he be from our brethren of the Khazraj clan, if you so command us, it will be done."

Then Saʿd ibn ʿUbādah stood up. Now, he was the chieftain of the Khazraj and otherwise an upright man, but the Era of Ignorance still had a hold on him. He said to Saʿd ibn Muʿādh, "By the Everlasting God! You will never slay him, and nor could you even if you tried!"

Usayd ibn Ḥudayr, Saʿd ibn Muʿādh's cousin, then stood and addressed Saʿd ibn ʿUbādah, "By the Everlasting God, you lie! We will indeed slay him! You are but a hypocrite wrangling over hypocrites!"

The two clans, the Aws and the Khazraj, rose up in a furor and were on the verge of coming to blows. The Messenger of God remained at the pulpit working to settle them down until they became calm. The Prophet himself remained calm.

That day I stayed home. My tears flowed until they ran dry, and sleep's anti- 16.1.8
mony did not once touch my eyes. My parents feared that the weeping would rip my insides apart. While they sat with me as I was crying, a woman sought permission to visit me. I bade her enter, and she sat down next to me crying. While we were in this state, the Messenger of God came to us and sat with us. Now he had not sat with me since the affair began, for a month had passed without a revelation coming. The Messenger of God confessed the oneness of God when he sat, and then said, "As for the matter before us, ʿĀʾishah, word about you concerning a certain matter has reached me. If you are blameless, God will prove you blameless, but if you are guilty of sin, seek God's forgiveness and repent before him. Truly, if a servant recognizes his sin and repents, God shall accept his repentance." When the Messenger of God finished speaking, my tears subsided, and eventually I couldn't even tell I had been crying. I then asked my father, "Intercede for me with God's Messenger on the matter of which he spoke," but he answered, "By God, I know not what I would say to the Messenger of God." So I asked my mother, "Intercede for me with the God's Messenger!" But she too answered, "By God, I know not what I would

عنِّي رسول الله صلّى الله عليه وسلّم. قالت: والله ما أدري ما أقول لرسول الله صلّى الله عليه وسلّم. فقلتُ، وأنا جارية حديثة السنّ لا أقرأ من القرآن كثيرًا: إني والله لقد عرفتُ أنّكم قد سمعتم بهذا الأمر حتّى استقرّ في أنفسكم وصدّقتم به. فَلَئِن قلتُ لكم: إنّي بريئةٌ، واللهُ يعلم براءتي. لا تصدّقوني بذلك، ولئن اعترفت لكم بذنب، واللهُ يعلم أنّي بريئةٌ لتصدّقوني. وإنّي واللهِ ما أجد لي ولكم مثلاً إلّا كما قال أبو يوسف ﴿فَصَبْرٌ جَمِيلٌ وَٱللَّهُ ٱلْمُسْتَعَانُ عَلَىٰ مَا تَصِفُونَ﴾.

قالت: ثمّ تحوّلتُ فاضطجعت على فراشي. وأنا واللهِ حينئذ أعلم أنّي بريئةٌ وأنّ الله ٩،١،١٦
مبرّئي ببراءتي. ولكن والله ماكنتُ أظنّ أن يُنزل في شأني وحيٌ يُتلى. ولَشأني كان
أحقر في نفسي من أن يتكلّمَ الله فيّ بأمر يُتلى، ولكن كنتُ أرجو أن يرى رسول الله
صلّى الله عليه وسلّم في المنام رؤيا يبرّئني الله بها. قالت: فوالله ما رام رسول الله
صلّى الله عليه وسلّم مجلسه ولا خرج من أهل البيت أحدٌ حتّى أنزل الله على نبيّه
صلّى الله عليه وسلّم. فأخذه ماكان يأخذه من البُرحاء عند الوحي حتّى أنّه ليتحدّر
منه مثل الجمان من العرق[1] في اليوم الشات[2] من ثقل الوحي الّذي أنزل عليه. قالت:
فلمّا سُرّيَ عن رسول الله صلّى الله عليه وسلّم، وهو يضحك وكان أوّل كلمةٍ تكلّمَ
بها أن قال: أبشري، يا عائشة. أما والله قد أبرأك الله. فقالت لي أمّي: قومي إليه.
فقلتُ: لا، والله لا أقوم إليه ولا أحمدُ إلّا الله. هو الّذي أنزل براءتي.

قالت: فأنزل الله تبارك وتعالى ﴿إِنَّ ٱلَّذِينَ جَآءُو بِٱلْإِفْكِ عُصْبَةٌ مِّنكُمْ﴾ عشر آيات. فأنزل الله هذه الآيات في براءتي.

قالت: فقال أبو بكر، وكان يُنفق على مسطح لقرابته منه وفقره: والله لا أنفق عليه شيئًا أبدًا بعد الّذي قال بعائشة. فأنزل الله ﴿وَلَا يَأْتَلِ أُوْلُواْ ٱلْفَضْلِ مِنكُمْ وَٱلسَّعَةِ﴾ إلى قوله ﴿أَلَا تُحِبُّونَ أَن يَغْفِرَ ٱللَّهُ لَكُمْ﴾. فقال أبو بكر: والله إنّي لأحبُّ أن يغفر الله لي. فرجع إلى مسطح النفقة الّتي كان ينفق عليه. وقال: والله لا أنزعها أبدًا.

١ [من العرق] ح؛ ساقطة من مم، ط. ٢ مم؛ ح: اليوم الشاتي؛ اليوم لشاتي.

say to the Messenger of God." Now, I was just a young maiden—I could not yet recite much of the Qur'an—but I said, "By God, I know you have heard so much about this affair that now it has taken hold of your hearts and you believe it to be true! Indeed, even if I were to say to all of you, 'I am blameless, and God knows my innocence,' you would still not believe my words. But if I were to confess my sin before you all—though God knows I am blameless—you would surely believe my words. Truly, I swear by God, I can find no adage for you or me more suitable than the words of Joseph's father: «it is best to be patient: from God alone I seek help to bear what you are saying»."[195]

Then I turned and left to lie down on my bed. I swear by God that, at that **16.1.9**
moment, I knew I was blameless and that God would vindicate my innocence, yet I did not imagine that a revelation concerning my problems would descend and come to be recited. For in my heart I loathed the thought that God might address any matter concerning me in a revelation to be recited aloud. Rather, I hoped that the Messenger of God would have a vision in his sleep, by which God would vindicate me. By God, the Messenger of God refused to receive anyone, and not one person from his household went out, until God granted his Prophet a revelation. Suddenly the tremulous convulsions that took hold of him at the moment of revelation seized him, and soon beads of sweat began to run down him like pearls, even though it was a winter's day—because of the gravity of the revelation that had descended. When the convulsions had passed, he began laughing, and the first word he spoke was, "Good tidings, 'Ā'ishah! Indeed, by God, God has vindicated you!" My mother then said to me, "Go to him!" "No, by God," I said, "I will not, nor shall I praise any but God, for He is the one who revealed my innocence."

God, Blessed and Exalted be He, revealed, «It was a group from among you who concocted the slander» and ten more verses. [196] God revealed these verses about my innocence.

Abū Bakr, who used to provide Misṭaḥ with money because of their kinship and Misṭāḥ's poverty, said, "By God, never again shall I give him money after saying what he did about 'Ā'ishah!" But God revealed,

> «Those who have been graced with bounty and plenty should not swear that they will no longer give to kinsmen, the poor, those who emigrated in God's way: let them pardon and forgive. Do you not wish that God will forgive you?»[197]

قالت عائشة: وكان رسول الله صلّى الله عليه وسلّم سأل زينب ابنة جحش زوج ١٠،١،١٦
النبيّ صلّى الله عليه وسلّم عن أمري: ما علمت؟ أو، ما رأيت؟
فقالت: يا رسول الله أحمي سمعي وبصري. والله ما علمتُ إلّا خيرًا.
قالت عائشة: وهي الّتي كانت تُساميني من أزواج النبيّ صلّى الله عليه وسلّم.
فعصمها الله بالورع. وطفقتْ أختُها حمنة ابنة جحش تحارب لها، فهلكت فيمن هلك.
قال الزهريّ: فهذا ما انتهى إلينا من أمر هؤلاء الرهط.

٢،١٦

عبد الرزّاق عن ابنِ أبي يحيى عن عبدِ الله بن أبي بكر عن عمرة عن عائشة، قالت:

لمّا أنزل الله براءتها حدّ النبيّ صلّى الله عليه وسلّم هؤلاء النفر الّذين قالوا فيها ما قالوا.

٣،١٦

عبد الرزّاق عن معمر عن الزهريّ:

أنّ رسول الله صلّى الله عليه وسلّم حدّهم.

Abū Bakr then said, "By God, I indeed wish that God will forgive me," and he resumed providing Misṭaḥ with the money he used to provide, saying, "By God, never again will I withhold it."

ʿĀʾishah continued: The Prophet had asked Zaynab, the daughter of Jaḥsh and the Prophet's wife, about my situation: "What do you know?"—or, "What do you think?" 16.1.10

"I protect my ears and eyes from such things," Zaynab answered. "I swear by God, I know nothing but good of her."

ʿĀʾishah added: Zaynab was my biggest rival among the Prophet's wives, and God sealed her heart with piety. Her sister, Ḥamnah bint Jaḥsh, sought to turn her against me, but Ḥamnah only damned herself along with the others.

Al-Zuhrī said: This is all that has come down to us about those people.

ʿAbd al-Razzāq, on the authority of Ibn Abī Yaḥyā, on the authority of ʿAbd Allāh ibn Abī Bakr, on the authority of ʿAmrah, on the authority of ʿĀʾishah, who said: 16.2

When God vindicated her innocence with His revelation, the Prophet punished those who said about her what they said according to God's law.[198]

ʿAbd al-Razzāq, on the authority of Maʿmar, on the authority of al-Zuhrī: 16.3

The Messenger of God punished them according to God's law.

حَدِيثُ أَصْحَابِ الأُخْدُودِ

١،١٧ عبد الرزّاق عن معمر عن ثابت البنانيّ عن عبد الرحمن بن أبي ليلى عن صهيب، قال:

٢،١٧ كان رسول الله صلّى الله عليه وسلّم، إذا صلّى العصر، هَمَسَ. والهمسُ في قول بعضهم: يحرّك شفتيه كأنّه يتكلّم بشيء. فقيل له: يا نبيّ الله، إنّك إذا صلّيتَ العصر همستَ. فقال: إنّ نبيّاً من الأنبياء كان أُعجب بأمّته، فقال: من يقوم لهؤلاء؟ فأوحى إليه أن خيّرهم بين أن أنتقم منهم أو أسلِّط عليهم عدوّهم. فاختاروا النقمة، فسلَّط الله عليهم الموت. فمات منهم في يوم سبعون ألفاً.

٣،١٧ قال: وكان إذا حدّث بهذا الحديث حدّث بهذا الحديث الآخر، قال: وكان مَلِكٌ من الملوك، وكان لذلك الملك كاهنٌ يتكهّن له. فقال ذلك الكاهن: انظروا لي غلاماً فَطِناً— أو قال: لَقِناً— أعلِّمه علمي هذا، فإنّي أخاف أن أموت فينقطع منكم هذا العلم ولا يكون فيكم من يعلمه. قال: فنظروا له غلاماً على ما وصف، فأمروه أن يحضر ذلك الكاهن وأن يختلف إليه. فجعل يختلف إليه.[1]

٤،١٧ قال: وكان على طريق الغلام راهبٌ في صومعة. قال معمر: وأحسب أنّ أصحاب الصوامع يومئذ مسلمين. قال: فجعل الغلام يسأل ذلك الراهب كلّما مرّ به. فلم يزل حتّى أخبره، قال: إنّما أعبد الله، وجعل الغلام يمكث عند الراهب ويُبْطِئ عن الكاهن. قال: فأرسل الكاهن إلى أهل الغلام إنّه لا يكاد يحضرني. فأخبر الغلامُ الراهبَ بذلك، فقال له الراهب: إذا قال الكاهن: أين كنتَ؟ فقُل: كنتُ عند أهلي. وإذا قال لك أهلُك: أين كنتَ؟ فقُل: كنتُ عند الكاهن.

١ [فجعل يختلف إليه] تع؛ ساقطة من م.

The Story of the People of the Pit[199]

'Abd al-Razzāq, on the authority of Ma'mar, on the authority of Thābit al-Bunānī, on the authority of 'Abd al-Raḥmān ibn Abī Laylā, on the authority of Ṣuhayb, who said: 17.1

When the Messenger of God prayed the afternoon prayer, he used to murmur—"murmuring" means, one of them said, that he moved his lips as though he were saying something—so someone said to him, "O Prophet of God, whenever you pray the afternoon prayer, you murmur!" He replied, "One of the many prophets was more astounded by his community's conduct than the rest. He asked God, 'Who shall deal with these people?' And God revealed to him that the prophet should give the people a choice: either God could take vengeance upon them, or their enemies could be appointed to rule over them. They chose God's vengeance, and thus He appointed death to rule over them. Seven thousand of them died on a single day." 17.2

Whenever the Prophet would relate this tradition, he would also relate another tradition, saying: 17.3

Once there was a king, and that king possessed a diviner who practiced his craft in the king's service. One day that diviner said, "Seek out a clever"—or he said, "sharp"—"young boy that I might instruct him in this craft of mine. I fear that I shall soon die and that this knowledge will be cut off from you, leaving you with no one who knows it." They searched and found a young boy for him who matched his description, and they commanded the boy to meet that diviner and visit him frequently. Thus the boy began frequenting the diviner's residence.

Now there was a monk who lived in a hermitage that lay along the young man's path to the diviner—Ma'mar said: I believe that the inhabitants of the hermitage in those days were Muslims[200]—and the young man began to ask that monk questions whenever he passed by him. It was not long before he told the boy, "I worship God alone," and the young man began to stay with the monk and come late for his visits to the diviner. The diviner wrote a message to the young man's family, saying, "He hardly comes to see me!" The young man informed the monk about this, so the monk told him, "If the diviner says, 'Where have 17.4

قال: فبينا الغلام على ذلك، إذ مرّ بجماعةٍ من الناس كبيرةٍ قد حبستهم دابّةٌ. قال ٥،١٧
بعضهم: إنّ تلك الدابّة كان الأسد. وأخذ الغلام حجرًا، قال: اللّهمّ، إن كان ما يقول
الراهب حقًّا، فأسألك أن أقتل هذه الدابّة. وإن كان ما يقول الكاهن حقًّا، فأسألك
أن لا أقتلها. قال: ثمّ رماها، فقتل الدابّة.

فقال الناس: من قتلها؟

فقالوا: الغلام.

ففزع إليه الناس وقالوا: قد علم هذا الغلام علمًا لم يعلمه أحدٌ.

فسمع به أعمى، فجاءه، فقال له: إنْ أنت رددتَ عليّ بصري، فلك كذا وكذا.

فقال الغلام: لا أريد منك هذا، ولكن إنْ رُدَّ إليك بصرُك، أتؤمن بالّذي ردّه عليك؟

قال: نعم.

قال: فدعا الله، فردّ عليه بصرَه. قال: فآمن الأعمى.

فبلغ ذلك الملك أمرُهم، فبعث إليهم، فأُتِي بهم، فقال: لأقتلنّ كلّ واحد منكم قتلةً ٦،١٧
لا أقتلها صاحبه. قال: فأمر بالراهب وبالرجل الّذي كان أعمى، فوضع المنشار على
مفرق أحدهما، فقُتِل وقُتِل الآخر بقتلة أخرى. ثمّ أمر بالغلام، فقال: انطلقوا به
إلى جبل كذا وكذا، فألقوه من رأسه. فلمّا انطلقوا به إلى ذلك المكان الّذي أرادوا،
جعلوا يتهافتون من ذلك الجبل ويتردّون منه حتّى لم يبقَ إلّا الغلام. فرجع، فأمر به
الملكُ، فقال: انطلقوا به إلى البحر، فألقوه فيه. فانطُلِقَ به إلى البحر، فغرّق اللهُ من كان
معه وأنجاه اللهُ. فقال الغلام: إنّك لن تقتلني حتّى تصلُبَني وترميني وتقول إذا رَمَيْتَني:
باسم ربّ الغلام. أو قال: بسم الله ربّ الغلام. فأمر به، فصُلب. ثمّ رماه وقال:

you been?' then say, 'I've been with my family'; and when your family says to you, 'Where have you been?' then say, 'I've been with the diviner.'"

Meanwhile, the young man passed by a large gathering of people who were 17.5
trapped by a beast—one of the transmitters of the story said: this beast was a lion—so the young man grabbed several rocks and said, "O Lord, if what the monk says is true, then I beseech You to aid me to kill this beast; but if what the diviner says is true, then I beseech You to prevent me from killing it." Then he cast the stone and killed the beast.

"Who killed it?" someone asked.

"The young man," the others answered.

The people then rushed to him for protection and said, "This young man has knowledge known by no other!"

A blind man heard about him, so he came to the young man and said to him, "If you can restore my sight, then I shall give you such and such."

"I don't want such things from you," replied the young man. "Rather, if your sight is restored, will you have faith in the One who restored it to you?"

"Yes," he answered.

The young man then prayed to God, and He restored the man's sight. The blind man then became a believer.

When word of their affair reached the king, he sent for them, and they were 17.6
brought before him. The king declared, "Verily, I will cause each of you to die a different death than the one before him!" Then he ordered the monk and the man who had been blind to be brought before him. Placing a saw on the waist of one of the two men, he executed him, and the other he killed in a different manner. Then he issued his sentence against the young man, and when he was brought forward, he said, "Take him to such-and-such mountain and cast him from its summit!" When they had taken him to the intended place, they began to stumble over one another atop the mountain and fall from it until none remained but the young man. When he returned, the king sentenced him again, saying, "Take him and cast him into the sea!" Yet, once they had taken him to the sea, God drowned all those who were with him, but saved the young man. The young man declared, "Truly, you will never kill me unless you crucify me and shoot me through with arrows; and when I have been shot through with arrows, you must say, 'In the name of the young man's Lord'"—or, he said, "In the name of God, the young man's Lord." The king gave the sentence against him, and he was crucified. Later they shot him with arrows

بسم الله ربّ الغلام. قال: فرفع الغلام يده إلى صدغه. ثمّ مات، فقال الناس: لقد علم هذا الغلام علماً ما علمه أحدٌ، فإنّا نؤمن بربّ هذا الغلام.

٧،١٧ قال: فقيل للملك: أجزعتَ أن خالفك ثلاثة؟ فهذا العالم كلّهم قد خالفوك. قال: فخدّ الأخدود. ثمّ ألقى فيه الحطب والنار. ثمّ جمع الناس، فقال: من رجع إلى دينه تركناه، ومن لم يرجع ألقيناه في النار. فجعل يلقيهم في تلك الأخدود، قال: فذلك قول الله ﴿قُتِلَ أَصْحَٰبُ ٱلْأُخْدُودِ ٱلنَّارِ ذَاتِ ٱلْوَقُودِ﴾ حتّى بلغ ﴿ٱلْعَزِيزِ ٱلْحَمِيدِ﴾. قال: فأمّا الغلام، فإنّه دُفِنَ. قال: فيُذكر أنّه أُخرِجَ في زمن عمر بن الخطّاب، رحمه الله، وإصبعه على صدغه كما كان وضعها.[1]

قال عبد الرزّاق: والأخدود بنجران.

---

١ مم؛ تع: كما كان وضعها حين قتل.

and said, "In the name of God, the young man's Lord." The young man lifted his hand to his temple and then died. The people then cried out, "Verily, this young man knew knowledge known by none other, and we have faith in this young man's Lord."

Then someone said to the king, "Are you not worried that he shall defy you 17.7
a third time? Now the entire world defies you!" The king decreed, "Dig the pit, and then cast the wood and fire therein." The king assembled the people and said, "Whoever returns to his religion will be spared, and whoever does not return we will cast into the fire." Thus he began casting them into the pits. Concerning this, God decreed:

> «Accursed were the makers of the pit, The makers of the fuel-stoked fire! They sat down there to witness what they wrought against the believers. They exacted vengeance against them for naught but their faith in God, the Mighty, the Praiseworthy.»[201]

As for the young man, he was buried. It is said that he was exhumed from his grave in time of ʿUmar ibn al-Khaṭṭāb, and his finger was still on his temple just as he had placed it.

ʿAbd al-Razzāq said: "The Pit" is in Najrān.[202]

حَدِيثُ أَصْحَابِ الكُهْفِ

عبد الرزّاق عن معمر، قال: أخبرني إسماعيل بن شروس عن وهب بن منبّه، قال: ١،١٨

جاء رجلٌ من حواريّ عيسى بن مريم إلى مدينة أصحاب الكهف. فأراد أن ٢،١٨
يدخلها. فقيل: إنّ على بابها صنماً لا يدخلها أحدٌ إلّا سجد له. فكره أن يدخله، فأتى حمّاماً، فكان قريباً من تلك المدينة. وكان يعمل فيه، يؤاجر نفسه من صاحب الحمّام. ورأى صاحب الحمّام في حمّامه البركة والرفق.[١] وفوّض إليه وجعل يسترسل إليه. وعَلِقَه فتيةٌ من أهل المدينة، فجعل يُخبرهم عن خبر السماء والأرض وخبر الآخرة حتّى آمنوا به وصدّقوه وكانوا على مثل حاله في حسن الهيئة. وكان يشترط على صاحب الحمّام أنّ الليل لي ولا تحول بيني وبين الصلاة إذا حضرت.

وكان ذلك[٢] حتّى جاء ابن الملك بامرأة يدخل بها الحمّام. فعيّره الحواريّ، فقال: أنت ٣،١٨
ابن الملك وتدخل معك هذه الكذا وكذا؟! فاستحيى، فذهب. فرجع مرّةً أخرى، فقال له مثل قوله،[٣] فسبّه وانتهره. ولم يلتفت حتّى دخل، ودخلتْ معه المرأة. فباتا في الحمّام، فماتا فيه. فأتى الملك، فقيل: قتل ابنَك صاحبُ الحمّام![٤] فالتمس، فلم يُقْدَرْ عليه[٥] وهرب. فقال: من كان يصحبه؟ فسمّوا الفتية، فخرجوا من المدينة. فمرّوا بصاحب لهم في زرع له، وهو على مثل أمرهم. فذكروا له أنّهم التُمِسُوا، فانطلق معهم، ومعه كلب، حتّى آواهم الليل إلى كهف. فدخلوا فيه، فقالوا: نبيت هاهنا الليلة، ثمّ نُصبِح، إن شاء الله. ثمّ ترون رأيكم. قال: فضُرِب على آذانهم، فخرج الملك

---

١ مم؛ تع: في حمامه البركة ودر عليه الرزق. ٢ [وكان ذلك] تع؛ ساقطة من مم. ٣ [فقال له مثل قوله] تع؛ ساقطة من مم.
٤ [فأتى الملك فقيل قتل ابنك صاحب الحمّام] تع؛ ساقطة من مم. ٥ [عليه] تع؛ ساقطة من مم.

The Story of the Companions of the Cave[203]

ʿAbd al-Razzāq, on the authority of Maʿmar, who said: Ismāʿīl ibn Sharūs related to me on the authority of Wahb ibn Munabbih, who said: **18.1**

One of the Apostles of Jesus, the son of Mary, came to the city of the Companions of the Cave. He desired to enter the city, but was told that an idol stood at its gate and that none could enter without prostrating before it. Wishing, therefore, not to enter the city gate, he traveled to a bathhouse nearby. He worked there and earned his living from the owner of the bathhouse. When the owner of the bathhouse saw the blessing and profit in his bathhouse, he handed its management over to the Apostle and entrusted its affairs to him. A number of the youths had become devoted to the Apostle, and he began teaching them about all that the heavens and the earth contained and about the world to come. With time, they came to have faith and believed his message so that, like the Apostle, they became beautiful to behold. The Apostle would also stipulate to the owner of the bathhouse, "The evening belongs to me, so do not come between me and my prayers when the time for prayer approaches." **18.2**

Things continued thus until the prince brought a woman to take with him inside the bathhouse. The Apostle rebuked him, saying, "You are the king's son, and and you dare take this sort of girl inside with you?" The two were ashamed, and the prince went on his way. Then the prince returned another time, but even though the Apostle spoke to him as before, cursing him and trying to chase him off, the prince paid no heed and entered the bathhouse, and the woman entered with him. They spent the night in the bathhouse and died there. The king came and someone said, "The owner of the bathhouse has killed your son!" They searched but could not find him, for he had fled. The king asked, "Who were his companions?" and they named the youths. Now, the youths had left the city and come across one of their companions at a field he owned, and he was a man of faith like them. They told him that they were being pursued by the king, so he set out with them along with his dog, and eventually they took shelter in a cave for the evening. They entered the cave and said, "We'll pass the night until morning comes, God willing. Then we'll **18.3**

بأصحابه يتّبعونهم حتّى وجدهم. فدخلوا الكهف. فكلّما أراد الرجل منهم أن يدخل أرعِب، فلم يُطق أحدٌ أن يدخل.

فقال له قائلٌ: ألستُ قلتُ: لو كنت قدرت عليهم، قتلتهم؟

قال: بلى.

قال: فابنِ عليهم باباً للكهف، ودَعْهم يموتوا عطاشاً وجُوعاً.

ففعل، ثمّ غبروا زماناً.

٤،١٨ ثمّ إنّ راعي غنمٍ أدركه المطر عند الكهف، فقال: لو فتحت هذا الكهف وأدخلتُ غنمي من المطر، فلم يزل يعالجه حتّى فتح لغنمه. فأدخلها فيه، وردّ الله أرواحهم في أجسادهم من الغد حين أصبحوا، فبعثوا أحدهم بورق ليشتري لهم طعاماً. فلمّا أتى باب مدينتهم، جعل لا يُري أحداً من ورقه شيئاً إلّا استنكرها[١] حتّى جاء رجلاً فقال: بِعْني بهذه الدراهم طعاماً.

قال: ومن أين هذه الدراهم؟

قال: خرجتُ أنا وأصحابٌ لي أمس فآوانا الليل. ثمّ أصبحنا فأرسلوني.

فقال: هذه الدراهم كانت على عهد مُلك فلان، فأنى لك هذه الدراهم؟

فرفعه إلى الملك، وكان رجلاً صالحاً، فقال: من أين لك هذه الورق؟

قال: خرجتُ أنا وأصحاب لي أمس حتّى أدركنا الليل في كهف كذا وكذا. ثمّ[٢] أمرني أصحابي أن أشتري لهم طعاماً.

قال: وأين أصحابك؟

قال: في الكهف.

فانطلق معه حتّى أتى باب الكهف، فقال: دعوني حتّى أدخل على أصحابي قبلكم. فلمّا رأوه ودنا منهم، ضُرب على أذنه وآذانهم. فأرادوا أن يدخلوا عليهم، فجعل كلّما

١ مم؛ تع: فكلما أتى باب المدينة رأى شيئًا ينكره. ٢ [ثم] تع؛ ساقطة من مم.

discuss what to do." God then caused their ears to be sealed. The king set out with his aides to pursue them, and eventually he found them. They entered the cave, but whenever one of their men wanted to go farther in he would be filled with terror, so that none could bear to enter.

Someone then said to the king, "Didn't you say, 'If I can capture them, I'll kill them'?"

"Yes," he replied.

"Then block the mouth of the cave and leave them," said the man, "and they'll die of hunger and thirst."

Thus did the king act, and the eras passed.

One day, a shepherd with his flock was caught out in the rain and came to 18.4
the cave. "If only I could open this cave and shelter my sheep from the rain!" he exclaimed. The shepherd fumbled about at the mouth of cave, and he eventually opened it up for his sheep and sheltered them in it. The next day, God restored the souls of the youths to their bodies. When they awoke that morning, they sent one of their number with some silver coins to buy some food for them. When he came to the city gate, no one to whom he offered the silver pieces would accept them, until eventually he approached a man and said, "Sell me this food for these silver pieces."

"Where did you get these silvers?" the man replied.

"My companions and I left the city only yesterday," he answered, "and found shelter for the night, and when we woke up this morning, they sent me here."

"But these silvers are from the reign of King So-and-so! How did you ever come to possess these silvers?" the man replied.

He then took the matter to the king, a righteous man, who said, "Where did you obtain these silver pieces?"

"My companions and I left the city just yesterday," he answered, "and eventually we reached such-and-such cave in the evening. After that, my companions told me to buy some food for them."

"Where are these companions of yours?" the king inquired.

"In the cave!" he answered.

So the king set out with him and eventually came to the mouth of the cave. The youth said, "Allow me to go in after my companions before you do." When his companions saw him and he had drawn near, God caused their ears to be sealed with sleep. Though the king and his men wanted to enter to see them,

دخل رجلٌ منهم رُعِبَ، فلم يقدروا أن يدخلوا عليهم. فبنوا عندهم كنيسةً وبنوا مسجدًا يصلُّون فيه.[١]

١ مم؛ تع: واتخذوها مسجدًا يصلُّون فيه.

whenever a man would enter he would be overcome with fear, so they were unable to follow after them. Thus, they built a church where they rested and built a mosque to pray there.

بُنْيانُ بَيْتِ المَقْدِسِ

عبد الرزّاق عن معمر عن قتادة في قوله ﴿وَأَلْقَيْنَا عَلَىٰ كُرْسِيِّهِۦ جَسَدًا ثُمَّ أَنَابَ﴾ قال: ١،١٩

على كرسيّه شيطانٌ أربعين ليلةً حتّى ردّ اللهُ إليه ملكه.

قال معمر:[١] ولم يُسلّط على نسائه.

قال معمر: قال قتادة: ٢،١٩

إنّ سليمان قال للشياطين: إنّي أُمرت أن أبني مسجدًا، بيت المقدس، لا أسمع ١،٢،١٩
فيه صوت منقار ولا منشار. قالت الشياطين: إنّ في البحر شيطانًا، فلعلّك إن قدرت عليه يُخبرك بذلك. وكان ذلك الشيطان يرد كلّ سبعة أيام عينًا يشرب منها، فعمدت الشياطين إلى تلك العين، فنزحتها. ثمّ ملأتها خمرًا. فجاء الشيطان، فقال: إنّكِ لَطيبةُ الريح ولكنّك تُسفّهين الحليمَ وتزيدين السفيه سفهًا. ثمّ ذهب، فلم يشرب. فأدركه العطش، فرجع، فقال مثل ذلك ثلاث مرّات. ثمّ كرع، فشرب، فسكر. فأخذوه، فجاءوا به إلى سليمان. فأراه سليمان خاتمه. فلمّا أراه ذلك، وكان مُلك سليمان في خاتمه، فقال له سليمان: إنّي قد أمرت أن أبني مسجدًا شرط أن لا أسمع فيه صوت منقار ولا منشار. فأمر الشيطان بزجاجة، فصُنعت. ثمّ وضعت على بيض الهدهد. فجاء الهدهد للربض على بيضه، فلم يقدر عليه، فذهب. فقال الشيطان: انظروا ما يأتي به الهدهد، فخذوه. فجاء بالماس، فوضعه على الزجاجة، ففلقها. فأخذوا الماس، فجعلوا يقطعون به الحجارة قطعًا حتّى بنى بيت المقدس.

---

١ مم؛ زاد تع: قال الحسن.

The Construction of the Temple of Jerusalem[204]

'Abd al-Razzāq, on the authority of Maʿmar, on the authority of Qatādah concerning God's decree, «We placed a human form on his throne, but later he turned in repentance»,[205] saying: 19.1

A demon sat on his throne for forty nights until God restored to Solomon his rule.

Maʿmar said: But the demon did not exercise any authority over his wives.[206]

Maʿmar said: Qatādah said: 19.2

Solomon declared to the demons,[207] "Verily, God has commanded me to build a mosque in Jerusalem, but I must not hear there the sound of a saw or the clang of a hammer." The demons replied, "Truly in the sea lives a demon; perhaps he is able to accomplish this and will inform you how." That demon was accustomed to returning every seven days to a well to drink from it, so the demons embarked on a journey to this well. The demons dredged the well and filled it with wine. When the demon came to the well, he said, "Truly, yours is a fine aroma, but you make a fool of the crafty, and only add to the fool's folly." The demon then departed and did not drink, but when his thirst became acute he returned, repeating three times what he had said before. Finally he took a sip, and then continued to drink until he became drunk. The demons then seized him and brought him to Solomon. Solomon showed the demon his signet ring. When he showed him the ring—for Solomon's power to rule resided in his ring—Solomon declared to him, "Indeed, I have been commanded to build a temple, on the condition that I must not hear there the sound of a saw or the clang of a hammer." The demon requested a glass container, and it was crafted. The glass container was placed over the egg of the hoopoe. The hoopoe then came to nestle atop its egg but could not. When the hoopoe left, the demon said, "Watch now and see what the hoopoe brings, and then take it!" The hoopoe returned carrying a diamond and, placing it atop the glass container, split open the glass. The demons took the diamond and began carving stones until they had constructed the Jerusalem Temple. 19.2.1

قال: وانطلق سليمان يوماً إلى الحمّام، وقد كان فارق بعض نسائه في بعض المأثم. ٢،٢،١٩
فدخل الحمّام ومعه ذلك الشيطان. فلمّا دخل ذلك، أخذ الشيطان خاتمه، فألقاه في البحر. وألقى على كرسيّه جسداً، السرير، شبه سليمان. فخرج سليمان، وقد ذهب ملكه. وكان الشيطان على سرير سليمان أربعين ليلةً. فاستنكره أصحابه وقالوا: لقد فُتِنَ سليمان من تهاونه بالصلاة. وكان ذلك الشيطان يتهاون بالصلاة وبأشياء من أمر الدين. وكان معه من صحابة سليمان رجلٌ يشبّه بعمر بن الخطّاب في الجلد والقوّة. فقال: إنّي سائله لكم.

فجاءه، فقال: يا نبيّ الله، ما تقول في أحدنا يصيب من امرأته في الليلة الباردة، ثمّ ينام حتّى تطلع الشمس، لا يغتسل ولا يصلّي. هل ترى عليه في ذلك بأساً؟

قال: لا بأسَ عليه.

فرجع إلى أصحابه، فقال: لقد افتتن سليمان!

قال: فبينا سليمان ذاهبٌ في الأرض، إذ أوى إلى امرأة، فصنعت له حوتاً— أو ٣،٢،١٩
قال: فجاءته بحوت— فشقّت بطنه. فرأى سليمان خاتمه في بطن الحوت. فرفعه فأخذه فلبسه، فسجد له كلّ شيء لقيه من دابّة أو طير أو شيء. وردّ الله إليه ملكه. فقال عند ذلك ﴿رَبِّ ٱغۡفِرۡ لِي وَهَبۡ لِي مُلۡكٗا لَّا يَنۢبَغِي لِأَحَدٖ مِّنۢ بَعۡدِيٓ﴾.

قال قتادة: يقول لا تسلُبَنّه مرّةً أخرى.

قال معمر: قال الكلبي: ٣،١٩

فحينئذ سُخِّرَتْ[١] له الشياطينُ معاً والطير.[٢]

١ تع؛ م: سحرت. ٢ م؛ تع: الشياطين والرياح.

Now one day Solomon set off for the bathhouse, and he had withdrawn from one of his wives because of a certain sinful act she had committed.[208] When he entered the bathhouse, that demon entered with him. When the demon entered the bathhouse, he stole Solomon's ring and threw it into the sea. Then the demon cast a human form on his throne—his footstool—in the shape of Solomon, and Solomon's power to rule abandoned him. Thus the demon sat on Solomon's footstool forty nights, but Solomon's aides did not realize this and said, "Solomon has succumbed to temptation and neglected his prayers!"—but it was the demon who neglected the prayers and other matters pertaining to religion. Now among the companions of Solomon was a man of perseverance and strength, much like ʿUmar ibn al-Khaṭṭāb, and he said, "Indeed, I will ask Solomon about this on behalf of you all." 19.2.2

Thus he came to him, saying, "O Prophet of God, what would you say to one of us who enjoys his wife on a cold night, then sleeps until the sun rises—but he neither does his ablutions nor prays. Do you find any fault with him?"

"No," the demon answered, "he committed no fault." [209]

The man return to his companions and declared, "Solomon has been led astray!"

While Solomon traversed the earth he took shelter with a woman, and she placed before him a whale—or he said: she brought him a whale—and split open its belly. Solomon saw his signet ring in the belly of the whale. He removed it from its belly and put it on again. From then on, all the creatures he encountered prostrated themselves in obedience to him, whether beast or fowl, or any other creature, and God restored Solomon's power to rule. About this God has said: 19.2.3

> «He turned to us and prayed: "Lord forgive me! Grant me such power to rule as none after me will possess."»[210]

Qatādah said: Solomon was asking God not to dispossess him of his power to rule ever again.

Maʿmar said: al-Kalbī said: 19.3

At that time the demons and birds were made subservient to Solomon.

بَدْءُ مَرَضِ رَسُولِ اللهِ صلّى الله عليه وسلّم

عبد الرزّاق عن معمر عن الزهريّ، قال: أخبرني أبو بكر بن عبد الرحمن بن الحارث بن هشام عن أسماء بنت عميس، قالت: ١،٢٠

أوّل ما اشتكى رسول الله صلّى الله عليه وسلّم في بيت ميمونة، فاشتدّ مرضُه حتّى أُغْمِيَ عليه. قال: فتشاور نساؤه في لدّه، فلدّوه. فلمّا أفاق، قال: هذا فعل نساء جئن من هؤلاء، وأشار إلى أرض الحَبَشَة وكانت أسماء بنت عميس فيهنّ.

قالوا: كنّا نتّهم بك ذات الجنب، يا رسول الله!

قال: إنّ ذلك لداءٌ ما كان الله ليقذفني به. لا يَبْقَيَنَّ في البيت أحدٌ[١] إلّا التدّ إلّا عمّ رسول الله، يعني عبّاساً. قال: فلقد التدّت ميمونة يومئذ وإنّها لصائمة لعزيمة رسول الله صلّى الله عليه وسلّم.

قال الزهريّ: أخبرني عبيد الله بن عبد الله بن عتبة أنّ عائشة أخبرته، قالت: ٢،٢٠

أوّل ما اشتكى رسول الله صلّى الله عليه وسلّم في بيت ميمونة. فاستأذن أزواجه أن يمرّض في بيتي، فأذنّ له. قالت: فخرج ويدٌ له على الفضل بن العبّاس ويدٌ أُخرى على يد رجل آخر، وهو يخُطّ برجليه في الأرض.

فقال عبيد الله: فحدّثتُ به ابن عبّاس، فقال:

أَتدري من الرجل الّذي لم تسمِّ عائشةُ؟ هو عليّ بن أبي طالب ولكنّ عائشة لا تطيب له نفساً بخير.

---

١ ح، ط؛ م: ليبقين في البيت أحدًا.

The Beginning of the Messenger of God's Illness

'Abd al-Razzāq, on the authority of Ma'mar, on the authority of al-Zuhrī, who said: Abū Bakr ibn 'Abd al-Raḥmān ibn al-Ḥārith ibn Hishām related to me on the authority of Asmā' bint 'Umays, who said: 20.1

The onset of the Messenger of God's illness occurred while he was in the chamber of his wife Maymūnah. His illness became so severe that he lost consciousness. His wives then gathered to discuss whether or not they should treat him by pouring medicine into the corner of his mouth.[211] They administered the medicine, but when the Prophet had regained consciousness, he said, "This is the work of the women who came from those people!"—and he pointed in the direction of Abyssinia. Indeed, Asmā' bint 'Umays was there in their midst.

"O Messenger of God," they declared, "we suspected that you had pleurisy!"

"God would never cast such an affliction upon me," he retorted. "Leave no one untreated by this medicine except for the Messenger's uncle," by whom he meant 'Abbās. Even Maymūnah was given the medicine orally that day, though she was fasting, because the Messenger of God had commanded it.

Al-Zuhrī said: 'Ubayd Allāh ibn 'Abd Allāh ibn 'Utbah related to me that 'Ā'ishah informed him, saying: 20.2

The Messenger of God first fell ill in Maymūnah's chamber. He asked his wives' permission to be nursed in my quarters, and they granted him his request. When he set out, he placed one of his hands on al-Faḍl ibn al-'Abbās and the other in the hand of another man, and his feet dragged along the ground.

'Ubayd Allāh said: Ibn 'Abbās related to me the following, saying:

"Do you know who the person 'Ā'ishah did not name was? It was 'Alī ibn Abī Ṭālib," he answered, "but 'Ā'ishah found it displeasing to say so."[212]

قال الزهريّ: أخبرني عروة عن غيره عن عائشة، قالت: ٣،٢٠

قال رسول الله صلّى الله عليه وسلّم في مرضه الّذي مات فيه: صُبّوا عليّ من سبع قرب لم تحلَل أَوكيتُهنّ لعلّي أستريح فأعهد إلى الناس.

قالت عائشة: فأَجلسناه في مخضب لحفصة من نحاس وسكبنا عليه الماءَ حتّى طفق يشير إلينا أن قد فعلتنّ. ثمّ خرج.

قال الزهريّ: وأخبرني عبد الرحمن بن كعب بن مالك، وكان أبوه أحد الثلاثة الّذين تيب عليهم، عن رجل من ٤،٢٠ أصحاب النبيّ صلّى الله عليه وسلّم:

قام يومئذ خطيباً، فحمد الله وأثنى عليه، واستغفر للشهداء الّذين قتلوا يوم أُحُد، قال: إنّكم يا معشر المهاجرين! إنّكم تزيدون والأنصار لا يزيدون. الأنصار عيبتي الّتي أويتُ إليها، فأَكرموا كريمَهم وتجاوزوا عن مسيئهم.

قال الزهريّ: سمعتُ رجلاً يذكر: ٥،٢٠

أنّ النبيّ صلّى الله عليه وسلّم قال: إنّ عبداً خيّره ربُّه بين الدنيا والآخرة، فاختار ما عند ربِّه. ففطن أبو بكر أنّه يريد نفسه، فبكى. فقال له النبيّ صلّى الله عليه وسلّم: على رِسلك. ثمّ قال: سُدّوا هذه الأبواب الشوارع في المسجد إلّا باب أبي بكر، رحمه الله، فإنّي لا أَعلم رجلاً أحسن يداً عندي من الصحابة من أبي بكر.

قال الزهريّ: وأخبرني عبيد الله بن عبد الله بن عتبة أنّ عائشة وابن عبّاس أخبراه: ٦،٢٠

أنّ النبيّ صلّى الله عليه وسلّم، حين نزل به، جعل يلقي خميصةً له على وجهه. فإذا اغتمّ كشفها عن وجهه، وهو يقول: لعنة الله على اليهود والنصارى اتّخذوا قبور أنبيائهم مساجد.

تقول عائشة: يحذّر مثل الّذي فعلوا.

Al-Zuhrī said: ʿUrwah related to me on the authority of someone else, on the authority of ʿĀʾishah, who said: 20.3

During his fatal illness, the Messenger of God said, "Take seven waterskins whose strings have been unfastened and pour them over me so that I might recuperate and announce my testament to the people."

ʿĀʾishah continued: We sat him down in a copper tub that belonged to Ḥafṣah and poured the water over him until he began gesturing to us as if to say, "You have done enough." Then he came out.

Al-Zuhrī said: ʿAbd al-Raḥmān ibn Kaʿb ibn Mālik—whose father was one of three whose repentance was accepted[213]—related to me on the authority of one of the Prophet's Companions: 20.4

That day the Prophet stood up addressing the people. He offered praise to God and extolled His glory. Asking God to forgive those martyrs slain during the battle of Uḥud, he declared, "You, O assembly of Emigrants! You shall continue to increase, but the Allies shall not increase. The Allies are my trusted companions in whom I found refuge, so extol their noble deeds and overlook their misdeeds."

Al-Zuhrī said: I heard a man recall: 20.5

The Prophet said, "One of God's servants has been given a choice between the life of this world and that of the Hereafter, and he has chosen to be with his Lord." Abū Bakr surmised that the Prophet was speaking of himself and wept. "Be at ease," said the Prophet. Later he would also say, "Close the doors of the mosque that face the street except for the door of Abū Bakr, may God have mercy on him, for in my view, I know of no other man among the Companions who has so greatly aided me as has Abū Bakr."

Al-Zuhrī said: ʿUbayd Allāh ibn ʿAbd Allāh ibn ʿUtbah related to me that ʿĀʾishah and Ibn ʿAbbās both related to him: 20.6

Once the Prophet's illness descended upon him, he began placing a cloak[214] over his face. Whenever his body was racked with pain, he would remove it from his face and declare, "God's curse be upon the Christians and the Jews, for they have adopted the graves of their prophets as places of worship!"

ʿĀʾishah said: The Prophet was warning us against the like of what they actually did.[215]

قال معمر: قال الزهريّ: ٧،٢٠

وقال النبيّ صلّى الله عليه وسلّم لعبد الله بن زمعة: مُرِ الناس فليصلّوا.[١] فلقي عمر بن الخطّاب، فقال: يا عمر! صلِّ بالناس.

فصلّى عمر بالناس، فجهر بصوته، وكان جهير الصوت، فسمعه رسول الله صلّى الله عليه وسلّم.

فقال: أليس هذا صوت عمر؟

قالوا: بلى، يا رسول الله.

فقال: يأبى الله ذلك والمؤمنون! لِيُصَلِّ بالناس أبو بكر.

فقال عمر لعبد الله بن زمعة: بئسَ ما صنعتَ! كنتُ أرى أنّ رسول الله صلّى الله عليه وسلّم أمرك أن تأمرني.

قال: لا والله ما أمرني أن آمر أحداً.

قال الزهريّ: وأخبرني عبد الله بن عمر[٢] عن عائشة قالت: ٨،٢٠

لمّا ثقل رسول الله صلّى الله عليه وسلّم، قال: مروا أبا بكر، فليصلِّ بالناس. قالت: قلت: يا رسول الله![٣] إنّ أبا بكر رجلٌ رقيقٌ. إذا قرأ القرآن، لا يملك دمعه. فلو أمرتَ غير أبا بكر. قالت: واللهِ ما بي إلّا كراهيّة أن يتشاءم الناسُ أوّل من يقوم في مقام رسول الله صلّى الله عليه وسلّم. فراجعته مرّتين أو ثلاثاً، فقال: ليصلِّ بالناس أبو بكر، فإنّكن مثل صواحب يوسف!

قال الزهريّ: وأخبرني أنس بن مالك قال: ٩،٢٠

لمّا كان يوم الاثنين، كشف رسولُ الله صلّى الله عليه وسلّم ستر الحجرة. فرأى أبا بكر وهو يصلِّي بالناس. قال: نظرتُ إلى وجهه كأنّه ورقة مصحف وهو يبتسم.

---

١ مم: لعبد الله بن عباس مر الزمعة فليصلوا؛ والنص أعلاه من ح (رواية عبد الأعلى عن معمر).

٢ مم؛ ح: حمزة بن عبد الله بن عمر. ٣ ح ؛مم: يا أبا بكر برسول الله.

Maʿmar said: al-Zuhrī said: 20.7

The Prophet said to ʿAbd Allāh ibn Zamʿah, "Convey my command to the people that they ought to pray." ʿAbd Allāh ibn Zamʿah set out and, upon meeting ʿUmar ibn al-Khaṭṭāb, he told him, "Lead the people in the prayer."

ʿUmar then prayed with the people, but as he lifted his voice in prayer—for he had a booming voice—the Messenger of God overheard, so he asked, "Isn't this ʿUmar's voice?"

"O Messenger of God," they said, "indeed it is."

"God and the Believers reject this," he declared. "It is Abū Bakr who shall lead the people in prayer."

Later ʿUmar said to ʿAbd Allāh ibn Zamʿah, "What a foul thing you've done! I thought the Messenger of God had ordered you to command me."

"No," said ʿAbd Allāh ibn Zamʿah, "by God, he hadn't asked me to give such an order to anyone."

Al-Zuhrī said: ʿAbd Allāh ibn ʿUmar related to me on the authority of ʿĀʾishah, who said: 20.8

When the Messenger of God had become seriously ill, he said, "Command Abū Bakr to lead the people in prayer." I said, "O Messenger of God! Abū Bakr is a frail man. Whenever he reads the Qurʾan, he can't even hold back his tears—if only you would give the order to someone other than Abū Bakr." By God, I only hated the thought that people might wish ill toward the first person to occupy the place of the God's Messenger. I repeated this two times, or maybe three, but he said, "Abū Bakr shall lead the people in prayer. You women are like the mistresses of Joseph!"[216]

Al-Zuhrī said: Anas ibn Mālik related to me, saying: 20.9

On Monday the Messenger of God pulled the veil of his chamber aside and watched Abū Bakr lead the people in prayer.[217] Anas said: I gazed at his face as though it were the page of a book, and he smiled.

Anas continued: We were almost tempted to abandon our prayer because of the joy we felt upon seeing the Messenger of God. Whenever Abū Bakr would

قال: وكِدْنا أن نفتتن في صلاتنا فرحاً برؤية رسول الله صلّى الله عليه وسلّم. فإذا أبو بكر دار ينكُص، فأشار إليه النبيّ صلّى الله عليه وسلّم أن كما أنت. ثمّ أرخى الستر، فقبض من يومه ذلك. وقام عمر فقال: إنّ رسول الله صلّى الله عليه وسلّم لم يُمت ولكنّ ربّه أرسل إليه كما أرسل إلى موسى أربعين ليلةً فمكث عن قومه[1] أربعين ليلةً. والله إنّي لأرجو أن يعيش رسولُ الله صلّى الله عليه وسلّم حتّى يقطع أيدي رجال من المنافقين وألسنتهم يزعمون — أو قال: يقولون — إنّ رسول الله صلّى الله عليه وسلّم قد مات.

قال معمر: أخبرني أيّوب عن عكرمة قال: ١٠،٢٠

قال العبّاس بن عبد المطّلب: والله لأعلمنّ ما بقاءُ رسول الله صلّى الله عليه وسلّم فينا، فقلتُ: يا رسول الله، لو اتّخذتَ شيئاً تجلس عليه، يدفع عنك الغبار ويردّ عنك الخصم.

فقال النبيّ صلّى الله عليه وسلّم: لأدعَنَّهم ينازعُوني ردائي ويطئون عقبي، ويغشاني غبارُهم حتّى يكون اللهُ يُرِيحني منهم. فعلمتُ أنّ بقاءَه فينا قليل.

قال: فلمّا توفّي رسول الله صلّى الله عليه وسلّم، قام عمر فقال: إنّ رسول الله صلّى الله عليه وسلّم لم يمت ولكن صعق كما صعق موسى. والله إنّي لأرجو أن يعيش رسول الله صلّى الله عليه وسلّم حتّى يقطع أيدي رجال وألسنتهم من المنافقين، يقولون: إنّ رسول الله صلّى الله عليه وسلّم قد مات.

فقام العبّاس بن عبد المطّلب، فقال: أيّها الناس! هل أحد منكم عهدٌ أو عقدٌ من رسول الله صلّى الله عليه وسلّم؟

قالوا: اللّهمّ لا.

قال: فإنّ رسول الله صلّى الله عليه وسلّم لم يمت حتّى أحلّ الحلال، ثمّ حارب وواصل وسالم، ونكح النساء وطلّق، وتركَكم عن محجّة بيّنة وطريق ناهجة. فإن يكُ ما

١ [فمكث عن قومه] ح؛ ساقطة من م.

turn, thus delaying his prayer, the Prophet would gesture to him, as if to say, "As you were." Then the Prophet released the veil and was taken from us on that very day. ʿUmar stood up and said, "Verily, the Messenger of God has not died! Rather, his Lord has sent for him as He sent for Moses for forty nights! Thus did Moses remain away from his people for forty nights. By God, I expect the Messenger of God to live long enough to cut off the hands of the hypocrites and to cut out the tongues of those claiming"—or he said, "saying"—"that the Messenger of God has died."

Maʿmar said: Ayyūb related to me on the authority of ʿIkrimah, who said: **20.10**

Al-ʿAbbās ibn ʿAbd al-Muṭṭalib said, "I said to myself, 'By God, I must know for certain how much longer the Messenger of God will remain among us.' So I said to him, 'O Messenger of God, if only you were to take a chair to sit upon, then God would spare you the dust and keep petitioners away!'

"'I'll let them contend with me over a spot to sit on my robe even if they tread upon my heels,' the Prophet replied. 'Their dust shall cover me until God grants me a respite from them.' Then I knew that his time with us was short."[218]

When the Messenger of God passed away, ʿUmar stood up and said, "The Messenger of God has not died! Rather, he has merely been made to slumber as Moses slumbered! By God, I expect that the Messenger of God will live until he severs the hands and cuts out the tongues of these hypocrites who say, 'The Messenger of God has indeed died!'"

Then al-ʿAbbās ibn ʿAbd al-Muṭṭalib stood up and said, "O people! Do any of you possess a testament or covenant from the Messenger of God?"

"No, by God," they replied.

Al-ʿAbbās then said, "The Messenger of God did not die until he had made what was lawful lawful. Then he waged war, persevered, and made peace; he married women and divorced; and he left you on a clear path and a well-marked course. If the matter be truly as Ibn al-Khaṭṭāb says, then it will not exceed God's ability to exhume him and bring him back to us, so do not stand

تقول، يا ابن الخطّاب، حقّاً، فإنّه لن يُعجز الله أن يحثوعنه فيخرجه إلينا، وإلا فَخَلِّ بيننا وبين صاحبنا. فإنّه يأسن كما يأسن الناس.

قال الزهريّ: وأخبرني ابن كعب بن مالك عن ابن عبّاس قال: ١١،٢٠

خرج العبّاس وعليّ من عند رسول الله صلّى الله عليه وسلّم في مرضه. فلقيهما رجلٌ، فقال: كيف أصبح رسول الله صلّى الله عليه وسلّم، أبا حسن؟

فقال: أصبح رسول الله صلّى الله عليه وسلّم بارئاً.

فقال العبّاس لعليّ بن أبي طالب: أنت بعد ثلاث لعبد العصا.

ثمّ حلّ به،[١] فقال: إنّه يخيّل إليّ إنّي لأعرف وجوه بني عبد المطّلب عند الموت وإنّي خائفٌ ألّا يقوم رسول الله صلّى الله عليه وسلّم من وجعه هذا. فاذهب بنا إليه فنسأله. فإن يكُ هذا الأمر إلينا، علمنا ذلك. وإن لا يكُ إلينا، أمرناه أن يستوصي بنا خيراً.

قال له عليٌّ: أرأيتَ إذا جئناه، فلم يُعطِناها، أترى أنّ الناس يعطوها؟ والله لا أسأله إيّاها أبداً.

قال الزهريّ: قالت عائشة: ١٢،٢٠

فلمّا اشتدّ مرضُ رسول الله صلّى الله عليه وسلّم قال: في الرفيق الأعلى، ثلاث مرّات ثمّ فتر.

قال معمر: وسمعتُ قتادة يقول: ١٣،٢٠

آخرشيء تكلّم به رسول الله صلّى الله عليه وسلّم: اتّقوا الله في النساء وما مكلت أيمانُكم.

---

١ مم؛ بد: خلا به.

between us and our kinsman. For indeed, his flesh decays like any other person's."[219]

Al-Zuhrī said: Ibn Kaʿb ibn Mālik informed me that Ibn ʿAbbās said: 20.11

Al-ʿAbbās and ʿAlī went out from the Messenger of God's home while he was still ill, and a man encountered the two and said, "Abū Ḥasan, how fares the Messenger of God this morning?"

"The Messenger of God has recovered," ʿAlī replied.

Then al-ʿAbbās said to ʿAlī, "After three days, you will be the servant of the staff."[220]

Al-ʿAbbās dismounted at the Prophet's home and said, "I have this sense that I can perceive death in the faces of ʿAbd al-Muṭṭalib's progeny, and I fear that the Prophet will not recover from this affliction of his. Come with us to him so that we may question him. For if the right to rule is to be ours, then we will know for certain; and if it is not to be ours, then we will ask him to grant us his blessing."

But ʿAlī said to him, "What would you think if we were to go to him and he did not give it to us? Do you believe that the people will then give it to us? By God, I'll never ask it of him."

Al-Zuhrī said: ʿĀ'ishah said: 20.12

When the illness of the Messenger of God worsened, he said, "In the most exalted company!" three times and then went limp.

Maʿmar said: I heard Qatādah say: 20.13

The last words of the Prophet were, "Fear God in matters concerning women and those slave women your right hands possess."[221]

عبد الرزّاق عن معمر عن الزهريّ قال: أخبرنا أبو سلمة بن عبد الرحمن، قال: كان ابن عبّاس يحدّث: ١٤،٢٠

أنّ أبا بكر الصدّيق دخل المسجد وعمر يحدّث الناس. فمضى حتّى البيت الّذي توفّي فيه رسول الله صلّى الله عليه وسلّم، وهو في بيت عائشة، فكشف عن وجهه بُرْد حِبَرَة كان مُسَجّىً عليه. فنظر إلى وجه النبيّ صلّى الله عليه وسلّم، ثمّ أكبّ عليه فقبّله. ثمّ قال: والله لا يجمع الله عليك موتتين. لقد مُتَّ الموتة الّتي لا تموت بعدها أبداً.

ثمّ خرج أبو بكر إلى المسجد، وعمر يكلّم الناسَ. فقال له أبو بكر: اجلس يا عمر! فأبى أن يجلس، فكلّمه مرّتين أو ثلاثاً، فأبى أن يجلس. فقام أبو بكر فتشهّد، فأقبل الناس على أبي بكر وتركوا عمر. فلمّا قضى أبو بكر تشهُّدَه. قال: أمّا بعد، فمن كان يعبدُ محمّداً، فإنّ محمّداً قد مات. ومن كان منكم يعبد الله، فإنّ الله حيٌّ لا يموت. ثمّ تلا هذه الآية ﴿وَمَا مُحَمَّدٌ إِلَّا رَسُولٌ قَدْ خَلَتْ مِن قَبْلِهِ الرُّسُلُ﴾ الآية كلّها. فلمّا تلاها أبو بكر، رحمه الله، أيقن الناسُ بموت رسول الله صلّى الله عليه وسلّم وتلقّوها من أبي بكر حتّى قال قائلٌ من الناس: فلم يعلموا أنّ هذه الآية أُنزلت حتّى تلاها أبو بكر.

قال الزهريّ: وأخبرني سعيد بن المسيّب، قال: ١٥،٢٠

قال عمر: والله ما هو إلّا أن تلاها أبو بكر، وأنا قائم، فخررتُ إلى الأرض وأيقنتُ أنّ رسول الله صلّى الله عليه وسلّم قد مات.

أخبرنا عبد الرزّاق، قال: أخبرنا معمر عن الزهريّ، قال: أخبرني أنس بن مالك: أنّه سمع خطبة عمر، رحمه الله، الآخرة حين جلس على منبر النبيّ صلّى الله عليه وسلّم، وذلك الغد من اليوم توفّي رسول الله صلّى الله ١٦،٢٠

'Abd al-Razzāq, on the authority of Maʿmar, on the authority of al-Zuhrī, who said: Abū Salamah ibn 'Abd al-Raḥmān related to us, saying: Ibn al-'Abbās used to report that: 20.14

Abū Bakr al-Ṣiddīq entered the mosque while 'Umar was speaking to the people. He proceeded to walk until he reached the chamber in which the Messenger of God passed away—'Ā'ishah's chamber—and pulled back the *ḥibarah* cloak[222] in which his corpse had been shrouded. He gazed at the Prophet's face, leaned over him, and kissed him. Then he said, "By God, God will not cause you to suffer two deaths. You have already died the death after which you shall never die again."

Then Abū Bakr went out to the mosque while 'Umar was still speaking to the people. Abū Bakr said to him, "Sit down, 'Umar!" But he refused to sit. He told him two or three more times, but still he refused to sit. So Abū Bakr stood up and confessed the oneness of God, and the people turned toward Abū Bakr and left 'Umar. When Abū Bakr had finished confessing God's oneness, he said, "Now, whoever used to worship Muḥammad, truly Muḥammad has died; whoever among you worshipped God, truly God lives and has not died." Then he recited this verse:

> «Muḥammad is merely a messenger before whom many messengers have come and gone. If he died or was killed, would you revert to your old ways? If anyone does so, he will not harm God in the least. God will reward the grateful.»[223]

Abū Bakr, may God have mercy on him, recited the verse, and the people knew for certain that the Messenger of God had died. They received the verse from Abū Bakr in a way that caused some to declare that they had not known that this verse had been revealed until Abū Bakr recited it.

Al-Zuhrī said: Saʿīd ibn al-Musayyab related to me, saying: 20.15

'Umar said, "By God, hardly a moment passed after Abū Bakr recited the verse before I, standing there, immediately dropped prostrate to the ground, for then I knew for certain that the Messenger of God had died."

'Abd al-Razzāq related to us, saying: Maʿmar related to us on the authority of al-Zuhrī, who said: Anas ibn Mālik related to me that he heard the last sermon of 'Umar, may God have 20.16

عليه وسلّم. قال:

فتشهّد عمر، وأبو بكر صامتٌ لا يتكلّم. ثمّ قال عمر:

أمّا بعد، فإنّي قلتُ مقالةً وإنها لم تكن كما قلتُ. وإنّي والله ما وجدتُ المقالة الّتي قلتُ في كتاب الله تعالى ولا في عهدٍ عَهِدَه إليّ رسول صلّى الله عليه وسلّم. ولكنّي كنت أرجو أن يعيش رسول الله صلّى الله عليه وسلّم حتّى يَدْبُرَنا، يريد بذلك حتّى يكون آخرهم. فإن يكُ محمّداً قد مات، فإنّ الله قد جعل بين أظهركم نوراً تهتدون به. هذا كتاب الله. فاعتصموا به تهتدون لِماَ هدى الله به محمّداً صلّى الله عليه وسلّم. ثمّ إنّ أبا بكر، رحمه الله، صاحبُ رسول الله صلّى الله عليه وسلّم وثاني اثنين. وإنّه أولى الناس بأموركم. فقوموا، فبايعوه.

وكانت طائفةٌ منهم قد بايعوه قبل ذلك في سقيفة بني ساعدة، وكانت بيعة العامّة على المنبر.

قال الزهريّ: وأخبرني أنس، قال: ١٧،٢٠

لقد رأيتُ عمر يزعج أبا بكر إلى المنبر إزعاجاً.

عبد الرزّاق عن معمر عن الزهريّ عن عبيد الله بن عبد الله بن عتبة عن ابن عبّاس، قال: ١٨،٢٠

لمّا احتضر رسول الله صلّى الله عليه وسلّم، وفي البيت رجال فيهم عمر بن الخطّاب رضي الله عنه، فقال النبيّ صلّى الله عليه وسلّم: هَلُمُّوا أكتب لكم كتاباً لا تضلّوا بعده. فقال عمر: إنّ رسول الله صلّى الله عليه وسلّم قد غلب عليه الوجع، وعندكم القرآن. حسبنا كتاب الله. فاختلف أهل البيت واختصموا. فمنهم من يقول: قرّبوا يكتب لكم رسول الله صلّى الله عليه وسلّم كتاباً لا تضلّوا بعده. ومنهم من يقول ما قال عمر. فلمّا أكثروا اللغو والاختلاف عند رسول الله صلّى الله عليه وسلّم، قال رسول الله صلّى الله عليه وسلّم: قوموا!

mercy on him, which he delivered while seated on the Prophet's pulpit that day following the passing of the Messenger of God. He said:

ʿUmar confessed the oneness of God, and Abū Bakr remained silent and did not speak. Then ʿUmar spoke,

"Now, I have said something that was not as I said it was. By God, I had neither found what I said in God's Scripture, nor in a testament that the Messenger of God left to me. Rather, I expected that the Messenger of God would live until he outlasted us"—meaning that he would be the last of them—"but if it truly be that Muḥammad has died, then God has placed among you a light by which you might be guided: this Scripture of God. So hold fast to it, and take as your guide that by which God guided Muḥammad! Then hold fast to Abū Bakr. May God have mercy on him, the companion of the Prophet and the second of the two:[224] he is the most deserving of the people to manage your affairs. So rise up and give him your oaths of allegiance."

A group of them had given him the oaths of allegiance before that at the portico of the Sāʿidah clan, and the public oath was given at the pulpit.

Al-Zuhrī said: Anas related to me, saying: **20.17**

I saw ʿUmar ardently urging Abū Bakr to ascend the pulpit.

ʿAbd al-Razzāq, on the authority of Maʿmar, on the authority of al-Zuhrī, on the authority of **20.18**
ʿUbayd Allāh ibn ʿAbd Allāh ibn ʿUtbah, on the authority of Ibn ʿAbbās, who said:

When death came to take the Messenger of God, a number of prominent men were in his chamber, among them ʿUmar ibn al-Khaṭṭāb, and the Prophet said, "Draw near to me so that I may write you a testament, lest you go astray after my death." But ʿUmar said, "The Messenger of God has been overtaken by pain, and you all have the Qur'an. The Scripture of God is sufficient for us."[225] The household of the Prophet disagreed and began to dispute with one another. Among them was one who said, "Draw near so that the Messenger of God may write his testament for you, lest you go astray after he dies." Among them was another who said what ʿUmar had said. When the foolish talk and disagreements around the Messenger of God became acute, he commanded, "Leave, all of you!"

قال عبيد الله: فكان ابن عبّاس يقول: إنّ الرزيّة كلّ الرزيّة! ما حال بين رسول الله صلّى الله عليه وسلّم وبين أن يكتب لهم ذلك الكتاب من اختلافهم ولغطهم.

'Ubayd Allāh said: Ibn 'Abbās used to say, "A disaster! What a disaster! The only thing that prevented the Messenger of God from writing that testament down for them was the quarreling and clamor!"

بَيْعَةُ أَبِي بَكْرٍ رَضِيَ ٱللَّهُ تَعَالَىٰ عَنْهُ فِي سَقِيفَةِ بَنِي سَاعِدَة

عبد الرزّاق عن معمر عن الزهريّ عن عبيد الله بن عبد الله بن عتبة عن ابن عبّاس، قال: ١،٢١

كنت أقرئ عبد الرحمن بن عوف في خلافة عمر. فلمّا كان آخر حجّة حجّها عمرُ، ونحن بمنىً، أتاني عبد الرحمن بن عوف في منزلي عشيّاً. فقال: لو شهدتَ أمير المؤمنين اليوم! أتاه رجلٌ، فقال: يا أمير المؤمنين، إنّي سمعتُ فلاناً يقول: لو قد مات أمير المؤمنين، قد بايعت فلاناً. ١،١،٢١

فقال عمر: إنّي لقائمٌ العشيةَ[١] في الناس فمحذِرهم[٢] هؤلاء الرهط الّذين يريدون أن يغتصبوا المسلمين أمرهم.

قال: فقلت: يا أمير المؤمنين، إنّ الموسم يجمع رُعاع الناس وغوغاءهم، وإنّهم الّذين يغلبون على مجلسك. وإنّي أخشى إن قلت فيهم اليوم مقالةً أن يطّيّروا بها كلّ مطّيّر ولا يعوها ولا يضعوها على مواضعها. ولكن أمْهِل، يا أمير المؤمنين، حتّى تَقْدِم المدينة. فإنّها دار السنّة والهجرة، تخلص بالمهاجرين والأنصار فتقول ما قلتَ متمكِّناً، فيَعُوا مقالتك ويضعوها علىٰ مواضعها.

قال: فقال عمر: أمّا والله إن شاء الله لأقومنّ به في أوّل مقام أقومه في المدينة.

قال: فلمّا قدمنا المدينة وجاءت الجمعة، هجّرت لمّا حدّثني عبد الرحمن بن عوف. ٢،١،٢١
فوجدتُ سعيد بن زيد، قد سبقني بالتهجير جالساً إلى جنب المنبر. فجلست إلى جنبه

---

١ لش؛ مم: عشية. ٢ لش؛ مم: فحذرهم.

The Oath of Fealty to Abū Bakr at the Portico of the Sāʿidah Clan

ʿAbd al-Razzāq, on the authority of Maʿmar, on the authority of al-Zuhrī, on the authority 21.1
of ʿUbayd Allāh ibn ʿAbd Allāh ibn ʿUtbah, on the the authority of Ibn ʿAbbās, who said: 21.1.1

During ʿUmar's caliphate I used to teach the Qur'an to ʿAbd al-Raḥmān ibn ʿAwf. Now when ʿUmar undertook his final hajj, we were in Minā.[226] ʿAbd al-Raḥmān came to see me at my residence that evening and said, "If only you had witnessed the Commander of the Faithful today! A man went up to him and said, 'O Commander of the Faithful, I've heard so-and-so say, Were the Commander of the Faithful to die, I would certainly pledge my fealty to so-and-so.'[227]

"'I'll address the people this very night!' ʿUmar exclaimed. 'I must warn them of this band of men who seek to seize power over the Muslims by force!'"

Ibn ʿAbbās continued: "O Commander of the Faithful," I said, "the market now gathers together the vulgar mobs,[228] and they will overwhelm any assembly you convene. My fear is that, if you make a statement in their midst on the morrow, they will take your words as auguring all manner of bad things and thus not pay them heed nor give them their due. Rather, proceed carefully, O Commander of the Faithful, until you have arrived in Medina, for it is the abode of the Sunnah and the Hijrah. There you can speak with the Emigrants and the Allies alone and say whatever you wish in full command of an audience who will heed your words and give them their due."

"By God," ʿUmar replied, "if He so wills it, then I shall do so as soon as I set foot in Medina."

21.1.2 When we arrived in Medina, the time for the Friday Congregation[229] had come. I rushed off to the mosque when ʿAbd al-Raḥmān ibn ʿAwf told me, but I found that Saʿīd ibn Zayd had beaten me in the rush to get there and was seated next to the pulpit. I sat down next to him, my knee touching his. Once the sun had set, ʿUmar, God bless his soul, came out to meet us all, and as he approached I said, "By God, the Commander of the Faithful is certain to

تمسّ ركبتي ركبته. قال: فلمّا زالت الشمس، خرج علينا عمر، رحمه الله. قال: فقلتُ وهو مقبل: أمّا والله ليقولنّ أمير المؤمنين على هذا المنبر مقالاً لم يقل قبله. قال: فغضب سعيد بن زيد وقال: وأيّ مقالٍ يقول لم يقل قبله؟

قال: فلمّا ارتقى عمر المنبر، أخذ المؤذّن في أذانهم. فلمّا فرغ من أذانه، قام عمر، فحمد الله وأثنى عليه بما هو أهله. ثمّ قال:

أمّا بعد، فإنّي أريد أن أقول مقالةً قد قدّر لي أن أقولها. لا أدري لعلّها بين يدَيّ أجلي. فمن وعاها وعقلها وحفظها، فليحدّث بها حيث تنتهي راحلته. ومن خشي أن لا يعيها، فإنّي لا أحلّ لأحد أن يكذب عليّ.[1]

إنّ الله بعث محمّدًا صلّى الله عليه وسلّم بالحقّ وأنزل معه الكتاب. فكان ممّا أنزل الله عليه آية الرجم، فرجم رسول الله صلّى الله عليه وسلّم، ورجمنا بعده. وإنّي خائفٌ أن يطول بالناس زمانٌ، فيقول قائلٌ: والله ما الرجم في كتاب الله. فيضلّ أو يترك فريضةً أنزلها الله. ألا وإنّ الرجم حقٌّ على من زنى إذا أحصن وقامت البيّنةُ وكان الحمل أو الاعتراف. ثمّ قد كنّا نقرأ ﴿وَلا تَرْغَبُوا عَنْ آبَائِكُمْ فَإِنَّهُ كُفْرٌ بِكُمْ﴾ أو ﴿فَإِنَّ كُفْرًا بِكُمْ أَنْ تَرْغَبُوا عَنْ آبَائِكُمْ﴾.

ثمّ إنّ رسول الله صلّى الله عليه وسلّم قال: لا تُطْرُوني كما أَطْرَتِ النصارى ابنَ مريم، صلوات الله عليه، فإنّما أنا عبدُ الله، فقولوا: عبد الله ورسوله.

ثمّ إنّه بلغني أنّ فلانًا منكم[2] يقول إنّه لو قد مات أمير المؤمنين قد بايعت فلانًا.[3] فلا يغرّنّ امرأً أن يقول: إنّ بيعة أبي بكرٍ كانت فَلْتَةً. وقد كانت كذلك إلّا أنّ الله وقى شرّها، وليس فيكم من تُقطع إليه الأعناق مثل أبي بكر. إنّه كان من خيرنا حين توفّي رسول الله صلّى الله عليه وسلّم، وإنّ عليًا والزبير ومن معه تخلّفوا عنه في بيت فاطمة،

١ [فمن وعاها . . . أن يكذب علي] من لش؛ ساقطة من مم. ٢ [فلانا منكم] في مم؛ بل: الزبير (معمر عن الزهري في رواية غير عبد الرزّاق). ٣ [فلانا] في مم؛ بل: عليًا (معمر عن الزهري في رواية غير عبد الرزّاق).

say something the like of which has never been said from the pulpit before!" Angered, Sa'īd ibn Zayd said, "And what exactly will he say that hasn't been said before?"

When 'Umar had ascended the pulpit, the muezzin began the call to prayer. Once he had finished the call to prayer, 'Umar stood up and praised and extolled God, as is His due, and then he spoke:

> Now to the heart of the matter: I wish to make a statement that God has ordained me to say. I know not for certain whether the hour of my death soon arrives. Let whoever heeds, understands, and remembers my words repeat them wherever his journeys may take him; but whoever fears that he shall not heed my words, let him not spread lies against me.
>
> Indeed, God sent Muḥammad, God bless him and keep him, with the Truth and revealed through him the Scripture. One of God's revelations was the verse on stoning.[230] The Messenger of God stoned adulterers, and we stoned adulterers after him. I fear that in times to come men will say, "By God, stoning is not in God's Book." Thus they shall go astray or neglect a command God has revealed. For indeed, stoning is the just punishment for the adulterer, if one has married and the evidence is present, be it pregnancy or confession. We used to read in the Qur'an: «Yearn not for ancestors other than your own, as it is an affrontery to faith for you», or «For you it is an affrontery to faith to yearn for ancestors other than your own».[231]
>
> The Messenger of God also said, "Do not praise me to excess as the Christians did to Mary's son,[232] God's blessings upon him, for I am but a servant of God. Rather, say 'the servant of God and His Messenger.'"
>
> Now it has also reached me that a man from your ranks says, "Were the Commander of the Faithful to die, then I would certainly pledge my fealty to so-and-so." But do not be deceived by a man[233] who says, "The oath of fealty to Abū Bakr was a hasty decision!"[234] Though it was indeed so, God dispelled its evil, and there is no one among you for whom men have risked their necks as they have for Abū Bakr. He was the best of us when the Messenger of God passed, even though 'Alī and al-Zubayr withdrew to Fāṭimah's

وتخلّفت عنّا الأنصار بأسرهم في سقيفة بني ساعدة. واجتمع المهاجرون إلى أبي بكر، رحمه الله، فقلتُ: يا أبا بكر، انطلق بنا إلى إخواننا من الأنصار. فانطلقنا نؤمُّهم، فلقينا رجلين صالحين من الأنصار قد شهدا بدراً. فقالا: أين تريدون، يا معشر المهاجرين؟ قلنا: نريد إخواننا هؤلاء من الأنصار. قالا: فارجعوا، فاقْضوا أمركم بينكم. قال: قلتُ: فامضوا،[١] لنأتينّهم. فأتيناهم، فإذا هم مجتمعون في سقيفة بني ساعدة، بين أظهرهم[٢] رجلٌ مزمّل. قلتُ: من هذا؟ فقالوا: هذا سعد بن عبادة. قلتُ: وما شأنه؟ قالوا: هو وجع.

قال: فقام خطيب الأنصار، فحمد الله وأثنى عليه بما هو أهله. ثمّ قال: أمّا بعد، فنحن الأنصار وكتيبة الإسلام. وأنتم، يا معشر قريش، رهطٌ منّا وقد دفّت إلينا دافّةٌ منكم.

فإذا هم يريدون أن يختزلونا من أصلنا ويحضونا من الأمر. وكنتُ قد زوّرتُ[٣] في نفسي مقالةً،[٤] وكنتُ أريد أن أقوم بها بين يدي أبي بكر، وكنت أداري من أبي بكر بعض الحدّ. وكان هو أوقرمنّي وأجلّ. فلمّا أردتُ الكلام، قال: على رِسْلك. فكرهتُ أن أعصيه.

فحمد الله أبو بكر، رضي الله عنه، وأثنى عليه بما هو أهل، ثمّ قال، واللهِ ما ترك كلمةً كنتُ زوّرتُها في نفسي إلّا جاء بها، أو بأحسن منها في بديهته. ثمّ قال: أمّا بعد، فما ذكرتم فيكم من خيرٍ، يا معشر الأنصار، فأنتم له أهل. ولن تعرف العرب هذا الأمر إلّا لهذا الحيّ من قريش. فهم أوسط العرب داراً ونسباً. وإنّي قد رضيت لكم هذين الرجلين، فبايعوا أيّهما شئتم. قال: فأخذ بيدي وبيد أبي عبيدة بن الجرّاح.

---

١ مم: فاقضوا؛ وساقطة في لش. ٢ لش؛ مم: أظهركم. ٣ لش؛ مم: رويت. ٤ [مقالة] من لش؛ ساقطة من مم.

house and the Allies withdrew from us with their kinsmen into the Portico of the Sāʿida clan. It was the Emigrants who gathered before Abū Bakr, God show him mercy, whereupon I said, "Abū Bakr! Come with us to see our brethren, the Allies!" Thus we went with him leading the way, and we encountered two righteous men from the Allies who had witnessed the Battle of Badr. They asked, "O assembly of Emigrants, what do you seek?" We replied, "We seek out these brethren of ours from the Allies." "Return!" they said. "Settle on who will lead you among yourselves." I then replied, "Make way, for we won't be stopped." We came to them and, lo, they had gathered together at the Portico of the Sāʿida clan and in their midst was a man wrapped in a cloak. "Who is that?" I asked. "That's Saʿd ibn ʿUbādah," they answered. "What's wrong with him?" "He's taken ill," they said.

The spokesman for the Allies rose and, after praising and extolling God as is His due, had his say: "We the Allies are the Legion of Islam. You, O company of Quraysh, are but a troop in our ranks, a band of which wandered out of the desert into our midst."

By these words did they seek to rip us out by the roots and wrest power away from us. In my heart, I had prepared something to say and planned to say it in front of Abū Bakr so that he might help soften its harshness since his bearing was grander and more dignified than mine. When I wanted to speak, he said, "Rest easy," and I was loath to defy him.

Abū Bakr, God be pleased with him, offered praises to God as is His due, and then he spoke. By God, he neglected not a single word that I had prepared in my heart without uttering its like or, in his perceptive way, something even better. Then he said, "O company of Allies, you have mentioned your virtues, and you deserve as much, but the Arabs will not recognize the rule of any tribe save that of the Quraysh, for they are the noblest of Arabs in lineage and abode. Indeed, it would please me to offer you either of these two men, so pledge your fealty to whomever you wish." Then he took hold of my hand and the hand of Abū ʿUbaydah ibn al-Jarrāḥ.

قال: فوٱللهِ ماكرهت ممّا قال شيئاً إلّا هذه الكلمة. كنت لأن أقدم فتُضرب عنقي لا يُقرّبني ذلك إلى إثمٍ أحبُّ إليّ من أن أؤمّر على قومٍ فيهم أبو بكر.

فلمّا قضى أبو بكر مقالته، قام رجلٌ من الأنصار، فقال: أنا جُذَيلها المُحَكَّك وعذيقُها المرجّب. منّا أميرٌ ومنكم أميرٌ، يا معشر قريش، إلّا أجلبنا الحرب فيما بيننا وبينكم جذعاً.

قال معمر: قال قتادة: ٣،١،٢١

فقال عمر بن الخطّاب: لا يصلُح سيفان في غمد واحد، ولكنّ منّا الأُمراء ومنكم الوزراء.

قال معمر: قال الزهريّ في حديثه بالإسناد: ٤،١،٢١

فارتفعت الأصوات بيننا وكثر اللغط حتّى أشفقت الاختلاف. فقلت: يا أبا بكر، أبسط يدك أبايعك. قال: فبسط يده فبايعتُه، فبايعه المهاجرون وبايعه الأنصار.

قال: ونزونا على سعد حتّى قال قائلٌ: قتلتم سعداً! قال: قلتُ: قتل ٱلله سعداً.

وإنّا وٱللهِ ما رأينا فيما حضرنا من أمرنا أمراً كان أقوى من مبايعة أبي بكر. خشينا إن فارقنا القوم أنّ يُحدِثُوا بيعةً بعدنا. فإمّا أن نبايعهم على ما لا نرضى، وإمّا أن نخالفهم فيكون فساداً. فلا يَغُرّنّ امرأً أن يقول إنّ بيعة أبي بكر كان فلتةً. فقد كانت كذلك، غير أن ٱلله وقى شرّها وليس فيكم من تُقطع إليه الأعناق مثل أبي بكر.

فمن بايع رجلاً عن غير مشورة من المسلمين، فإنّه لا يبايع، ولا هو ولا الّذي بايعه[١] تغرّةً، أن يُقتلا.

---

١ لش؛ مم: لا يبايع هؤلاء الذين بايعه.

Naught but these words did I find objectionable, for I would have preferred to have stepped forward to be beheaded, were it not a sin, than to rule over a people in whose midst was Abū Bakr.

When Abū Bakr finished his speech, a man from the Allies stood up and cried, "I am the stout rubbing post and the short palm heavily laden with fruit:[235] Choose a leader from among yourselves, O company of Quraysh, and we shall choose one from our own ranks, lest war break out from our dispute and ensnare us once again!"

Maʿmar said: Qatādah said: 21.1.3

ʿUmar ibn al-Khaṭṭāb replied, "Two swords cannot fit in a single scabbard; rather, the commanders are to come from our ranks and the aides[236] from yours."

Maʿmar said: al-Zuhrī continued with his story according to his authorities: 21.1.4

As the people began lifting their voices from both directions and the clamor heightened until the dispute turned dangerous, I said, "Abū Bakr! Stretch out your hand so that I may pledge my fealty to you!" Abū Bakr stretched out his hand, and once I had pledged my fealty to him, the Emigrants and Allies did likewise. We pounced on Saʿd until someone cried out, "You've killed Saʿd!" "May God kill Saʿd!" I said.

Indeed, by God, of all the things that transpired during these events, we saw nothing more grave than the oath of fealty pledged to Abū Bakr. We feared that, had we left the Allies to their own devices, they would have pledged their own oath of fealty immediately after our departure. In that case, we would have had to pledge fealty to someone we could not abide, or we would have had to oppose them. In either case, chaos would have ensued. So let not a man be deceived into saying, "The oath of fealty to Abū Bakr was a hasty decision." Though it was indeed so, God dispelled its evil, and there is no one among you for whom men have risked their necks as they have for Abū Bakr.

If someone were to pledge fealty to a man from the Muslims without consultation,[237] his pledge of fealty would be invalid and both would be subject to death.

قال معمر: قال الزهريّ: ٢،٢١

وأخبرني عروة أنّ الرجلين الّذين لقياهم من الأنصار: عويم بن ساعدة ومعن بن عديّ. والّذي قال: أنا جذيلها المحكّك وعذيقها المرجّب، الحباب بن المنذر.

عبد الرزّاق عن معمر عن ليث عن واصل الأحدب عن المعرور بن سويد عن عمر بن الخطّاب، قال: ٣،٢١

من دعا إلى إمارة نفسه أو غيره، من غير مشورة من المسلمين، فلا يحلّ لكم إلّا أن تقتلوه.

عبد الرزّاق عن معمر عن ابن طاووس عن أبيه عن ابن عبّاس: ٤،٢١

قال عمر: اعقل عنّي ثلاثاً: الإمارة شورى، وفي فداء العرب مكان كلّ عبد عبدٌ، وفي ابن الأمة عبدان.

وكتم ابن طاووس الثالثة.

عبد الرزّاق عن معمر، قال: أخبرني محمّد بن عبد الله بن عبد الرحمن القاريّ عن أبيه: ٥،٢١

أنّ عمر بن الخطّاب ورجلاً من الأنصار كانا جالسين، فجاء عبد الرحمن بن عبد القاريّ، فجلس إليهما. فقال عمر: إنّا لا نحبّ أن يجالسنا من يرفع حديثاً. فقال له عبد الرحمن: لست أجالس أولئك، يا أمير المؤمنين! فقال عمر: بل، فجالس هؤلاء وهؤلاء ولا ترفع حديثاً. ثمّ قال عمر للأنصاريّ: من ترى الناس يقولون يكون الخليفة بعدي؟ فعدّد رجالاً من المهاجرين ولم يسمّ عليّاً. فقال عمر: فما لهم من أبي الحسن؟ فوالله إنّه لأحراهم، إن كان عليهم، أن يقيم على طريقة من الحقّ.

قال معمر: وأخبرني أبو إسحاق عن عمرو بن ميمون الأوديّ، قال: ٦،٢١

Maʿmar said: al-Zuhrī said: 21.2

ʿUrwah related to me that the two men from the Allies who met them were ʿUwaym ibn Sāʿidah and Maʿn ibn ʿAdī, and the one who said, "I am the stout rubbing post and the short palm heavy laden with fruit" was al-Ḥubāb ibn al-Mundhir.

ʿAbd al-Razzāq, on the authority of Maʿmar, on the the authority of Layth, on the authority 21.3
of Wāṣil al-Aḥdab, on the authority of al-Maʿrūr ibn Suwayd, on the authority of ʿUmar ibn al-Khaṭṭāb, who said:

With regard to a man who summons others to recognize his own political authority or that of another without consulting the Muslims, the only permissible course of action for you is to kill him.

ʿAbd al-Razzāq, on the authority of Maʿmar, on the authority of Ibn Ṭāwūs, on the authority 21.4
of his father, on the authority of Ibn ʿAbbās:

ʿUmar said, "Take to heart three of my instructions. Authority derives from Shura.[238] In the ransom customs of the Arabs, each slave is redeemed for another, and the son of a slave woman with two slaves . . ."[239]

Ibn Ṭāwūs kept the third to himself.

ʿAbd al-Razzāq, on the authority of Maʿmar, who said: Muḥammad ibn ʿAbd Allāh ibn ʿAbd 21.5
al-Raḥmān al-Qārī related to me on the authority of his father:

ʿUmar ibn al-Khaṭṭāb and a man from the Allies were sitting together, and ʿAbd al-Raḥmān ibn ʿAbd al-Qārī came and sat next to them. ʿUmar then said, "We do not wish to sit with those who spread rumors," to which ʿAbd al-Raḥmān replied, "Nor would I sit with the likes of such people, O Commander of the Faithful!" So ʿUmar said, "Rather those sorts of people sit with these sorts of people, so do not spread what is said." ʿUmar then spoke to the Allies: "Who do the people say shall be caliph after me?" The Allies proceeded to list several men from the Emigrants, but did not name ʿAlī. "What do they say of Abū l-Ḥasan?"[240] ʿUmar queried, "By God, were he to lead them, he would certainly be the most capable of keeping them on the path of Truth."

Maʿmar said: Abū Isḥāq reported to me on the authority of ʿAmr ibn Maymūn al-Awdī, 21.6
who said:

كنت عند عمر بن الخطّاب حين ولى الستّة الأمر، فلمّا جازوا اتبّعهم بصره. ثمّ قال: لئن ولّوها الأُجَيْلِح ليركبنّ بهم الطريق، يريد عليّاً.

I was at the house of ʿUmar ibn al-Khaṭṭāb when he granted authority to the Six,[241] and as they left his gaze followed them, whereupon he said, "If only they were to entrust the rule to little baldy, he could lead them along the True Path"—by whom he meant ʿAlī.

قَوْلُ عُمَرَ فِي أَهْلِ ٱلشُّورَى[1]

عبد الرزّاق عن معمر عن قتادة، قال: ١،٢٢

اجتمع نفرٌ فيهم المغيرة بن شعبة، فقالوا: من ترَوْن أمير المؤمنين مستخلِفاً؟ ١،١،٢٢

فقال قائلٌ: عليّ.

وقال قائلٌ: عثمان.

وقال قائلٌ: عبد الله بن عمر، فإنّ فيه خلفاً.

فقال المغيرة: أفلا أعلم لكم ذاك؟

قالوا: بلى.

قال: وكان عمر يركب كلّ سبت إلى أرض له. فلمّا كان يوم السبت، ذكر المغيرة إبّانه. فوقف على الطريق، فمرّ به على أتان له، تحته كساءٌ قد عطّفه عليها. فسلّم عمر، فردّ عليه المغيرة، ثمّ قال: يا أمير المؤمنين، أتأذن لي أن أسير معك؟

قال: نعم.

فلمّا أتى عمر ضيعته، نزل عن الأتان وأخذ الكساء، فبسطه واتّكأ عليه. وقعد المغيرة بين يديه فحدّثه. ثمّ قال المغيرة: يا أمير المؤمنين، إنّك والله ما تدري ما قدّر أجلك. فهلا حددت للناس أحداً. أو علّمت لهم عَلَماً ينتهون إليه؟

٢،١،٢٢ قال: فاستوى عمر جالساً، ثمّ قال: هيه، اجتمعتم، فقلتم: من ترون أمير المؤمنين مستخلفاً؟ فقال قائلٌ عليّاً، وقال قائلٌ عبدَ الله بن عمر، فإنّ فيه خَلَفاً. قال: فلا يأمنوا يُسأل عنها رجلان من آل عمر؟

فقلت: أنا لا أعلم لك ذلك.

قال: قلت: فاستخلِف.

قال: من؟

What ʿUmar Said about the Members of the Shura[242]

ʿAbd al-Razzāq, on the authority of Maʿmar, on the authority of Qatādah, who said: **22.1**

A group gathered together, and al-Mughīrah ibn Shuʿbah was among them. **22.1.1** They said, "Whom do you suppose the Commander of the Faithful will designate as his successor?"

"ʿAlī," said one.

"ʿUthmān," said another.

Yet another suggested, "ʿAbd Allāh ibn ʿUmar, for he's the caliph's son."

Then al-Mughīrah said, "Why don't I find out for you all?"

"Yes, do so!" they answered.

ʿUmar was accustomed to riding out on the Sabbath to a plot of land he owned, so when the Sabbath arrived, al-Mughīrah kept its time in mind and waited by the side of the road. ʿUmar passed by him seated on the jenny ass that he owned; beneath him was a cloth, which he had folded and placed atop the jenny ass. ʿUmar greeted him with peace, and al-Mughīrah returned the greeting and said, "O Commander of Faithful, might you permit me to walk alongside you?"

"Yes," he said.

When ʿUmar arrived at his estate, he descended from the jenny ass, removed the cloth, unfolded it, and reclined on it. Al-Mughīra sat down in front of him and related his story, after which he said, "O Commander of the Faithful, by God, you know not when the hour of your death has been ordained, so haven't you set some guideline for the people, or given them some indication that they might follow?"

ʿUmar sat up straight and said, "I see, so you've all gathered together and **22.1.2** said, 'Whom do you think the Commander of the Faithful will designate as his successor?' One of you said 'ʿAlī', and someone else said, 'ʿAbd Allāh ibn ʿUmar, for he's the caliph's son.' Didn't they feel safe enough to ask that of two men from ʿUmar's family?"

"That," I said, "I cannot tell you."

Then I said, "You must designate a successor!"

قلت: عثمان.

قال: أخشى عقده وأثرته.

قال: قلت: عبد الرحمن بن عوف.

قال: مؤمن ضعيف.

قال: فقلت: فالزبير.

قال: ضَرِسٌ.

قال: قلت: طلحة بن عبيد الله.

قال: رضاؤه رضاءُ مؤمنٍ، وغضبه غضبُ كافرٍ. أمّا إنّي لو ولَّيتُها إيّاه لجعل خاتمه في يد امرأته.

قال: قلت: فعليٌّ؟

قال: أمّا إنّه أحراهم، إن كان عليهم[1] أن يقيم على سنّة نبيّهم صلّى الله عليه وسلّم، وقد كنّا نعيب عليه مزاحةً كانت فيه.

عبد الرزّاق عن معمر عن الزهريّ عن سالم عن ابن عمر، قال: ٢،٢٢

دخلت على حفصة، فقالت: علمت أنّ أباك غير مستخلف؟

قال: قلت: ما كان ليفعل.

قالت: إنّه فاعل.

قال: فحلفت أن أكلّمه في ذلك. فسكتّ حتّى غزوت، ولم أكلّمه. قال: وكنت كأنّما أحمل بيميني جبلاً حتّى رجعت، فدخلت عليه. فسألني عن حال الناس، وأنا أخبره، ثمّ قلت له: إنّي سمعتُ الناس يقولون مقالةً، فآليت أن أقولها لك: زعموا أنّك غير مستخلف. وإنّه لو كان لك راعي إبلٍ أو راعي غنمٍ. ثمّ جاءك وتركها، رأيت أن قد ضيّع. فرعاية الناس أشدّ.

١ [عليهم] أنا؛ ساقطة من م.

"Who?" he asked.

"ʿUthmān," I said.

"I fear his bond to his tribe and his cupidity,"[243] he said.

"ʿAbd al-Raḥmān ibn ʿAwf," I said.

"A weak believer," he said.

"Then al-Zubayr?" I asked.

"Too stubborn,"[244] he answered.

"Ṭalḥah ibn ʿUbayd Allāh," I suggested.

"His calmness is that of a believer, but his anger is that of an infidel. Were I to place him in charge of the caliphate, then I might as well have handed the caliphal seal to his wife."

"What about ʿAlī then?" I asked.

"Indeed, he's the most capable of them—if it were he—to rule according to the Prophet's Sunnah, but we used to rebuke him for the touch of foolishness that was in him."

ʿAbd al-Razzāq, on the authority of Maʿmar, on the authority of al-Zuhrī, on the authority of Sālim, on the authority of Ibn ʿUmar, who said: **22.2**

I went in to see my sister Ḥafṣah, and she said, "Did you know that your father is not going to designate a successor?"

"He surely won't do that!" I said.

"Indeed, he will," she replied.

Thus I made an oath that I would speak to him of this, but I remained quiet until after I had returned from a military expedition, and I did not speak to him. Until I returned, it was as though I had been carrying a mountain in my right hand, so I went to see him. He asked about the affairs of the people. I told him whatever news I knew, and then I said, "I have heard the people making certain statements that I swore I would report to you: They claim that you will not designate a successor. Now, say you had a shepherd tending to camels, or one who tended sheep, and he came to you and left his flocks behind. Wouldn't you have considered them lost? Shepherding people is an even more serious matter!"

قال: فوافقه قولي، فوضع رأسه ساعةً، ثمّ رفعه إليّ. فقال: إنّ الله يحفظ دينه، وإنّي إن لا أستخلف، فإنّ رسول الله صلّى الله عليه وسلّم لم يستخلف. وإن أستخلف، فإنّ أبا بكر قد استخلف. قال: فما هو إلّا أن ذكر رسول الله صلّى الله عليه وسلّم وأبا بكر، فعلمت أنّه لم يكن ليعدل برسول الله صلّى الله عليه وسلّم وأنّه غير مستخلف.

He agreed with what I had said and lowered his head for some time. When he lifted his head to me, he said, "Certainly God will preserve His religion, even if I do not designate my successor. Indeed, the Messenger of God did not designate a successor. Were I to designate my successor—well, Abū Bakr also designated his successor. The matter only requires that one keep in mind the Messenger of God and Abū Bakr." At that point, I knew that he would not deviate from the Messenger of God's precedent and that he would not be designating a successor.

اسْتِخلَافُ أَبي بَكْرٍ عُمَرَ رَحِمَهما اللهُ

١،٢٣ عن الرزّاق عن معمرعن الزهريّ عن القاسم بن محمّد عن أسماء بنت عميس، قالت:

دخل رجلٌ على أبي بكر، رحمه الله، وهو شاكٍ، فقال: استخلفتَ عمر وقد كان عتا علينا ولا سلطانَ له. فلو قد ملكنا لكان وعثاً علينا وأعتى. فكيف تقول لله إذا لقيتَه؟

فقال أبو بكر: أجلسوني. فأجلسوه، فقال: هل تفرّقني إلّا بالله؟ فإنّي أقول إذا لقيتُه: استخلفتُ عليهم خيرَ أهلك.

٢،٢٣ قال معمر: فقلت للزُّهريّ: ما قول: خير أهلك؟ قال: خير أهل مكّة.

Abū Bakr's Designation of 'Umar as His Successor

'Abd al-Razzāq, on the authority of Ma'mar, on the authority of al-Zuhrī, on the authority of al-Qāsim ibn Muḥammad, on the authority of Asmā' bint 'Umays, who said: 23.1

A man from the Emigrants came to see Abū Bakr, God grant him mercy, while he was stricken ill, and he said, "You have designated 'Umar to succeed you. He has been harsh with us, even though he lacked authority. If he is to rule over us, then he will certainly be stern with us and even harsher. How will you tell this to God when you meet Him?"

"Help me sit up," said Abū Bakr, and so they sat him upright. He then spoke: "Who else but God can you mention to frighten me? Indeed, this is what I will say when I meet him: 'I designated the best of your people to rule over them!'"

Ma'mar said: I asked al-Zuhrī, "What did he mean when he said 'the best of 23.2
your people'?" He answered, "The best of the Meccans."

بَيْعَةُ أَبِي بَكْرٍ رَضِيَ اللهُ عَنْهُ

عبد الرزّاق عن معمر عن أيّوب عن عكرمة، قال: ١،٢٤

لمّا بويع لأبي بكر تخلّف عليٌّ في بيته. فلقيه عمرُ، فقال: تخلّفتَ عن بيعة أبي بكر؟ فقال: إنّي آليتُ يمين حين قُبض رسول الله صلّى الله عليه وسلّم ألّا أرتدي برداءٍ إلّا إلى الصلاة المكتوبة حتّى أجمع القرآن، فإنّي خشيتُ أن يتفلّت القرآن. ثمّ خرج، فبايعه.

عبد الرزّاق عن معمر عن أبي إسحاق عن العلاءِ بن عرار،[1] قال: سألتُ ابن عمر عن عليّ وعثمان، فقال: ٢،٢٤

أمّا عليٌّ، فهذا بيته، يعني بيته قريبٌ من بيت النبيّ صلّى الله عليه وسلّم في المسجد. وسأحدّثك عنه، يعني عثمان، وأمّا عثمان، رحمه الله، فإنّه أذنب فيما بينه وبين الله ذنباً عظيماً، فغفر له. وأذنب فيما بينه وبينكم ذنباً صغيراً، فقتلتموه.

أخبرنا عبد الرزّاق، قال: أخبرنا ابن مبارك عن مالك بن مغول عن ابن أَبجر، قال: ٣،٢٤

لمّا بويع لأبي بكر رضي الله عنه، جاء أبو سفيان إلى عليّ. فقال: غلبَكم على هذا الأمر أذلّ أهل بيت في قريش! امّا والله لأملأنّها خيلاً ورجالاً. قال: فقلتُ: ما زلتَ عدوّاً للإسلام وأهله، فما ضرّ ذلك الإسلام وأهله شيئاً. إنّا رأينا أبا بكر لها أهلاً.

أخبرنا عبد الرزّاق، قال: أخبرنا معمر عن أيوب عن ابن سرين، قال:[2] ٤،٢٤

---

١ مم: عيزار. ٢ [قال:] أنا؛ ساقطة من مم.

The Oath of Fealty Pledged to Abū Bakr

ʿAbd al-Razzāq, on the authority of Maʿmar, on the authority of Ayyūb, on the authority of ʿIkrimah, who said: **24.1**

When the oath of fealty was pledged to Abū Bakr, ʿAlī withdrew to his house. ʿUmar met him and said, "So you've withdrawn to avoid pledging fealty to Abū Bakr?" ʿAlī replied, "I swore an oath when the Messenger of God was taken from this world that I would not don a coat until I had collected the Qur'an, except to perform the required prayers, for I feared that the Qur'an would slip away."[245] After that he came out and pledged his fealty to Abū Bakr.

ʿAbd al-Razzāq, on the authority of Maʿmar, on the authority of Abū Isḥāq, on the authority of al-ʿAlāʾ ibn ʿArār, who said: **24.2**

I asked Ibn ʿUmar about ʿAlī and ʿUthmān, and he said, "As for ʿAlī, that there is his house"—meaning that ʿAlī's house was near the Prophet's house in the mosque—"and I will tell you a story about the other"—meaning ʿUthmān. "As for ʿUthmān," he continued, "God grant him mercy. He committed a grave sin against God, but God forgave him; he committed but a minor sin against all of you, but you all murdered him."[246]

ʿAbd al-Razzāq related to us, saying: Ibn Mubārak related to us on the authority of Mālik ibn Mighwal, on the authority of Ibn Abjar, who said: **24.3**

When the oath of fealty was pledged to Abū Bakr, Abū Sufyān came to ʿAlī and said, "The lowliest households of the Quraysh have seized this power to rule over all of you. By God, I will fill the city with horses and men!" ʿAlī replied, "I have said before that you remain an enemy to Islam and its people. This brings no harm to Islam and its people and, indeed, we regard Abū Bakr as worthy."

ʿAbd al-Razzāq related to us, saying: Maʿmar related to us, on the authority of Ayyūb, on the authority of Ibn Sīrīn: **24.4**

قال رجل لعليّ: أخبرني عن قريش. قال: أوزننا أحلاماً إخوتنا بني أميّة. وأنجدُنا عند اللقاء وأسخانا بما ملكت اليمينُ فهم بنو هاشم. وريحانة قريش الّتي تشمّ بها بنو المغيرة. إليك عنّي سائر اليوم.

٥،٢٤ أخبرني عبد الرزّاق، قال: أخبرنا معمر، قال:

قال رجلٌ لعليّ: أخبرني عن قريش. قال: أمّا نحن، فأنجد أمجاد هداة أجواد. وأمّا إخواننا بنو أميّة، قادة ذادة. وريحانة قريش الّتي تشمّ بها بنو المغيرة.

A man once said to ʿAlī, "Tell me about the Quraysh." ʿAlī replied, "Our most cunning in political strategy are our brethren, the Umayyah clan; the bravest of us at the moment of battle and the most generous with the spoils is the Hāshim clan; the sweet-smelling flower that perfumes the Quraysh is the Mughīrah clan. Away with you now, that's enough for today."

ʿAbd al-Razzāq related to us, saying: Maʿmar related to us, saying: **24.5**

A man once said to ʿAlī, "Tell me about the Quraysh." ʿAlī replied, "As for us, the Hāshim clan, we are the braves, the men of distinction, the leaders, and the virtuous; as for our brethren, the Umayyah clan, they are the vanguards of the defense; and the sweet-smelling flower that perfumes the Quraysh is the Mughīrah clan."

غَزوةُ ذاتِ السَّلاسِلِ وَخبَرُ عَلِيٍّ وَمُعاوِيَة

عبد الرزّاق عن معمر عن الزهريّ، قال: ١،٢٥

ثمّ إنّ رسول الله صلّى الله عليه وسلّم بعدما هاجر وجاء الّذين كانوا بأرض ١،١،٢٥
الحبشة، بعث بعثين قِبَل الشام، إلى كلب وبلقين وغسّان وكفّار العرب الّذين في مشارف الشام. فأمّر رسول الله صلّى الله عليه وسلّم على أحد البعثين أبا عبيدة بن الجرّاح، وهو أحد بني فِهر، وأمّر على البعث الآخر عمرو بن العاص. فانتدب في بعث أبي عبيدة أبو بكر وعمرُ. فلمّا كان عند خروج البعثين، دعا رسول الله صلّى الله عليه وسلّم أبا عبيدة بن الجرّاح وعمرو بن العاص، فقال لهما: لا تَعاصيا. فلمّا فصلا عن المدينة، جاء أبو عبيدة. فقال لعمرو بن العاص: إنّ رسول الله صلّى الله عليه وسلّم عهد إلينا أن لا تعاصيا، فإمّا أن تُطيعني وإمّا أن أطيعك. فقال عمرو بن العاص: بل أَطِعْني.

فأطاعه أبو عبيدة، فكان عمرو أمير البعثين كليهما. فوجد من ذلك عمر بن الخطّاب وجداً شديداً، فكلّم أبا عبيدة، فقال: أتُطيع ابن النابغة وتؤمّره على نفسك وعلى أبي بكر وعلينا؟ ما هذا برأي!

فقال أبو عبيدة لعمر بن الخطّاب: ابن أمّ، إنّ رسول الله صلّى الله عليه وسلّم عَهِدَ إليّ وإليه أن لا تعاصيا. فخشيت إن لم أطِعه أن أعصي رسول الله صلّى الله عليه وسلّم ويدخل بيني وبينه الناس، وإنّي والله لأطيعنّه حتّى أقفل.

فلمّا قفلوا، كلّمَ عمرُ بن الخطّاب[1] رسول الله صلّى الله عليه وسلّم وشكى إليه ذلك.

---

١ [رسول الله . . . عمر بن الخطاب] ساقطة من م؛ النص أعلاه من رواية غير معمر عن الزهري في تاريخ مدينة دمشق لابن عساكر واقتضاه السياق.

The Expedition of Dhāt al-Salāsil and the Story of ʿAlī and Muʿāwiyah[247]

ʿAbd al-Razzāq, on the authority of Maʿmar, on the authority of al-Zuhrī, who said: 25.1

After the Messenger of God had undertaken the Hijrah and those who had 25.1.1
been in the land of Abyssinia had arrived in Medina, the Prophet dispatched two expeditions into Syria against the Kalb, Bal-Qayn, and Ghassān tribes, as well as the infidel Arabs who dwelled along the Syrian steppe. He appointed Abū ʿUbaydah ibn al-Jarrāḥ, a member of the Fihr clan, to be commander of the first expedition, and appointed ʿAmr ibn al-ʿĀṣ as the commander of the second. Abū Bakr and ʿUmar left Abū ʿUbaydah in charge of his expedition.

At the time of the two expeditions' departure, the Messenger of God called for Abū ʿUbaydah ibn al-Jarrāḥ and ʿAmr ibn al-ʿĀṣ to come to see him. "Do not defy one another's commands," he ordered. When they had left Medina behind, Abū ʿUbaydah approached ʿAmr ibn al-ʿĀṣ and said, "The Messenger of God charged us not to defy one another's commands; either you should submit to my command, or I should submit to yours." ʿAmr ibn al-ʿĀṣ answered, "Nay, submit to my command."

Thus did Abū ʿUbaydah submit to the command of ʿAmr, leaving ʿAmr the chief commander of both expeditions. That exasperated ʿUmar ibn al-Khaṭṭāb, who said to Abū ʿUbaydah, "Are you actually going to heed the commands of Ibn al-Nābighah, and recognize him not as just your commander, but as Abū Bakr's and ours as well? What is this nonsense?"

"Listen, brother!" Abū ʿUbaydah replied. "The Messenger of God made us both swear that we would not defy one another's commands. I fear that if I don't submit to his command, not only will I disobey God's Messenger but the people will involve themselves in our dispute as well. So, by God, I am determined to submit to his command until I return."

When they had returned, ʿUmar ibn al-Khaṭṭāb spoke to the Messenger of God and complained to him about the matter. The Messenger of God answered, "I would never bestow authority on anyone over you without first giving you precedence." By "you" he meant the Emigrants.

فقال رسول الله صلّى الله عليه وسلّم: ما أنا بموثِر بها عليكم إلّا بعدكم، يريد المهاجرين.

وكانت تلك الغزوة تُسمّى ذات السلاسل، أسر فيها ناسٌ كثيرٌ من العرب وسُبُوا.
ثمّ أمّر رسول الله صلّى الله عليه وسلّم بعد ذلك أسامة بن زيد، وهو غلامٌ شابٌّ، فانتدب في بعثة عمر بن الخطّاب والزبير بن العوّام. فتوفّي رسول الله صلّى الله عليه وسلّم قبل أن يفصل ذلك البعث. فأنفذه أبو بكر الصدّيق بعد رسول الله صلّى الله عليه وسلّم.

٢،١،٢٥ ثمّ بعث أبو بكر حين وَلِيَ الأمر بعد وفاة رسول الله صلّى الله عليه وسلّم ثلاثة أمراء إلى الشام: وأمّر خالد بن سعيد على جند، وأمّر عمرو بن العاص على جند، وأمّر شرحبيل بن حسنة على جند، وبعث خالد بن الوليد على جند قِبَل العراق.

ثمّ إن عمر كلّم أبا بكر، فلم يزل يكلّمه حتّى أمّر يزيد بن أَبي سفيان على خالد بن سعيد وجنده. وذلك من موجدةٍ وجدها عمر بن الخطّاب على خالد بن سعيد حين قدم من اليمن بعد وفاة رسول الله صلّى الله عليه وسلّم. فلقي عليَّ بن أبي طالب خالد بن سعيد، فقال: أغُلبتم يا بني عبد مناف على أمركم؟ فلم يحملها عليه أبو بكر، وحملها عليه عمر. فقال عمر: إنّك لتترك إمرته على التغالب. فلمّا استعمله أبو بكر، ذكر ذلك. فكلّم أبا بكر، فاستعمل مكانه يزيد بن أبي سفيان. فأدركه يزيد أميرًا بعد أن وصل الشام بذي المروة.

وكتب أبو بكر إلى[1] خالد بن الوليد، فأمره بالمسير إلى الشام بجنده، ففعل. فكانت الشام على أربعة أمراء حتّى توفّي أبو بكر.

٣،١،٢٥ فلمّا استخلف عمر، نزع خالد بن الوليد وأمّر مكانه أبا عبيدة بن الجرّاح. ثمّ قدم الجابية، فنزع شرحبيل بن حسنة، وأمر جنده أن يتفرّقوا في الأمراء الثلاثة.

فقال شرحبيل بن حسنة: يا أمير المؤمنين، أعجزتُ أم خُنتُ؟

قال: لم تعجزْ ولم تخُنْ.

قال: ففيمَ عزلتَني؟

١ [إلى] أنا: ساقطة من م.

That expedition was named Dhāt al-Salāsil.[248] During that expedition large numbers of Arabs were taken into bondage as captives. Then, after that expedition, the Messenger of God appointed Usāmah ibn Zayd as commander, though he was still a young man, and he placed ʿUmar ibn al-Khaṭṭāb and al-Zubayr ibn al-ʿAwwām in command of a contingent as well; but the Prophet passed away before he was able to specify the mission of those forces. Hence, it fell to Abū Bakr al-Ṣiddīq to accomplish the task after the Messenger of God.

When Abū Bakr later assumed the leadership of the community, after 25.1.2 the death of God's Messenger, he dispatched three commanders to Syria: he appointed Khālid ibn Saʿīd over one army, ʿAmr ibn al-ʿĀṣ over another army, and Shuraḥbīl ibn Ḥasanah over a third army. Lastly, he dispatched Khālid ibn al-Walīd to Iraq at the head of an army.

Afterward ʿUmar spoke with Abū Bakr, continually pressing him to appoint Yazīd ibn Muʿāwiyah in command over Khālid ibn Saʿīd and his army. ʿUmar ibn al-Khaṭṭāb did that because he held a grudge against Khālid ibn Saʿīd. When Khālid had returned from Yemen after the Prophet's death, he met with ʿAlī ibn Abī Ṭālib and protested, "O Sons of ʿAbd Manāf! Have you been forced to relinquish your leadership?"[249] Abū Bakr bore him no ill will for that, but ʿUmar did and said, "And so shall you be forced to relinquish command!"[250] Hence, when Abū Bakr made Khālid a general, ʿUmar reminded Abū Bakr of this and pressed him until he appointed Yazīd ibn Abī Sufyān in his place.[251] Yazīd granted Khālid ibn Saʿīd the rank of commander once he had arrived in Syria at Dhū l-Marwah.

Abū Bakr then wrote to Khālid ibn al-Walīd and ordered him to march his army toward Syria, and so he did. Thus was Syria under the authority of four different commanders until Abū Bakr passed away.

Once ʿUmar assumed the caliphate, he dismissed Khālid ibn al-Walīd and 25.1.3 appointed Abū ʿUbaydah ibn al-Jarrāḥ in his place as commander. Later, ʿUmar went to al-Jābiyah and dismissed Shuraḥbīl ibn Ḥasanah and ordered his army to be dispersed among the remaining three commanders.

"O Commander of the Faithful," said Shuraḥbīl ibn Ḥasanah, "was I inept or disloyal?"

"You were neither inept nor disloyal," answered ʿUmar.

Shuraḥbīl pressed him, "Why then did you remove me from command?"

"I'd be remiss," ʿUmar replied, "were I to keep you in command after having found someone stronger than you."

قال: تحرّجت أن أؤمّرك وأنا أجد أقوى منك.

قال: فاعْذُرْني، يا أمير المؤمنين.

قال: سأفعل، ولو علمت غير ذلك، لم أفعل. قال: قام عمر فعذره، ثمّ أمر عمرو بن العاص بالمسير إلى مصر.

وبقي الشام على أميرين: أبي عبيدة بن الجرّاح ويزيد بن أبي سفيان. ثمّ توفّي أبو عبيدة بن الجرّاح، فاستخلف خالداً وابن عمّه عياض بن غنم. فأقرّه عمر، فقيل لعمر: كيف تقرّ عياض بن غنم وهو رجل جواد لا يمنع شيئاً يسأله وقد نزعت خالد بن الوليد في أن كان يعطي دونك؟ فقال عمر: إنّ هذه شيمة عياض في ماله حين يخلص إلى ماله، وإنّي مع ذلك لم أكن لأغيّر أمراً قضاه أبو عبيدة بن الجرّاح.

قال: ثمّ توفّي يزيد بن أبي سفيان، فأمّر مكانه معاوية. فنعاه عمر إلى أبي سفيان، فقال: احتسب يزيد، يا أبا سفيان.

قال: يرحمه الله، فمن أمّرت مكانه؟

قال: معاوية.

قال: وصلتك رحم.

قال: ثمّ توفّي عياض بن غنم، فأمّر مكانه عمير بن سعد الأنصاري، فكانت الشام على معاوية وعمير حتّى قُتل عمر.

٤،١،٢٥ فاستخلف عثمان بن عفّان، فعزل عميراً وترك الشام لمعاوية. ونزع المغيرة بن شعبة عن الكوفة وأمّر مكانه سعد بن أبي وقّاص. ونزع عمرو بن العاص عن مصر وأمّر مكانه عبد الله بن سعد بن أبي سرح. ونزع أبا موسى الأشعريّ وأمّر عبد الله بن عامر بن كريز. ثم نزع[1] سعد بن أبي وقّاص من الكوفة وأمّر الوليد بن عقبة. ثمّ شُهد على الوليد، فجلده ونزعه، وأمّر سعيد بن العاص مكانه.

---

[1] مم: أمر.

"O Commander of the Faithful," Shuraḥbīl asked, "will you vouch for my honor?"

"I will," answered ʿUmar, "and indeed, I would not do so if I knew it not to be true." Thus ʿUmar stood before the people and vouched for Shuraḥbīl's honor. Subsequently he ordered ʿAmr ibn al-ʿĀṣ to march against Egypt.

Two commanders retained their authority over Syria: Abū ʿUbaydah ibn al-Jarrāḥ and Yazīd ibn Abī Sufyān. Soon thereafter Abū ʿUbaydah passed away, leaving Khālid and his paternal cousin, ʿIyāḍ ibn Ghanm, as his successors. ʿUmar confirmed ʿIyāḍ as commander, but someone complained to him, "How is it that you have confirmed ʿIyāḍ ibn Ghanm, when he's an openhanded man who gives away whatever is asked of him, but you have dismissed Khālid ibn al-Walīd because he gave without your permission?"[252] ʿUmar replied, "That's just the way ʿIyāḍ treats his wealth whenever he happens upon it. Even so, far be it from me to alter a command issued by Abū ʿUbaydah ibn al-Jarrāḥ!"

When Yazīd ibn Abī Sufyān passed away, ʿUmar appointed his brother Muʿāwiyah in his place. ʿUmar brought news of his death to Abū Sufyān, saying, "Abū Sufyān, God has taken Yazīd."[253]

"May God grant him mercy," he answered. "Whom have you appointed in his place?"

"Muʿāwiyah,"said ʿUmar.

"May the bonds of kinship keep you," he replied.[254]

Then ʿIyāḍ ibn Ghanm passed away, so ʿUmar appointed ʿUmayr ibn Saʿd the Ally in his place as commander. Thus were ʿUmayr and Muʿāwiyah in command of Syria until ʿUmar was murdered.

ʿUthmān ibn ʿAffān then assumed the caliphate and removed ʿUmayr, leaving Syria to Muʿāwiyah. He dismissed al-Mughīrah ibn Shuʿbah from Kūfah and appointed Saʿd ibn Abī Waqqāṣ as commander in his place. He dismissed ʿAmr ibn al-ʿĀṣ from Egypt and appointed ʿAbd Allāh ibn Saʿd ibn Abī Sarḥ as commander in his place. He dismissed Abū Mūsā l-Ashʿarī and appointed ʿAbd Allāh ibn ʿĀmir ibn Kurayz as commander. Later on he also dismissed Saʿd ibn Abī Waqqāṣ from Kūfah and appointed al-Walīd ibn ʿUqbah as commander in his place, but when charges of misconduct were brought against al-Walīd, ʿUthmān had him scourged and dismissed him,[255] appointing Saʿīd ibn al-ʿĀṣ in his place as commander. 25.1.4

In the events to follow, the people began to grumble and soon plunged headlong into the Civil War. Saʿīd ibn al-ʿĀṣ left for hajj, but when later he

ثمّ قال الناس ونشبوا في الفتنة. فحجّ سعيد بن العاص، ثمّ قفل من حجّه. فلقيته خيل العراق، فأرجعه من العذيب. وأخرج أهل مصر عبد الله بن سعد بن أبي سرح، وأقرّ أهل البصرة عبد الله بن عامر بن كريز.

٥،١،٢٥ فكان ذلك أوّل الفتنة حتّى إذا قُتل عثمان، رحمه الله. بايع الناس عليّ بن أبي طالب، فأرسل إلى طلحة والزبير: إن شئتما، فبايعاني. وإن شئتما، بايعتُ أحدكما. قالا: بل نبايعك. ثمّ طمرا[١] إلى مكّة، وبمكّة عائشة زوج النبيّ صلّى الله عليه وسلّم تكلّم بما يتكلّمان به، فأعانتهما على رأيهما. فأطاعهم ناس كثير من قريش، فخرجوا قِبَل البصرة يطلبون بدم ابن عفّان. وخرج معهم عبد الرحمن بن أبي بكر، وخرج معهم عبد الرحمن بن عتّاب بن أسيد وعبد الرحمن[٢] بن الحارث بن هشام وعبدالله بن الزبير ومروان بن الحكم في أناس من قريش. كلّموا أهل البصرة، وحدّثوهم أنّ عثمان قُتل مظلوماً وأنّهم جاءوا تائبين ممّا كانوا غلوا به في أمر عثمان. فأطاعهم عامّة أهل البصرة واعتزل الأحنف بمن معه من تميم. وخرجت عبد القيس إلى عليّ بن أبي طالب بعامّة من أطاعها.

وركبت عائشة جملاً لها، يقال له عسكر، وهي في هودج قد ألبسته الدفوف، يعني جلود البقر، فقالت: إنما أريد أن يحجز بين الناس مكاني. فقالت: ولم أحسب أن يكون بين الناس قتال. ولو علمت ذلك، لم أقف ذلك الموقف أبداً. قالت: فلم يسمع الناس كلامي، ولم يلتفتوا إليّ.

وكان القتال. فقُتل يومئذٍ سبعون من قريش، كلُّهم يأخذ بخطام جمل عائشة حتّى يقتل. ثمّ حملوا الهودج حتّى ادخلوه منزلاً من تلك المنازل. وجُرح مروان جراحاً شديدةً، وقُتل طلحة بن عبيد الله يومئذ وقُتل الزبير بعد ذلك بوادي السباع.

١ [طمرا] أنا؛ ساقطة من م. ٢ أنا؛ م: عبد الله.

returned from his hajj, he encountered a band of cavalry from Iraq that forced him to return from al-ʿUdhayb. The settlers in Egypt[256] also exiled ʿAbd Allāh ibn Saʿd ibn Abī Sarḥ, but the settlers in Basra remained loyal to ʿAbd Allāh ibn ʿĀmir ibn Kurayz.

Thus began the Civil War, and eventually ʿUthmān, God grant him mercy, **25.1.5** was murdered. The people pledged their allegiance to ʿAlī ibn Abī Ṭālib, and he sent a letter to Ṭalḥah and al-Zubayr: "If you two wish, pledge me your allegiance; but if you prefer, I shall pledge my allegiance to one of you." "Nay," they replied, "rather we shall pledge allegiance to you." Soon thereafter, the two fled to hide in Mecca. There in Mecca, ʿĀʾishah, the Prophet's wife, made common cause with al-Zubayr and Ṭalḥah and aided them in their scheme. A great number of the Quraysh heeded them and set off for Basra, calling for vengeance for the spilling of ʿUthmān's blood. Those who set off with them were, among others from the Quraysh, ʿAbd al-Raḥmān ibn Abī Bakr, ʿAbd al-Raḥmān ibn ʿAttāb ibn Asīd, ʿAbd al-Raḥmān ibn al-Ḥārith ibn Hishām,[257] ʿAbd Allāh ibn al-Zubayr, and Marwān ibn al-Ḥakam. They addressed the settlers in Basra and informed them that ʿUthmān had been murdered without just cause and that they had come as penitents, repentant of all excesses they had committed during ʿUthmān's reign. Most of Basra's settlers heeded them, but al-Aḥnaf withdrew along with his supporters from the Tamīm tribe. The ʿAbd al-Qays tribe went out to join ʿAlī ibn Abī Ṭālib with all those people who would heed them.

ʿĀʾishah rode atop a camel of hers named ʿAskar, and she sat inside a howdah covered by *dufūf*—meaning cowskin. She called out, "My only wish is that my presence will restrain the people." She later said, "Little did I know that hostilities would break out between them. Had I known that, I would have never have put myself in that position." ʿĀʾishah continued, "The people did not heed my words and paid me no mind."

Thus the battle ensued. Seventy Quraysh were killed that day, and each of them grabbed onto the halter of ʿĀʾishah's camel until it had been slain in battle. Then they carried the howdah away and placed it inside one of the encampments nearby. Marwān was severely wounded, Ṭalḥah ibn ʿUbayd Allāh was slain during the battle,[258] and al-Zubayr was murdered after the battle in Wādi l-Sibāʿ.[259] ʿĀʾishah and Marwān made the return journey along with the remaining Quraysh, and when they had approached Medina, ʿĀʾishah left them behind and headed toward Mecca. Marwān and al-Aswad ibn Abī

وقفلت عائشة ومروان بمن بقي من قريش، فقدموا المدينة. وانطلقت عائشة، فقدمت مكّة. فكان مروان والأسود بن أبي البختريّ على المدينة وأهلها، يغلبان عليها.

٢٥، ١، ٦ وهاجت الحرب بين عليّ ومعاوية. فكانت بعوثهما تقدم المدينة وتقدم مكّة للحجّ. فأيّهما سبق، فهو أمير الموسم أيّام الحجّ للناس. ثمّ إنّها أرسلت أمّ حبيبة زوج النبيّ صلّى الله عليه وسلّم إلى أمّ سلمة، قالت إحداهما للأخرى: تعاليَ نكتب إلى معاوية وعليّ أن يقلعا عن هذه البعوث الّتي تروع الناس حتّى تجتمع الأمّة على أحدهما. فقالت أمّ حبيبة: كفيتك أخي معاوية. وقالت أمّ سلمة: كفيتك عليّاً. فكتبت كلّ واحدة منهما إلى صاحبها، وبعث وفداً من قريش والأنصار. فأمّا معاوية، فأطاع أمّ حبيبة. وأمّا عليّ، فهمّ أن يطيع أمّ سلمة، فنهاه الحسن بن عليّ عن ذلك. فلم تزل بعوثهما وعمّالهما يختلفون إلى المدينة ومكّة حتّى قُتل عليّ، رحمه الله تعالى. ثمّ اجتمع الناس على معاوية، ومروان وابن البختريّ يغلبان على أهل المدينة في تلك الفتنة.

٢٥، ١، ٧ وكانت مصر في سلطان عليّ بن أبي طالب، فأمّر عليها قيس بن سعد بن عبادة الأنصاريّ. وكان حامل راية الأنصار مع رسول الله صلّى الله عليه وسلّم يوم بدر وغيرها،[١] وكان قيس من ذوي الرأي من الناس إلّا ما غلب عليه من أمر الفتنة. فكان معاوية وعمرو بن العاص جاهدين على إخراجه من مصر، ويغلبان على مصر. وكان قد امتنع منهما بالدهاء والمكيدة، فلم يقدرا على أن يفتحا مصر حتّى كاد معاوية قيس بن سعد من قِبَل عليّ.

قال: فكان معاوية يحدّث رجلاً من ذوي الرأي من قريش، فيقول: ما ابتدعت من مكيدة قطّ أعجب عندي من مكيدة كايدتُ بها قيس بن سعد من قِبَل عليّ، وهو بالعراق، حين امتنع منّي قيس. فقلت لأهل الشام: لا تسبّوا قيساً ولا تَدْعوني

---

١ أنا؛ مم: وعيره سعد بن عبادة.

l-Bakhtarī then seized authority over Medina and its inhabitants and dominated its affairs.

War then broke out between ʿAlī and Muʿāwiyah. Their expeditionary forces had reached Medina at the same time as both approached Mecca for the hajj. Whichever of the two arrived first would provide the leader for the people to undertake the rites of the hajj season. Umm Ḥabībah, the Prophet's wife, sent a message to Umm Salamah, and each said to the other, "Come now, let's write to Muʿāwiyah and ʿAlī to convince them to stop terrifying the people with these armies until the community has reached a consensus on which of them shall lead." "You will handle my brother, Muʿāwiya," said Umm Ḥabībah. "And you will handle ʿAlī," replied Umm Salamah. Each wrote to the man she had chosen and sent a delegation of Quraysh and the Allies. As for Muʿāwiyah, he paid heed to Umm Ḥabībah, but as for ʿAlī, he was on the verge of heeding Umm Salamah, but al-Ḥasan ibn ʿAlī dissuaded him from doing so. Thus did their expeditions and their leaders continue to head for Medina and Mecca until ʿAlī, God Almighty grant him mercy, was murdered. It was then that the people reached a consensus on Muʿāwiyah, with Marwān and Ibn al-Bakhtarī dominating the inhabitants of Medina throughout the Civil War. 25.1.6

Egypt had been under the authority of ʿAlī ibn Abī Ṭālib, and over it he had appointed Qays ibn Saʿd ibn ʿUbādah the Ally as commander. He had been the bearer of the banner of the Allies alongside the Messenger of God at the Battle of Badr and at other battles as well. The sage counsel of Qays was greatly esteemed by the people, except when he became embroiled in the Civil War. Muʿāwiyah and ʿAmr ibn al-ʿĀṣ were struggling to eject Qays from Egypt and thus overrun the country, but Qays successfully repelled them with wile and guile. The two were unable to conquer Egypt until Muʿāwiyah hatched a plot against Qays ibn Saʿd to thwart ʿAlī. 25.1.7

Once when Muʿāwiyah was conversing with a Qurashī man known for his sage counsel, he said, "Never did I conceive of a gambit more daring than the one I used to ensare Qays ibn Saʿd in order to thwart ʿAlī. ʿAlī was in Iraq, and at the time Qays prevented me from taking Egypt. So I said to the Syrians, 'Don't provoke Qays, and don't call on me to undertake a raid against him. Qays has now joined our partisans. Several of his letters have come to us containing his counsel. See now how he treats your brethren who are with him at Kharbatā, how he continues to hand out their salaries and rations, and how he ensures

إلى غزوه، فإنّ قيساً لنا شيعة تأتينا كتبه ونصيحته ألا ترون ما يفعل بإخوانكم الّذين عنده من أهل خربتا يجري عليهم أعطياتهم وأرزاقهم ويؤمّن سربهم ويُحسن إلى كلّ راغب قدم عليه، فلا نستنكره في نصيحته.

قال معاوية: وطفقتُ أكتب بذلك إلى شيعتي من أهل العراق، فسمع بذلك مني جواسيس عليّ الّذين عندي من أهل العراق.

فلمّا بلغ ذلك علياً، ونماه إليه عبد الله بن جعفر ومحمّد بن أبي بكر الصدّيق، اتّهم قيسَ بن سعد وكتب إليه يأمره بقتال أهل خربتا، وأهل خربتا يومئذ عشرة آلاف. فأبى قيس أن يقاتلهم وكتب إلى عليّ:

أنّهم وجوه أهل مصر وأشرافهم وذوي الحِفاظ منهم، وقد رضوا منّي بأن أؤمّن سربهم وأجري عليهم أعطياتهم وأرزاقهم. وقد علمتُ أنّ هواهم مع معاوية. فلستُ مكايدهم بأمر أهونَ عليّ وعليك من أن نفعل ذلك بهم اليوم. ولو دعوتهم إلى قتالي، كانوا قرناء، هم أسود العرب وفيهم بُسر بن أرطأة ومسلمة بن مخلّد ومعاوية بن حديج الخولانيّ. فذرني ورأيي فيهم، وأنا أعلم بما أداري منهم.

فأبى عليه عليٌّ إلّا قتالهم. فأبى قيس أن يقاتلهم وكتب قيس إلى عليّ: إن كنت تتّهمني، فاعتزلني عن عملك وأرسلْ إليه غيري.

فأرسل الأشتر أميراً على مصر حتّى إذا بلغ القلزم شرب بالقلزم شربةً من عسل. فكان فيها حتفه. فبلغ ذلك معاوية وعمرو بن العاص، فقال عمرو بن العاص: إنّ لله جنوداً من عسل. فلمّا بلغت علياً وفاة الأشتر، بعث محمّد بن أبي بكر أميراً على مصر.

فلمّا حُدّث به قيس بن سعد قادماً أميراً عليه، تلقّاه فخلا به وناجاه وقال: إنّك قد جئت من عند امرئ لا رأي له في الحرب، وإنّه ليس عزلكم إيّايَ بمانعي أن أنصح

the safety of their passage throughout his territory. He treats kindly any who wish to approach him, and he begrudges no one any counsel he has to offer.'"

Muʿāwiyah also said, "I took to writing this to my partisans among the Iraqis, and ʿAlī's spies who had infiltrated the Iraqis on my side soon heard of this."

When word reached ʿAlī—and it was ʿAbd Allāh ibn Jaʿfar and Muḥammad ibn Abī Bakr al-Ṣiddīq who brought it to his attention—he made accusations against Qays ibn Saʿd and wrote to him ordering him to attack those who had settled in Kharbatā. At the time, the fighting men settled in Kharbatā numbered ten thousand. Qays refused to engage them in battle and wrote to ʿAlī,

> They are the leaders of the warriors settled in Egypt and their nobles are known for their dastardly cunning. They are content with me as long as I ensure the safety of their passage and continue to distribute their salaries and rations. Indeed, I know their sympathies lie with Muʿāwiyah, but I cannot conceive of any strategy easier for you or me than that we continue to deal with them as we do now. Were I to call them to engage me in battle, they would become united, and these are the basest men of the Arabs, such as Busr ibn Arṭa'ah, Maslamah ibn Mukhallad, and Muʿāwiyah ibn Ḥudayj al-Khawlānī. So let me deal with them as I see fit, for I know best because of my acquaintance with them.

But ʿAlī insisted that he engage them in battle. Qays refused to engage them in battle and wrote again to ʿAlī, saying, "If you harbor doubts against me, then remove me from my post and send someone else in my place."

Thus ʿAlī sent al-Ashtar as his commander over Egypt. Eventually al-Ashtar reached al-Qulzum, and there he drank a draft made from honey that bore within it his demise. When the news reached Muʿāwiyah and ʿAmr ibn al-ʿĀṣ, ʿAmr exclaimed, "God's armies can even be found in honey!" But when news of al-Ashtar's death reached ʿAlī, he dispatched Muḥammad ibn Abī Bakr to be the commander over Egypt.

When Qays ibn Saʿd was informed that Muḥammad ibn Abī Bakr was approaching to take command, he went out to meet him in a secluded place so he could confide in him. Qays said, "You've just come from the company of a man with no knack for conducting war. Now, just because you're removing me from office doesn't prevent me from offering you sound advice. I have quite a bit of insight into your present situation, so I'll let you in on the strategy I've

لكم، وإنّي من أمركم على بصيرةٍ، إنّي أدلّك على الّذي كنتُ أكايد به معاوية وعمرو بن العاص وأهل خربتا. فكايدهم به، فإنّك إن كايدتَهم بغيره، تهلك. فوصف له قيس المكايدة الّتي كايدهم بها. فاغتشّه محمّد بن أبي بكر، وخالفه في كلّ شيء أمره به. فلمّا قدم محمّد بن أبي بكر مصر، خرج قيس قِبَل المدينة، فأخافه مروان والأسود بن أبي البختريّ حتّى إذا خاف أن يُؤخذ ويقتل. ركب راحلته فظهر إلى عليّ.

فكتب معاوية إلى مروان والأسود بن أبي البختري يتغيّظ عليهما، ويقول: أمددتما عليّاً بقيس بن سعد وبرأيه ومكايدته. فوالله لو أمددتماه بمائة ألف مقاتل، ما كان ذلك بأغيظ لي من إخراجكما قيس بن سعد إلى عليّ.

فقدم قيس بن سعد إلى عليّ. فلمّا بان له الحديث وجاءه قتلُ محمّد بن أبي بكر، عرف عليّ أنّ قيس بن سعد كان يداري منهم أموراً عِظاماً من المكايدة الّتي قصّر عنها رأي عليّ ورأي من كان يؤازره على عزل قيس. فأطاع عليّ قيساً في الأمر كلّه وجعله على مقدّمة أهل العراق ومن كان بأذربيجان وأرضها وعلى شرطة الخمسين الّذين انتدبوا للموت. وبايعوا ألفاً كانوا بايعوا عليّاً على الموت. فلم يزل قيس بن سعد يسدّ بمكيدته ذلك الثغر حتّى قُتل عليّ.

٨،١،٢٥ واستخلف أهل العراق الحسن بن عليّ على الخلافة، وكان الحسن لا يريد القتال، ولكنّه كان يريد أن يأخذ لنفسه ما استطاع من معاوية. ثمّ يدخل الجماعة ويبايع. فعرف الحسن أنّ قيس بن سعد لا يوافقه على ذلك، فنزعه وأمّر مكانه عبيد الله بن العبّاس. فلمّا عرف عبيد الله بن العبّاس الّذي يريد الحسن أن يأخذ لنفسه، كتب عبيد الله إلى معاوية يسأله الأمان ويشترط لنفسه على الأموال الّتي أصاب. فشرط ذلك معاوية له[١] وبعث إليه ابن عامر في خيل عظيمة، فخرج إليهم عبيد الله

١ [له] أنا؛ ساقطة من م.

been using to get the better of Muʿāwiyah, ʿAmr ibn al-ʿĀṣ, and those settled in Kharbatā. Use this strategy against them, because you will surely perish if you seek to dupe them by other means." Qays proceeded to describe to him the stratagem by which he had duped them, but Muḥammad ibn Abī Bakr thought him dishonest and did the opposite of everything that Qays said he should do. So when Muḥammad ibn Abī Bakr arrived in Egypt, Qays set off in the direction of Medina. However, Marwān and al-Aswad ibn Abī l-Bakhtarī made him fear for his safety until he even feared that he would be arrested or killed. Qays then took his mount and headed up to ʿAlī.

Muʿāwiyah wrote to Marwān and al-Aswad ibn Abī l-Bakhtarī in a fury, saying, "So you two are now aiding ʿAlī by sending him Qays ibn Saʿd, along with his counsel and strategic skill? By God, if you had sent a thousand warriors to his aid, that would have infuriated me less than exiling Qays ibn Saʿd to ʿAlī!"

Qays ibn Saʿd approached ʿAlī, and when he explained what had happened and when news of the murder of Muḥammad ibn Abī Bakr had arrived, ʿAlī realized that Qays had all along seen through the formidable guile of the gambit, which ʿAlī and all of those who advised him to dismiss Qays had failed to perceive. ʿAlī then heeded Qays's counsel for the rest of the war and placed him over the vanguard of the army of Iraq and those in Azerbaijan and its hinterlands. ʿAlī also made him the leader of his elite vanguard,[260] who had pledged to die in battle. Thus did the four thousand men who pledged to die for ʿAlī also pledge allegiance to him. Qays ibn Saʿd's strategies continued to secure the frontier until ʿAlī was murdered.

The Iraqis then chose al-Ḥasan ibn ʿAlī to be ʿAlī's successor as caliph. 25.1.8
Al-Ḥasan was averse to war, but wished, rather, to gain for himself whatever wealth he could procure from Muʿāwiyah and only then to join the community in solidarity and pledge his allegiance. Because al-Ḥasan knew that Qays ibn Saʿd would not agree to this, he removed him from command and appointed ʿUbayd Allāh ibn al-ʿAbbās as commander in his stead. Once ʿUbayd Allāh ibn al-ʿAbbās discovered what al-Ḥasan wanted to take for himself, ʿUbayd Allāh wrote to Muʿāwiyah seeking a guarantee of safety and stipulating that he should be able to keep for himself whatever wealth and property he had gained as spoils. Muʿāwiyah accepted his stipulations and dispatched Ibn ʿĀmir against him in command of a mighty host of cavalry. ʿUbayd Allāh went out to meet them at night, eventually joining their ranks and leaving his own

ليلاً حتّى لحق بهم وترك جنده الّذين هو عليهم لا أميرَ لهم، ومعهم قيس بن سعد. فأمّرت شرطة الخمسين قيس بن سعد، وتعاهدوا وتعاقدوا على قتال معاوية وعمرو بن العاص حتّى يشترط لشيعة عليّ ولمن كان اتّبعه على أموالهم ودمائهم وما أصابوا من الفتنة. فخلص معاوية حين فرغ من عبيد الله والحسن إلى مكايدة رجل هو أهمّ الناس عنده مكيدةً، وعنده أربعون ألفًا. فنزل بهم معاوية وعمرو وأهل الشام أربعين ليلةً. يُرسل معاوية إلى قيس، ويذكّره الله، ويقول: على طاعة من تقاتلني؟ ويقول: قد بايعني الّذي تقاتل على طاعته. فأبى قيس أن يقرّ له حتّى أرسل معاوية بسجلّ قد ختم له أسفله. فقال: اكتب في هذا السجلّ، فما كتبت فهو لك.

فقال عمرو لمعاوية: لا تعطِه هذا وقاتله. فقال معاوية وكان خير الرجلين: على رسلك، يا أبا عبد الله! فإنّا لن نخلص إلى قتال هؤلاء حتّى يُقتل عددهم من أهل الشام. فما خير الحياة بعد ذلك؟ وإنّي والله لا أقاتله حتّى لا[١] أجدَ من ذلك بدًّا. فلمّا بعث إليه معاوية بذلك السجلّ، اشترط قيس بن سعد لنفسه ولشيعة عليّ الأمان على ما أصابوا من الدماء والأموال. ولم يسأل معاوية في ذلك مالاً، فأعطاه معاوية ما اشترط عليه، ودخل قيس ومن معه في الجماعة.

٩،١،٢٥ وكان يُعَدّ في العرب حتّى ثارت الفتنة الأولى خمسةٌ يقال لهم ذوو رأي العرب ومكيدتهم: يُعدّ من قريش معاوية وعمرو، ويعدّ من الأنصار قيس بن سعد، ويعدّ من المهاجرين عبد الله بن بديل بن ورقاء الخزاعيّ، ويعدّ من ثقيف المغيرة بن شعبة. فكان مع عليّ منهم رجلان: قيس بن سعد وعبد الله بن بديل. وكان المغيرة معتزلاً بالطائف وأرضها.

١٠،١،٢٥ فلمّا حُكّم الحكمان، فاجتمعا بأذرح وافاهما المغيرة بن شعبة. وأرسل الحكمان إلى عبدالله بن عمر وإلى عبدالله بن الزبير، ووافى رجال كثير من قريش، ووافى معاوية

١ [لا] أنا: ساقطة من م.

forces without a commander. Qays ibn Saʿd was in their midst, and the elite vanguard chose Qays as their commander. They swore a convenant with one another to wage war against Muʿāwiyah and ʿAmr ibn al-ʿĀṣ until Muʿāwiyah agreed to guarantee to ʿAlī's partisans and all who followed them their wealth, their lives, and all that they had gained as spoils in the course of the strife. When Muʿāwiyah had finished with ʿUbayd Allāh and al-Ḥasan, he devoted his full attention to besting a man whose cunning he regarded as without equal. Muʿāwiyah had four thousand men at his command. He, ʿAmr, and the settlers of Syria made camp with them for forty nights, while Muʿāwiyah wrote to Qays urging him to remember God and saying, "By whose command do you seek to make war against me?" Muʿāwiyah also said, "The one under whose authority you fight has pledged me his allegiance!" But Qays refused to recognize him until Muʿāwiyah sent him a scroll with his seal placed at the bottom. "Write whatever you wish in this scroll," said Muʿāwiyah, "for I've written nothing in it. That's for you to do."

ʿAmr said to Muʿāwiyah, "Don't give him the scroll! Fight him instead!" But Muʿāwiyah, who was the better of the two men, replied, "Easy now, Abū ʿAbd Allāh! We're not going to waste our time fighting these men until just as many Syrians as they are slain. What good would it do to go on living then? By God, I will not fight them unless I find no other alternative." When Muʿāwiyah sent him that scroll, Qays ibn Saʿd stipulated his own conditions and demanded immunity for ʿAlī's partians from reprisal for the blood they had spilled and the property they had seized. Qays asked for no additional wealth in that scroll, and Muʿāwiyah granted all the conditions he stipulated. Thus did Qays and those with him join the community in solidarity.

Until the First Civil War had broken out, five men were famed among the 25.1.9 Arabs as men esteemed for their sage counsel and cunning. Numbered among the Quraysh were Muʿāwiyah and ʿAmr; among the Allies was Qays ibn Saʿd; among the Emigrants was ʿAbd Allāh ibn Budayl ibn Warqāʾ al-Khuzāʿī; and among the Thaqīf tribe was al-Mughīrah ibn Shuʿbah. Two of these men sided with ʿAlī: Qays ibn Saʿd and ʿAbd Allāh ibn Budayl. Al-Mughīrah, however, withdrew to Taif and its environs.

When the two Arbiters were appointed, they met at Adhruḥ.[261] Al-Mughīrah 25.1.10 ibn Shuʿbah journeyed to visit them both, and the two Arbiters also sent for ʿAbd Allāh ibn ʿUmar and ʿAbd Allāh ibn al-Zubayr to come. Many other men from the Quraysh came as well. Muʿāwiyah journeyed there along with the

بأهل الشام، ووافى أبو موسى الأشعريّ وعمرو بن العاص، وهما الحكمان. وأبى عليٌّ وأهل العراق أن يوافوا. فقال المغيرة بن شعبة لرجال من ذوي رأي أهل قريش: هل ترون أحداً يقدر على أن يستطيع أن يعلم، أيجتمع هذان الحكمان، أم لا؟ فقالوا له: لا نرى أنّ أحداً يعلم ذلك. قال: فوالله إنّي لأظنّني سأعلمه منهما حين أخلو بهما فأراجعهما.

فدخل على عمرو بن العاص، فبدأ به، فقال: يا أبا عبدالله، أخبرني عمّا أسألك عنه. كيف ترانا معشر المعتزلة؟ فإنّا قد شككنا في هذا الأمر الّذي قد تبيّن لكم في هذا القتال، ورأينا نستأني ونتثبّت حتّى تجتمع الأمّة على رجل. فندخل في صالح ما دخلت فيه الأمّة.

فقال عمرو: أراكم معشر المعتزلة خلف الأبرار ومعشر الفجّار!

فانصرف المغيرة ولم يسأله عن غير ذلك حتّى دخل على أبي موسى الأشعري. فخلا به فقال له نحواً ممّا قال لعمرو.

فقال أبو موسى: أراكم أثبت الناس رأياً وأرى فيكم بقيّة المسلمين. فانصرف، فلم يسأله عن غير ذلك.

قال: فلقي أصحابه الّذين قال لهم ما قال من ذوي رأي قريش. قال: أقسم لكم، لا يجتمع هذان على رأي واحد، وليدعُوَنّ كلّ واحد إلى رأيه.

فلمّا اجتمع الحكمان وتكلّما خاليين، فقال عمرو: يا أبا موسى، أرأيت أوّل ما نقضي به في الحقّ. علينا أن نقضي لأهل الوفاء بالوفاء، ولأهل الغدر بالغدر.

فقال أبو موسى: وما ذاك؟

قال: ألست تعلم أنّ معاوية وأهل الشام قد وافوا للموعد الّذي وعدناهم إيّاه؟

فقال: بلى.

settlers from Syria. Abū Mūsā l-Ashʿarī and ʿAmr ibn al-ʿĀṣ, who were the two Arbiters, also journeyed there, but ʿAlī and the settlers from Iraq refused to make the journey. Al-Mughīrah ibn Shuʿbah asked several Qurashī men of sage judgment, "Do you reckon that it's possible to know whether or not these two arbiters will reach an agreement?" "No one knows for sure," they replied, so he said, "Then, by God, I suppose I'll find it out myself once I have the chance to speak to them and interrogate them one-on-one."

Al-Mughīrah went to see ʿAmr ibn al-ʿĀṣ and took the matter up with him. He began by saying, "Abū ʿAbd Allāh, answer my questions: How do you regard those of us who have remained neutral? Indeed, we have had our doubts about this whole affair, even though it has seemed crystal clear to the rest of you throughout the fighting. Our view is that we should wait and remain resolute until the community agrees on a single man, and then join in solidarity with the community."

"I regard your pack of neutrals as being beneath the pious," ʿAmr answered, "and even beneath that insolent throng of ʿAlī's!"[262]

Al-Mughīrah departed, having asked ʿAmr nothing else, and went to see Abū Mūsā al-Ashʿarī. When he was alone with him, he asked the same question he had asked ʿAmr.

"I consider your judgment the most reliable," Abū Mūsā said, "and I believe the rest of the Muslims are with you." Al-Mughīrah then departed, having asked him no further questions.

Al-Mughīrah met again with his sage companions from the Quraysh with whom he had spoken before and declared, "I swear before you all, these two will never arrive at a consensus, and that's even if one were to call the other to his own opinion!"

When the two Arbiters met together and had begun to negotiate on their own, ʿAmr said, "Abū Mūsā, don't you think that before we determine the truth of any other matter we should first determine who is loyal and thus deserves loyalty and who is treacherous and thus deserves to be betrayed?"

"And who would that be?" Abū Mūsā retorted.

ʿAmr continued, "Do you not realize that Muʿāwiyah and the Syrians have journeyed to the location that we had specified for them?"

"Yes," he answered.

"Write this down then," said ʿAmr, and Abū Mūsā wrote it down. ʿAmr continued, "Are we not also determined to name a man who will rule over the

فقال:[١] فاكتبها. فكتبها أبو موسى، فقال عمرو: قد أخلصنا أنا وأنت على أن نسمّي رجلاً يلي أمر هذه الأمّة.[٢] فسمّ يا أبا موسى، فإنّي أقدر على أن أتابعك على أن تتابعني.

فقال أبو موسى: أسمّي عبد الله بن عمر بن الخطّاب. وكان عبد الله بن عمر فيمن اعتزل.

فقال عمرو: فأنا أسمّي لك معاوية بن أبي سفيان!

فلم يبرحا من مجلسهما ذلك حتّى اختلفا واستبّا. ثمّ خرجا إلى الناس. ثمّ قال أبو موسى: يا أيّها الناس، إنّي قد وجدت مثل عمرو بن العاص مثل الّذي قال الله تبارك وتعالى ﴿وَٱتْلُ عَلَيْهِمْ نَبَأَ ٱلَّذِيٓ ءَاتَيْنَٰهُ ءَايَٰتِنَا فَٱنسَلَخَ مِنْهَا﴾ حتّى بلغ ﴿لَعَلَّهُمْ يَتَفَكَّرُونَ﴾.

وقال عمرو بن العاص: يا أيّها الناس، إني وجدتُ مثل أبي موسى مثل الّذي قال الله تبارك وتعالى ﴿مَثَلُ ٱلَّذِينَ حُمِّلُوا۟ ٱلتَّوْرَىٰةَ ثُمَّ لَمْ يَحْمِلُوهَا كَمَثَلِ ٱلْحِمَارِ يَحْمِلُ أَسْفَارًۢا﴾ حتّى بلغ ﴿ٱلظَّٰلِمِينَ﴾.

ثمّ كتب كلّ واحد منهما بالمثل الّذي ضرب لصاحبه إلى الأمصار.

وقال الزهريّ عن سالم عن ابن عمر؛ ٢،٢٥

قال معمر: أخبرني ابن طاووس عن عكرمة بن خالد عن ابن عمر، قال:

فقام معاوية عشيّةً، فأثنى على الله بما هو أهله. ثمّ قال: أمّا بعد، فمن كان متكلّماً في هذا الأمر فليطلع لي قرنه. فوالله لا يطلع فيه أحدٌ إلّا كنت أحقّ به منه ومن أبيه.

١ [بلى. فقال:] أنا؛ ساقطة من م. ٢ [الأمّة] أنا؛ ساقطة من م.

Community? So, Abū Mūsā, name your man. I'm willing to agree with you if you are willing to agree with me."

"I nominate ʿAbd Allāh ibn ʿUmar ibn al-Khaṭṭāb," declared Abū Mūsā, and indeed Ibn ʿUmar was one of those who had remained neutral.

But ʿAmr said, "I nominate to you Muʿāwiyah ibn Abī Sufyān!"

The two of them met for a long time until, completely at odds, they began to hurl insults at one another. Then they went out to address the people. Abū Mūsā declared, "Listen everyone! I've found ʿAmr ibn al-ʿĀṣ to be the like of which the Almighty and Glorious God said:

> «Tell them the story of the man to whom We gave Our messages: he sloughed them off, so Satan took him as a follower and he went astray—if it had been Our will, We could have used these signs to raise him high, but instead he clung to the earth and followed his own desires—he was like a dog that pants with a lolling tongue whether you drive it away or leave it alone. Such is the image of those who reject Our signs. Tell them the story so that they may reflect.»"[263]

ʿAmr ibn al-ʿĀṣ declared, "Listen everyone! I've found Abū Mūsā to be the like of which the Almighty and Glorious God said:

> «Those who have been charged to obey the Torah, but do not do so, are like asses carrying books: how base such people are who disobey God's revelations! God does not guide people who do wrong.»"[264]

Then each of the two Arbiters wrote a message conveying the same description of his fellow Arbiter to the garrison cities.

Al-Zuhrī said on the authority of Sālim, on the authority of Ibn ʿUmar; 25.2

Maʿmar said: Ibn Ṭāwūs related to me on the authority of ʿIkrimah ibn Khālid, on the authority of Ibn ʿUmar, who said:

One evening Muʿāwiyah rose to speak and, praising God as is His due, said, "Whoever has a claim over the rule of this community, let him show his face. I swear by God, no one who shows his face will have a more rightful claim to it than I, be it he or his father!" Thus did Muʿāwiyah provoke ʿAbd Allāh ibn ʿUmar.[265]

قال: يعرّض بعبد الله بن عمر، قال عبد الله بن عمر: فأطلقت حَبْوتي، فأردت أن أقوم إليه. فأقول: يتكلّم فيه رجال قاتلوك وأباك على الإسلام. ثمّ خشيت أن أقول كلمةً تفرّق بين الجمع وتُسفك فيها الدماء، وأحمل فيه على غير رأي. فكان ما وعد الله تبارك وتعالى في الجنان أحبّ إليّ من ذلك كلّه. قال: فلمّا انطلقت إلى منزلي، أتاني حبيب بن مسلمة. فقال: ما الّذي منعك أن تتكلّم حين سمعت الرجل يتكلّم؟ فقلت له: لقد أردت ذلك، ثمّ خشيت أن أقول كلمةً تفرّق بين الجمع وتسفك فيها الدماء وأحمل فيه على غير رأي. فكان ما وعد الله تبارك وتعالى في الجنان أحبّ إليّ من ذلك كلّه. فقال حبيب بن مسلمة لعبد الله بن عمر: فداك أبي وأمّي! فإنّك عُصمت وحفظت ممّا خفت غرّته.

ʿAbd Allāh ibn ʿUmar said, "I threw off my outer cloak, ready to stand against him and say, 'You speak of men who vanquished you and your father for the sake of Islam!' But then I was afraid to say anything, lest I risk threatening the unity of community and cause blood to be shed because I acted against my better judgment. Almighty God's promise of Paradise was far dearer to me than all else. After I had returned to my encampment, Ḥabīb ibn Maslamah came to me and said, 'What prevented you from speaking up when you heard that man speak thus?' 'Indeed I wanted to,' I told him, 'but I feared I would say something that would risk threatening the unity of the community and cause bloodshed and lead me to act against my better judgment. Almighty God's promise of Paradise was far dearer to me than all else.' Ḥabīb ibn Maslamah then said to ʿAbd Allāh ibn ʿUmar, 'My father and mother's life for yours! God has protected you from sin and preserved you from the ruin you feared.'"

حَدِيثُ الحَجّاجِ بنِ عِلاط

عبد الرزّاق عن معمرعن ثابت البنانيّ عن أنس بن مالك، قال: ١،٢٦

لمّا افتتح رسول الله صلّى الله عليه وسلّم خيبر، قال الحجّاج بن علاط: يا رسول الله، إنّ لي بمكّة مالاً وإنّ لي بها أهلاً، وإنّي أريد أن آتيهم. فأنا في حلّ إن أنا نلت منك. أوقلت شيئاً؟ فأذن له رسول الله صلّى الله عليه وسلّم على أن يقول ما يشاء. فأتى امرأته حين قدم، فقال: اجمعي لي ما كان عندك، فإنّي أريد أن أشتري من غنائم محمّد صلّى الله عليه وسلّم وأصحابه. فإنهم قد استُبيحوا، وأصيبت أموالهم، وفشا ذلك بمكّة. فانقمع المسلمون، وأظهر المشركون فرحاً وسروراً. قال: وبلغ الخبر العبّاس بن عبد المطّلب، فقعد وجعل لا يستطيع أن يقوم.

قال معمر: فأخبرني عثمان الجزريّ عن مقسم، قال: ٢،٢٦

فأخذ ابناً له يشبه رسول الله صلّى الله عليه وسلّم، يقال له قثم. فاستلقى، فوضعه على صدره، وهو يقول:

حِبّي قُثَمْ ☆ شَبِيهُ ذِي الأَنْفِ الأَشَمّْ ☆ نَبِيُّ رَبِّ ذِي النِّعَمْ ☆ بِرَغْمِ أَنْفِ مَنْ رَغِمْ

قال ثابت: قال أنس: ٣،٢٦

ثمّ أرسل غلاماً له إلى الحجّاج: ماذا جئت به وماذا تقول؟ فما وعد الله خير ممّا جئت به. قال: فقال الحجّاج بن علاط: اقرأ على أبي الفضل السلام وقل له: فَلْيَخْلُ في بعض بيوته لآتيه. فإنّ الخبر على ما يسرّه. قال: فجاءه غلامه. فلمّا بلغ باب الدار،

The Story of al-Ḥajjāj ibn ʿIlāṭ

ʿAbd al-Razzāq, on the authority of Maʿmar, on the authority of Thābit al-Bunānī, on the authority of Anas ibn Mālik, who said: 26.1

When the Messenger of God had conquered Khaybar, al-Ḥajjāj ibn ʿIlāṭ said, "O Messenger of God, in Mecca I still have property and family. I want to go to them, but am I at liberty to claim I defeated you or say something similar?" God's Messenger granted al-Ḥajjāj permission to say whatever he wished, so when he arrived in Mecca, he went to his wife and said, "Gather together all that you have, for I want to purchase some of the spoils seized from Muḥammad and his companions. They've been pillaged, and their wealth has been seized." As the news spread around Mecca, the Muslims retreated to their homes in despair, and the Pagans openly celebrated with delight. Word reached al-ʿAbbās ibn ʿAbd al-Muṭṭalib, and he sat down as though unable to ever stand again.

Maʿmar said: ʿUthmān al-Jazarī reported to me on the authority of Miqsam, who said: 26.2

Al-ʿAbbās took in his arms a son of his named Qutham who looked just like the Messenger of God. Lying down, he placed him on his chest saying:

Beloved Qutham,
    Likeness of him with a noble face,
Prophet of the Lord of abounding grace
    In spite of their hatred for him.

Thābit continued: Anas said: 26.3

Al-ʿAbbās then sent his slave boy to al-Ḥajjāj with a message: "What ill news have you brought? What do you have to say? For indeed, what God has promised is greater than whatever news you bring." Al-Ḥajjāj replied, "Convey my greetings of peace to Abū l-Faḍl and tell him that he should seclude himself in one of the chambers of his house so that I may come see him, for he will find reason to rejoice from the news I bring." Al-ʿAbbās's slave boy returned to

قال: أبشر، يا أبا الفضل. قال: فوثب العبّاس فرحاً حتّى قبّل بين عينيه. فأخبره بما قال الحجّاج، فأعتقه.

قال: ثمّ جاءه الحجّاج، فأخبره أنّ رسول الله صلّى الله عليه وسلّم قد افتتح خيبر وغنم أموالهم، وجرت سهام الله تبارك وتعالى في أموالهم. واصطفى رسول الله صلّى الله عليه وسلّم صفيّة ابنة حيّ، فأخذها لنفسه وخيّرها بين أن يعتقها وتكون زوجه أو تلحق بأهلها. فاختارت أن يعتقها وتكون زوجه. ولكنّي جئت لما كان لي هاهنا. أردت أن أجمعه فأذهب به. فاستأذنت رسول الله، فأذن لي أن أقول ما شئت وأخفِ عنّي ثلاثاً. ثمّ اذكر ما بدا لك. قال: فجمعت امرأته ما كان عندها من حلي ومتاع، فدفعته إليه. ثمّ انشمر به.

فلمّا كان بعد ثلاث، أتى العبّاس امرأة الحجّاج، فقال: ما فعل زوجك؟

فأخبرته أن قد ذهب يوم كذا وكذا، وقالت: لا يخزيك الله، يا أبا الفضل. لقد شقّ عليه الّذي بلغك.

قال: أجل، فلا يخزيني الله، ولم يكن بحمد الله إلّا ما أحببنا. فتح الله تبارك وتعالى خيبر على رسوله صلّى الله عليه وسلّم، وجرت سهام الله تعالى في أموالهم. واصطفى رسول الله صلّى الله عليه وسلّم صفيّة لنفسه. فإن كان لك حاجة في زوجك، فالحقي به.

قالت: أظنّك والله صادقاً.

قال: فإنّي والله صادق، والأمر على ما أخبرتك.

قال: ثمّ ذهب حتّى أتى مجالس قريش، وهم يقولون إذا مرّ بهم: لا يصيبك إلّا خير، يا أبا الفضل! قال: لم يصِبني إلّا خير بحمد الله. قد أخبرني الحجّاج بن علاط أنّ خيبر فتحها الله على رسوله صلّى الله عليه وسلّم وجرت فيها سهام الله، واصطفى رسول الله صلّى الله عليه وسلّم صفيّة لنفسه. وقد سألني أن أخفي عنه ثلاثاً، إنّما جاء ليأخذ وما له، ماله من شيء هاهنا. ثمّ يذهب.

him, and when he reached the door of the house, he declared, "Good tidings, Abū l-Faḍl!" Al-ʿAbbās then sprang up so joyfully that he kissed the boy right between the eyes, and when he had told al-ʿAbbās all that al-Ḥajjāj had said, al-ʿAbbās freed the slave then and there.

Later, al-Ḥajjāj came to al-ʿAbbās and informed him that the Messenger of God had conquered Khaybar and plundered the possessions of its inhabitants; thus did the arrows of God divide their wealth:[266] "The Messenger of God singled out Ṣafiyyah bint Ḥuyayy and took her for himself. He gave her a choice: either she could be freed from bondage and become his wife, or she could rejoin her people. She chose to be freed and become his wife. However, I came here for what belongs to me. I wanted to gather it all together and leave with it, so I sought the Messenger of God's permission, which he granted me, to say whatever I had to say. Keep my secret for three nights, then spread the word as you see fit." The wife of al-Ḥajjāj gathered what jewels and belongings she had with her and handed them over to him, after which al-Ḥajjāj hastened to depart.

After the third night, al-ʿAbbās came to the wife of al-Ḥajjāj and asked, "What has your husband done?"

She told him that he had left on such-and-such day, saying, "God will not bring you shame, Abū l-Faḍl. We were greatly aggrieved over what happened to you."

"No," al-ʿAbbās replied, "God will not bring me shame. Praise God, only what we had hoped for came to pass. God the Blessed and Exalted conquered Khaybar for his Messenger, and God's arrows apportioned the shares of their possessions. The Messenger of God singled out Ṣafiyyah, the daughter of Ḥuyayy, and he took her for himself. If you have need of your husband, go join him."

"I reckon that you speak the truth," she replied.

"Indeed, I swear by God that I do speak the truth," al-ʿAbbās responded, "for the matter is just as I told you."

Al-ʿAbbās then left and came upon the assemblies of the Quraysh, who commented as he passed by them, "Naught but good will come to you, Abū l-Faḍl!" "Naught but good has come to me, praise be to God!" he replied. "Al-Ḥajjāj ibn ʿIlāṭ informed me that God has given his Messenger victory at Khaybar, that God's arrows have apportioned its wealth, and that the Messenger of God singled out Ṣafiyyah for himself. Al-Ḥajjāj asked me to keep his secret for three nights, for he had only come to reclaim his wealth and property here. After that, he went on his way!"

قال: فردّ الله تبارك وتعالى الكآبة الّتي كانت بالمسلمين على المشركين، وخرج المسلمون ممّن كان دخل بيته مكتئباً حتّى أتوا العبّاس. فأخبرهم الخبر، وسُرّ المسلمون، وردّ الله تبارك وتعالى ما كان من[1] كآبة أو غيظ أو حزن على المشركين.

١ ح، ط: ساقطة من م.

So God the Almighty and Exalted removed the Muslims' despair and cast it back upon the Pagans. Those Muslims who had entered their homes distraught now came out to see al-ʿAbbās so he could tell them the news. The Muslims were overjoyed, and God the Almighty and Exalted cast whatever despair, rage, or sorrow they had suffered back onto the Pagans.

خُصُومَةُ عَلِيّ وَالعَبَّاس

عبد الرزّاق عن معمر عن الزهريّ عن مالك بن أوس بن الحدثان النصريّ، قال: ١،٢٧

١،١،٢٧ أرسل إليّ عمر بن الخطّاب أنّه قد حضر المدينة أهل أبيات من قومك وإنّا قد أمرنا لهم برضخ، فاقسمه بينهم.

فقلت: يا أمير المؤمنين! مُرْ بذلك غيري.

قال: اقبضه أيّها المرءُ.

قال: فبينا أنا كذلك، جاءه مولاه، فقال: هذا عثمان وعبد الرحمن بن عوف وسعد بن أبي وقّاص والزبير بن العوّام — قال: ولا أدري أذكَرَ طلحة أم لا — يستأذن عليك.

قال: ائذن لهم.

قال: ثمّ مكث ساعةً. ثمّ جاء، فقال: هذا العبّاس وعليّ يستأذنان عليك.

قال: ائذن لهما.

قال: ثمّ مكث ساعةً. قال: فلمّا دخل العبّاس، قال: يا أمير المؤمنين، اقضِ بيني وبين هذا وهما يومئذ يختصمان فيما أفاء الله على رسوله صلّى الله عليه وسلّم من أموال بني النضير.

فقال القوم: اقضِ بينهما، يا أمير المؤمنين، وأرِح كلّ واحد منهما من صاحبه. فقد طالت خصومتهما.

فقال عمر: أنشدكم الله الّذي بإذنه تقوم السماوات والأرض. أتعلمون أنّ رسول الله صلّى الله عليه وسلّم قال: لا نُورَث، ما تركنا صدقةٌ؟

قالوا: قد قال ذلك.

ثمّ قال لهما مثل ذلك، فقالا: نعم.

٢،١،٢٧ قال لهم: فإنّي سأخبركم عن هذا الفيء. إنّ الله تبارك وتعالى خصّ نبيّه صلّى الله

The Dispute between ʿAlī and al-ʿAbbās[267]

ʿAbd al-Razzāq, on the authority of Maʿmar, on the authority of al-Zuhrī, on the authority of Mālik ibn Aws ibn al-Ḥadathān al-Naṣrī, who said: 27.1

ʿUmar ibn al-Khaṭṭāb sent me a message saying, "The leaders of the households of your tribe have convened in Medina, and before us lies the task of giving them a small bit of compensation. You are to divide it between them." 27.1.1

"O Commander of the Faithful," I objected, "ask someone else!"

"Come now, man, take it," he responded.

While I was thus occupied, ʿUmar's slave-client came to him and said, "It's ʿUthmān, ʿAbd al-Raḥmān ibn ʿAwf, Saʿd ibn Abī Waqqāṣ, and al-Zubayr ibn al-ʿAwwām"—I don't know if he mentioned Ṭalḥah or not—"and they all request permission to see you."

"Bid them enter, then," said ʿUmar.

After a while ʿUmar's slave-client came again and said, "It's al-ʿAbbās and ʿAlī requesting permission to see you."

"Bid the two to enter," ʿUmar answered.

After a while, al-ʿAbbās entered and said, "O Commander of the Faithful, render your judgment between me and this man!" Indeed, in those days he and ʿAlī were embroiled in a dispute over the spoils that God had granted to his Messenger from the properties once belonging to the Naḍīr clan.

Those present said, "Give them your judgment, O Commander of the Faithful, for their dispute has lasted far too long."

"I abjure you by God, by Whose leave the Heavens and the Earth stand!" ʿUmar then declared. "Do all of you not know that the Messenger of God said, 'We prophets leave no heirs; whatever we leave behind is for charity.'?"[268]

"Yes," they affirmed, "he indeed said that."

Next he said something similar to ʿAlī and al-ʿAbbās, and they too answered, "Yes."

ʿUmar then said to them, "I will tell you about these spoils. God, the Almighty and Exalted, sanctified his Prophet by these spoils by granting him a portion that He bestowed on none other. Thus He decreed «You believers did not have 27.1.2

عليه وسلّم منه بشيءٍ لم يعطه غيره. فقال: ﴿وَمَآ أَفَآءَ ٱللَّهُ عَلَىٰ رَسُولِهِۦ مِنۡهُمۡ فَمَآ أَوۡجَفۡتُمۡ عَلَيۡهِ مِنۡ خَيۡلٖ وَلَا رِكَابٖ وَلَٰكِنَّ ٱللَّهَ يُسَلِّطُ رُسُلَهُۥ عَلَىٰ مَن يَشَآءُ﴾. فكانت هذه لرسول الله صلّى الله عليه وسلّم خاصّةً. ثمّ والله ما احتازها دونكم، ولا استأثر بها عليكم. لقد قسم والله بينكم وبثها فيكم حتّى بقي منها هذا المال. فكان ينفق على أهله منه سنةً. قال: وربّما قال: ويحبس قوت أهله منه سنةً. ثمّ يجعل ما بقي من مجعل مال الله. فلمّا قبض رسول الله صلّى الله عليه وسلّم، قال أبو بكر: أنا وليّ رسول الله صلّى الله عليه وسلّم بعده. أعمل فيه بما كان يعمل رسول الله صلّى الله عليه وسلّم فيها.

ثمّ أقبل على عليّ والعبّاس، فقال: وأنتما تزعمان أنّه فيه ظالم فاجر؟ والله يعلم أنّه فيها صادق بارّ تابع للحقّ!

ثم وَلِيتُها بعد أبي بكر سنتين من إمارتي. فعملت فيها بما عمل رسول الله صلّى الله عليه وسلّم وأبو بكر. وأنتما تزعمان أنّي فيها ظالم فاجر؟ والله يعلم أنّي فيه صادق بارّ تابع للحقّ.[١] ثمّ جئتماني، وجاءني هذا — يعني العبّاس — يسألني ميراثه من ابن أخيه. وجاءني هذا — يعني عليّاً — يسألني ميراث امرأته من أبيها. فقلتُ إليكما: إنّ رسول الله صلّى الله عليه وسلّم قال: لا نورث، ما تركنا صدقةٌ. ثمّ بدا لي أن أدفعها إليكما، فأخذت عليك عهد الله وميثاقه لَتعملان فيه بما عمل فيها رسول الله صلّى الله عليه وسلّم وأبو بكر وأنا ما وَلِيتُها. فقلتما: ادفعها إلينا على ذلك. أتريدان منّا قضاءً غير ذلك؟ والّذي بإذنه تقوم السماء والأرض، لا أقضي بينكما بقضاء غير هذا: إن كنتما عجزتما عنها، فادفعاها إليّ.

٣،١،٢٧ قال: فغلبه عليٌّ عليها، فكانت بيد عليّ، ثمّ بيد حسن، ثمّ بيد حسين، ثمّ بيد علي بن حسين، ثمّ بيد حسن بن حسن، ثمّ بيد زيد بن حسن.

قال معمر: ثمّ بيد عبد الله بن حسن، ثمّ أخذها هؤلاء، يعني بني العبّاس.

١ [للحقّ] من بس؛ ساقطة من م.

to spur on your horses or your camels for whatever spoils God turned over to His Messenger from them. God gives authority to His messengers over whomever He will.»[269] Hence these spoils were for God's Messenger specifically, and then, by God, he did not hoard them from you and claim them as his alone; rather, by God, he divided it all between you and distributed it among you until nothing remained of it save this property. His household would receive payment from it annually"—or he perhaps said, "His household would take their nourishment from it annually"—"then he would consecrate what remained for God's charitable cause. When the Messenger of God was taken from this world, Abū Bakr said, 'I am the steward of the Messenger of God's property after his death, and I shall act in accordance with the actions of the Messenger of God.'"

ʿUmar then turned to face ʿAlī and al-ʿAbbās and declared, "You two claim that in doing so he acted as a brazen usurper! But God knows that he acted devoutly and earnestly while following the Truth."

"After this," ʿUmar continued, "I became steward over the property after Abū Bakr, and two years of my rule have now passed. I acted in accordance with the actions of God's Messenger and Abū Bakr, and you claim that I too act as a brazen usurper! But God knows that I have acted devoutly and earnestly while following the Truth. Now this man"—by whom he meant al-ʿAbbās—"has come to me asking for his inheritance from his nephew; and this man"—by whom he meant ʿAlī—"has come to me asking for the inheritance of his wife from her father. So I said, 'The Messenger of God said, "We leave no heirs; whatever we leave behind is for charity."' To me it seemed prudent to hand it over to the two of you after I had taken your oath and bond that you would manage it in accordance with the practices of the Messenger of God, Abū Bakr, and myself while I acted as its steward.[270] You two answered, 'Hand it over to us on that condition.' Now do you want us to render a different judgment? I swear by Him by Whose leave the Heavens and Earth stand, I shall not grant any further judgment than that. If you are unable to manage the property, then hand it back to me."

Al-Zuhrī added: ʿAlī would later seize control of the estate, and thus it fell 27.1.3
into his hands. Later it fell into hands of al-Ḥasan, then al-Ḥusayn, then ʿAlī ibn al-Ḥusayn, then Ḥasan ibn al-Ḥasan, and finally into the hands of Zayd ibn al-Ḥasan.

Maʿmar added: And then the property fell into the hands of ʿAbd Allāh ibn al-Ḥasan. Later, those people would seize it—meaning the Abbasids.[271]

عبد الرزّاق عن معمر عن الزهريّ عن عروة وعمرة، قالا: ٢،٢٧

إنّ أزواج النبيّ صلّى الله عليه وسلّم أرسلن إلى أبي بكر يسألن ميراثهنّ من رسول الله صلّى الله وسلّم. فأرسلت إليهنّ عائشة: ألا تتّقين الله؟ ألم يقُل رسول الله صلّى الله وسلّم: لا نورث، ما تركنا صدقةٌ. قال: فرضين بقولها وتركن ذلك.

عبد الرزّاق عن عروة عن عائشة: ٣،٢٧

أنّ فاطمة والعبّاس أتيا أبا بكر يلتمسان ميراثهما من رسول الله صلّى الله عليه ١،٣،٢٧
وسلّم. وهما حينئذ يطلبان أرضه من فدك وسهمه من خيبر. فقال لهما أبو بكر: سمعت رسول الله صلّى الله عليه وسلّم يقول: لا نورث، ما تركنا صدقةٌ. إنّما يأكل آل محمّد صلّى الله عليه وسلّم من هذا المال، وإنّي والله لا أدع أمرًا رأيت رسول الله صلّى الله عليه وسلّم يصنعه إلّا صنعتُه.

قال: فهجرته فاطمة، فلم تكلّمه في ذلك حتّى ماتت. فدفنها عليٌّ ليلاً ولم يؤذن بها أبا بكر. قالت عائشة: وكان لعليّ وجه[١] من الناس حياةَ فاطمة حبوه.[٢] فلمّا توفّيت فاطمة، انصرف وجوه الناس عنه. فمكثت فاطمة ستّة أشهر بعد رسول الله صلّى الله عليه وسلّم ثمّ توفّيت.

قال معمر: فقال رجلٌ للزهريّ: فلم يبايع عليٌّ ستّة أشهر؟

قال: لا، ولا أحد من بني هاشم حتّى بايعه عليّ.

فلمّا رأى عليّ انصراف وجوه الناس عنه، أسرع[٣] إلى مصالحة أبي بكر. فأرسل ٢،٣،٢٧
إلى أبي بكر أن ائتنا ولا تأتِنا معك بأحد. وكره أن يأتيه عمر لما يعلم من شدّته. فقال عمر: لا تأتِهم وحدك!

فقال أبو بكر: والله لآتينّهم وحدي، وما عسى أن يصنعوا بيّ؟

قال: فانطلق أبو بكر، فدخل على عليّ، وقد جمع بني هاشم عنده. فقام عليٌّ، فحمد الله وأثنى عليه بما هو أهله، ثمّ قال:

١ [وجه] من تط؛ ساقطة من م. ٢ م؛ ساقطة من تط. ٣ م؛ تط: ضرع.

ʿAbd al-Razzāq, on the authority of Maʿmar, on the authority of al-Zuhrī, on the authority of ʿUrwah and ʿAmrah, who said: 27.2

The Prophet's wives sent a message to Abū Bakr requesting their inheritance from the Messenger of God. ʿĀʾishah replied to them, "Don't you women fear God? Did the Messenger of God not say, 'We leave no heir; whatever we leave behind is for charity'?" They were satisfied with her reply and abandoned their request.

ʿAbd al-Razzāq, on the authority of Maʿmar, on the authority of al-Zuhrī, on the authority of ʿUrwah, on the authority of ʿĀʾishah: 27.3

Fāṭimah and al-ʿAbbās came to Abū Bakr demanding their inheritance from the Messenger of God. At the time, they were demanding his land in Fadak and his share of Khaybar. Abū Bakr said to them, "I heard the Messenger of God say, 'We leave no heirs; whatever we leave behind is for charity.' Only Muḥammad's family can support themselves from this property, and by God, there is no policy pursued by the Messenger of God that I'll neglect to pursue myself." 27.3.1

Fāṭimah refused to meet with Abū Bakr after that, and she would not speak to him about the matter for the rest of her life. ʿAlī buried her at night and did not announce her death to Abū Bakr. ʿĀʾishah said, "ʿAlī enjoyed a certain amount of sympathy among the people who admired him while Fāṭimah was alive, but when Fāṭimah passed away, the sympathies of the people left him. Fāṭimah outlived the Messenger of God by six months, and then she passed away."

Maʿmar said: A man asked al-Zuhrī, "So ʿAlī didn't pledge his allegiance for six months?"

"No," answered al-Zuhrī, "and neither did anyone else from the Hāshim clan until ʿAlī had pledged his allegiance."

When ʿAlī saw that he had lost the sympathy of the people, he hastened to reconcile with Abū Bakr. He sent a message to Abū Bakr saying, "Come to us, but do not bring anyone else with you." ʿUmar objected to Abū Bakr going to ʿAlī because he knew him to be relentless, so ʿUmar said, "Do not go to them alone." 27.3.2

"By God," replied Abū Bakr, "I will go see the Hāshim clan on my own—what could they possibly do to me?"

Abū Bakr set off to see ʿAlī at his residence, where all the Hāshim clan had gathered. ʿAlī then stood and, praising God as is His due, spoke:

أمّا بعد، يا أبا بكر، فإنّه لم يمنعنا أن نبايعك إنكار لفضيلتك ولا نفاسة عليك بخير ساقه الله إليك. ولكنّا نرى أنّ لنا في هذا الأمر حقّاً، فاستبددتم به علينا.

قال: ثمّ ذكر قرابته من رسول الله صلّى الله عليه وسلّم وحقّهم، فلم يزل يذكر ذلك حتّى بكى أبو بكر.

فلمّا صمت عليٌّ، تشهّد أبو بكر، فحمد الله وأثنى عليه بما هو أهله، ثمّ قال:

أمّا بعد، فوالله لَقرابة رسول الله صلّى الله عليه وسلّم أحرى إليّ[١] أن أصل من قرابتي. والله ما ألوت في هذه الأموال الّتي كانت بيني وبينكم عن الخير، ولكنّي سمعت رسول الله صلّى الله عليه وسلّم يقول: لا نورث، ما تركنا صدقةٌ. وإنّما يأكل آل محمّد صلّى الله عليه وسلّم في هذا المال، وإنّي والله لا أذكر أمراً صنعه رسول الله صلّى الله عليه وسلّم فيه إلّا صنعتُه إن شاء الله.

ثم قال عليٌّ: موعدك العشيّة للبيعة.

فلمّا صلّى أبو بكر الظهر، أقبل على الناس، ثمّ عذر عليّاً ببعض ما اعتذر به. ثمّ قام عليٌّ فعظّم من حقّ أبي بكر رضي الله عنه وفضيلته وسابقته. ثمّ مضى إلى أبي بكر، فبايعه. فأقبل الناس إلى عليّ، فقالوا: أصبتَ وأحسنتَ. فقالت: فكان الناس[٢] قريباً إلى عليّ حين قارب الأمر والمعروف.[٣]

---

١ مم؛ تط: أحبّ إليّ. ٢ [الناس] من تط؛ وساقطة من مم. ٣ مم؛ تط: الحقّ والمعروف.

"Now to the heart of the matter, Abū Bakr—it has not been due to any refusal to recognize your excellence, nor because of an effort to outstrip the virtue God has bestowed upon you, that we have not pledged our allegiance to you. Rather, we regard our leadership of this community as a right that you have usurped from us."

ʿAlī then spoke of his own kinship with the Messenger of God and the rights of the Hāshim clan; he did not cease speaking until Abū Bakr wept.

When ʿAlī grew silent, Abū Bakr confessed the Oneness of God and praised God as is His due, and then he declared:

"Now, I swear by God, kinship with the Messenger of God is more precious to me than even my own ties of kinship. By God, I stopped at nothing to do right by you all and this property, but I had heard the Messenger of God say, 'We leave no heir; whatever we leave behind is for charity.' Only Muḥammad's family can support themselves from this property. By God, I recall no policy pursued by God's Messenger regarding this property that I myself will not pursue, God willing."

ʿAlī then said, "Nightfall will be the time when you receive the pledge."

When Abū Bakr had finished the noon prayer, he turned to address the people and proceeded to pardon ʿAlī for that for which he had previously sought pardon. Afterward, ʿAlī stood to speak. He extolled the right of Abū Bakr, may God be pleased with him, as well as his excellence and precedence in Islam, and then ʿAlī walked over to Abū Bakr and pledged his allegiance to him. The people turned to ʿAlī and said, "You have done what is right and good."

ʿĀʾishah commented, "And thus did the people draw near to ʿAlī when he drew near to Abū Bakr's rule and to right conduct."

حَدِيثُ أَبِي لُؤْلُؤَةَ قَاتِلِ عُمَرَ رَضِيَ اللهُ عَنْهُ

عبد الرزّاق عن معمر عن الزهريّ، قال: ١٠٢٨

كان عمر بن الخطّاب لا يترك أحدًا من العجم يدخل المدينة. فكتب المغيرة بن شعبة إلى عمر أنّ عندي غلامًا نجّارًا نقّاشًا حدّادًا، فيه منافع لأهل المدينة. فإن رأيتَ أن تأذن لي أن أرسل به، فعلتُ.

فأذن له، وكان قد جعل عليه كلّ يوم درهمين، وكان يُدعى أبا لؤلؤة وكان مجوسيًّا في أصله. فلبث ما شاء الله، ثمّ إنّه أتى عمر يشكو إليه كثرة خراجه. فقال له عمر: ما تحسن من الأعمال؟

قال: نجّار نقّاش حدّاد.

فقال عمر: ما خراجك بكبير في كنه ما تحسن من الأعمال.

قال: فمضى وهو يتذمّر.

ثمّ مرّ به وهو قاعد، فقال: ألم أحدَّث أنّك تقول: لو شئتُ أن أصنع رحىً تطحن بالريح، فعلتُ؟

فقال أبو لؤلؤة: لأصنعنّ رحىً يتحدّث بها الناس!

قال: ومضى أبو لؤلؤة، فقال عمر: أمّا العبد، فقد أوعدني آنفًا.

فلمّا أزمع بالّذي أزمع به، أخذ خنجرًا، فاشتمل عليه. ثمّ قعد لعمر في زاوية من زوايا المسجد، وكان عمر يخرج بالسحر فيوقظ الناس بالصلاة. فمرّ به، فثار إليه، فطعنه ثلاث طعنات، إحداهنّ تحت سرّته وهي الّتي قتلته. وطعن اثنا عشر رجلًا من أهل المسجد، فمات منهم ستّة وبقي منهم ستّة. ثمّ نحر نفسه بخنجره، فمات.

The Story of Abū Lu'lu'ah, 'Umar's Assassin[272]

'Abd al-Razzāq, on the authority of Ma'mar, on the authority of al-Zuhrī, who said: 28.1

'Umar would not permit a single non-Arab to enter Medina, but al-Mughīrah ibn Shu'bah wrote to 'Umar, saying, "I own a slave who's a carpenter, artisan, and smith; he can be of great benefit to the inhabitants of Medina. If you deem it fit to permit me to send him, consider it done."

'Umar granted him permission, and al-Mughīrah levied a payment of two silver pieces per day from this slave. The slave was called Abū Lu'lu'ah, and he was originally a Zoroastrian. He remained in Medina as long as God willed, but then one day he came to 'Umar complaining about the severity of the levy on his work, so 'Umar asked him, "In which crafts do you excel?"

"I am a carpenter, an artisan, and a smith," he replied.

'Umar then declared, "Considering the extent to which you excel in your crafts, your levy is not so great!"

Abū Lu'lu'ah then walked away grumbling.

Another time, the slave passed by 'Umar while he was seated, and 'Umar said, "Is it true what I've been told: that you say, 'If you want me to fashion a mill that uses the wind to grind grain, I can'?"

"Indeed," replied Abū Lu'lu'ah, "I shall build a mill about which the people shall never cease to speak!"

As Abū Lu'lu'ah left, 'Umar exclaimed, "Did that slave just threaten me with violence?"

When Abū Lu'lu'ah resolved to do the deed, he took a dagger and concealed it. Then he crouched down in one of the corners of the mosque waiting for 'Umar. 'Umar had set out before daybreak to wake the people for prayer, and when he passed by, Abū Lu'lu'ah lunged toward him and stabbed him three times. One of the wounds was under 'Umar's navel and that was the one that killed him. Abū Lu'lu'ah stabbed twelve other men in the mosque; six of them died, and six survived. Then he slit his own throat with his dagger and died.

٢،٢٨ قال معمر: وسمعت غير الزهريّ يقول:

ألقى رجلٌ من أهل العراق عليه بُرنُساً، فلمّا اغتمّ فيه، نحر نفسه.

٣،٢٨ قال معمر: قال الزهريّ:

فلمّا خشي عمر النزف، قال: لِيُصلِّ بالناس عبد الرحمن بن عوف.

٤،٢٨ قال الزهريّ: فأخبرني عبد الله بن عبّاس، قال:

فاحتملنا عمر أنا ونفرٌ من الأنصار حتّى أدخلناه منزله. فلم يزل في غشية واحدة حتّى أسفر. فقال رجل: إنّكم لن تفزعوه بشيء إلّا بالصلاة.

قال: فقلنا: الصلاة، يا أمير المؤمنين!

قال: ففتح عينيه ثمّ قال: أصلّى الناس؟

قلنا: نعم.

قال: أمّا إنّه لا حظّ في الإسلام لأحد ترك الصلاة. وربّما قال معمر: أضاع الصلاة. ثمّ صلّى وجرحه يثعب دماً.

قال ابن عبّاس: ثمّ قال لي عمر: اخرج، فاسأل الناس من طعنني. فانطلقت فإذا الناس مجتمعون، فقلت: من طعن أمير المؤمنين؟

فقالوا: طعنه أبو لؤلؤة عدوّ الله، غلام المغيرة بن شعبة.

فرجعتُ إلى عمر وهو يستأني أن آتيه الخبر. فقلت: يا أمير المؤمنين، طعنك عدوّ الله أبو لؤلؤة.

فقال عمر: اللهُ أكبر! الحمد لله الّذي لم يجعل قاتلي يخاصمني يوم القيامة في سجدةٍ سجدها لله. قد كنت أظنّ أنّ العرب لن تقتلني.

ثمّ أتاه طبيب، فسقاه نبيذاً. فخرج منه، فقال الناس: هذه حمرة الدم. ثمّ جاءه آخر، فسقاه لبناً يصلد. فقال له الّذي سقاه اللبن: اعهدْ عهدك، يا أمير المؤمنين.

فقال عمر: صدقني أخو بني معاوية.

Ma'mar commented: I heard someone other than al-Zuhrī say: 28.2

An Iraqi settler threw a burnoose over him, and when he was caught inside, he slit his own throat.

Ma'mar said: al-Zuhrī said: 28.3

When 'Umar began to fear that he would bleed to death, he said, "Have 'Abd al-Raḥmān ibn 'Awf lead the people in prayer."

Al-Zuhrī said: 'Abd Allāh ibn al-'Abbās related to me, saying: 28.4

A group of the Allies and I carried 'Umar to his residence and laid him down inside. He remained unconscious until dawn. A man said, "Only if you mention the prayer will you be able to frighten him back to his senses!"

So we said, "O Commander of the Faithful, the prayer!"

'Umar then opened his eyes and asked, "Have the people prayed?"

"Yes," we replied.

"Islam will not bring good fortune to those who abandon prayer"—or perhaps 'Umar said, according to Ma'mar, "those who neglect prayer." After that he prayed, though his wound bled profusely.

Ibn 'Abbās continued: Then 'Umar told me, "Go out and ask the people who stabbed me." I set out, and when I came upon the people gathered together, I said, "Who has stabbed the Commander of the Faithful?"

"Abū Lu'lu'ah, the enemy of God and al-Mughīrah ibn Shu'bah's slave—he stabbed him!" they answered.

I returned to 'Umar, who was waiting for me to bring the report. I said, "O Commander of the Faithful, God's enemy Abū Lu'lu'ah stabbed you!"

"God is Great!" exclaimed 'Umar. "Praise be to God, who ensured that my assassin would not vie with me on the Day of Resurrection over a single prostration made to God![273] I did not suspect that the Arabs would kill me."

Shortly thereafter a doctor came to see him. He poured 'Umar date wine to drink,[274] and it came out from his belly. "This is the redness of blood," the people said. Later a different doctor came to him and poured him milk to drink, and the milk came out glistening white. The one who poured the milk for him then said to him, "Make your testament, O Commander of the Faithful."

"The man from the Mu'āwiyah clan[275] has told me the truth," 'Umar responded.

قال الزهريّ عن سالم عن ابن عمر: ٥،٢٨

ثمّ دعا النفر الستّة: علياً وعثمان وسعداً وعبد الرحمن والزبير. ولا أدري أذكَرَ طلحة أم لا. فقال: إنّي نظرت في الناس فلم أرَ فيهم شقاقاً. فإن يكن شقاق، فهو فيكم. قوموا، فتشاوروا، ثمّ أمّروا أحدكم.

قال معمر: قال الزهريّ: فأخبرني حميد بن عبد الرحمن عن المسور بن مخرمة، قال: ٦،٢٨

أتاني عبد الرحمن بن عوف ليلة الثالثة من أيام الشورى، بعدما ذهب من الليل ما شاء الله. فوجدني نائماً، فقال: أيقظوه. فأيقظوني، فقال: ألا أراك نائماً؟ والله ما اكتحلتُ بكثير نوم هذه الثلاث. اذهبْ، فادعُ لي فلاناً وفلاناً، ناساً من أهل السابقة من الأنصار. فدعوتُهم، فخلا بهم في المسجد طويلاً، ثمّ قاموا. ثمّ قال: اذهبْ، فادعُ لي الزبير وطلحة وسعداً. فدعوتهم فناجاهم طويلاً، ثمّ قاموا من عنده. ثمّ قال: ادعُ لي علياً. فدعوته، ناجاه طويلاً، ثمّ قام من عنده. ثمّ قال: ادعُ لي عثمان. فدعوته، فجعل يناجيه فما فرّق بينهما إلّا أذان الصبح.

ثمّ صلّى صهيب بالناس. فلمّا فرغ، اجتمع الناس إلى عبد الرحمن، فحمد الله وأثنى عليه. ثمّ قال:

أمّا بعد، فإنّي نظرت في الناس، فلم أرهم يعدلون بعثمان. فلا تجعل، يا عليُّ، على نفسك سبيلاً. ثمّ قال: عليك، يا عثمان، عهدُ الله وميثاقه وذمّته وذمّة رسول الله صلّى الله عليه وسلّم أن تعمل بكتاب الله وسنّة نبيّه صلّى الله عليه وسلّم وبما عمل به الخليفتان من بعده؟

قال: نعم.

Al-Zuhrī said, on the authority of Sālim, on the authority of Ibn 'Umar: 28.5

Next 'Umar called for the group of six: 'Alī, 'Uthmān, Sa'd, 'Abd al-Raḥmān, and al-Zubayr—I don't know if he mentioned Ṭalḥah or not. Then 'Umar declared, "I have examined the people, and I have not seen discord in their midst. If discord does arise, then it shall be from you. Arise now, convene to consult one another, and appoint one of your number as Commander of the Faithful."

Ma'mar said: al-Zuhrī said: Ḥumayd ibn 'Abd al-Raḥmān related to me on the authority of 28.6
Miswar ibn Makhramah, who said:

'Abd al-Raḥmān ibn 'Awf came to see me on the third night that the Shura was being held.[276] After as much time had passed into the night as God willed, he found me asleep. He said, "Wake him up!" They woke me up, whereupon he said, "Did I just find you sleeping? By God, sleep has hardly touched my eyes these past three nights. Go now, and call these persons to come see me"—all of whom were either early converts to Islam or from the Allies. I called for them to come, and 'Abd al-Raḥmān spoke to them alone inside the mosque for a long time. Later, when they stood up to leave, 'Abd al-Raḥmān said, "Call for al-Zubayr to come, as well as Ṭalḥah and Sa'd." I called for them to come, and he conferred with them for some time. Again they stood up to leave, and 'Abd al-Raḥmān said to me, "Call for 'Alī to come." I called for him to come, and 'Abd al-Raḥmān conferred with him for a long time. Then 'Alī stood to leave, and 'Abd al-Raḥmān said to me, "Call for 'Uthmān to come." I called for him to come, and when 'Abd al-Raḥmān began to confer with 'Uthmān nothing interrupted them until the call for the morning prayer.

Ṣuhayb then led the people in prayer.[277] When he had finished, the people gathered around 'Abd al-Raḥmān, who praised God and then proceeded to declare:

"Now, I have examined the people, and I have found none among them equal to 'Uthmān. And you, 'Alī, take care not to expose yourself to reproach. You, 'Uthmān, do you accept the burden of God's testament and His covenant, His pact and that of His Messenger, and that you shall act in accord with God's Scripture and the practice of His Prophet and with the precedent of the two caliphs who came after him?"

"Yes," answered 'Uthmān.

فمسح على يده، فبايعه. ثمّ بايعه الناس، ثمّ بايعه عليّ.

ثمّ خرج، فلقيه ابن عبّاس، فقال: خُدعتَ. فقال عليّ: أَوَخديعة هي؟

قال: فعمل بعمل صاحبيه ستًّا لا يخرم شيئاً إلى ستّ سنين، ثمّ إنّ الشيخ رقّ وضعف، فغُلب على أمره.

٧،٢٨ قال الزهري: فأخبرني سعيد بن المسيّب:

أنّ عبد الرحمن بن أبي بكر، ولم نجرّب عليه كذبةً قطّ، قال حين قُتل عمر: انتهيت إلى الهرمزان وجفينة وأبي لؤلؤة، وهم نجيٌّ فبغتُّهم. فثاروا وسقط من بينهم خنجر له رأسان، نصابه في وسطه. فقال عبد الرحمن: فانظروا بما قُتل عمر. فنظروا، فوجدوه خنجرًا على النعت الّذي نعت عبد الرحمن.

قال: فخرج عبيد الله بن عمر مشتملاً على السيف حتّى أتى الهرمزان. فقال: اصحبني حتّى ننظر إلى فرس لي. وكان الهرمزان بصيراً بالخيل، فخرج يمشي بين يديه. فعلاه عبيد الله بالسيف. فلمّا وجد حرّ السيف، قال: لا إله إلّا الله، فقتله.

ثمّ أتى جفينة، وكان نصرانيًّا، فدعاه. فلمّا أشرف له علاه بالسيف، فصلّب بين[1] عينيه.

ثمّ أتى ابنة أبي لؤلؤة، جارية صغيرة تدّعي الإسلام، فقتلها. فأظلمت المدينة يومئذ على أهلها.

ثمّ أقبل بالسيف صلتاً في يده، وهو يقول: والله لا أترك في المدينة سبيًّا إلّا قتلتُه وغيرهم! وكأنّه يعرّض بناس من المهاجرين. فجعلوا يقولون له: ألقِ السيف! ويأبى ويهابونه أن يقربوا منه حتّى أتاه عمرو بن العاص. فقال: أعطِني السيف، يا ابن أخي! فأعطاه إيّاه، ثمّ ثار إليه عثمان، فأخذ برأسه، فتناصيا حتّى حجز الناس بينهما.

---

١ [بين] أنا؛ ساقطة من م.

'Abd al-Raḥmān then placed his hand on 'Uthmān's and pledged him his allegiance, and the people pledged their allegiance soon thereafter, as did 'Alī.

Later, as 'Alī left, Ibn 'Abbās met up with him and said, "You were deceived."

"Was that indeed deception?" 'Alī replied.

'Uthmān acted in accordance with the precedent of his predecessors for six years, falling short in nothing for a full six years; however, after that the old man became feeble and frail and others dominated his rule.

Al-Zuhrī said: Sa'īd ibn al-Musayyab reported to me that: 28.7

'Abd al-Raḥmān ibn Abī Bakr—whom we've never known to lie—said at the time that 'Umar was killed, "I once came upon Hurmuzān, Jufaynah, and Abū Lu'lu'ah as they were discussing something in secret. I startled them, so they jumped up, and out from their midst fell a dagger with a blade on both ends, its handle in the middle." 'Abd al-Raḥmān later said, "Look to see with what type of weapon 'Umar was killed." They looked and found the dagger just as 'Abd al-Raḥmān had described it.

Thus it was that 'Ubayd Allāh ibn 'Umar set off with his sword sheathed until he reached Hurmuzān, whereupon he said, "Get up. Let's take a look at one of my horses." Hurmuzān had extensive knowledge of horses, so he set out walking in front of 'Ubayd Allāh. 'Ubayd Allāh then raised his sword to strike him, and when he felt sting of the sword, he cried, "There is no god but God!" and 'Ubayd Allāh killed him.

Next he went to Jufaynah, who was a Christian. 'Ubayd Allāh summoned him over and when Jufaynah got within striking distance, he attacked him with his sword, and Jufaynah made the sign of the cross between his eyes.

Lastly he came to Abū Lu'lu'ah's daughter, a small girl who claimed to have embraced Islam, and killed her. Thus did a dark shadow fall over Medina and its people that day.

'Ubayd Allāh then turned around with his sword blazing in his hand, "By God I won't leave a single captive alive in Medina, or anyone else!" and it seemed as though he was alluding to certain individuals from the Emigrants.[278] They started to say, "Throw down your sword!" but he refused, and they were too terrified to go near him. At last 'Amr ibn al-'Āṣ came and said, "Give me the sword, nephew!" 'Ubayd Allāh gave 'Amr the sword, and then 'Uthmān jumped up and grabbed him by the head, and the two scuffled with one another[279] until the people stepped between them.

فلمّا وُلِّيَ عثمان، قال: أشيروا عليّ في هذا الرجل الّذي فتق في الإسلام ما فتق، يعني عبيد الله بن عمر. فأشار عليه المهاجرين أن يقتله، وقال جماعةٌ من الناس: أَقُتِلَ عمر أمس وتريدون أن تتبعوه ابنه اليوم؟ أبعد الله الهرمزان وجفينة!

قال: فقام عمرو بن العاص، فقال: يا أمير المؤمنين، إنّ الله قد أعفاك أن يكون هذا الأمر ولك على الناس من سلطان، إنّما كان هذا الأمر ولا سلطان لك. فاصفح عنه، يا أمير المؤمنين. قال: فتفرّق الناس على خطبة عمرو وودى عثمان الرجلين والجارية.

قال الزهريّ: وأخبرني حمزة بن عبد الله بن عمر أنّ أباه قال: ٨،٢٨

يرحم الله حفصة إن كانت لمن شجع عبيد الله على قتل الهرمزان وجفينة.

قال الزهريّ: وأخبرني عبد الله بن ثعلبة، أو قال ابن حليفه، الخزاعيّ، قال: ٩،٢٨

رأيتُ الهرمزان رفع يده يصلّي خلف عمر.

قال معمر: وقال غير الزهريّ: ١٠،٢٨

فقال عثمان: أنا وليُّ الهرمزان وجفينة والجارية، وإنّي قد جعلتهم ديةً.

When 'Uthmān was made ruler, he declared, "Lend me your counsel concerning this man, who has sowed such dissension in Islam"—by whom he meant 'Ubayd Allāh ibn 'Umar. The Emigrants advised 'Uthmān to kill him, but the majority of the people said, "'Umar was killed only yesterday—do you wish to make his son follow him to his grave today? God damn Hurmuzān and Jufaynah!"

'Amr ibn al-'Āṣ stood and declared, "May God spare you of this matter while you have authority over the people! Indeed, this matter did not transpire when you were in power. Pardon him, O Commander of the Faithful!" The people dispersed after hearing 'Amr's oration, and 'Uthmān paid the blood price for the two men and the girl.

Al-Zuhrī said: Ḥamzah ibn 'Abd Allāh ibn 'Umar reported to me that his father, 'Abd Allāh ibn 'Umar, said: 28.8

May God have mercy on Ḥafṣah if she was indeed the one who spurred on 'Ubayd Allāh to kill Hurmuzān and Jufaynah.[280]

Al-Zuhrī said: 'Abd Allāh ibn Tha'labah—or he said, "the son of his tribe's ally"—al-Khuzā'ī, who said: 28.9

I saw al-Hurmuzān raise his hand as he prayed behind 'Umar.

Ma'mar said: someone other than al-Zuhrī said: 28.10

'Uthmān said, "I will assume responsibility for al-Hurmuzān, Jufaynah, and the girl, and will pay their blood price."

حَدِيثُ ٱلشُّورَىٰ[١]

١،٢٩ عبد الرزّاق عن معمر عن الزهريّ عن سالم عن ابن عمر، قال:

دعا عمر حين طُعن عليّاً وعثمان وعبد الرحمن بن عوف والزبير. قال: وأحسبه قال: سعد بن أبي وقّاص. فقال: إنّي نظرت في أمر الناس، فلم أرَ عندهم شقاقاً، فإن يكُ شقاق، فهو فيكم. ثمّ إنّ قومكم إنّما يؤمّرون أحدكم أيّها الثلاثة. فإن كنت على شيء من أمر الناس، يا عليّ، فاتّق الله ولا تحمل بني هاشم على رقاب الناس.

٢،٢٩ قال معمر: وقال غير الزهريّ:

لا تحمل بني أبي ركانة على رقاب الناس.

٣،٢٩ قال معمر: وقال الزهريّ في حديثه عن سالم عن ابن عمر، قال:

وإن كنت، يا عثمان، على شيء، فاتّق الله ولا تحمل بني أبي معيط على رقاب الناس. وإن كنت على شيء من أمور الناس، يا عبد الرحمن، فاتّق الله ولا تحمل أقاربك على رقاب الناس. فتشاوروا، ثمّ أمّروا أحدكم. قال: فقاموا ليتشاوروا.

قال عبد الله بن عمر: فدعاني عثمان فشاورني، ولم يُدخلني عمر في الشورى. فلمّا أكثر أن يدعوني، قلتُ: ألا تتّقون الله؟ أتؤمّرون وأمير المؤمنين حيٌّ بعد؟ قال: فكأنّما أيقظت عمر، فدعاهم، فقال: أمهلوا ليُصَلِّ بالناس صهيب. ثمّ تشاوروا، ثمّ أجمعوا أمركم في الثلاث. واجمعوا أمراء الأجناد، فمن تأمّركم من غير مشورة من المسلمين، فاقتلوه.

The Story of the Shura[281]

ʿAbd al-Razzāq, on the authority of Maʿmar, on the authority of al-Zuhrī, on the authority of Sālim, on the authority of Ibn ʿUmar, who said: **29.1**

When ʿUmar had been stabbed, he called for ʿAlī, ʿUthmān, ʿAbd al-Raḥmān ibn ʿAwf, and al-Zubayr—and I believe he also mentioned Saʿd ibn Abī Waqqāṣ—and said, "I have examined the state of the people and have not found any discord in their midst. If discord does appear, then it shall be from you. What's more, your people will recognize one of you as Commander of the Faithful in three days' time. And you, ʿAlī, if you find yourself in power over the affairs of the people, be mindful of God and do not burden them with the yoke of the Hāshim clan!"

Maʿmar said: someone other than al-Zuhrī said: **29.2**

Do not burden the people with the yoke of the Abū Rukānah clan![282]

Maʿmar said: al-Zuhrī continued his report related on the authority of Sālim, from Ibn ʿUmar: **29.3**

ʿUmar said, "And you, ʿUthmān, if you find yourself in power, be mindful of God and do not burden the people with the yoke of the Abū Muʿayṭ clan![283] And you, ʿAbd al-Raḥmān, if you find yourself in power over the people's affairs, be mindful of God and do not burden the people with the yoke of your kin. Go now, assemble the Shura, and appoint one of you as Commander of the Faithful." They then rose up to convene the Shura.

ʿAbd Allāh ibn ʿUmar said, "ʿUthmān called on me to come participate in the Shura, for ʿUmar had not appointed me to the assembly. When they persisted in calling me to attend, I replied, 'Do you not fear God? Will you appoint a new ruler while the Commander of the Faithful still lives?' It was as if my words awakened ʿUmar, for he then called for them and commanded, 'Proceed slowly and let Ṣuhayb lead the people in prayer; then convene the

قال ابن عمر: والله ما أحبّ أنّي كنت معهم، لأنّي قلّ ما رأيت عمر يحرّك شفتيه إلّا كان بعض الّذي يقول.

٤،٢٩ قال الزهريّ:

فلمّا مات عمر، اجتمعوا. فقال لهم عبد الرحمن بن عوف: إن شئتم، اخترتُ لكم منكم. فولّوه ذلك. قال المسور: فما رأيت مثل عبد الرحمن. والله ما ترك أحدًا من المهاجرين والأنصار، ولا غيرهم[١] من ذوي الرأي، إلّا استشارهم تلك الليلة.

١ أنا؛ مم: ولا ذوي غيرهم.

Shura. By the third day, you must come to a consensus on who will lead you, and also on who will command the armies; but if anyone attempts to lead without convening a Shura of Muslims, kill him!'"

Ibn 'Umar continued, "By God, I am glad I was not with them, for I barely saw 'Umar's lips move except to say what words he uttered then."[284]

Al-Zuhrī said: 29.4

When 'Umar died, they gathered together. 'Abd al-Raḥmān ibn 'Awf said to them, "If you all wish, I can choose one of your number," and so they appointed him to the task. Al-Miswar said, "Never have I seen the like of 'Abd al-Raḥmān. By God, there was not a single Emigrant, or Ally, or anyone else known for their sage judgment, with whom he did not consult that night."

غَزْوَةُ ٱلْقَادِسِيَّة وَغيرِهَا

عبد الرزّاق عن معمر عن الزهريّ، قال: ١،٣٠

أمّر رسول الله صلّى الله عليه وسلّم أسامةَ بن زيد على جيش، فيهم عمر بن الخطّاب والزبير، فقُبض النبيّ صلّى الله عليه وسلّم قبل أن يمضي ذلك الجيش. فقال أسامة لأبي بكر حين بويع له، ولم يبرح أسامة حتّى بويع لأبي بكر، فقام فقال: إنّ النبيّ صلّى الله عليه وسلّم وجّهني لما وجّهني له، وإنّي أخاف أن ترتدّ العرب. فإن شئت، كنتُ قريباً منك حتّى تنظر.

فقال أبو بكر: ما كنت لأردّ أمرًا أمر به رسول الله صلّى الله عليه وسلّم، ولكن إن شئت أن تأذن لعمر، فافعل.

فأذن له وانطلق أسامة بن زيد حتّى أتى المكان الّذي أمره رسول الله صلّى الله عليه وسلّم. فقال: أخذتهم الضبابة حتّى جعل الرجل منهم لا يكاد يبصر صاحبه. قال: فوجدوا رجلاً من أهل تلك البلاد. قال: فأخذوه يدلّهم الطريق حيث أرادوا، وأغاروا على المكان الّذي أمروا. قال: فسمع بذلك الناس، فجعل بعضهم يقول لبعض: تزعمون أنّ العرب قد اختلفت وخيلهم بمكان كذا وكذا؟ قال: فردّ الله تبارك وتعالى بذلك عن المسلمين.

فكان يُدْعَى بالإمارة حتّى مات، يقولون: بعثه رسول الله صلّى الله عليه وسلّم ولم ينزعه حتّى مات.

عبد الرزّاق عن معمر عن الزهري، قال: ٢،٣٠

لمّا استخلف عمر نزع خالد ابن الوليد، فأمّر أبا عبيدة بن الجرّاح وبعث إليه بعهده، وهو بالشام يوم اليرموك. فمكث العهد مع أبي عبيدة شهرين لا يعرّفه إلى خالد

The Expeditions to al-Qādisiyyah and Elsewhere

ʿAbd al-Razzāq, on the authority of Maʿmar, on the authority of al-Zuhrī, who said: 30.1

The Messenger of God appointed Usāmah ibn Zayd as the commander of an army in whose ranks were ʿUmar ibn al-Khaṭṭāb and al-Zubayr, but the Prophet was taken from this world before that army could proceed. Usāmah, who did not set out until after Abū Bakr had been given the pledge of allegiance, said to Abū Bakr when he pledged his allegiance, "The Prophet ordered me to go and do what had to be done, but now I fear that the Arabs will soon apostatize.[285] Still, if you wish, I will remain by your side until you see what transpires."

"Far be it from me to cancel a command issued by the Messenger of God," Abū Bakr replied, "but if you wish to give leave to ʿUmar to stay, then do so."

Usāmah gave ʿUmar leave to stay and then set out, eventually arriving at the place the Messenger of God had commanded him to go. A thick fog overtook them so that each man could barely see his comrade. They found a man who lived in that land, and captured him so he would show them the path to their destination. Thus they raided the place they had been commanded to raid. When the people heard that, they began to say to one another, "You all claim that the Arabs have become disunited, but their cavalry is in such-and-such place?" But God spared the Muslims from that.

Usāmah was called "the Commander" until he died. People would say, "The Messenger of God commissioned him, and no one dismissed him until he died."

ʿAbd al-Razzāq, on the authority of Maʿmar, on the authority of al-Zuhrī, who said: 30.2

When ʿUmar became caliph, he dismissed Khālid ibn al-Walīd and appointed Abū ʿUbaydah ibn al-Jarrāḥ as commander. ʿUmar dispatched his edict to Abū ʿUbaydah while he was in Syria at the Battle of Yarmūk. The edict

حياءً منه. فقال خالد: اخرجْ أيّها الرجل عهدك! نسمع لك ونطيع. فلعمري لقد مات أحبُّ[1] الناس إلينا، ووُلّيَ أبغض الناس إلينا. فجعله أبو عبيدة على الخيل.

عبد الرزّاق عن معمر عن الزهريّ عن سالم عن ابن عمر؛ ٣،٣٠

قال معمر: وأخبرني ابن طاووس عن عكرمة بن خالد عن ابن عمر، قال:

دخلت على حفصة ونوساتها تنطف فقلت: قد كان من أمر الناس ما ترين، ولم يُجعل لي من الأمر شيءٌ.

قالت: فالحقّ بهم فإنّهم ينتظرونك. والّذي أخشى أن يكون في احتباسك عنهم فرقةً. فلم تدعه حتّى يذهب. فلمّا تفرّق الحكمان، خطب معاوية، فقال: من كان متكلّماً فليُطلع قرنه.

عبد الرزّاق عن معمر عن أيّوب السختيانيّ عن حميد بن هلال، قال: ٤،٣٠

لمّا كان يوم القادسيّة، كان على الخيل قيس بن مكشوح العبسيّ، وعلى الرجّالة المغيرة بن شعبة الثقفيّ، وعلى الناس سعد بن أبي وقّاص.

فقال قيس: قد شهدتُ يوم اليرموك ويوم أجنادين ويوم بيسان[2] ويوم فحل، فلم أرَ كاليوم عديداً ولا حديداً ولا صنعةً لقتال. والله ما يُرى طرفاهم.

فقال المغيرة بن شعبة: إنّ هذا زَبَدٌ من زبد الشيطان، وإنّا لو قد حملنا عليهم قد جعل الله بعضهم على بعض. فلا أُلْفِيَنَّكَ إذا حملت عليهم برجّالتي أن تحمل عليهم بخيلك في أقفيتهم. ولكن تكفّ عنّا خيلك، واحمل على من يليك.

قال: فقام رجل، فقال: الله أكبر، إنّي لأرى الأرض من ورائهم.

فقال المغيرة: اجلس، فإنّ القيام والكلام عند القتال فشل. وإذا أراد أحدكم أن يبل فليبل في مركز رمحه. ثمّ قال: إنّي هازٌّ رايتي ثلاثاً. فإذا هززتها المرّة الأولى،

---

١ [أحبُّ] أنا: ساقطة من م. ٢ مم: عبس.

remained with Abū ʿUbaydah for two months, and he did not inform Khālid of its existence out of deference to him. Khālid then said, "Listen, man, produce your edict! We will heed you and obey. By my life, the dearest of people to us has died, and now the most malicious toward us rules!"[286] Abū ʿUbaydah then placed Khālid in command of the cavalry.

ʿAbd al-Razzāq, on the authority of Maʿmar, on the authority of al-Zuhrī, on the authority of Sālim, on the authority of Ibn ʿUmar: 30.3

Maʿmar said: Ibn Ṭāwūs also related to me on the authority of ʿIkrimah ibn Khālid, on the authority of Ibn ʿUmar, who said:

I entered Ḥafṣah's house, even though her hair still dangled in wet locks, and said, "The leadership of the people has been decided just as you suspected, and I now have nothing to do with the affair!"

"Go join them," Ḥafṣah said, "for they are expecting you. I fear that conflict will arise if you remove yourself from them." She would not leave him be until he went. Once the two arbiters disagreed, Muʿāwiyah delivered his oration, saying, "Whoever has a claim to make, let him show his face!"[287]

ʿAbd al-Razzāq, on the authority of Maʿmar, on the authority of Ayyūb al-Sakhtiyānī, on the authority of Ḥumayd ibn Hilāl, who said: 30.4

At the battle of al-Qādisiyyah, Qays ibn Makshūḥ al-ʿAbsī was in command of the cavalry and al-Mughīrah ibn Shuʿbah in command of the infantry. Saʿd ibn Abī Waqqāṣ was in command of all the forces.

Qays said, "I witnessed the battles of Yarmūk, Ajnādayn, Baysān, and Faḥl, but never have I seen such numbers as today, nor such an array of iron and warcraft. I swear by God that the army stretches as far as the eye can see."

Al-Mughīrah said, "This is merely Satan frothing at the mouth! If we attack them, then God will cause them to turn against one another. Surely I'll never find you if I attack them with my infantry and then you attack with your cavalry from the rear. Rather, keep your cavalry at the ready, and attack whoever draws near to you."

A man then stood and declared, "God is great! I see the earth behind them!"

"Be seated!" al-Mughīrah retorted. "Standing and talking before battle will lead to failure. If any of you wishes to flee, let him flee no farther from where his spear is planted." Later al-Mughīrah said, "I shall wave my banner three times.

فتهيَّؤوا. ثمّ إذا هززتها الثالثة، فتهيّؤوا للحملة — أو قال: احملوا — فإنّي حامل.

قال: فهزّها الثالثة، ثمّ حمل وإنّ عليه لدرعين. قال: فما وصلنا لنفسه حتّى أثأى فيهم بطعنتين وفُقِئَت عينُه. وكان الفتح. قال: فجعل الله بعضهم على بعض حتّى يكونوا رُكاماً، فما تشاء أن تأخذ برجلين أو واحد منهم فتقتله إلّا فعلت.[1]

[1] النص من (وصلنا . . .) حتى آخر الخبر مصحّف في مم؛ فلعلّ قراءتي أعلاه غير مثبوتة.

When I wave it the first time, make ready for battle. When I wave it a third time, ready yourselves to attack"—or he said, "Attack!"—"for I will attack."

Al-Mughīrah waved his banner the third time and then attacked, and he was wearing two coats of mail. We didn't reach him until he had twice inflicted piercing attacks into their ranks and his eye had been gouged out. Then the victory came. God caused them to fall upon one another until they formed a great heap, such that whoever wanted to seize one or two of them to kill could easily do so.

تَزْوِيجُ فَاطِمَةَ رَحْمَةَ اللهِ عَلَيْهَا

١،٣١ عبد الرزّاق عن معمرعن أيّوب عن عكرمة وأبي يزيد المديني، أو أحدهما - شكّ أبو بكر - أنّ أسماء ابنة عميس قالت:

لمّا أُهديت فاطمة إلى[١] عليّ، لم نجد في بيته إلّا رملاً مبسوطاً ووسادةً حشوها ليف وجرّةً وكوزاً. فأرسل النبيّ صلّى الله عليه وسلّم إلى عليّ:[٢] لا تُحْدِثَنّ حدثاً—أو قال: لا تقربنّ أهلك—حتّى آتيك. فجاء النبيّ صلّى الله عليه وسلّم، فقال: أثَمَّ أخي؟ فقالت أمّ أيمن، وهي أمّ أسامة بن زيد وكانت حبشيّةً وكانت امرأةً صالحةً: يا نبيّ الله، هو أخوك وزوّجته ابنتك؟ وكان النبيّ صلّى الله عليه وسلّم آخى بين أصحابه وآخى بين عليّ ونفسه. فقال: إنّ ذلك يكون، يا أمّ أيمن.

قال: فدعا النبيّ صلّى الله عليه وسلّم بإناءٍ فيه ماء، فقال فيه ما شاء الله أن يقول، ثمّ مسح به[٣] صدر عليّ ووجهه. ثمّ دعا فاطمة، فقامت إليه تعثر في مرطها من الحياء. فنضح عليها من ذلك الماء وقال لها ما شاء الله أن يقول. ثمّ قال لها: أمّا أنّي لم آلُكِ، أنكحتك أحبّ أهلي إليّ.

ثمّ رأى رسول الله صلّى الله عليه وسلّم سواداً من وراء الستر، أو من وراء الباب، فقال: من هذا؟

قالت: أسماء.

قال: أسماء بنت عميس؟

قالت: نعم، يا رسول الله!

قال: أجئتِ كرامةً لرسول الله صلّى الله عليه وسلّم مع ابنته؟

---

١ [إلى] من ط؛ ساقطة من م. ٢ [عليّ] من ط؛ ساقطة من م. ٣ [مسح به] من ط؛ ساقطة من م.

The Marriage of Fāṭimah

ʿAbd al-Razzāq, on the authority of Maʿmar, on the authority of Ayyūb, on the authority of ʿIkrimah and Abū Yazīd al-Madīnī, or one of the two (the doubt is Abū Bakr's),[288] that Asmāʾ bint ʿUmays said: 31.1

When Fāṭimah was brought to ʿAlī as a bride, we found nothing in his house save a floor of packed sand, a pillow stuffed with palm fibers, and a single earthen jar and jug. The Prophet sent ʿAlī a message saying, "Don't plan to do anything"—or he said: "Stay away from your kin"—"until I come to see you." When the Prophet came, he said, "Is my brother there?" Umm Ayman, a righteous woman from Abyssinia who was the mother of Usāmah ibn Zayd, said, "O Prophet of God! ʿAlī is your brother, and you have married your daughter to him?" For indeed, the Prophet had sealed a pact of brotherhood between his companions, and he had made the brotherhood pact between ʿAlī and himself.[289] "That is so, Umm Ayman," the Prophet replied.

The Prophet then called for a vessel filled with water, and uttering over it whatever words God willed him to say, he anointed ʿAlī with the water on his chest and face. Next he called for Fāṭimah, and as she stood up, she was so bashful that she stumbled over the hem of her garment. The Prophet sprinkled some of the water on her and spoke to her as God willed, and finally he said, "I have not neglected you. I have married you to the man who is the dearest to me of all my people."

Later on the Prophet saw a dark shape from beyond the partition—or from beyond the door—so he said, "Who is it?"

"Asmāʾ," she responded.

"Asmāʾ bint ʿUmays?" he asked.

"Yes, O Messenger of God."

"Have you come to honor God's Messenger and his daughter?" he asked her.

"Yes," said Asmāʾ, "for tonight the girl's marriage shall be consummated, and she should have a woman by her side. Should the need arise, she can let her know."

قالت: نعم، إنّ الفتاة ليلة يُبنى به، لا بدّ لها من امرأة تكون قريباً منها،[١] إن عرضت حاجة، أفضت بذلك إليها.

فقالت: فدعا لي دعاءً إنّه لأوثق عملي عندي. ثمّ قال لعليّ: دونك أهلك. ثمّ خرج، فولّى. قالت: فما زال يدعو لهما حتّى توارى في حجره.

٢،٣١ عبد الرزّاق عن يحيى بن العلاء البجليّ عن عمّه شعيب بن خالد عن حنظلة بن سبرة[٢] بن المسيّب عن أبيه عن جدّه عن ابن عبّاس، قال:

١،٢،٣١ كانت فاطمة تُذكر لرسول الله صلّى الله عليه وسلّم، فلا يذكرها أحد إلّا صدّ عنه حتّى يئسوا منها. فلقي سعد بن معاذ عليّاً، فقال: إنّي والله ما أرى رسول الله صلّى الله عليه وسلّم يحبسها إلّا عليك.

قال: فقال له عليّ: لِمَ ترى ذلك؟ قال: فوالله ما أنا بواحد من الرجلين. ما أنا بصاحب دنيا يلتمس ما عندي، وقد علم ما لي صفراء ولا بيضاء، ولا أنا بالكافر الّذي يترفّق بها عن دينه—يعني يتألّفه بها—إنّي لأوّل من أسلم.

فقال سعد: فإنّي أعزم عليك لتفرّجنّها عنّي فإنّ في ذلك فرجاً.

قال: فأقول ماذا؟

قال: تقول: جئتُ خاطباً إلى الله وإلى رسوله صلّى الله عليه وسلّم فاطمة بنت محمّد.

قال: فانطلق عليّ، فعرض على النبيّ صلّى الله عليه وسلّم وهو يصلّي وهو[٣] ثقيلٌ حَصِرٌ. فقال النبيّ صلّى الله عليه وسلّم: كأنّ لك حاجةً، يا عليّ؟

قال: أجل، جئتُ خاطباً إلى الله ورسوله فاطمة ابنة محمّد.

فقال له النبيّ صلّى الله عليه وسلّم: مرحباً، كلمةً ضعيفةً.

٢،٢،٣١ ثم رجع عليّ إلى سعد بن معاذ، فقال له: ما فعلتَ؟

قال: فعلتُ الّذي أمرتَني به، فلم يزِد على أن رحّب بي كلمةً ضعيفةً.

---

١ [منها] من ط؛ ساقطة من م. ٢ أنا؛ م: سمرة. ٣ [وهو] من ط؛ ساقطة من م.

The Prophet then prayed an invocation to God on my behalf, and indeed this deed is the one for which I'm most certain God will reward me. Later he said to ʿAlī, "Take your wife unto yourself." Then the Prophet departed and turned away, but did not cease praying to God on their behalf until he had disappeared behind the walls of his home.

ʿAbd al-Razzāq, on the authority of Yaḥyā ibn al-ʿAlāʾ al-Bajalī, on the authority of his uncle Shuʿayb ibn Khālid, on the authority of Ḥanẓalah ibn Sabrah ibn al-Musayyab, on the authority of his father, from his grandfather, on the authority of Ibn ʿAbbās, who said: 31.2

Men would often ask the Messenger of God for Fāṭimah's hand, but the Prophet turned away every single man who asked until, eventually, they gave up all hope of marrying her. Saʿd ibn Muʿādh met with ʿAlī and said, "By God, I think the Messenger of God only withholds her for your sake." 31.2.1

"What makes you think that?" asked ʿAli. "I am neither a man who possesses great wealth to which I can lay claim—he knows I have neither gold nor silver—nor am I an infidel who will be swayed to abandon his religion for her"—that is, to have his heart turned by her—"Rather," he continued, "I am the first to have embraced Islam!"

"I beg of you," Saʿd said, "only you can grant me solace from the thought of her—that would be a great relief to me."

"What should I say?" asked ʿAlī.

"You should say," Saʿd answered, "'I have come to God and His Messenger to ask for the hand of Fāṭimah bint Muḥammad!'"

ʿAlī went before Muḥammad while he was in prayer, but he was dumbfounded and unable to speak. "ʿAlī, are you in need of something?" asked the Prophet.

"Yes," he answered, "I have come to God and His Messenger to ask for the hand of Fāṭimah bint Muḥammad!"

The Prophet answered him with a feeble "Welcome."

ʿAlī then returned to Saʿd ibn Muʿādh, who asked him, "What did you do?" 31.2.2

"I did just as you instructed me," ʿAlī answered, "but he said no more than a feeble 'Welcome.'"

"By the One who sent him with Truth," Saʿd exclaimed, "he's given her to you in marriage! There's no turning back now, and he never lies. I adjure you!

فقال سعد: أنكحك، والّذي بعثه بالحقّ! إنّه لا خلف الآن ولا كذب عنده. عزمتُ عليك لتأتينه غداً، فتقولنّ: يا نبيّ الله، متى تبنيني؟

قال عليّ: هذه أشدّ من الأولى! أولا أقول: يا رسول الله حاجتي؟

قال: قل كما أمرتك.

فانطلق عليّ، فقال: يا رسول الله! متى تبنيني؟

قال: الثالثة، إن شاء الله.

ثمّ دعا بلالاً، فقال: يا بلال، إنّي زوّجت ابنتي ابن عمّي وأنا أحبّ أن يكون من سنّة أمّتي إطعام الطعام عند النكاح، فأتِ الغنم،فخذ شاةً وأربعة أمداد أو خمسةً، فاجعل لي قصعةً. لعلّي أجمع عليها المهاجرين والأنصار. فإذا فرغت منها، فأذني بها، فانطلق، ففعل ما أمره. ثمّ أتاه بقصعة فوضعها بين يديه. فطعن رسول الله صلّى الله عليه وسلّم في رأسها. ثمّ قال: أدخل عليَّ الناس زفّةً زفّةً ولا تغادرنّ زفّةً إلى غيرها—يعني إذا فرغت زفةٌ لم تعُد ثانيةً. فجعل الناس يردون، كلّما فرغت زفّة وردت أخرى حتّى فرغ الناس. ثمّ عمد النبيّ صلّى الله عليه وسلّم إلى ما فضل منها، فتفل فيه وبارك. وقال: يا بلال! احملها إلى أمّهاتك وقل لهنّ: كلن وأطعمن من غشيكنّ!

ثمّ إنّ النبيّ صلّى الله عليه وسلّم قام حتّى دخل على النساء، فقال: إنّي قد زوّجت ٣،٢،٣١
ابنتي ابن عمّي وقد علمتنّ منّي، وإنّي دافعها إليه الآن إن شاء الله. فدونكنّ ابنتكنّ، فقام النساء فغلّفنها من طيبهنّ وحُلِيّهنّ. ثمّ إنّ النبيّ صلّى الله عليه وسلّم دخل، فلمّا رآه النساء ذهبن وكانت بينهنّ وبين النبيّ صلّى الله عليه وسلّم سُترة. وتخلّفت أسماء ابنة عميس، فقال لها النبيّ صلّى الله عليه وسلّم: على رسلك، من أنت؟

فقالت: أنا الّتي أحرس ابنتك فإنّ الفتاة ليلة يُبنى بها، لا بدّ لها من امرأة تكون قريباً منها. إن عرضت لها حاجة وإن أرادت شيئاً، أفضت بذلك إليها.

فقال: فإنّي أسأل إلهي أن يحرسكِ من بين يديكِ ومن خلفك وعن يمينك وعن شمالك من الشيطان الرجيم.

Tomorrow you must go to him and say, 'O Prophet of God, when will you permit me to consummate the marriage?'"

"This is even more unbearable than the first," ʿAlī replied. "Can't I just say, 'O Messenger of God, I am in need'?"

"Say what I instructed you to say," Saʿd insisted.

ʿAlī set out to see the Prophet and said, "O Messenger of God, when shall you permit me to consummate the marriage?"

"The third night, God willing," he answered.

Soon thereafter the Prophet called for Bilāl, saying, "Bilāl, I have wedded my daughter to my cousin, and it would please me if the holding of a feast in celebration of matrimony were to become my community's established custom. So bring a sheep and get hold of a lamb, too, as w ell as four or five measures of grain; then bring me a wide bowl. Perhaps I will gather the Emigrants and Allies together. When you've finished, let me know." Bilāl departed and did all he had commanded him, and at last brought him the bowl and placed it in front of him. The Messenger of God then plunged his hand into the bowl, saying, "Let the people enter to see me group by group, and do not permit any group to leave and go somewhere else!"—meaning that, once a group had finished, it would not go out again. The people started to arrive, and when one group finished, another would arrive until, eventually, everyone had finished. Next the Prophet chose the choicest portion of the feast, which he spat upon and blessed,[290] saying, "Bilāl, take this to your Mothers, the Mothers of the Believers,[291] and tell them, 'Eat, and feed whoever comes to you.'"

The Prophet then rose up to go and visit his wives. He said, "I have wedded 31.2.3
my daughter to my cousin, and you know her stature in my eyes. Now I shall present her to him, God willing, so go prepare your daughter." The women then set about adorning her with their perfumes and jewelry. The Prophet entered, and when the women saw him, they went behind the curtain that separated them from the Prophet. Asmāʾ bint ʿUmays stayed behind, so the Prophet said to her, "Be at ease. Who are you?"

"I am the one who will keep watch over your daughter," she answered, "for tonight the girl's marriage is to be consumated. She will need a woman to be by her side so that, if a problem arises and she wants something, she can let her know."

The Prophet replied, "I shall ask my God to watch over you, protecting you from your front and back and your right and left from Satan the Accursed."[292]

ثمّ صرخ بفاطمة، فأقبلت. فلمّا رأت عليّاً جالساً إلى جنب النبيّ صلّى الله عليه وسلّم، خفرت وبكت وأشفق النبيّ صلّى الله عليه وسلّم أن يكون بكاؤها لأنّ عليّاً لا مال له. فقال النبيّ صلّى الله عليه وسلّم: ما يُبْكِيكِ، فما ألوتك في نفسي. وقد طلبت لكِ خير أهلي. والّذي نفسي بيده، لقد زوّجتكه سعيداً في الدنيا، وإنّه في الآخرة لمن الصالحين.

٤،٢،٣١ فلازمتها، فقال النبيّ صلّى الله عليه وسلّم: ائتيني بالمخضب فاملَيه ماءً. فأتت أسماء بالمخضب، فملأته ماءً. ثمّ مَجَّ النبيّ صلّى الله عليه وسلّم فيه وغسل فيه قدميه ووجهه. ثمّ دعا فاطمة، فأخذ كفّاً من ماء، فضرب به على رأسها وكفّاً بين ثدييها. ثمّ رشّ جلده وجلدها. ثمّ التزمها، فقال: اللّهمّ إنّها منّي، وأنا منها. اللّهمّ كما أذهبت عنّي الرجس وطهّرتني، فطهِّرها.

ثمّ دعا بمخضب آخر. ثمّ دعا عليّاً، فصنع به كما صنع بها، ودعا له كما دعا لها. ثمّ قال إنْ قُوما إلى بيتكما. جمع الله بينكما وبارك في سرّكما، وأصلح بالكما. ثمّ قام فأغلق عليهما بابهما بيده.

قال ابن عبّاس: فأخبرتني أسماء بنت عميس أنّها رمقت رسول الله صلّى الله عليه وسلّم، فلم يزل يدعو لهما خاصّةً، لا يُشركهما في دعائه أحداً حتّى توارى في حجره.

٣،٣١ عبد الرزّاق عن وكيع بن الجرّاح، قال: أخبرني شريك عن أبي إسحق:

أنّ عليّاً لمّا تزوّج فاطمة، قالت للنبيّ صلّى الله عليه وسلّم: زوّجتنيه أعيمش عظيم البطن!

فقال النبيّ صلّى الله عليه وسلّم: لقد زوّجتكه وإنّه لأوّل أصحابي سلماً وأكثرهم علماً وأعظمهم حلماً.

٤،٣١ عبد الرزّاق عن معمر عن الزهريّ عن عروة بن الزبير أنّ أسامة بن زيد أخبره:

The Prophet then called out for Fāṭimah. She drew near, and when she saw ʿAlī seated next to the Prophet, she hesitated and wept. Worried that her weeping was because ʿAlī had no wealth, the Prophet said, "Why do you cry? My heart has not neglected you. I have sought out for your sake the man dearest to me of all my people. I swear by Him whose hand holds my soul, I married you to one blessed in this life and who shall number among the righteous in the next."

Asmāʾ then joined Fāṭimah, and the Prophet said, "Bring me a basin and fill 31.2.4
it with water." Asmāʾ brought the basin and filled it with water. The Prophet spat in the basin and cleansed his feet and face therein. Next he called for Fāṭimah and, taking a handful of water, he poured it over her head and then poured another handful over her bosom. After that he sprinkled his skin and her skin with water and then, having finished the task, he said, "O Lord, she is from me, and I am from her. O Lord, as you have cleansed me of filth and have purified me, so purify her."[293]

The Prophet then called for another basin and called ʿAlī over. He did to ʿAlī as he had done to Fāṭimah, and prayed over him just as he had prayed over her. "Rise, go to your chamber," he said, "for God has made you one. He has hallowed your union and brought you to a good life." Then he stood and closed the door behind them himself.

Ibn ʿAbbās said: Asmāʾ bint ʿUmays related to me that she watched the Prophet as he continued to pray for them alone, mentioning no one else in his prayer, until he disappeared behind the walls of his home.

ʿAbd al-Razzāq, on the authority of Wakīʿ ibn al-Jarrāḥ, who said: Sharīk reported to me on 31.3
the authority of Abū Isḥāq that:

When ʿAlī married Faṭimah, she said to the Prophet, "You've married me to a little bleary-eyed man with a big belly!"

"Rather," the Prophet replied, "I married you to a man who was the first of my companions to become a Muslim, a man possessing a mind more learned and a bearing more formidable than them all."

ʿAbd al-Razzāq, on the authority of Maʿmar, on the authority of al-Zuhrī, on the authority of 31.4
ʿUrwah ibn al-Zubayr, who said that Usāmah ibn Zayd related to him that:

أنّ النبيّ صلّى الله وسلّم ركب حمارًا على إكاف تحته قطيفة فدكيّة. وأردف وراءه أسامة بن زيد، وهو يعود سعد بن عبادة في بني الحارث بن الخزرج، وذلك قبل وقعة بدر، حتّى مرّ بمخلط فيه من المسلمين والمشركين وعبدة الأوثان واليهود. وفيهم عبد الله بن أبيّ بن سلول، وفي المجلس عبد الله بن رواحة.

فلمّا غشيت المجلس عجاجة الدابّة خمّر عبد الله بن أبيّ أنفه بردائه، ثمّ قال: لا تغبّروا علينا. فسلّم النبيّ صلّى الله عليه وسلّم، ثمّ وقف فنزل فدعاهم إلى الله وقرأ عليهم القرآن. فقال له عبد الله بن أبيّ: أيّها المرء، ألا أحسن من هذا، إن كان ما تقول حقًّا. فلا تؤذِنا في مجلسنا، وارجع إلى رحلك، فمن جاءك منّا، فاقصص عليه.

فقال ابن رواحة: أغشنا في مجالسنا. فإنّا نحبّ ذلك.

فاستبّ المسلمون والمشركون واليهود حتّى همّوا أن يتواثبوا. فلم يزل رسول الله صلّى الله عليه وسلّم يخفضهم. ثمّ ركب دابّته حتّى دخل على سعد بن عبادة، فقال: أيْ سعد، ألم تسمع ما يقول أبو حباب؟ يريد عبد الله بن أبيّ. قال: كذا وكذا.

قال سعد: اعفُ عنه، يا رسول الله صلّى الله عليه وسلّم، واصفح. فوالله لقد أعطاك الله الّذي أعطاك، ولقد اصطلح أهل هذه البحيرة أن يُتوّجوه، يعني يملّكوه، فيعصّبوه بالعصابة. فلمّا ردّ الله تبارك وتعالى ذلك بالحقّ الّذي أعطاكه، شرِق بذلك. فلذلك فعل بك ما رأيت، فعفا عنه رسول الله صلّى الله عليه وسلّم.

آخر كتاب المغازي

والحمد لله وحده وصلّى الله على سيّدنا محمّد وآله وصحبه

The Prophet was riding on a donkey saddled with velvet from Fadak, and Usāmah was following close behind him. He was paying a visit to Saʿd ibn ʿUbādah in the quarter of the clan of al-Ḥārith ibn al-Khazraj, and this was before the Battle of Badr. Eventually he passed by a mixed assembly of Muslims, pagan idolaters, and Jews. ʿAbd Allāh ibn Ubayy ibn Salūl was in their midst, and at the assembly too was ʿAbd Allāh ibn Rawāḥah.

When the beast kicked up dust into the assembly, ʿAbd Allāh ibn Ubayy covered his nose with his cloak, saying, "Don't cover us in dust!" The Prophet greeted them with peace and stopped, after which he dismounted and began to call them to worship God and recited the Qur'an to them. ʿAbd Allāh ibn Ubayy then said to him, "Listen, man, if what you say is true, then wouldn't it be better not to trouble us at our assembly? Go back to your mount, and if one of us comes to you, then tell them your stories!"

Ibn Rawāḥah retorted, "Come to our assembly, for we enjoy it."

The Muslims, the Pagans, and the Jews all began to curse one another until they resolved to fight it out, but the Prophet worked long and hard to calm them down. He then got back on his donkey and eventually arrived at Saʿd ibn ʿUbādah's home. "O Saʿd," he said, "did you hear what Abū Ḥubāb said?"—by whom he meant ʿAbd Allāh ibn Ubayy—"He said this and that."

"Pardon him, O Messenger of God," Saʿd pleaded, "and be forgiving. By God, God has now given you that which He has given you, but the people of this settlement had previously decided to crown him as their ruler"—meaning to make him their king—"and to crown him with the leader's turban. The Almighty and Blessed God brought these plans to naught through the Truth He bestowed upon you, and that's stuck in his craw; so that is why he treated you as you saw today. So pardon him, O Messenger of God."

Here ends the *Book of Expeditions*

Praise be to God, the One, and may God's blessing be upon our Master Muḥammad, his Kinsfolk, and his Companions.

Notes

1 I.e., the sacred precincts encompassing the cultic centerpiece of Mecca: the cubed structure known as the Kaaba. Tradition asserts that at this time the Kaaba had not yet become the object of a monotheistic cult of worship but rather was the principal cultic site of the local pagan religion focused on the worship of idols housed therein. As a cultic center, it was forbidden to wage war within its environs. The early tradents of this tradition thus regarded the siege as a sacrilegious one.

2 "the Elephant Troop" (Ar. *aṣḥāb al-fīl*): see Q 105, Sūrat al-Fīl, which alludes to Mecca's deliverance from a Christian army remembered for its war elephant. Islamic historical and exegetical tradition relates these events, imbuing them with legendary details that are often contradictory and irreconcilable. The historical personality that led the Elephant Troop was a Christian regent for Abrahah, the negus of Axum (located in modern Ethiopia). From his base in Yemen, he ostensibly marched against Mecca to destroy the Kaaba in order to secure unrivaled cultic status for his recently constructed cathedral of al-Qullays (or al-Qalīs). Cf. de Prémare, "L'attaque de la Kaʿba," 261–367 (esp. 325 ff.): most notable here for Muḥammad's biography is that al-Zuhrī, and thus Maʿmar, reject the notion that Muḥammad was born in the year of these events, called the "Year of the Elephant"—often dated, likely incorrectly, to AD 570. Cf. *EI3*, art. "Abraha" (U. Rubin). Recent research suggests that Abraha's campaign against Mecca, if historical, likely dates to shortly after the year AD 558. See Robin, "Abraha et la Reconquête de l'Arabie déserte," 75 f.

3 "House" (Ar. *al-bayt*): i.e., "the house" wherein the divinity abides. All references to the House in this text refer to Mecca's cultic centerpiece, the Kaaba.

4 "their cross": a reference to the Christian identity of the attackers. The cross as an object of reverence among Abrahah's troops is a common theme of the historiography of the events; e.g., see de Prémare, "L'attaque de la Kaʿba," 325–26 and Tottoli, "Muslim Attitudes towards Prostration," 12. Abraha's usage of the iconography of the cross is also confirmed by epigraphic evidence; see Robin, "Abraha et la Reconquête de l'Arabie déserte," 14.

5 Purposely ambiguous, the text makes no mention of the identity of the visitor. Implied here, however, is that the visitor is divine, semidivine, or angelic in nature. Other early Muslim historians, such as Ibn al-Kalbī (204/819), portray ʿAbd al-Muṭṭalib as an adherent of the cult of the idol Hubal, to which the Kaaba was ostensibly dedicated during his

time. In Maʿmar's version, the ambiguity of the language may imply that this detail has been expurgated.

6 "most honored shaykh": often identified with Ishmael, the son of Abraham and regarded at this time as the progenitor of the inhabitants of Arabia, or "Ishmaelites"; cf. Gen. 16, 21:8–21 and Millar, "Hagar, Ishmael, Josephus, and the Origins of Islam."

7 "between the viscera and blood" (Ar. *bayna'l-farth wa-l-dam*): an idiomatic phrase used to describe the inedible contents of the animal's innards, as opposed to the consumable flesh of the slaughtered animal.

8 "altars" (Ar. *anṣāb*): the term may also be rendered as "idols"; however, these were not just any idols, but stone idols upon which sacrifices were made. Tradition attributes their establishment to Abraham, who erected them under Gabriel's guidance. See Q Māʾidah 5:3 and Crone, "The Religion of the Qurʾānic Pagans," 169.

9 In the ancient world, the inhabitants of Arabia were renowned for their ability to speak to and divine the behavior of animals; see Schäfer, *The Jewish Jesus*, 221 f.

10 "mosque" (Ar. *masjid*); lit. "where one does prostrations (in worship)": the word "mosque" here is a catchall term for all places of congregational worship, and thus is not used in the narrower sense as a Muslim place of worship. See al-Aqṣā Mosque in the glossary.

11 "swords . . . buried in the well Zamzam": an omen of the conquests soon to come with the advent of Islam.

12 Presumably, ʿAbd al-Muṭṭalib receives this injunction from a deity or angel, although the language here is again circumspect, leaving the meaning ambiguous.

13 "I shall cast lots for them": the casting of lots reflects an ancient Near Eastern method for determining the will of a deity. Here, ʿAbd al-Muṭṭalib employs arrows, a popular technique that survived the coming of Islam, though not without controversy. See Crone and Silverstein, "Lot-Casting."

14 The episode of ʿAbd al-Muṭṭalib's vow to sacrifice his son and his subsequent ransoming of him constitutes a subtle parallel with Islamic literary traditions regarding Abraham and his nearly sacrificed son, Isaac/Ishmael (Islamic tradition is conflicted on the identity of the son Abraham attempted to sacrifice to God). Indeed, this parallelism is noted by early purveyors of the *sīra* tradition, as well as evidenced by reference to Muḥammad as *ibn al-dhabīḥayn*—i.e., "the descendant of the two sacrifices," ʿAbd Allāh ibn ʿAbd al-Muṭṭalib and Ishmael (cf. Ṭabarī, *Taʾrīkh*, 1:291)—as the Meccans were seen to be the descendants of Abraham (see Q Ḥajj 22:78).

15 This light is prophetic and represents the unborn Muḥammad; below, this light will be transferred to Muḥammad's mother who, after the prophet's birth, witnesses the light

"fill the castles of Syria." The story here plays off a well-known prophetological trope in Late Antique accounts of Moses; see Lowin, *The Making of a Forefather*, 243–46.

16 Arabian custom, and subsequently Islamic law, recognizes not only kinship through blood relations but also via milk relations. Children nursed from the same woman are regarded as siblings and are therefore forbidden to intermarry but allowed to socialize. See Giladi, *Infants, Parents, and Wetnurses*.

17 "One of the diviners" (Ar. *kāhin min al-kuhhān*): the *kuhhān* were diviners who spoke in oracular, rhyming utterances via contact with a familiar spirit and who acted as the main representatives of Arabian, polytheistic religious authority; e.g., see van Gelder, *Anthology*, 110–13. In the *sīra-maghāzī* literature, the *kuhhān* usually regard Muḥammad as a threat, in stark contrast to the righteous monotheists (usually monks or rabbis) who herald Muḥammad's future role as a Prophet.

18 "her house": other traditions state more explicitly that Muḥammad's milch-mother was a Bedouin woman to whom his birth mother had handed over her son to acquaint him with the customs of the desert nomads. The theme of surrogacy is also salient to the Late Antique "prophetic lives" of Abraham and Moses—accounts after which the present one appears to have been modeled. See Lowin, *The Making of a Forefather*, 234–38.

19 Cf. Q 94, Sūrat al-Sharḥ, which seems to have inspired the story. The story, only briefly told here, expands in subsequent retellings and details how angelic beings were sent down to split open the infant Muḥammad's breast and purify his heart in preparation for his future as God's Messenger. See Rubin, *Eye of the Beholder*, 59 ff. This story is rooted in a common literary topos of late antique hagiography; see Sizgorich, "The Martyrs of Najran," 130 f.

20 "palaces of Syria" (Ar. *quṣūr al-Shām*): Āminah's vision is an omen of the Prophet's future destiny to conquer Syria.

21 A foreshadowing of the destiny of Muḥammad and his community to overtake the Levant, this anecdote also mirrors similar Muslim traditions concerning the threat of Saul to the young, soon-to-be-king David; see Maghen, "Davidic Motifs," 104.

22 "cornerstone" (Ar. *al-rukn*): the black stone at the base of the Kaaba and, according to pious legend, present at every iteration of the Kaaba's construction since Abraham and regarded to be of heavenly origin.

23 Cf. Gen. 36:7.

24 The mention of Khadījah's sister is odd here, insofar as it potentially leaves the impression that the *muntashiyah* who acted as a matchmaker between the couple was in fact Khadījah's sister. However, given that the *muntashiyah* was slave-born (Ar. *muwalladah*) and not a full Qurashī, this is highly unlikely. Some traditionists identify this

matchmaker with Nafīsah bint Munyah, the sister of a tribal ally (*ḥalīf*) of the Nawfal ibn ʿAbd Manāf clan of Quraysh named Yaʿlā ibn Munyah al-Tamīmī. However, other narrations do in fact place Khadījah's sister, Hālah bint Khuwaylid, in the role of facilitating the marriage. In the story about Hālah, though, Khadījah's sister constructs a gambit to ensure that her uncle, ʿAmr ibn Asad, is inebriated (and *not* her father, as this account, unlike Maʿmar's, assumes Khuwaylid ibn Asad has passed away) so that he will agree to marry Khadījah off to a penniless Muḥammad. In Maʿmar's narrative, the implication seems to be that Khadījah's sister brokers the marriage arrangements for Khadījah and Muḥammad with her father Khuwaylid, but not the initial agreement and proposal between Khadījah and Muḥammad. Rather, this initial agreement is brokered by the unnamed slave-born woman described by Maʿmar in other traditions as a "dark-skinned woman" (*imrāʾah sawdāʾ*). See Balādhurī, *Ansāb*, 1:243–44 and al-Zubayr ibn Bakkār, *Muntakhab*, 27–29.

25 "*rajaz*-poets" (Ar. *rujjāz*): this refers to the simplest, and thus easiest, meter of Arabic poetry, traditionally regarded as the poetic meter of the common folk and simple songs and thus viewed with lower regard than the more complex meters of Arabic poetic verse. Cf. van Gelder, *Anthology*, 93–108.

26 Pherkad: romanized from the Arabic *al-farqad* ("oryx calf"), refers to one of two stars, either γ or β of Ursa Minor, known as "the two oryx calves" (*al-farqadān*) in Arabic astronomy.

27 "acts of religious devotion" (Ar. *al-taḥannuth*): used as a technical term in *maghāzī* and *ḥadīth* to designate acts of religious devotion (including prayer and feeding the poor) specific to a group of Arabian monotheists who, despite their rejection of polytheism, refrained from converting to either Christianity or Judaism. It has no historical relation with the Hebrew *teḥinnoth*, which postdates this Arabic word by centuries. See Goitein, *Studies in Islamic History*, 93, and Kister, "*Al-taḥannuth*."

28 "true vision" (Ar. *al-ruʾyā al-ṣādiqah*): the term could also be plausibly rendered as "dream," and other tradents contemporary with Maʿmar, such as Ibn Isḥāq, specify that Muḥammad had been sleeping during his first "dreaming-vision" (cf. Ibn Hishām, 1:236; trans. Guillaume, 106). On this episode see Rubin, "*Iqrāʾ bi-ismi rabbika*," and Schoeler, *Biography*, 38–79.

29 Q ʿAlaq 96:1–5; cf. Is. 40:6: the angel's command "Read!" (*iqraʾ*) can also be translated as "Recite!" However, I have chosen to render the verb as "read" because of the implied celestial text, which appears as a golden scroll in Ibn Isḥāq's account, following the interpretation of Neuwirth, *Der Koran I*, 267–71, 274 ff. As phrased by Maʿmar, Muḥammad's response, "I cannot read" (*mā anā bi-qāriʾ*; lit. "I am not a reader"), appears to highlight

Muḥammad's inability to read. The illiteracy of Muḥammad later becomes a key doctrine in Islamic theology, which regarded his illiteracy as an ideal precondition for the miracle of his reception of the Qur'an. See Goldfeld, "The Illiterate Prophet."

30 "returned with these words" (*rajaʿa bihā*): the phrase "these words" is a conjectural reading of preposition *-hā*, which has no clear antecedent.

31 Cf. Q 73, Sūrat al-Muzzammil.

32 In other words, Muḥammad's conduct conformed to the pinnacle of Arabian ideals of moral behavior; see Kister, "'God Will Never Disgrace Thee.'"

33 "written as much of the Gospels in Arabic": a passage often, but tendentiously, used to argue for the existence of an Arabic translation of the Gospels in circulation prior to the advent of Islam. However, other versions of this story state that, rather than writing the Gospels in Arabic (*al-ʿarabiyyah*), Waraqah wrote them in Hebrew (*al-ʿibrāniyyah*); see Wensinck, *Concordance*, 4:118. There is similar anecdotal and literary evidence, but neither documentary nor linguistic evidence from the surviving Arabic translations of the Gospels suggest that there existed formal, complete translations of the Gospels into Arabic until the Abbasid period. See Griffith, *The Bible in Arabic*.

34 "the Nomos" (Ar. *al-nāmūs*); from the Greek *nómos*: the word likely entered Arabic via a Palestinian Aramaic or Syriac intermediary *nāmūsā*; cf. Müller-Kessler and Sokoloff, *A Corpus of Christian Palestinian Aramaic*, 2a:279b and 2b, 251b, s.v. *n.y.m.w.s.* Although the Greek *nómos* most often refers to customary conduct or behavioral norms of community (thus often translated as "law," "practice," "order"), the association of *nómos* with the angel of revelation in the Islamic tradition perhaps arises from a conflation of the angel with the Law (i.e., *nómos*) of Moses he reputedly revealed to the prophet, even though the Torah does not mention an angelic intermediary and Talmudic authorities later polemicized against this idea. In general, see *EQ*, s.v. "Nāmūs" (H. Motzki) and *TDNT*, s.v. νόμος (Kleinknecht, Gutbrod): there is a precedent for the angelic-personification of *nómos*, however, in Syriac homiletic literature; see Griffith, "The Gospel in Arabic," 148–89.

35 This narrative contains curious parallels to the autobiographical opening sections of the Nag Hammadi tractate *Zostrianos*, a heavenly ascension apocalypse of Platonic and Sethian provenance likely dating at least as early as the third century AD. In this apocalypse, the holy man Zostrianos adopts the life of a recluse pondering the mysteries of the universe and offering worship and sacrifices to the gods. Despairing over "the pettiness" of his world, Zostrianos relates that he dared to deliver himself over to death by the wild beasts of the deserts. Zostrianos's would-be suicide is thwarted, however, by the appearance of an angel, who consoles him with the news that he has been chosen to receive the

revelations of the heavenly realms, whereupon the angel takes him on a celestial journey. See Burns, "The Apocalypse of Zostrianos," 31.

36 Cf. Q 73, Sūrat al-Muzzammil and 74, Sūrat al-Muddaththir. See Rubin, "The Shrouded Messenger."

37 "reeds . . . reeds of pearl" (Ar. *qaṣab . . . qaṣab min al-lu'lu'*): the hadith scholars are divided on how to interpret the widespread hadith that Khadījah's heavenly home would be fashioned from *qaṣab*—a word that usually means "reeds." Here, as translated above, Maʿmar seems to explain the reeds as fashioned of pearl—other interpretations include "an expansive, hollowed pearl (*mujawwafah wāsiʿah*)," "reeds adorned with jewels, pearls and rubies (*al-qaṣab al-manẓūm bi-l-durr wa-l-lu'lu' wa-l-yāqūt*)," or suggest the reeds represent that "she passed through life with great success because she was quick to have faith (*aḥrazat qaṣab al-sabq li-mubādaratihā ilā īmān*)." These examples, among others, are from Ibn Hajar, *Fatḥ*, 8:138.

38 "publicly to abandon idols": the word "abandon" is absent in the manuscript, but I have filled in the apparent lacuna here with an alternative transmission from Maʿmar's *Expeditions* as indicated in the textual apparatus. Possibly, the original text asserted that Islam was preached only in secret, whereas in public Muḥammad still sanctioned idol worship. Such an assertion would run directly contrary to the traditional and orthodox narratives of Muḥammad's life.

39 See Q Furqān 25:7, 41, and Crone, "Angels versus Humans as Messengers of God," 317 f.

40 There is a qur'anic prohibition against the consumption of carrion; see Q Baqarah 2:173.

41 ʿUmar here mockingly refers to Muḥammad as a descendant of the somewhat legendary Abū Kabshah. See "Ibn Abī Kabshah" in the glossary.

42 Q ʿAnkabūt 29:48–49.

43 Q Raʿd 13:43.

44 "the saying of 'Peace!' . . .": the five ritual prayers—none of which were instituted at this point in Muḥammad's prophetic career—all culminate with the phrase *al-salām ʿalaykum wa-raḥmatu'llāh* (lit., "God's mercy and peace be upon you (pl.)") uttered once to the right and once to the left. See Melchert, "The Concluding Salutation."

45 "has abandoned his religion" (Ar. *ṣaba'a*); lit. "ʿUmar has become a Sabaen": Sabaens (Ar. *ṣābi'ūn*), although mentioned in the Qur'an, remain somewhat mysterious beyond their belief in "God and the Last Day" (Q Baqarah 2:62, Anʿām 6:69). Later tradition often identifies them merely with those who abandon their ancestral religion. See de Blois, "The 'Sabians' (Ṣābi'ūn) in Pre-Islamic Arabia."

46 "assemblies" (Ar. *majālis*): lit., the "sitting sessions" in which the Quraysh's elders deliberate.

47 There seems to be a lacuna in the text here.

48 "al-Ṣiddīq": Abū Bakr is traditionally known by this sobriquet; the explanation given for it here is one of many, albeit the most famous, and implies that it derives from his faithful affirmation of the truth (Ar. *taṣdīq*) of Muḥammad's story when many would not. The word is qur'anic and often applied to prophets (Q Yūsuf 12:46; Maryam 19:41, 56; and Mā'idah 5:75) and believers (Ḥadīd 57:19 and Nisā' 4:65).

49 Q Qāf 50:29.

50 "public bath" (Ar. *dīmās*): the Arabic word comes from the Greek *dēmósion*, suggesting the possibility of a Christian source for the tradition.

51 "I was given the choice": in Arabic the construction is passive (*qīla lī*, "it was said to me"); hence, the identity of the speaker—whether the speaker was divine or angelic—remains ambiguous here.

52 "humankind's original faith" (Ar. *al-fiṭrah*): a technical term that refers to humankind's inborn nature, predisposing every human being to worship the one true God and follow the truth of his revealed religion.

53 The events of this chapter considerably postdate those mentioned in the previous section. Tradition places the Ḥudaybiyah expedition in the month of Dhū l-Qaʿdah, six years after Muḥammad and his fledgling community of Meccan believers undertook the Hijrah to Medina—i.e., during March–April AD 628; however, al-Zuhrī provides the slightly different date of Shawwal 6/February–March AD 628 (see 6.3 below). Whereas the last narrative presents Muḥammad to us in his most vulnerable state, this narrative relates events that transpire after the tables had turned considerably in his favor. Politically, the Quraysh were severely weakened by their conflicts with Muḥammad's Medinese polity. As he marches to undertake a pilgrimage here, the negotiations transpire at a time in which the political rise and eventual dominance of Muḥammad's Medinese polity over the Hejaz seems inexorable and close.

54 "He donned the seamless garments . . . a pilgrimage to Mecca": that is, Muḥammad outwardly donned the *iḥrām* garments designating that he and his followers had ritually consecrated themselves for a pilgrimage to Mecca. This pilgrimage was nonseasonal—i.e., an *ʿumrah* as opposed to the hajj, which must be undertaken during the month of Dhū l-Hijjah. The point here is that the nonaggressive intentions of Muḥammad as he approached Mecca would have been plain to the Meccan Quraysh, who were intimately familiar with this custom, even if the Meccans may have suspected the *ʿumrah* to be a ruse.

55 "hired troops" (Ar. *aḥābīsh*): confederate mercenaries of the Meccan Quraysh, these were often recruited from the Bedouin and Abyssinians who had settled in the Arabian Peninsula. See Wansbrough, "Notes on Aḥābīš Qurayš."

56 *Ḥal*: the voice command to urge a camel to rise.

57 "the war elephant" (Ar. *al-fīl*): the elephant of the so-called "Elephant Troop" (Ar. *aṣḥāb al-fīl*) that marched against Mecca to destroy the Kaaba. See n. 2.

58 Cf. Num. 20:11.

59 'Urwah speaks as a leader from the Thaqīf tribe of the city of Taif allied with the Meccan Quraysh; this is also the reason he is able to act as a mediator between them and Muḥammad's people in what follows.

60 "murdered and took their wealth": it is strange that 'Urwah does not immediately recognize al-Mughīrah, for most historians claim that the former was the uncle of the latter. 'Urwah does know all too well, however, the story of al-Mughīrah's crime. 'Urwah and al-Mughīrah were both from the city of Taif, whose inhabitants exiled al-Mughīrah for his treacherous crime.

61 "Caesar and Khosroes and the Negus": the Byzantine, Sassanid, and Abyssinian rulers were frequently called by the name Caesar (Ar. *qayṣar*), Khosroes (Ar. *kisrā*), or the Negus (Ar. *al-najāshī*) regardless of their actual names and regnal titles.

62 "crying out the pilgrims' invocation": viz., they cried out the *talbiyah*, an invocation made by pilgrims when entering into the state of *iḥrām* prior to entering the sacred precincts—the invocation here being, "Here we are, O Lord! Here we are! (*labbayka allāhumma labbayka*)."

63 "Your cause has just become easier for you": this statement is a play on Suhayl's name, which derives from the word *sahula*, "to be easy."

64 "In the name of God, the Merciful and the Compassionate" (Ar. *bismillāh al-raḥmān al-raḥīm*): this statement serves as an important consecrating act and has pre-Islamic precedents—a fact on display here in Suhayl's subsequent insistence on Muḥammad employing its pre-Islamic equivalent: *bismika llāhumma*, "In your Name, O God."

65 A common trope is that the Pagans opposed to Muḥammad worshipped God as Allah prior to Islam but refused to refer to God under the epithet *the Merciful* (*al-raḥmān*) used by the Christians and Jews of pre-Islamic Arabia. See Robin, "Arabia and Ethiopia," pp. 304 ff. The trope is rooted in Q Furqān 25:60, but recent scholarship strongly suggests that the dichotomy between Allah and *al-raḥmān* is more rhetorical than historical. See Crone, "The Religion of the Qur'ānic Pagans," pp. 166–69.

66 After the Muslims' initial Hijrah to Medina in AD 622, the subsequent undertaking of a Hijrah to the Prophet's city functioned as an act affirming and actualizing one's

conversion to Islam, and even became obligatory. Abū Jandal's dismay reflects (1) the belief that forcing one to return to Mecca was tantamount to denying him the chance to convert to Islam and join the community of Muslims, and (2) the belief that the Muslims could no longer provide a safe haven for their coreligionists who suffered imprisonment and deprivation in Mecca at the hands of the unbelieving Quraysh.

67 "Abū Jandal ibn Suhayl ibn ʿAmr": Abū Jandal is Suhayl's son—the man with whom the Prophet negotiates. Suhayl, like others opposed to Muḥammad's religion, shackled and imprisoned his son in his home in order to prevent him from joining the Muslims in Medina and to convince him to return to his people's religion. See Anthony, "The Domestic Origins of Imprisonment," 580–82.

68 Q Mumtaḥana 60:10.

69 This brief reference refers to the blockade of the Quraysh's trade routes to the north undertaken by Abū Jandal and Abū Baṣīr who, alongside many other Meccan Muslims unable to undertake their Hijrah to Medina because of the Ḥudaybiyah agreement, set up their own rogue encampment from which they employed banditry to intercept Qurashī caravans. See Rubin, "Muḥammad's Curse of Muḍar," 252–54 and Anthony, "The Domestic Origins of Imprisonment," 582–84.

70 Q Fatḥ 48:24–26.

71 "they would say it was ʿUthmān": as noted in the introduction, Maʿmar studied with al-Zuhrī in Syria when he resided in Ruṣāfah, the favorite residence of the Umayyad caliph Hishām ibn ʿAbd al-Malik. The Umayyads were keenly interested in emphasizing the importance of the first caliph to come from their clan of Quraysh: the third caliph ʿUthmān ibn ʿAffān. Muslim rebels murdered ʿUthmān in 35/656, and the Umayyads used this event as a basis for seizing the caliphate and establishing the legitimacy of their rule.

72 Hereafter follow two narrations concerning Heraclius, emperor of Byzantium from AD 610 to 641. The story is a set piece for early Muslim kerygmatic storytelling and reflects the extent to which Muslims assimilated and interacted with Byzantine and Christian narratives and perceptions in the Umayyad period. The frame story is a Muslim adaptation of a popular tale regarding Heraclius's premonition of the coming of the Islamic conquests. A version of it appears in many non-Muslim chronicles as well, the earliest of which dates to the late-seventh century AD; see *Chr. Fredegar*, 53–55 (§§ 65–66). See also Conrad, "Heraclius in Early Islamic Kerygma," and Esders, "Herakleios, Dagobert und die 'beschnitten Völker.'"

73 "a seer" (Ar. *ḥazzā'*): the word for "seer" here is likely derived from the Syriac *ḥazāyā* (also cf. Heb. *ḥōzeh*). On the emperor's interest in astrology, see Esders, "Herakleios, Dagobert und die 'beschnitten Völker,'" 260–63.

74 "king of the circumcised" (Ar. *malik al-khitān*): I have followed one current of the tradition that reads *malik al-khitān*, although one may also read *mulk al-khitān*, i.e., "the kingdom/dominion of the circumcised" (see Ibn Ḥajar, *Fatḥ*, 1:42 and Kister, "'. . . And He Was Born Circumcised . . .'" 19). Cf. Matt. 2:2, Luke 1:33.

75 Although not explicitly stated in this account, other accounts place these events in Bostra in Syria, and thus connect Heraclius's statement to the impending conquest of Syria rather than Constantinople.

76 "the sin of the tenants" (Ar. *ithm al-arīsīn*): the reference here is to Jesus's "parable of the tenants" found in Mark 12:1–12, Matt. 21:33–46, and Luke 20:9–19. The letter warns that, like the wicked tenants in the gospel parable, the Romans will be dispossessed of the lands over which God has made them stewards because they acted wickedly and scorned the landowner's son/Messenger. Though traditionally interpreted christologically, here the gospel parable is clearly applied to Muḥammad. The Arabic word here for tenant, *arīs*, is exceedingly rare and reveals the story's Levantine provenance since it derives from the Palestinian Aramaic translation of the New Testament, whose term for the tenant, *arīs* (pl. *arīsīn*), appears only in the extant lectionaries from this region and not in any of the Syriac translations of the New Testament. See Müller-Kessler and Sokoloff, *A Corpus of Christian Palestinian Aramaic*, 2a:222a, s.v. *ā.r.y.s* and Conrad, "Heraclius in Early Islamic Kerygma," 129–30.

77 Q Āl ʿImrān 3:64.

78 The first of the grand "thematic battles" of the Prophet's biography during the Medinese period, this first battle transpired between Muḥammad's early followers from Mecca (the "Emigrants") and his Medinese followers (the "Allies"), on the one side, and Muḥammad's Meccan opponents from the Quraysh on the other. Because they won though greatly outnumbered, the Muslims' victory is seen as proof of God's support of the believers and his punishment of the Quraysh for their misdeeds; themes salient to the narratives of this section.

79 Q Anfāl 8:19.

80 E.g., see Q Anfāl 8:5–9, Ḥajj 22:39–40.

81 16 (17) Ramadan 2/12 (13) March AD 624; other dates given include 17, 19, or 21 Ramadan 2/13, or 15, 17 March AD 624.

82 "the day of manifest redemption" (Ar. *yawm al-furqān*): cf. Q Anfāl 8:41 where the Muslims' victory at Badr is also called *yawm al-furqān*. My translation of the phrase follows the one most conventionally favoured for this verse (Rubin, "On the Arabian Origins of the Qur'ān," 427–28.); however, as Walid Saleh argues ("A Piecemeal Qur'ān"), *yawm al-furqān* may simply convey the meaning of "the day of distinction"—i.e., the

day that the Believers willing to fight distinguished themselves from those unwilling to fight (at Badr).

83 "Whenever the slaves . . . you leave them alone?": Maʿmar's version of the narrative is a bit opaque, but in the version given by Ibn Isḥāq, the rationale for the behavior is more clearly laid out. According to Ibn Isḥāq's narrative, the slaves belonged to Quraysh's warriors who had left Mecca to aid Abū Sufyān's caravan, and the Muslims beat them because they wanted the slaves to admit that they actually belonged with Abū Sufyān's caravan. See Ibn Hishām, 1:616 f; trans. Guillaume, 295. The point of the narrative to follow is to demonstrate that Muḥammad is the equal of the cunning Abū Sufyān as a strategist. This is displayed by Muḥamamd's clever use of seemingly innocuous questions to surmise key information about the fighting numbers of the Quraysh.

84 "Birk al-Ghimād" (also "al-Ghumād") "of Dhū Yaman": medieval geographers differ over which location this story refers to; however, given the context and intention behind the statement, a territory in the far reaches of the Yemen is likely intended. The phrase means something like "we will follow you to the ends of the Earth." See 12.3.1.

85 "Arab diebs" (Ar. *dhu'bān al-ʿarab*): the Bedouin nomads of the desert (lit., "the wolves of the Arabs") who, as opposed to the oasis dwellers, were disdained for their viciousness and barbarity; cf. Q Tawbah 9:97.

86 "his brother Shaybah . . . stood up": ʿUtbah comes forward to fight with his son and brother in defiance of Abū Jahl's slander against his courage. Because ʿUtbah is a Qurashī from the ʿAbd Shams clan, Muḥammad asks his Medinese supporters to sit down in order to give ʿUtbah a suitable contest with members from his own tribe of Quraysh. The men chosen by Muḥammad are his believing relatives from the Qurashī clan of Hāshim: ʿAlī is his paternal cousin, Ḥamzah his paternal uncle, and ʿUbaydah shares Muḥammad's great-grandfather ʿAbd Manāf. The MS has ʿUbaydah's name as ʿUbaydah ibn al-Ḥārith ibn *ʿAbd* al-Muṭṭalib, thus making him the Prophet's cousin, but this is a corruption—and a seemingly common one at that: see Balādhurī, *Ansāb*, 1(2):720 and ibid., 3:285.

87 Cf. Q Zalzalah 99:6.

88 This narrative constitutes the earliest martyrology, or "martyr story," of the Islamic tradition, and thus focuses on the fate of two martyrs from the Medinese Allies (ʿĀṣim ibn Thābit and Khubayb ibn ʿAdī) and the miracles accompanying their deaths. There exists a wide variance in the dating of these events in the *sīra-maghāzī* literature, and our text only specifies that it transpired after Badr. Ibn Isḥāq merely places the events after the battle of Uḥud in 3/625 without further specifying an exact date, whereas Wāqidī places the events in Safar 4/July–August 625. See Jones, "The Chronology of the Maghāzī,"

249. On the incident more generally, see Motzki, Boekhoff-van der Voort, and Anthony, *Analysing Muslim Traditions*, ch. 6 and Anthony, *Crucifixion*, 35 ff.

89 "to trim his pubic hair with it" (Ar. *yastaḥiddu bihā*): Islamic law regulates the hygienic maintenance and grooming of the human body, including hair dressing. The trimming of hair under the arms and in the pubic region falls into this category. See *EI2*, art. "Shaʿr, 2. Legal aspects regarding human hair" (A. K. Reinhart). The point here is that Khubayb, an ideal martyr, remained as scrupulously attentive to the ritual aspects of Islamic faith as possible, even in the face of certain death.

90 "the Sacred Precincts (Ar. *al-ḥaram*) to kill him": executions always took place outside the perimeter of Mecca's Sacred Precincts due to the ancient prohibition on shedding blood therein.

91 "he prayed two prostrations' worth of prayers" (Ar. *ṣallā rakʿatayni*): viz., he prayed two *rakʿah*s. A *rakʿah* is the basic unit of prayer gestures for the Muslim ritual prayer. It consists of a bending of the torso from an upright position followed by two prostrations; different prayers at different appointed times of the day, and occasionally under different conditions (such as travel or fear for one's life), require a different number of *rakʿah*s.

92 "Reckon my killers' number": i.e., "Hold them accountable for killing me on the Day of Judgment!" Khubayb's prayer is a discrete reference to Q Maryam 19:94–95.

93 Q Furqān 25:27–29.

94 This incident is the first of the stories relating Muḥammad and the Muslim community's fraught relationship with the largest Jewish clans in Medina. Traditionally, three Jewish clans are mentioned in the *sīra-maghāzī* literature: the Qaynuqāʿ, the Naḍīr, and the Qurayẓah; however, Maʿmar's text only relates the stories of the Naḍīr and the Qurayẓah and lacks any mention of the Qaynuqāʿ.

95 "six months": i.e., the month of Rabiʿ I in 3 (September–October AD 624).

96 Q Ḥashr 59:1–2.

97 "the first time in this earthly life that the Jews were banished": the word for banishment here, *al-ḥashr*, also means "to gather," but particularly in the sense of herding together as a congregation to one location, viz., a deracination. Thus is the word used in the Qur'an to refer to the gathering of humankind on the Day of Judgment and the consignment of the damned to Hell (e.g., Q Baqarah 2:203 and Āl ʿImrān 3:19). "This earthly life" (Ar. *al-dunyā*) specifies this life as opposed to the afterlife. Notably, other references to exile in this text use not *al-ḥashr*, but the less ambiguous term *al-jalāʾ*.

98 "the attendants of your womenfolk . . . golden anklets": golden anklets (*al-khalākhil*) were often worn by women and were idiomatically referred to as their "servants" or

"attendants." By threatening the attendants of the womenfolk of al-Naḍīr, the Meccan Quraysh made a not-so-veiled threat against the Jews' womenfolk. On this theme in pre-Islamic poetry, see Hamori, *Mutanabbī's Panegyrics*, 79.

99 The clan of al-Naḍīr lived half a day's march from Medina. The Qurayẓah clan was another prominent Jewish tribe of Yathrib, so Muḥammad secures a pact with them prior to his siege of al-Naḍīr to ensure that they will not interfere.

100 Muslim legends of the "lost tribes of Israel" winding their way to Arabia abound from quite an early date (see Rubin, *Between Bible and Quran*, 46–48), but it is ambiguous whether this text places the Naḍīr clan among these lost tribes or not. The exile mentioned by the text likely comes from anti-Jewish polemics found in Christian writings, which regarded the Romans' destruction of the Jerusalem Temple under the emperor Titus in AD 70 and the Jews' supposed "exile" from Palestine as divine punishment for the crucifixion of Jesus. The Jewish presence in Palestine throughout the Roman period, even well into late antiquity, contradicts these sentiments, but they were widespread nonetheless and subsequently adapted by the Islamic tradition, particularly in the interpretation of Q Isrā' 17:2–8. See Yuval, "The Myth of the Jewish Exile," and Busse, "The Destruction of the Temple."

101 "the fate of the Qurayẓah clan": in the events to follow, the Jewish clan of Qurayẓah would likewise be accused of treachery, leading to the slaughter of their men and sale of the women and children into captivity. These events are related in ch. 8.

102 Q Ḥashr 59:1–6.

103 "favored him thereby": the orchards thus became the Prophet's personal property to the exclusion of all others.

104 Q Ḥashr 59:6.

105 "fifteen years": which is to say that, according to al-Zuhrī's calculations, Muḥammad was called to be a Prophet fifteen years prior to undertaking the Hijrah from Mecca to Medina in 622. Given that these calculations are in lunar rather than solar years, this means that al-Zuhrī dates Muḥammad's encounter with Gabriel at Mount Ḥirā' to ca. AD 608. On the typological models behind the dating of the major events in Muḥammad's life, see Rubin, *Eye of the Beholder*, 190 ff.

106 Q Ḥijr 15:95, 91.

107 Q Ḥijr 15:94.

108 I.e., 21 September 622, a Tuesday. This differs from the date given by Ibn Isḥāq for Muḥammad's arrival on 12 Rabiʿ I. The problem is that Ibn Isḥāq also states that Muḥammad arrived on a Monday, but 12 Rabiʿ I (24 September 622) falls on a Friday.

Hence, the date given here is likely more correct. See *EI2*, art. "Hiḏjra" (W. Montgomery Watt).

109 Q Anfāl 8:7.

110 Q Qamar 54:45.

111 Q Mu'minūn 23:64.

112 Q Āl ʿImrān 3:127, 128.

113 After emigrating to Medina, the Prophet's followers began to raid Meccan caravans traveling on the route between Mecca and Syria. The Battle of Badr began with one such raid, this time against a caravan of Abū Sufyān ibn Ḥarb returning to Mecca from Syria. The Meccans reinforced Abū Sufyān's caravan with relief forces under the leadership of Abū Jahl. Thus, it is Abū Jahl and his relief forces who fight, and lose, against the Muslims at the Battle of Badr, not Abū Sufyān's caravan. Cf. *EI3*, "Badr" (Khalil Athamina).

114 Q Ibrāhīm 14:28.

115 Q Baqarah 2:243.

116 Q Āl ʿImrān 3:13.

117 Q Anfāl 8:42.

118 "the day on which al-Ḥaḍramī was slain": i.e., the Raid of Nakhlah in Rajab 2/January AD 624, in which the Muslims raided a Qurashī caravan in which ʿAmr ibn al-Ḥaḍramī was killed and thus violated the sanctity of the month of Rajab, an act ostensibly condoned by prophetic revelation (cf. Q Baqarah 2:217). The killing of Ibn al-Ḥaḍramī served as the Meccans' pretext for their offensive against the Muslims at Badr even after they had secured and protected Abū Sufyān's caravan from Muslim raiders. Maʿmar's version of the story of the Nakhlah raid survives, but in ʿAbd al-Razzāq's Qur'an commentary rather than the *Kitāb al-Maghāzī*. See ʿAbd al-Razzāq, *Tafsīr*, 1:87–88; cf. Balādhurī, *Ansab*, 1:929–31 and Jones, "The Chronology of the Maghāzī," 247.

119 Q Baqarah 2:194.

120 Q Mu'minūn 23:77.

121 Q Mu'minūn 23:78.

122 I.e., 27 May AD 632, a Wednesday. Other traditions from al-Zuhrī place his death on a Monday (e.g., Bayhaqī, *Dalā'il*, 6:234). On the varying dates given by Muslim tradition for the date of Muḥammad's death, cf. Rubin, *Eye of the Beholder*, 190–94.

123 Abū Bakr led the hajj in Dhū l-Hijjah 9/March–April 631, so according to al-Zuhrī the expedition against Tabūk must have occurred either in Muharram 10/April–May 631 or shortly thereafter. This date conflicts with Ibn Isḥāq's reckoning, since he places Tabūk earlier, in Rajab 9/October–November 630. See Jones, "The Chronology of the Maghāzī," 257 f.

124 The battle that transpired at Uḥud is the second of the grand thematic battles of the Prophet's life, taking place after the Battle of Badr and before the Battle of the Trench. It also marks an important turning point in the Medinese career of Muḥammad, for it is his first and only real defeat in battle. Being a defeat, Uḥud raised many questions about the nature God's providence and why he allowed his prophet to suffer defeat. This narrative offers many answers to these questions, but some of its most central themes are that of the community's disobedience to the prophet and the wisdom of God behind the trial suffered by the community in the course of Uḥud.

125 Which is to say, the Naḍīr clan's exile transpired in Rabīʿ I 3/September–October 624 and the Battle of Uḥud transpired six months later, in Shawwāl 3/March–April 625. The dating of these events relative to one another is problematic. Later scholars of the Islamic tradition place the expulsion of the Naḍīr clan *after* Uḥud; see the comments in Jones, "The Chronology of the Maghāzī," 249, 268.

126 Q Āl ʿImrān 3:152.

127 I.e., the omen is a boon, for many will sacrifice themselves for God's cause; cf. Q Ṣāffāt 37:102.

128 "ʿAbd Allāh ibn Ubayy . . . third of the army": the Muslims' defeat by Meccans at Uḥud is often laid at the feet of Ibn Ubayy due to a decision to prematurely *withdraw* from the field of battle. Here, by contrast, he seems to have simply remained behind to ensure Medina would be protected in the event of a Muslim defeat on the battlefield. However, the ductus of the text is also ambiguous. I have chosen to read it as "he remained behind" (*inkhazala*), a reading most strongly supported by the transmission of the text and flow of the narrative; however, one could feasibly read it as "he withdrew" (*inkhadhala*) instead.

129 "One of the Messenger of God's teeth" (*rubāʿiyah*): lit., one of the incisors next to the canines.

130 "had his chest rent open": the vicitim is unidentified here, but subsequent tradition identifies this person with the Prophet's believing uncle, Ḥamzah ibn ʿAbd al-Muṭṭalib.

131 Q Āl ʿImrān 3:173.

132 Q Āl ʿImrān 3:172.

133 The speaker here is ʿAbd al-Razzāq's pupil, Isḥāq al-Dabarī. See the Note on the Text.

134 The narrative of the final major battle of the Prophet before the conquest of Mecca, the incident of the United Clans, or the Battle of the Trench, relates the story of the Meccans' largest all-out assault on Medina. The Muslims triumph by surviving the siege but then face a threat from within Medina itself. They must confront the last remaining large Jewish clan of Medina: Qurayẓah. An alliance between Qurayẓah and the Prophet's enemies is uncovered, and he resolves to punish them harshly for their perfidy.

135 I.e., the Battle of the Trench (al-Khandaq) transpired no earlier than Shawwal 5 AH/ February–March AD 627; cf. Jones, "The Chronology of the Maghāzī," 251.

136 Q Aḥzāb 33:25.

137 "perfumed himself" (*istajmara*): the Arabic might also be translated "he cleaned himself with stones"—i.e., he performed an act of ritual purification called for after attending to the call of nature (Ar. *al-istinjā'*).

138 "the sun had set . . .": the late-afternoon prayer, or *ṣalāt al-ʿaṣr*, must be prayed before sunset, the concern often being expressed that undertaking the prayer during sunset could potentially be misconstrued as sun worship. See Rubin, "Morning and Evening Prayers."

139 "brethren of apes and pigs": in the Qur'an, God punished Jews who violated the Sabbath by transforming them into apes and pigs (Q Baqarah 2:65, Mā'idah 5:60, Aʿrāf 7:166); cf. Rubin, *Between Bible and Qur'ān*, 213 ff.

140 "bound like a captive atop a jenny ass" (*asīran ʿalā atān*): Saʿd ibn Muʿādh appears here to have been brought bound, and thus against his will, in order to utter a sentence approved by the Prophet himself. Saʿd ibn Muʿādh may have been bound to keep him propped up because he suffered from a fatal arrow wound, from which he purportedly died soon after the massacre of the Qurayẓah clan. The account of al-Zuhrī, however, does not mention these wounds. Contrast his reticence here in al-Zuhrī's account with Saʿd's sanguine participation in the Qurayẓah's sentencing as depicted in Ibn Hishām, 2:239–40; trans. Guillaume, 463 f. Cf. Kister, "The Massacre of the Banū Qurayẓah," 62–63, 90–91.

141 Cf. Q Āl ʿImrān 3:154.

142 The conquest of the Jewish settlement north of Medina known as Khaybar represents in our text a fulfillment of promised glory after the disappointment of Ḥudaybiyah. The narrative of Khaybar's conquest is, notably, followed by the fulfillment of the Prophet's promise that they indeed would undertake another lesser pilgrimage (*ʿumrah*) a year after Ḥudaybiyah (see ch. 2).

143 Q Fatḥ 48:20.

144 "under the tree" (*taḥta l-shajarah*): on the day of al-Ḥudaybiyah, some 1,500 men renewed their oath of fealty to Muḥammad under an acacia tree (*samura*). See Juynboll, *Canonical Ḥadīth*, 496a, 578b. The phrase is also used in connection with the pledge at al-ʿAqabah that set the stage for Muḥammad and the Emigrants' Hijrah to Medina; see Rubin, *Eye of the Beholder*, 182–83.

145 "took the fifth portion as was his right" (*khammasa*): this passage refers to Muḥammad having enacted the *khums* (or "fifth share") law stipulated in Q Anfāl 8:41. In essence, the

khums is the Prophet's share of the battle gains to be used for charity and the common good of the community.

146 "month of Dhū l-Qaʿdah": i.e., in March AD 629 and over a full year after al-Ḥudaybiyah.

147 "order him to leave": what al-Zuhrī describes here harkens back to the stipulations agreed to in the treaty of al-Ḥudaybiyah (see chapter 2 above).

148 "thirteenth of Ramadan": viz., 13 Ramadan 8 = 3 January AD 630.

149 This narrative relates the nearly bloodless conquest of Muḥammad's native city of Mecca and, finally, the integration of his most implacable enemies from the Meccan Quraysh into the community of believers. Particularly conspicuous in our text is the great deal of attention dedicated to the experiences of Abū Sufyān as he converts to Islam (an event telescoped in the narrative of his encounter with Heraclius in 2.7), since he is the forefather of the Umayyad caliphal dynasty that patronized the scholarship of Maʿmar's principal teacher, al-Zuhrī. Even more intriguing is that Abū Sufyān's companion throughout is the Prophet's uncle, al-ʿAbbās, the progenitor of the Abbasid caliphal dynasty that would supplant the Umayyads in 132/750.

150 "his approach from Syria": viz., the Meccan Quraysh sent this message to him on his return journey from Syria and after his having spoken with Heraclius about the prophetic claims of his kinsman Muḥammad.

151 "Red Death" (*al-mawt al-aḥmar*): a particularly striking metaphor for slaughter.

152 "so ready for war and so arrayed in their tribes" (*ṣabāḥ qawmin fī diyārihim*): absent in the English rendering is that the conquest transpired in the early morning as "a morning incursion" (*sabāḥ*).

153 "had returned to him": meaning that al-ʿAbbās was negotiating with the Meccans, and the Prophet and his followers were waiting for al-ʿAbbās to send his envoy back to Muḥammad with word of the status of the negotiations.

154 "what the Thaqīf did . . .": i.e., the Thaqīf tribe murdered ʿUrwah, who was a Muslim at the time; see his entry in the glossary.

155 The Khuzāʿah and Bakr clans were allied with the Medinese Muslims and Meccan Quraysh, respectively, and in the course of the conquest a battle broke out between the two clans. See *EI2*, art. "Khuzāʿa" (M. J. Kister).

156 "and a woman": tradition records at least two women killed, so the identity of the woman referred to here is uncertain. One likely possibility is the second of Ibn Khaṭal's two singing-girls, Fartanā and Arnab (or Qarībah). Fartanā allegedly repented at Mecca's conquest, but Arnab remained defiant and was murdered. The second possibility is a slave girl named Sārah, who joined Muḥammad in Medina as a Muslim but later apostatized from Islam and returned to Mecca. After her return, she sang songs impugning

Muḥammad. Sārah was reputedly killed by ʿAlī ibn Abī Ṭālib (Balādhurī, *Ansāb*, 1:900 f.); however, other accounts give Sārah another, similarly woeful, death, claiming that though Muḥammad spared her life, she was later trampled to death by horses at al-Abṭaḥ in Mecca during the reign of the second caliph ʿUmar ibn al-Khaṭṭāb (Ṭabarī, *Tārīkh*, 1:1641). On the other figures mentioned, see the Glossary.

157 Q 110, Sūrat al-Naṣr.

158 "the rear of the Hawāzin tribe" (Ar. *ʿUjz Hawāzin*): in speaking of the "rear" (*ʿujz*) of Hawāzin the account refers specifically to three of its clans: Jusham ibn Muʿāwiyah ibn Bakr, Naṣr ibn Muʿāwiyah ibn Bakr, and Saʿd ibn Bakr. See *EI2*, "Hawāzin" (W. M. Watt).

159 Q Tawbah 9:25.

160 "caused their hearts to turn" (Ar. *yata'allafuhum*): a reference to "those whose hearts were caused to turn (*al-mu'allafah qulūbuhum*)" in Q Tawbah 9:60, a verse interpreted as referring to those Meccan leaders, such as Abū Sufyān and his sons, who received payment from the Prophet's share of the spoils from Ḥunayn as a reward for their reconciliation with him at the conquest of Mecca.

161 "a coat of mail": contrast this to the Prophet's approach toward Mecca in the garments of a pilgrim in chapter 2, on al-Ḥudabiyah.

162 "leather stirrup" (Ar. *gharz*): this is perhaps an anachronism, since the usage of stirrups seems to have been a late-Umayyad innovation. See Kennedy, *Armies of the Caliphs*, 171–72.

163 "companions of the acacia tree" (Ar. *aṣḥāb al-samura*): viz., those 1,500 or so who gave their oath of fealty, known as *bayʿat al-riḍwān*, to the Prophet under the acacia tree after the events of Ḥudaybiyah (see above).

164 "furnace": in Arabic *waṭīs*, a play on the name of the valley of Awṭās, where the encampment of Ḥawāzin was situated prior to the battle at Ḥunayn.

165 "the invocations preceding the early morning prayer" (Ar. *qunūt ṣalāt al-ghadāh*): the word for invocations here, *qunūt*, is a technical term for either invocations or curses integrated into the five ritual prayers between the recitation of the Qur'an and the full prostration (*sajdah*).

166 "imprisoning them": probably in their homes or other makeshift structures rather than a formal prison. See Anthony, "The Domestic Origins of Imprisonment."

167 "twice a day, morning and evening" (*ṭarafay al-nahār bukratan wa ʿashiyyatan*): the times of day associated with prayer, cf. Q Hūd 11:114, Maryam 19:11, 61.

168 "the two fields of lava rock" (Ar. *al-ḥarratayn*): the topography of Yathrib (later: Medina) was famous for its marshy lands where its inhabitants cultivated date palms,

and for two stretches of lava rock that lay adjacent to the city, creating its most conspicuous natural boundary.

169 I.e., Asmāʾ used one *niṭāq* to tie the leather pouch filled with provisions for the Hijrah and another to tie her dress around her waist. The title "Dhāt al-Niṭāqayn," however, may have first appeared as a pejorative designation with vague sexual insinuations that the Umayyads concocted to besmirch the dignity of the mother of the "counter-caliph" ʿAbd Allāh ibn al-Zubayr, who sought to overthrow the dynasty from 63/683 to 73/692. See Bitan, "Asmāʾ *Dhāt al-Niṭāqayn*."

170 Q Anfāl 8:30.

171 Cf. 1 Sam. 24:2–7 and Maghen, "Davidic Motifs," 106 ff.

172 "A bounty . . ." (Ar. *diyah*): usually the wergild, being the standard compensation for an individual's wrongful death, often set at one hundred camels of specific types (see Juynboll, *Canonical Ḥadīth*, 78a), but in this case, it is a reward offered by the Quraysh for killing an undesirable, renegade kinsman.

173 "divining arrows" (Ar. *al-azlām*): special arrows lacking both feathers and arrowheads, and used for lot-casting.

174 That the Jews of the Hejaz lived in towering structures is a common theme of both the Hadith and the Qur'an; e.g., see Q Aḥzāb 33:26 and Dhāriyāt 51:2.

175 I.e., in September AD 622; on the symbolism of Monday, see Rubin, *Eye of the Beholder*, 191.

176 Cf. Q Tawbah 9:108.

177 "load of Khaybar": Khaybar's load was that of dates and the riches of their sale, as opposed to the load of bricks, whose value to God and the believers far outstripped their otherwise paltry material worth.

178 The issue of the Prophet's recitation of poetry is a particularly sensitive one, as his enemies often denounced him as a mere poet (Ar. *shāʿir*; see Q Anbiyāʾ 21:5, Ṭūr 52:30); thus, al-Zuhrī emphasizes that this instance during the construction of Medina's mosque was a unique case; an exception to the rule. The Qur'an vehemently denies that the revelation is poetry and that its prophet is in any way a poet (Q Yā Sīn 36:69–70). It also speaks of poets as mendacious sinners inspired by demons (Q Shuʿarāʾ 26:221–4). The relationship between the poets and Islam was not hopelessly fraught, though, as the Qur'an speaks well of poets who believe (227), and Muḥammad famously employed poets such as his bard Ḥassān ibn Thābit. See Gilliot, "Poète ou prophète?"

179 Q Ḥajj 22:39.

180 "as God decreed": an allusion to Q Anfāl 8:7, «Remember how God promised you that one of the two enemy groups would fall to you: you wanted the unarmed group to be

yours, but it was God's will to establish truth according to His Word and to finish off the disbelievers.»

181 "he did not enroll them in a military register" (Ar. *lā yajmaʿuhum dīwān*): the narrator, Kaʿb ibn Mālik, here refers to the *dīwān al-jund*, the "military roll," established by the second caliph ʿUmar ibn al-Khaṭṭāb during the Islamic conquests and wherein all the participants in the Islamic conquests were registered according to their precedence in Islam (*al-sābiqah*) and tribal genealogy (*al-nasab*). The military registry was also the means whereby the warriors' pay and rations were distributed and calculated.

182 Q Tawbah 9:118.

183 "final third of the night" (Ar. *thulth al-layl*): the night in Islamic law began with the sunset prayer (*ṣalāt al-maghrib*) and ended with the daybreak prayer (*ṣalāt al-fajr*), with the intervening time being divided into thirds.

184 Q Tawbah 9:117–8.

185 Q Tawbah 9:119.

186 Cf. Q Tawbah 9:96.

187 "appointed . . . as his vicegerent" (Ar. *istakhlafa ʿalaynā*): i.e., he made ʿAlī the authority in his absence. The verb *istakhlafa* means that ʿAli was Muḥammad's "caliph" (Ar. *khalīfa*) during his absence, an action often cited by the Shiʿah to prove that Muḥammad intended his son-in-law ʿAlī to be his *direct* successor after his death.

188 Cf. Q Mujādilah 58:26–33.

189 An episode containing a story that extols the loyalty and fighting prowess of the Khazraj, one of the two main tribal faction of the Medinese Allies. The story exhorts as much as it entertains. In a thorough study of these events and the multitude of traditions thereon, Harald Motzki has demonstrated that the original story belongs to the earliest stratum of *maghāzī* materials to survive; see his "The Murder of Ibn Abī Ḥuqayq."

190 The story of Kaʿb's assassination by the Aws is not recorded by ʿAbd al-Razzāq in his recension of Maʿmar's *Kitāb al-Maghāzī*, but it does appear in his Qur'an commentary; see ʿAbd al-Razzāq, *Tafsīr*, 1: 164–65. See also Rubin, "The Assassination of Kaʿb b. al-Ashraf," and Kaʿb's entry in the glossary.

191 "He's gone" (Ar. *fāẓa*): the text here reproduces the accent of the Jews of Khaybar by having the man's wife say *fāẓa* rather than the more "correct" *fāḍa* [*rūḥuh*].

192 Cf. Q Aḥzāb 33:28–34, 28–53.

193 Cf. Q Baqarah 2:10.

194 "divorce his wife" (Ar. *firāq ahlihi*): here, as in what immediately follows, the word rendered variously as "wife" or "household" translates the Arabic *ahl*, literally meaning family or household. Note in the passages to follow how Usāmah's reference to the

Prophet's "household" rather than directly naming ʿĀʾishah follows the cultural protocol requiring one to speak only in an indirect manner about a man's wife, out of deference to his or her honor. Note also that the following passage discreetly reveals ʿAlī's thinly veiled contempt for ʿĀʾishah when ʿAlī directly references ʿĀʾishah as "her."

195 Q Yūsuf 12:18.

196 Q Nūr 24:11, 12–21.

197 Q Nūr 24:22.

198 "punished . . . according to God's law" (Ar. *ḥaddahum*): the reference here is to Q Nūr 24:4–5, «As for those who accuse chaste women of fornication, and then fail to provide four witnesses, strike them eighty times, and reject their testimony ever afterwards: they are lawbreakers, except for those who repent later and make amends—God is most merciful and forgiving.»

199 Here begins a section encompassing chapters 17–19 in which Maʿmar adds additional narrative materials not transmitted from al-Zuhrī and relating to the so-called "stories of the prophets" (Ar. *qiṣaṣ al-anbiyāʾ*), which are expansions of narratives found in, or alluded to by, the Qurʾan.

200 "were Muslims" (*kānū muslimīn*): Maʿmar here does not intend to speak anachronistically per se; rather, he asserts—as does the Qurʾan—that they followed the true faith of Islam, which is timeless and therefore also practiced by many prophets before Muḥammad, such as Abraham, Moses, and Jesus and his followers (see, e.g., Q Āl ʿImrān 3:52, 67).

201 Q Burūj 85:4–8.

202 By placing these events in Najrān, ʿAbd al-Razzāq explicitly connects this legend not only to Q 85, Sūrat al-Burūj, but also to the Christian martyrdom stories that circulated regarding the South Arabian martyrs of the fifth to sixth centuries AD, such as Azqīr, St. Arethas (Ar. al-Ḥārith), and the so-called "sixty martyrs" of Najrān executed by the Jewish king Dhū Nuwās in AD 523. See Beeston, "The Martyrdom of Azqir"; Sizgorich, "The Martyrs of Najran"; and Beaucamp, Briquel-Chatonnet, and Robin, *Juifs et chrétiens en Arabie*. For a survey of Muslim versions of the story, see D. Cook, "The *Aṣḥāb al-Ukhdūd*."

203 An Islamic adaptation of a Christian legend known as "The Seven Sleepers of Ephesus" placed in the reign of the Roman emperors Decius (r. 249–51) and Theodosius II (r. 408–50), the story circulated in many versions in both the Christian and Islamic worlds. This early Arabic retelling, however, seems to be most directly dependant on that of the Syriac-speaking historian Zacharias Rhetor of Mytilene (ca. AD 465–536).

See Griffith, "Christian Lore and the Arabic Qur'ān"; Reynolds, *The Qur'ān and Its Biblical Subtext*, 167–85.

204 Whereas previous tales related by Maʿmar seem to have arrived into the Islamic tradition via Christian sources, the story of Solomon related here has its closest parallels in rabbinic tales of the demon Asmodeus (e.g., see b.*Giṭṭīn* 7.68 and y.*Sanhedrīn*, 2.20c). On other Muslim versions of the story, see Klar, "*And We cast upon his throne a mere body.*"

205 Q Ṣād 38:34.

206 "But [the demon] did not exercise any authority over his wives" (*lam yusalliṭ ʿalā nisāʾih*): that it is the demon who did not excerise authority over Solomon's wives and not Solomon himself is made clear in a longer account preserved by Ibn ʿAsākir, *Dimashq*, 2:250, *wa-malaka kulla shayʾin kāna yamlikuhu Sulaymān illā annahu lam yusalliṭ ʿalā nisāʾih.*

207 Here, the account provides an Islamic perspective on the depiction of Solomon as an esoteric king with dominion and mastery over demons and occult knowledge, an image that had become increasingly prominent in the Late Antique world prior to the rise of Islam, and one addressed directly by the Qur'an (e.g., Q Baqarah 2:106, Anbiyāʾ 21:81–82, Sabaʾ 34:12–14). See Torijano, *Solomon, the Esoteric King.*

208 Cf. Q Nisāʾ 4:34.

209 In Islamic law, both coitus and sleep require one to undertake ritual washing (*ghusl*) and ablutions (*wuḍūʾ*), respectively, before undertaking prayer; here, the demon, having assumed the guise of Solomon, shows no concern for any of these matters.

210 Q Ṣād 38:35.

211 "Pouring medicine into the corner of his mouth" (Ar. *fī laddihi*): the term *ladd* here refers to administering an Abyssinian medicine known as *ladūd*; it was apparently a type of balm applied orally. See Ullmann, *Wörterbuch*, 2:436–37, 439.

212 "found it displeasing to say so" (*lā taṭību lahā nafsan bi-khayr*): i.e., ʿĀʾishah wished not to mention ʿAlī due to her well-known antipathy toward him.

213 I.e., Kaʿb ibn Mālik; this is a reference to the story related in ch. 13.

214 "cloak" (Ar. *khamīṣah*): a garment usually described as a black cloak with adorned edges, worn by both women and men and often used as a sleeping garment. See Stillman and Stillman, *Arab Dress*, 13.

215 Visiting and mourning at gravesites was a fraught practice in early Islam and remained highly contested among later scholars. On this topic, see Diem and Schöller, *The Living and the Dead in Islam*, 2:11–167 and Halevi, *Muḥammad's Grave*.

216 "mistresses of Joseph" (Ar. *ṣawāḥib Yūsuf*): the Prophet's comment alludes to an episode in the story of the prophet Joseph found in Q Yūsuf 12:30–34. In this episode, the mistress of the house invites several women over for a feast, but her true intent is to

show the ladies the irresistible beauty of her slave, Joseph, whom she had attempted to seduce. In the Qur'an, the episode demonstrates the formidable wiles (Ar. *kayd*) of women (cf. 28). Muḥammad thus likens ʿĀ'ishah to these women because she, by objecting to Abū Bakr leading the prayer, is only pretending to be concerned about Abū Bakr's frailty. In fact, she frets over any bad luck that may result from him becoming the Prophet's successor. In this way, the Prophet's statement reveals that he sees through her gambit and perceives the true source of her objections.

217 The Prophet's house was a part of the structure of the central mosque in Medina, so he could easily watch the goings-on from inside the chamber where he lay ill. See Halm, "Der *Masǧid* des Propheten."

218 An outer garment known as a *ridāʾ*, here translated as "robe," could double as a mat for sitting upon the dusty ground. Seeing Muḥammad sitting on the ground atop his *ridāʾ*, al-ʿAbbās suggests that he sit on a chair instead and thus be spared the dust kicked up from petitioners and litigants coming to see him to settle their disputes. That Muḥammad, so weak and weary from his sickness, cares not whether they struggle to sit even upon his own *ridāʾ* and rudely trample upon his heels reveals to al-ʿAbbās that the hour of his death draws near.

219 The corruptibility of the Prophet's corpse became a matter of controversy in subsequent centuries, but here the humanity of the Prophet is staunchly affirmed. On this issue and the initial expectations that Muḥammad might rise from the dead, see Szilágyi, "A Prophet like Jesus?"

220 "servant of the staff" (Ar. *ʿabd al-ʿaṣā*): meaning that the Prophet will die in three days, after which the leadership of the community will fall to someone other than ʿAlī. The image here is that of a slave subject to being beaten harshly with a staff by an unsympathetic master, and therefore unquestioning in his obedience.

221 "those . . . your right hand possesses": i.e., those whom you own. The phrasing is taken from the Qur'an (e.g., Q Nisāʾ 4:24, Mu'minūn 23:6, Aḥzāb 33:52).

222 "*ḥibarah* cloak": a woolen cloth, probably covered with striped designs; see Stillman and Stillman, *Arab Dress*, 14–15.

223 Q Āl ʿImrān 3:144.

224 "second of the two" (Ar. *thānī al-ithnayn*): a reference to Q Tawbah 9:40b «When the two of them were in the cave, he said to his companion, "Do not worry, God is with us," and God sent His calm down to him, aided him with forces invisible to you, and brought down the disbelievers' plan». As traditionally interpreted, this verse refers to Muḥammad and Abū Bakr hiding from the Meccans in the cave called Thawr during the Hijrah from Mecca to Medina. See Rubin, "The Life of Muḥammad and the Qur'ān."

225 "testament . . . The Scripture of God": the word for testament and scripture in this passage is the same: *kitāb*, meaning simply a book or piece of writing. The anxiety expressed here is that, if Muḥammad writes down a *kitāb* as his testament, it could be confused with God's *Kitāb*, the Qur'an, which alone is Scripture.

226 "we were in Minā": the Hāshim clan of the Quraysh, the clan of the Prophet of which Ibn ʿAbbās was a member, had their residences near a piedmont (Ar. *shiʿb*) in Minā.

227 "a man of your ranks . . . to so-and-so": in an alternative transmission from Maʿmar, these persons are named. The speaker is the Prophet's companion al-Zubayr ibn al-ʿAwwām, and it is ʿAlī ibn Abī Ṭālib to whom he pledges to swear his oath of fealty. Maʿmar's text, therefore, might have been censored here by ʿAbd al-Razzāq. See Balādhurī, *Ansāb*, 2:8.

228 "the market . . . vulgar mobs": the hajj season and the busiest season of the markets naturally coincided, bringing with them masses of people whose behavior and conduct could lead to unpredictable results. Ibn ʿAbbās wisely advises ʿUmar to avoid inflaming any disputes in this tinderbox.

229 "Friday Congregation" (Ar. *al-jumuʿah*): the day for the collective prayer in which a sermon is delivered in the main mosque.

230 "the verse on stoning" (Ar. *āyat al-rajm*): ʿUmar here discusses a verse famously alleged to have been omitted from the Qur'an. Here his comments foreshadow the verse's exclusion from the collection of the Qur'an commissioned by his successor, ʿUthmān ibn ʿAffān.

231 ʿUmar gives two versions of the verse on stoning, both of which he abbreviates. The full verse reads: «Do not yearn for ancestors other than your own, for it is an effrontery to faith. If a man and woman advanced in years commit adultery, then stone the two and such is the decisive punishment from God; God is almighty and all wise (*lā targhibū ʿan ābaʾikum fa-innahu kufran bikum al-shaykh wa'l-shaykhah idhā zaniyā fa'rjamūhumā al-battata nakālan min Allāh wa'Llāhu ʿazīzun ḥakīmun*).» Where the verse once stood in the Qur'an is a matter of disagreement in the tradition, the two main options offered being Q 33, Sūrat al-Aḥzāb or 24, Sūrat al-Nūr. See Nöldeke, et al., *History of the Qur'ān*, 199–201.

232 "Mary's son": Jesus the son of Mary, so called in order to emphasize the humanity of Jesus despite being born of a Virgin (e.g., Q Āl ʿImrān 3:45–59 and Maryam 19:17–21), and thus to eschew the Christian practice of calling him "the Son of God."

233 The speaker here again, according to an alternative transmission of the report from Maʿmar, is al-Zubayr ibn al-ʿAwwām. See Balādhurī, *Ansāb*, 2:8.

234 "hasty decision" (Ar. *faltah*): the term here, *faltah,* suggests an ad hoc solution and thus indicates that the action, though undertaken by one of exemplary station, does not establish a precedent worthy of emulation.

235 A "stout rubbing post" (*al-judhayl al-muḥakkak*) provides relief for a camel with an itch; a "short palm heavy laden with fruit" (*al-ʿudhayq al-murajjab*) is the pride of its owner. The speaker here, al-Ḥubāb ibn Mundhir, compares himself to both, presuming that he has found the solution to the conflict before them.

236 "commanders . . . aides" (Ar. *umarāʾ . . . wuzarāʾ*): the Allies, as their Arabic name "Anṣār" literally suggests, are to be the aides to the Quraysh. In calling the Anṣār aides to the Quraysh, ʿUmar uses the word *wazīr,* a word that has been Anglicized as vizier. However, he does not use it in the sense that it assumes in the Abbasid period—i.e., a powerful administrative magnate of the caliph—but rather in its qurʾanic sense, in which Aaron is called the aide (*wazīr*) to Moses (Q Ṭā Hā 20:29, Furqān 25:35).

237 "consultation" (Ar. *mashwarah*): ʿUmar here means to emphasize the importance of deciding a leader by means of a Shura. For a description of the procedures and purpose of the Shura, see the glossary and Crone, "*Shūrā* as an Elective Institution."

238 Cf. Q Shūrā 42:38 and n. 242 below.

239 "two slaves" (Ar. *ʿabdān*): in a separate transmission of this report, the reading "two riding-camels (*baʿīrān*)" appears in place of "two slaves"; see Abū ʿUbayd, *Amwāl,* 220 (no. 361). However, the reading above is supported from another report attributed to ʿUmar in which he states, *jaʿaltu fī l-ʿabd ʿabdayn wa-fī ʾbn al-amah ʿabdayn*; see Ibn Saʿd, *Ṭabaqāt,* 3:353.

240 "Abū l-Ḥasan": ʿAlī ibn Abī Ṭālib, known as Abū l-Ḥasan after his eldest son al-Ḥasan ibn ʿAlī.

241 "the Six": the six members of the Shura ʿUmar appointed on his deathbed to determine the next leader of the community; see the following chapter.

242 On his deathbed ʿUmar appointed six of the most prominent Companions of Muḥammad to choose one of their own number as the next leader of the community by means of a Shura. Tradition is at odds as to who exactly numbered among the six—indeed, only five names are mentioned in Maʿmar's account from al-Zuhrī here (but cf. 28.6 below; see also Crone, "*Shūrā* as an Elective Institution," p. 5 for the other alleged candidates)—but tradition is more or less unanimous in asserting that the two main candidates were Muḥammad's son-in-law from the Umayyad clan, ʿUthmān ibn ʿAffān, and Muḥammad's son-in-law and first cousin from the Hāshim clan, ʿAlī ibn Abī Ṭālib. The practice of deciding leadership via a Shura is attested to in the Qurʾan (see Q Āl ʿImrān 3:159 and Shūrā 42:38), but the application of this process of adjudication to determining the

leadership of the Muslim community is an innovation by ʿUmar, aimed at preventing the outbreak of civil strife between the competing candidates, whom he seems to have regarded as equally capable (or incapable) of acting as the Commander of the Faithful. In any case, although the Shura was often called for in subsequent decades, ʿUmar's institution never again decided the leadership of the Islamic polity as seen here and virtually disappeared into obsolescence within a century's time. This event is revisited at 28.6 and ch. 29.

243 "his bond . . . and his cupidity" (Ar. *ʿaqdahu wa-atharatahu*): ʿUthmān's loyalty to the Umayyah clan of the Quraysh, who rise to become the first caliphal dynasty that his subsequent reign facilitates, was notorious, as was his fondness for wealth.

244 "Too stubborn" (Ar. *ḍaris*): more precisely, to be stubborn to the point of irascibility; the image conveyed by the word is that of a man with his teeth set on edge.

245 ʿAlī's collected Qur'an mentioned here never became the standard codex (*muṣḥaf*) as did ʿUthmān's; however, among ʿAlī's partisans, the Shiʿah, his codex, and the superiority thereof to ʿUthmān's have been frequently debated. Cf. Modarressi, *Tradition and Survival*, 2–4 and Kohlberg and Amir-Moezzi, *Revelation and Falsification*.

246 The caliphate of ʿUthmān ibn ʿAffān ended in Dhū l-Hijjah 35/June 656 with his assassination by a faction of Muslims who cited as justification for their actions his misrule of the community and his refusal to abdicate.

247 In terms of chronological scope, this chapter is by far the most sweeping. It covers the last expeditionary raids ordered by the Prophet, offers a brief chronological overview of the reigns of his four successors (Abū Bakr, ʿUmar, ʿUthmān, and ʿAlī), and culminates in a narrative of the Great Civil Strife (Ar. *al-fitnah al-kubrā*) that ensued after the assassination of ʿUthmān in Dhū l-Hijjah 35/June 656. The narrative then recounts the conflicts ʿAlī ibn Abī Ṭālib engaged in throughout his bid to become recognized as the sole legitimate Commander of the Faithful: the Battle of the Camel and the Battle of Ṣiffīn. The end of the hostilities—marked by Muʿāwiyah ibn Abī Sufyān's appeasement of ʿAlī's party after the latter's assassination in Ramadan 40/January 661 and his consolidation of power over the Muslim community from his base in Damascus, Syria—is regaled in Muslim historiography as the "Year of Communal Solidarity" (Ar. *ʿām al-jamāʿah*). A key theme throughout the narrative is the polar opposition of civil strife (*fitnah*) and communal solidarity (*jamāʿah*).

248 According to other accounts, ʿAmr's expeditionary force is sent first, on account of his kinship ties with the tribes of the region, but fearing the hazards he encounters there, he sends a request for reinforcements from the Prophet. It is the auxiliary forces subsequently dispatched to ʿAmr's aid that Abū ʿUbaydah commands and that, presumably,

he hands over to ʿAmr's command. See Kister, "On the Papyrus of Wahb b. Munabbih," 557 ff.

249 "O sons of ʿAbd Manāf . . .": ʿAlī and Khālid belonged to the Hāshim and Umayyad clans of the Quraysh, respectively, and both clans belonged to ʿAbd Manāf, putatively the strongest and most important branch of Quraysh. Neither of the first two rulers to succeed Muḥammad, Abū Bakr and ʿUmar, belonged to this powerful branch of Quraysh, and thus their leadership is interpreted by Khālid as an affront to both the Hāshim and Umayyah clans. Incidentally, the two dynasties of caliphs, the Umayyads and Abbasids, both came from these descendants of ʿAbd Manāf.

250 "So shall you be forced to relinquish command" (Ar. *innaka la-tatraku imratahu ʿalā al-taghālub*): a more literal rendering would say "his appointment over you as commander," wherein "his" refers to the Prophet's appointment of Khālid ibn Saʿīd as a commander (*amīr*) over an expeditionary force to Yemen.

251 According to other accounts, Khālid approached ʿUthmān ibn ʿAffān with the same concerns as he did ʿAlī and delayed pledging his allegiance to Abū Bakr as Commander of the Faithful for two months. See Donner, *The Early Islamic Conquests*, 113–14 and Balādhurī, *Ansāb*, 2:17.

252 ʿUmar's antipathy toward Khālid ibn al-Walīd is legendary, but many accounts attribute the caliph's decision to dismiss Khālid to his use of the booty of the conquest to enrich himself and other tribal notables, while neglecting the poor; see ʿAthamina, "The Appointment and Dismissal of Khālid ibn al-Walīd," 260 ff.

253 "God has taken Yazīd" (Ar. *iḥtasib Yazīda*): the phrase *iḥtasib* is said to one bereaved of a child and literally means "take care to seek God's reward." As an admonition, it serves as a warning not to mourn the death of one's child excessively and, instead, to show forbearance. Abū Sufyān's measured reply shows his piety. See Halevi, *Muḥammad's Grave*, 114 ff.

254 "May the bonds of kinship keep you" (Ar. *waṣalatka raḥim*): an expression of gratitude.

255 Al-Walīd ibn ʿUqbah's offense was drunkenness; see Anthony, *The Caliph and the Heretic*, 36–37.

256 "the settlers in Egypt" (Ar. *ahl Miṣr*): the word translated as settlers here literally means "people" or "inhabitants," but here the references are not to the local inhabitants of Egypt per se, but rather to the Arabian tribesmen who settled in the conquered territories in the newly established garrison cities, such as al-Fusṭāṭ in Egypt (near the site of modern-day Cairo) and Basra and Kūfah in Iraq.

257 The manuscript reads "'Abd Allāh ibn al-Ḥārith ibn Hishām," which seems to be an error given that 'Abd al-Raḥmān ibn al-Ḥārith ibn Hishām was the famed participant in the Battle of the Camel. See Balādhurī, *Ansāb*, 5:240.

258 Ṭalḥah did indeed die during the battle, but only after it had been lost and, even then, at the hands of his supposed ally Marwān ibn al-Ḥakam. See Balādhurī, *Ansāb*, 2:225–26; cf. Madelung, *Succession*, 171 f.

259 "murdered . . . Wādī l-Sibā'": that is, Ibn al-Zubayr did not die on the field of battle. Tradition is unanimous that al-Zubayr fled the field of battle and, for his cowardice after having led Muslims into war against one another, was tracked down in Wādī l-Sibā' and killed by Ibn Jurmūz. See Madelung, *Succession*, 170 f.

260 "elite vanguard": the *shurṭat al-khamīs* of 'Alī, consisting of several thousand warriors willing to give their lives for 'Alī. See Ebstein, "*Shurṭa* Chiefs," 106–7.

261 The two arbiters mentioned here are 'Amr ibn al-'Āṣ and Abū Mūsā l-Ash'arī, who were appointed by Mu'āwiyah and 'Alī, respectively, to settle the differences between their two warring parties peacefully. The arbitration took place during the period after the stalemate at the Battle of Ṣiffīn in Safar 36/July 657. See Hinds, "The Ṣiffīn Arbitration Agreement."

262 I.e., 'Amr has even more contempt for al-Mughīrah and his ilk than he does for 'Alī and his partisans.

263 Q A'rāf 7:175–6.

264 Q Jumu'ah 62:5.

265 Recognizing Ibn 'Umar as a potential rival, Mu'āwiyah sought to provoke him into open confrontation by claiming an even greater right to lead the Muslims than his father, 'Umar ibn al-Khaṭṭāb.

266 Lots were cast using divining arrows, here called "the arrows of God" (*sihām Allāh*), to determine God's portion—the fifth, or *khums*—apart from that of the conquering army. See Crone and Silverstein, "Lot-Casting," 428–29.

267 In this chapter, the narratives detail the disaffection that spread among the members of the Prophet's clan, the Hāshimites, after and because of the appointment of Abū Bakr as Commander of the Faithful. In particular, those who voice grievances are the Prophet's uncle al-'Abbās, his daughter Fāṭimah, and his son-in-law and cousin 'Alī. Such disaffection, the narratives relate, was not limited to the Hāshim clan's disagreements with Abū Bakr; it also produced rancor among the clan members themselves. Abū Bakr and 'Umar, the narratives emphasize, did their best to placate the parties while remaining unyieldingly faithful to the Prophet's instructions, but even their sagacious and discerning measures did not resolve all the matters.

268 "We prophets leave no heir; whatever we leave behind is for charity" (Ar. *lā nūrithu mā taraknā ṣadaqatun*): this saying and its interpretation is much contested between the Sunnīs and the Shiʿah as well as their respective forebears. In versions of the prophetic hadith favorable to the claims of ʿAlī and Fāṭimah, the rendering of the sentence changes slightly, so as to read "What we prophets have left behind for charity cannot be inherited (*lā yūrath mā taraknā ṣadaqatan*)"—with the consequence of rendering all property otherwise possessed by Muḥammad heritable by his descendants. See Goldziher, *Muslim Studies*, 2:102 f.

269 Q Ḥashr 59:6.

270 I.e., merely to provide for the necessities of life for the Prophet's family and for charity.

271 This passage firmly dates Maʿmar's reception of the story from al-Zuhrī to the reign of the Umayyad caliph Hishām ibn ʿAbd al-Malik. Maʿmar's subsequent comments also suggest that the transmission of his materials to ʿAbd al-Razzāq postdates the revolt of ʿAbd Allāh ibn al-Ḥasan's sons Muḥammad al-Nafs al-Zakiyyah (killed in 145/762) and Ibrāhīm ibn ʿAbd Allāh (killed in 146/763), after which the Abbasid caliph al-Manṣūr seized the properties from ʿAlī's descendants. The caliph al-Mahdī returned the estates to Alids during his reign from 158/775 to 169/785, but Maʿmar died long before, in 153/770. See Samhūdī, *Wafā'*, 3:416–17.

272 ʿUmar's leadership as Commander of the Faithful ended abruptly with his assassination at the hands of a slave. The slave was a Persian taken captive during the Islamic conquests in the East and had been transported to Medina for his skill as a craftsman. The story is a prescient and tragic example of an emerging tension in the early Islamic polity: the presence of massive numbers—tens of thousands, if not more—of non-Arabs enslaved as captives of war and now required to assimilate and work in the elite conquest culture of their new masters. These non-Arabs are called *mawālī* (sg. *mawlā*) in Arabic, a word usually rendered as "slave-client," but that entails a much more formal relationship of servitude and patronage. A tribal patron essentially guarantees a client access to Muslim society via captivity, slavery, or conversion. As this process was often forced upon the clients as the result of captivity and/or enslavement, it is hardly surprising that this created a situation with the potential for conflagration. Revisited here as well is the process behind ʿUmar's Shura that led, much to the dismay of the Hāshim clan, to the appointment of ʿUthmān ibn ʿAffān as the next Commander of the Faithful. See also the previous narrative in ch. 21.

273 "a single prostration made to God" (Ar. *sajdah sajadahā li-Llāh*): ʿUmar expresses his gratitude to God that he was killed by a non-Muslim rather than by a Muslim whose prostrations in prayer could have potentially outnumbered his.

274 "He gave 'Umar date wine to drink" (Ar. *saqāhu nabīdhan*): the consumption of alchohol and intoxicants is, generally speaking, expressly forbidden in Islamic law, but there is ambiguity over whether the scriptural prohibition of wine (Ar. *khamr*) in Q Mā'idah 5:90 applies only to beverages fermented from grapes or to all intoxicating drinks. Some early jurists, therefore, allowed the consumption of date wine (*nabīdh*), but not grape wine (*khamr*). 'Umar's consumption of date wine is explained as either reflecting the view that only grape wine (*khamr*) was forbidden or by asserting that the so-called *nabīdh* here refers not to wine but, rather, to a drink made by steeping dates in water without permitting the fermentation process to begin. See Anthony, "The Assassination of 'Umar," 222 and Haider, "Contesting Intoxication," 158 ff.

275 "The man from the Mu'āwiyah clan" (Ar. *akhū banī mu'āwiyah*): i.e., the second doctor who poured milk for him. The first doctor is said to have been from the Allies. The Mu'āwiyah clan referred to here is not to be confused with Mu'āwiyah ibn Abī Sufyān; it is, rather, a subtribe of the Kindah of Yemen. Cf. Ibn Sa'd, *Ṭabaqāt*, 3:346 and Balādhurī, *Ansāb*, 5:381–82.

276 "the third night . . .": i.e., its final night; cf. 29.1.

277 Although 'Umar had previously designated 'Abd al-Raḥmān ibn 'Awf as the prayer leader, here the leader of the prayer is Ṣuhayb ibn Sinān, known as "the Byzantine" (Ar. al-Rūmī; lit., "Roman"), an early Companion of Muḥammad numbered among the so-called *ahl al-subbāq*, or "forerunners," who are the first of their peoples to convert to Islam. The *ahl al-subbāq* are Muḥammad, Salmān, Ṣuhayb, and Bilāl, representing the Arabs, Persians, Byzantines, and Abyssinians, respectively. See Bashear, *Arabs and Others*, 17, 25. Ṣuhayb leads the prayer because, as a non-Qurashī, he is ineligible to be the community's leader, and thus his leadership of the prayers during the proceedings of the Shura does not bias the candidacy of any of its participants as, for instance, Abū Bakr al-Ṣiddīq's leading of prayers during Muḥammad's illness purportedly biased the community in favor of his leadership. Cf. Ṭabarī, *Tārīkh*, 2:2724.

278 'Ubayd Allāh implicates certain prominent Qurashīs, and probably 'Alī in particular, in a conspiracy to murder his father, 'Umar. Cf. Madelung, *Succession*, 69 f. and Anthony, "The Assassination of 'Umar," 220 f.

279 "the two scuffled with one another" (Ar. *tanāṣayā*): lit., "they grabbed each other by the forelock."

280 "God have mercy on Ḥafṣah": this is an allusion to a report not recorded here that asserts that it was in fact 'Umar's daughter Ḥafṣah who instigated her brother 'Ubayd Allāh to go on his killing spree. See Anthony, "The Assasination of 'Umar," 220.

281 See n. 242 above.

282 The meaning is essentially the same: the Abū Rukānah clan is a branch of the Hāshim clan descended from Hāshim's son ʿAbd Yazīd. ʿAbd Yazīd had a son known as Rukānah al-Muṭṭalibī who, though famed for his manly prowess and matchless skill as a wrestler, was bested by the Prophet in a wrestling match. See Guillaume, *Life*, 178.

283 I.e., the Umayyah clan. ʿUmar here foreshadows the rise of Umayyad dynasty of caliphs. ʿUthmān's favoritism of his clan, the Umayyads, during his caliphate notoriously laid the groundwork for their rise to power under Muʿāwiyah ibn Abī Sufyān. However, the account also implies that neither ʿAlī nor ʿAbd al-Raḥmān ibn ʿAwf would have been any better in this regard had they assumed leadership of the community as Commander of the Faithful.

284 I.e., Ibn ʿUmar, the narrator of the account, states that he is glad to have been absent from the Shura because it enabled him to be at his father's bedside as he lay dying from a stab wound. At his father's side, Ibn ʿUmar was able to hear these precious last words of ʿUmar.

285 "the Arabs will soon apostatize" (Ar. *an tartadda l-ʿarab*): Abū Bakr's caliphate was predominately occupied with the so-called Riddah, or Apostasy, Wars—irredentist conflicts in which he fought to keep the Arabian tribes united under the banner of Islam.

286 Abū Bakr has died, and ʿUmar, famed for his hatred of Khālid, now rules.

287 See 25.2 above.

288 "the doubt is Abū Bakr's": ʿAbd al-Razzāq al-Ṣanʿānī, whose *kunyah* is Abū Bakr, doesn't recall if Maʿmar related the tradition on Ayyūb's authority from both ʿIkrimah and Abū Yazīd or just one of the two.

289 The allusion here is the pact of brotherhood (Ar. *al-mu'ākhāh*) formed between key individuals from the Medinese Allies and the Meccan Emigrants to cement the new alliance minted after the Hijrah. Muḥammad, rather than adopting a Medinese as his brother, instead chose ʿAlī as his brother, an event highlighted by the Shiʿah as indicative of ʿAlī's unparalleled bond with the Prophet. See Ibn Hishām, 1:504 ff. (trans. Guillaume, 234) and Balādhurī, *Ansāb*, 1:641 ff.

290 Saliva was regarded as a key medium for transmitting blessings from one person to another. The Hadith are filled with anecdotes in which people bring their children to be blessed or healed with the saliva of the Prophet. See Chelhod "Le *baraka* chez les Arabes"; Giladi, "Some Notes on *Taḥnīk*"; and the miracles of Jesus in Mark 8:22 and John 9:6.

291 I.e., the Prophet's wives, to whom the Qur'an explicitly refers as the Believers' Mothers; see Q Aḥzāb 33:6.

292 "Satan the Accursed" (*al-shayṭān al-rajīm*): "Al-Rajīm" appears in the Qur'an as an epithet of Satan, but its precise meaning is somewhat obscure. Other meanings include "pelted with stones" and "accuser." Cf. Silverstein, "On the Original Meaning of *al-shayṭān al-rajīm*."

293 The water here not only removes filth but also serves as a means of conveying the purity, and hence the blessing, of the Prophet to Fāṭimah and ʿAlī.

Glossary of Names, Places, and Terms

Note: Where possible, I have relied on *EI2* or *EI3* for identifying the names of persons and toponyms; however, for more obscure entries, I have relied heavily on Islamic tradition. In particular, for identifying persons I used al-Balādhurī's *Ansāb al-ashrāf*, Jamāl al-Dīn al-Mizzī's *Tahdhīb al-Kamāl*, and Ibn Ḥajar al-ʿAsqalānī's *al-Iṣābah fī tamyīz al-ṣaḥāba*. For toponyms, I have predominately relied on al-Samhūdī's *Wafāʾ al-Wafā bi-akhbār dār al-Muṣṭafā* and Yāqūt's *Muʿjam al-buldān*. Finally, in arranging the entries in alphabetical order the Arabic definite article "al-" as well as the Arabic letters *hamzah* and *ʿayn* have been disregarded. Oft-used terms, such as Mecca, Medina, Companion, Ally, and Emigrant are not cross-referenced.

ʿAbbās ibn ʿAbd al-Muṭṭalib, al- (d. ca. 32/653) Muḥammad's uncle and the eponymous ancestor of the Abbasid line of the Hāshim clan. His descendants would later dominate the caliphate as the Abbasid dynasty, ruling over the heartlands of Islamic civilization from 132/750 to 656/1258.

ʿAbd Allāh ibn ʿAbd al-Muṭṭalib (fl. sixth century AD) Father of Muḥammad, he died while trading in Medina prior to the Prophet's birth. See Genealogical Table.

ʿAbd Allāh ibn Abī Bakr (ibn Abī Quḥāfah) (d. ca. 12/633) Son of Abū Bakr al-Ṣiddīq (q.v.), famous for helping his father and Muḥammad escape from Mecca during the Hijrah and his valor at the conquest of Taif.

ʿAbd Allāh ibn Abī Bakr (ibn Muḥammad ibn ʿAmr ibn Ḥazm) (d. ca. 130/747–48 or 135/752–53) Nephew of ʿAmrah bint ʿAbd al-Raḥmān (q.v.), tradent and Medinese jurist.

ʿAbd Allāh ibn ʿĀmir ibn Kurayz (d. 57/677 or 59/679) Qurashī noble of the ʿAbd Shams clan and governor of Basra from 29/649–50 to 35/656 under his maternal cousin ʿUthmān ibn ʿAffān (q.v.), and again from 41/661 to 44/664 under Muʿāwiyah ibn Abī Sufyān. He sided with ʿĀʾishah, Ṭalḥah, and al-Zubayr against ʿAlī at the Battle of the Camel in 36/656.

ʿAbd Allāh ibn ʿAtīk Medinese Ally from the Khazraj tribe famous for leading the expedition into Khaybar (q.v.) to assassinate Ibn Abī l-Ḥuqayq (q.v.).

He is said to have died fighting at the Battle of Yamāmah in 11/632 or with ʿAlī (q.v.) at the Battle of Ṣiffīn in 36/657.

ʿAbd Allāh ibn Ḥasan (ibn al-Ḥasan ibn ʿAlī ibn Abī Ṭālib al-Maḥḍ) Leader of the Hāshim clan at the outset of the Abbasid period, he was killed in an Iraqi prison by the caliph al-Manṣūr (r. 136–58/754–75) in ca. 144–5/762–3 during the revolt of his two sons, Muḥammad and Ibrāhīm.

ʿAbd Allāh ibn Jaʿfar (ibn Abī Ṭālib) (d. between 80/699 and 90/709) Son of the Prophet's cousin Jaʿfar (q.v.) and Asmāʾ bint ʿUmays (q.v.), he became a staunch supporter of his uncle ʿAlī in the Civil War but later eschewed politics. He maintained a reputation for liberality and patronage in Medina, earning him the nickname "the Ocean of Generosity" (*baḥr al-jūd*).

ʿAbd Allāh ibn Masʿūd (d. 32/65–63) Companion and famed Qur'an reader.

ʿAbd Allāh ibn Rawāḥah Medinese Ally from the Khazraj tribe and poet who participated in all the major battles of the Prophet until martyred fighting against the Byzantines in the Battle of Mu'tah in 8/629.

ʿAbd Allāh ibn Ubayy ibn Salūl (d. 9/631) Powerful chieftain from the Khazraj tribe remembered as a leading figure among the so-called "Hypocrites" (*al-munāfiqūn*) who either opposed or offered merely lukewarm support to Muḥammad in Medina.

ʿAbd Allāh ibn ʿUmar ibn al-Khaṭṭāb (d. ca. 73/693) Companion and brother-in-law to the Prophet. Eleven years old at the time of the Hijrah, he first participated in battle at al-Khandaq in 5/627, after which he participated in all of the subsequent campaigns of the Prophet and even in an illustrious string of battles during the conquests. He remained neutral during the First Civil War.

ʿAbd Allāh ibn al-Zubayr ibn al-ʿAwwām Son of the Companion and Emigrant al-Zubayr (q.v.), first Muslim child born after the Hijrah in 2/624, and counter-caliph in Mecca for nine years prior to his defeat by the Umayyads in 73/692.

ʿAbd Allāh ibn Unays (al-Juhanī) Medinese Ally who led the expedition to assassinate the Jewish merchant Ibn Abī l-Ḥuqayq (q.v.); he died in 54/674 or 80/699–700.

ʿAbd Manāf Ancestor of Muḥammad and eponymous progenitor of the branch of the Quraysh that included its two most powerful clans: the Umayyah clan (ʿAbd Shams) and the Hāshim clan. See Genealogical Table.

ʿAbd al-Muṭṭalib (ibn Hāshim ibn ʿAbd Manāf) Muḥammad's grandfather, into whose care he and his mother fell after the death of Muḥammad's father. See Genealogical Table.

ʿAbd al-Qays Eastern Arabian tribe, many of whose members settled in Basra during the early Islamic conquests.

ʿAbd al-Raḥmān (ibn ʿAbd Allāh) ibn Kaʿb ibn Malik (d. ca. 96–125/715–43) Medinese tradent and great-grandson of the Ally Kaʿb ibn Malik (q.v.).

ʿAbd al-Raḥmān ibn ʿAttāb ibn Asīd (d. Jumada II 36/November–December 656) Qurashī notable of the ʿAbd Shams clan, whose father ʿAttāb, though he only converted after the conquest of Mecca, served the Prophet and the first caliph Abū Bakr (q.v.) as governor of Mecca and Taif (q.vv.). ʿAbd al-Raḥmān died fighting against ʿAlī (q.v.) at the Battle of the Camel.

ʿAbd al-Raḥmān ibn ʿAwf (d. 31/652) Emigrant Companion from the Zuhrah clan of the Quraysh, famed for the fortune he earned as a merchant and for his role as kingmaker at the Shura convened by the caliph ʿUmar ibn al-Khaṭṭāb (q.v.). See Genealogical Table.

ʿAbd al-Raḥmān ibn Azhar Nephew of ʿAbd al-Raḥmān ibn ʿAwf (q.v.) and Companion, he witnessed the conquest of Mecca and the Battle of Ḥunayn as a youth. He reportedly died during the Umayyads' siege of Medina, at the Battle of al-Ḥarrah, in 63/683.

ʿAbd al-Raḥmān ibn al-Ḥārith ibn Hishām (al-Makhzūmī) (d. before 60/680) Qurashī notable and son-in-law of the caliph ʿUthmān ibn ʿAffān (q.v.), who commissioned him to aid in the project to codify the Qur'an. He fought against ʿAlī (q.v.) at the Battle of the Camel in 36/656. See Abū Bakr ibn ʿAbd al-Raḥmān.

ʿAbd al-Raḥmān ibn Mālik al-Mudlijī (fl. first/seventh century) Nephew of Surāqah ibn Juʿshum (q.v.) and al-Zuhrī's source for the story about him.

ʿAbd al-Razzāq al-Ṣanʿānī (d. 211/826) Yemeni tradent, legal scholar, Qur'an exegete, and the transmitter (*rāwī*) of Maʿmar's book *The Expeditions*.

Abraham (Ibrāhīm) Patriarch of biblical fame revered in the Qur'an and Islamic tradition as a prophet, ancient monotheist (*ḥanīf*), founder of the Kaaba cult in Mecca, and progenitor of the Jews and Arabs through his sons Isaac (Isḥāq) and Ishmael (Ismāʿīl), respectively.

Abū ʿAmr ibn al-ʿAlāʾ (d. 154/771 or 157/773–74) Baṣran authority on the Qur'an revered as one of "seven Qur'an reciters."

Abū l-ʿĀṣ ibn Rabīʿ Nephew of Khadījah bint Khuwalyid (q.v.) to whom Muḥammad married his daughter Zaynab (q.v.) prior to being called to prophethood. Although Abū l-ʿĀṣ fought against Muḥammad at the Battle of Badr and was taken captive, Zaynab freed him by paying his ransom. Only after the conquest of Mecca did Abū l-ʿĀṣ, seeking refuge with his former wife, become a Muslim.

Abū Bakr (ibn Abī Quḥāfah) al-Ṣiddīq First caliph after Muḥammad (r. 10–13/632–4) and his father-in-law, he was a wealthy Qurashī merchant and counted among the first converts, if not the first, to Islam among the Meccans. See Genealogical Table.

Abū Bakr ibn ʿAbd al-Raḥmān ibn al-Ḥārith ibn Hishām (d. ca. 93/711–12) Qurashī notable from the Makhzūm clan and one of the famed seven jurists of Medina, known as "the monk of the Quraysh" (*rāhib Quraysh*) because of his piety. See ʿAbd al-Raḥmān ibn al-Ḥārith.

Abū Baṣīr (ibn Asīd ibn Jāriyah al-Thaqafī) (d. before 10/632) Companion numbered among "the oppressed" (*al-mustaḍʿafūn*) who were imprisoned in Mecca and prevented from making the Hijrah to join Muḥammad in Medina.

Abū Hurayrah (d. 59/678) Companion and the most prolific tradent of Prophetic hadith from the first generation of Muslims.

Abū Isḥāq (ʿAmr ibn ʿAbd Allāh al-Sabīʿī) (d. 129/746–47) Tradent from Kūfah.

Abū Jahl ibn Hishām (d. 2/624) Uncle of the Prophet killed at Badr, whose actual name was Abū l-Ḥakam ʿAmr ibn Hishām ibn al-Mughīrah. "Abū Jahl" means "father of ignorance" and is a pejorative name given to him for his inveterate and often cruel opposition to Muḥammad and his early followers.

Abū Jandal ibn Suhayl ibn ʿAmr Qurashī Companion numbered those "oppressed" (*al-mustaḍʿafūn*) who were imprisoned in Mecca and prevented from making the Hijrah to join Muḥammad in Medina. He died at the age of thirty-eight fighting at the Battle of Yamāmah in 11/632.

Abū Kabshah See Ibn Abī Kabshah.

Abū Khaythamah (al-Sālimī) Medinese Ally said to have witnessed Uḥud and who died during the caliphate of Yazīd I ibn Muʿāwiyah (r. 64–65/683–4).

Abū Lubābah (ibn ʿAbd Mundhir?) Medinese Ally who died soon after the assassination of the caliph ʿUthmān (q.v.) in 35/656.

Abū Luʾluʾah Slave-client of al-Mughīrah ibn Shuʿbah (q.v.) and the assassin of the second caliph ʿUmar ibn al-Khaṭṭāb (q.v.).

Abū Mūsā l-Ashʿarī, ʿAbd Allāh ibn Qays (d. 52/672) Companion from the Yemeni tribe of al-Ashʿar, he was a prominent figure in the early Islamic conquests and twice appointed governor of Kūfah, once under ʿUmar (q.v.) in 22/642–43 and again under ʿUthmān (q.v.) in 34/654–55. He is also remembered as one of the two arbitrators, alongside ʿAmr ibn al-ʿĀṣ, appointed at Ṣiffīn in 37/657 and charged with settling the dispute between ʿAlī and Muʿāwiyah.

Abū l-Qāsim See al-Qāsim.

Abū Qatādah (al-Ḥārith ibn Ribʿī) (d. ca. 54/674) Medinese Ally from the Khazraj tribe and cousin to Kaʿb ibn Malik (q.v.).

Abū Ruhm ibn ʿAbd al-Muṭṭalib ibn ʿAbd Manāf Qurashī notable and uncle of the Prophet. See Umm Misṭaḥ.

Abū Salamah ibn ʿAbd al-Raḥmān (ibn ʿAwf al-Zuhrī) (d. 94/712–13 or 104/722–23) Son of the prominent companion ʿAbd al-Raḥmān ibn ʿAwf, he was also a prominent tradent, jurist, and judge (*qāḍī*) in Medina.

Abū Sufyān ibn Ḥarb (ibn Umayyah ibn ʿAbd Shams ibn ʿAbd Manāf) (d. ca. 32–34/653–5) Qurashī notable, merchant, and chief opponent of Muḥammad during the Medinese period, Abū Sufyān converted to Islam just prior to the conquest of Mecca. His sons Yazīd and Muʿāwiyah (q.vv.) were instrumental in the early Islamic conquests. See Genealogical Table.

Abū Sufyān ibn al-Ḥārith ibn ʿAbd al-Muṭṭalib (d. 8/630) Muḥammad's cousin and milch-brother, who converted after the conquest of Mecca and was slain at the Battle of Ḥunayn.

Abū Ṭālib ibn ʿAbd al-Muṭṭalib, Abū l-Faḍl (d. ca. AD 619) Paternal uncle of Muḥammad and his caregiver after the death of ʿAbd al-Muṭṭalib. See Genealogical Table.

Abū ʿUbayda ibn al-Jarrāḥ Emigrant and Qurashī notable from the wealthy Fihr clan, he served under ʿUmar as the supreme commander of the forces in Syria until he perished in the Emmaus Plague in 18/639. See Genealogical Table.

Abū Umāmah Asʿad ibn Zurārah (d. 1/623) Medinese Ally from the Khazraj tribe and the first Medinese to pledge fealty to Muḥammad at ʿAqabah.

Abū Yazīd al-Madīnī (fl. end of the seventh century AD) Early tradent of Basra.

Abū Zamīl Simāk (ibn al-Walīd) al-Ḥanafī (d. before 120/738) Early tradent of Kūfah.

Abyssinia In Arabic, "Ḥabash" or "Ḥabashah"; a name of South Arabian origin used in reference to the land and peoples of Abyssinia, it was the destination of several preliminary Hijrahs of the persecuted Meccan Believers prior to the Hijrah to Medina in AD 622. See Negus.

Adhruḥ Located in the south of modern-day Jordan between Petra and Maʿān, it served as the location for arbitration of the conflict between Muʿāwiyah ibn Abī Sufyān and ʿAlī ibn Abī Ṭālib (q.vv.).

Age of Ignorance (Ar. al-jāhiliyyah) Catchall term for humankind's plight before God revealed the religion of Islam to humanity through the Prophet Muḥammad with special reference to Arabian paganism.

Aḥnaf ibn Qays, al- (d. 67/686) Chief of the Tamīm tribe in Basra. He refused to participate in the Battle of the Camel, though he subsequently joined ʿAlī ibn Abī Ṭālib during his conflict with Muʿāwiyah ibn Abī Sufyān (q.vv.).

ʿĀʾishah bint Abī Bakr (d. 58/678) Wife of the Prophet Muḥammad and daughter of the first caliph Abū Bakr (q.v), she married the Prophet three years prior to the Hijrah. See Genealogical Table.

Ajnādayn Battle between Byzantine and Muslim forces during the conquest of Palestine dated to ca. Jumada I or II 13/July–August 634. Modern geographers have placed the battle in Wādī al-Ṣamt some nine kilometers north of Bet Guvrim.

ʿAlāʾ ibn ʿArār al-Khārifī, al- Minor tradent from Kufah and authority for Abū Isḥāq al-Sabīʿī (q.v.).

ʿAli ibn Abī Ṭālib (ibn ʿAbd al-Muṭṭalib), Abū l-Ḥasan (d. 40/661) Muḥammad's cousin and son-in-law, married to his daughter Fāṭimah, ʿAlī numbered among the earliest converts to Islam and is regarded by Sunnis as the last of the four rightly guided caliphs and by the Shiʿah as the first imam and Muḥammad's true successor. See Genealogical Table.

ʿAlī ibn al-Ḥusayn (ibn ʿAlī ibn Abī Ṭālib) (ca. 38/358–59 to 95/713) Great-grandson of the Prophet and fourth imam of the Twelver Shiʿah; known as Zayn al-ʿĀbidīn, "The Ornament of the Worshippers."

ʿAlī ibn Zayd ibn Judʿān (d. ca. 131/749) Tradent from Basra.

Allāt One of the so-called "daughters of God" mentioned in Q Najm 53:19–20 and said to have been worshipped by the Quraysh prior to Islam. See al-ʿUzzā, Hubal.

Allies (Anṣār; sg. Anṣārī) Also "Helpers," the term *anṣār* is from the Qur'an and is the principle moniker for the Medinese Arabs of the Aws and Khazraj tribes (q.v.) who believed in Muḥammad and gave refuge to the Emigrants (q.v.) from Mecca (q.v.; Q Tawbah 9:100, Q Tawbah 9:117). The title is also applied to the disciples of Jesus Christ (Q Āl ʿImrān 3:52, Q Ṣaff 61:14).

ʿAlqamah ibn Waqqāṣ (d. before 80/700) Minor Medinese tradent.

Āmina bint Wahb ibn ʿAbd Manāf ibn Zuhrah (d. ca. AD 577) Muḥammad's mother. Though she reportedly foresaw her son's future glory, she died while he was still a boy. See Genealogical Table.

ʿĀmir ibn Fuhayrah (al-Taymī) (d. Ṣafar 4/July–August 625) Freedman (*mawlā*) of Abū Bakr and early convert to Islam, he died at the expedition of Biʾr Maʿūnah.

ʿĀmir ibn Luʾayy Clan of the Quraysh.

ʿĀmir ibn Mālik (fl. seventh century AD) Known as "The Lover of Spears" (*mulāʿib al-asinnah*; lit., "The One Who Plays with Spears") and a chieftain of the ʿĀmir ibn Ṣaʿṣaʿah tribe, he offers the Prophet his protection for an expedition of Muslims to Najd. The protection is not honored by his fellow tribesmen and leads to the massacre at Biʾr Maʿūnah.

ʿĀmir ibn al-Ṭufayl Bedouin poet, warrior, and fierce opponent to Muḥammad who instigated the massacre at Biʾir Maʿūnah alongside his uncle ʿĀmir ibn Mālik (q.v.).

ʿAmr ibn Abī Sufyān al-Thaqafī (fl. late seventh and early eighth century AD) Early Medinese tradent.

ʿAmr ibn al-ʿĀṣ (d. ca. 42–43/662–4) Companion famous for his political cunning, both as the conqueror of Egypt and as a formidable foe to ʿAlī ibn Abī Ṭālib (q.v.) alongside Muʿāwiyah ibn Abī Sufyān (q.v.) in the Civil War. He is the founder of Fusṭāṭ, the precursor of modern Cairo, established after the conquest of Egypt.

ʿAmr ibn ʿAwf clan Major clan of Medina's Aws tribe (q.v.).

ʿAmr ibn Maymūn al-Awdī (d. ca. 74–77/693–7) Kūfan tradent and early convert from Yemen; companion of Muʿādh ibn Jabal (q.v.).

ʿAmr ibn Umayyah al-Ḍamrī d. ca. 40–60/660–80) Companion and sole survivor of the expedition to Biʾr Maʿūnah (q.v.).

ʿAmr ibn al-Zubayr (d. ca. 64/683–84) Son of the prominent Companion al-Zubayr ibn al-ʿAwwām (q.v.).

ʿAmrah (bint ʿAbd al-Raḥmān) (d. 98/716) Paternal niece of ʿĀʾishah bint Abī Bakr (q.v.) and important female tradent.

Aʿnaqa Liyamūt See al-Mundhir ibn ʿAmr.

Anas ibn Mālik (d. 92/711) Companion, scribe of the Prophet and long-lived, prolific tradent of Basra.

ʿAqabah, al- A mountain road between Minā and Mecca where Muḥammad held secret meetings with men from Medina, who pledged him their allegiance prior to his undertaking the Hijrah there in 1/622.

Aqṣā Mosque, al- (Ar. al-masjid al-aqṣā; lit., "the Farthest Mosque") A location mentioned Q Isrāʾ 17:1 and usually identified with the Temple Esplanade in Jerusalem by subsequent tradition. Today it is also the name of a mosque built on the same location.

Ashtar, Mālik ibn al-Ḥārith al-Nakhāʿī al- (d. ca. 37/658) Virulent opponent of the third caliph ʿUthmān ibn ʿAffān (q.v.) and fiercely loyal partisan and general of ʿAlī ibn Abī Ṭālib (q.v.), he received his nickname "al-Ashtar" (the split-eyed) from an injury he received fighting the Byzantines at the Battle of Yarmuk (q.v.) in 15/636.

Ashṭāṭ, al- Pool of water near ʿUsfān (q.v.).

ʿĀṣim ibn Thābit First of the Medinese Allies to be martyred by the Liḥyānīs at al-Rajīʿ (q.v.), he was also the maternal grandfather of ʿĀṣim ibn ʿUmar ibn al-Khaṭṭāb al-ʿAdawī (q.v.), the son of the second caliph, ʿUmar ibn al-Khaṭṭāb (q.v.).

ʿĀṣim ibn ʿUmar ibn al-Khaṭṭāb al-ʿAdawī (d. ca. 70/689–90) Qurashī notable, son of ʿUmar ibn al-Khaṭṭāb (q.v.) and grandson (or nephew, some early scholars say) of the Ally ʿĀṣim ibn Thābit (q.v.) via his mother, Jamīlah bint [ʿĀṣim ibn] Thābit ibn Abī l-Aqlaḥ al-Anṣārī. He was the maternal grandfather of the Umayyad caliph ʿUmar (II) ibn ʿAbd al-ʿAzīz (r. 99–101/717–20), who was greatly revered by the Medinese.

Asmāʾ bint Abī Bakr (Dhāt al-Niṭāqayn) (d. 73/693) Daughter of the first caliph and half sister to ʿĀʾishah, she married the Companion al-Zubayr ibn al-ʿAwwām (q.v.) after the Hijrah (q.v.), a marriage that ended in divorce but from which were born ʿAbd Allāh ibn al-Zubayr, a claimant to the caliphate, and ʿUrwah ibn al-Zubayr (q.v.), a seminal scholar of prophetic biographical traditions.

Asmāʾ bint ʿUmays al-Khathʿamiyyah (d. 39/659–60) Widow of Jaʿfar ibn Abī Ṭālib (q.v.), who subsequently married Abū Bakr and then ʿAlī ibn

Abī Ṭālib (q.vv.). She had been among those early Meccan followers of Muḥammad who undertook the preliminary emigrations to Abyssinia to flee persecution in Mecca.

Assembly House (dār al-nadwah) In pre-Islamic times, the main meeting hall of Mecca located north of the Kaaba and where the elders of the Quraysh gathered to plan and adjudicate.

Aswad ibn Abī l-Bakhtarī, al- (fl. seventh century AD) Qurashī notable who converted to Islam after the conquest of Mecca, he fought alongside ʿĀʾishah (q.v.) at the Battle of the Camel and subsequently changed his allegiance to Muʿāwiyah ibn Abī Sufyān (q.v.).

Aws and Khazraj The two main tribes of Yathrib from whose ranks the Allies (q.v.) were drawn and who gave refuge to Muḥammad and his earliest Meccan Believers after the Hijrah (q.v.).

Awṭās Wadi where the Battle of Ḥunayn was fought in 8/630, located near the oasis of Taif.

Ayyūb al-Sakhtiyānī, al- (d. ca. 131–2/748–50) Prominent tradent and legal authority from Basra.

Badr The site of the first of the grand thematic battles of the Prophet's biography in Ramadan 2/March 624 during the Medinese period, located some 159 kilometers southwest of Medina and nearly 50 kilometers inland from the Red Sea coast.

Bal-Qayn Arabian tribe of southern origin descended from Quḍāʿah and whose territories lay in the regions between Wādī l-Qurā and Taymāʾ (q.v.) as well as farther north.

Barīrah Handmaiden to ʿĀʾishah (q.v.).

Basra (al-Baṣrah) Garrison city founded in 17/638 during the Islamic conquests of southern Iraq and located near the Shaṭṭ al-Arab river. See Kūfah.

Baysān (Bet Shean) Site of a battle between Byzantine and Muslim armies during the early Islamic conquests in ca. 13/634, located thirty kilometers south of Lake Tiberius.

Bilāl (ibn Rabāḥ) (d. ca. 17–21/638–42) Emigrant Companion of Abyssinian origin and the first muezzin.

Biʾr Maʿūnah Well located on the road from Mecca and Medina, remembered for a massacre committed against Muslims in ca. Safar 4/July–August 625.

Bostra (Ar. Buṣrā) Ancient fortified town located south of Damascus and approximately thirty kilometers north of the modern Syria–Jordan border.

Budayl ibn Warqāʾ al-Khuzāʿī (d. ca. 10/632) Meccan chieftain of Khuzāʿah who played a prominent role in the negotiations at Ḥudaybiyah (6/628) and converted to Islam after Mecca's conquest. He subsequently fought alongside the Muslims at Ḥunayn (8/630) and Tābūk (9/630).

Busr ibn Arṭaʾah (ca. 3–70/625–89) Qurashī notable from the ʿĀmir ibn Luʾayy clan (q.v.) and a notoriously vicious military commander for Muʿāwiyah ibn Abī Sufyān (q.v.).

Caliph (Ar. khalīfah, pl. khulafāʾ) See Commander of the Faithful.

Commander of the Faithful (Ar. amīr al-muʾminīn) Title borne by Muḥammad's first successors as the leaders of the Muslim community (*ummah*) that emphasizes their leadership of a religious community of believers and the military role that leadership entails. These leaders are often called caliphs (Ar. *khulafāʾ*, sg. *khalīfah*), meaning "successor" or "vicegerent."

Companion (Ar. ṣaḥābī, pl. ṣaḥābah) Honorific for Muḥammad's followers who either knew him intimately or met him prior to his death.

Ḍhāt al-Salāsil A location in the northern Ḥijāz and the target of a Muslim raid of the same name in ca. Jumada II 8/September 629.

Dhū l-Ḥulayfah Located at modern-day Abar ʿAlī, some ten kilometers from Medina, it is the location stipulated for Medineses to don the garments of pilgrimage and to enter the state of purity (*iḥrām*) required to initiate the rites of pilgrimage on the way to Mecca.

Dhū l-Majāz Market near ʿArafah, approximately twenty kilometers east of Mecca on the road to Taif. Alongside ʿUkāẓ, Majannah, and Minā, Dhū l-Majāz was one of the four markets where the Quraysh would hold their pilgrimage fairs.

Dhū l-Marwah Located in Wādī l-Qurā, "the Valley of Villages," in the northern Ḥijāz, approximately a four- or five-day journey from Medina.

Diḥyah (ibn Khalīfah) al-Kalbī (d. 50/670) Mysterious Companion and merchant, he delivered the Prophet's letter to the Byzantine Emperor Heraclius.

Emigrants (al-muhājirūn) Earliest Meccan converts to Islam, many of whom were from the Quraysh or their slave-clients (*mawālī*) and who followed or preceded Muḥammad in his Hijrah to Medina.

Fadak Small village near Khaybar, about a three-day journey from Medina. Fadak was known for its dates and cereals. The fate of the Prophet's share in the ownership of Fadak and its produce became a cause of disagreement between Abū Bakr and Fāṭimah (q.vv.). Fāṭimah claimed ownership of the land as her inherited right, a right denied her by Abū Bakr.

Faḍl ibn al-ʿAbbās, al- (ibn ʿAbd al-Muṭṭalib) Cousin to the Prophet, who accompanied him in his last hours and attended to his burial alongside ʿAlī ibn Abī Ṭālib (q.v.). He settled in Syria after the conquests, and died in the Emmaus Plague that struck the region in 18/639.

Faḥl (Pella) Located twelve kilometers southeast of Baysān, it was the location of a battle between Byzantines and Muslims during the early Islamic conquests in ca. Dhū l-Qaʿdah 13/January 635.

Farwah ibn Nufāthah al-Judhāmī (d. after 6/628?) Byzantine governor over the inhabitants of the hinterlands of ʿAmmān, or Maʿān, of al-Balqāʾ, who is said to have been crucified at the pool of ʿAfrā in Palestine by the Byzantines for confessing belief in the prophethood of Muḥammad.

Fāṭimah bint Muḥammad (al-Zahrāʾ) (d. 11/632) Youngest child of Muḥammad and his wife Khadījah (q.v.), and the first wife of ʿAlī ibn Abī Ṭālib (q.v.). She bore four children to ʿAlī: al-Ḥasan, al-Ḥusayn (q.vv.), Zaynab, and Umm Kulthūm.

Gabriel (Jibrīl, Jibrāʾīl) The angel who, in the Qurʾan, brings down the revelation to the Prophet's heart by God's leave (Q Baqarah 2:97) and who, in the Bible, interprets the prophet Daniel's vision (Dan. 8:16–12, 9:20–27) and announces the births of John the Baptist and Jesus (Luke 1:11–20, 26–38).

Ghamīm, al- A place between ʿUsfān and Mount Ḍajnān.

Ghassān Christianized tribal confederation of the Azd, who migrated from South Arabia and settled in the Levantine hinterlands of the Late Roman empire in the late fifth century and rose to power locally as allies to the Roman emperors. Their rulers, or phylarchs, are frequently referred as the "kings" (*mulūk*) of Ghassān in Islamic sources.

Ghaṭafān A group of Northern Arabian tribes whose lands lay in Najd between the Ḥijāz and the Shammar Mountains.

Ḥabīb ibn Maslamah (al-Fihrī) (d. ca. 42/662 or later) Qurashī notable and military commander of Muʿāwiyah ibn Abī Sufyān (q.v.).

Ḥafṣah (d. Shaʿban 45/October–November 665) Daughter of ʿUmar ibn al-Khaṭṭāb and Muḥammad's fourth wife, whom he wedded in Shaʿban 3/February 625; her copy of the Qurʾan, inherited from her father, purportedly served as the basis for the third caliph ʿUthmān ibn ʿAffān's codification thereof.

Hajj (Ar. al-ḥajj, al-ḥijjah) Seasonal pilgrimage to Mecca with many attendant rites, such as the donning of a simple white garment, circling around the Kaaba, and an animal sacrifice. It must be undertaken in the month of Dhū l-Hijjah.

Ḥajjāj ibn ʿIlāṭ, al- (d. soon after 13/634) Companion of the Sulaym clan who converted at the conquest of Khaybar and who settled in Ḥimṣ in Syria during the early Islamic conquests.

Ḥamnah bint Jaḥsh Sister of the Prophet's wife, Zaynab bint Jaḥsh (q.v.), she was wedded to Ṭalḥah ibn ʿUbayd Allāh (q.v.) after her first husband, Muṣʿab ibn ʿUmayr, was slain at Uḥud.

Ḥamrāʾ al-Asad Elevated location approximately sixteen kilometers south of Medina, visible from the ravine leading to Mecca.

Ḥamzah ibn ʿAbd al-Muṭṭalib (d. 3/625) Paternal uncle of the Prophet, early believers, and martyr at the Battle of Uḥud.

Ḥanẓalah ibn Sabrah ibn al-Musayyab (al-Fazārī) (fl. second/eighth century) Kūfan tradent and grandson of al-Musayyab ibn Najaba al-Fazārī, an early partisan of ʿAlī ibn Abī Ṭālib (q.v.).

Ḥarām ibn Milḥān Medinese Ally said to have been among those martyred at Biʾr Maʿūnah.

Ḥārith ibn ʿAbd al-Muṭṭalib, al- The eldest son of the Prophet's grandfather, ʿAbd al-Muṭṭalib; he died before the birth of Muḥammad. See Genealogical Table.

Ḥārith ibn ʿĀmir ibn Nawfal, al- (ibn ʿAbd Manāf) (d. 2/624) Powerful Meccan notable of the Quraysh slain by Khubayb the Ally at Badr and infamous for having stolen golden gazelles from the Kaaba before Islam.

Ḥārith ibn Ḥāṭib, al- (ibn al-Ḥārith al-Qurashī al-Jumaḥī) (d. ca. 65–86/685–705) One of the few Muslims born in Abyssinia during his parents' sojourn there while fleeing the persecution of the Meccans before the Hijrah.

Ḥārith ibn al-Khazraj, al- One of the five main clans of the Khazraj tribe in Medina.

Ḥasan ibn ʿAlī ibn Abī Ṭālib, al- (d. 49/669) Grandson of the Prophet and second imam of the Twelver Shiʿah, he ended the First Civil War by brokering an agreement with Muʿāwiyah ibn Abī Sufyān (q.v.) in 40/661 in the wake of the assassination of his father ʿAlī.

Ḥasan ibn al-Ḥasan, al- (ibn ʿAlī ibn Abī Ṭālib) (d. 97/715–16) Great-grandson of the Prophet and successor to his father al-Ḥasan ibn ʿAlī in managing the properties (*ṣadaqah*) of the ʿAlids under the Umayyads.

Ḥasan al-Baṣrī, al- (d. 110/728–29) Renowned traditionist, pietist, and scholarly authority of Basra.

Hawāzin A large northern Arabian tribe that included the Thaqīf and the Saʿd ibn Bakr (q.vv.), against whom the Muslims fought at the Battle of Ḥunayn following the conquest of Mecca.

Heraclius Byzantine/East Roman emperor from AD 610 to 641.

Hejaz (Ar. Ḥijāz) Region of northwestern Arabia running along the Red Sea coast and bordered to the East by the Sarāt Mountains, it is the sacred heartland and spiritual birthplace of Islam wherein Mecca and Medina lie.

Hijrah See Emigrants.

Hilāl ibn Umayyah (fl. first/seventh century) Medinese Ally whose repentance for not accompanying Muḥammad during his expedition against Tabūk was accepted.

Ḥirā' Mountain located northeast of Mecca where Muḥammad is said to have received his first revelation of the Qur'an.

Hishām ibn ʿUrwah (d. 146/763) Son of ʿUrwah ibn al-Zubayr (q.v.) and, after Ibn Shihāb al-Zuhrī (q.v.), the most important transmitter of ʿUrwah's *maghāzī* traditions.

Ḥubāb ibn al-Mundhir Medinese Ally from the Khazraj clan who witnessed Badr and reportedly died during the caliphate of ʿUmar ibn al-Khaṭṭāb (q.v.).

Hubal According to later tradition, a chief idol worshipped in Mecca (q.v.) as a deity and before whom the Meccans cast lots. Unlike the so-called "daughters of God," Hubal never receives mention in the Qur'an; however, tradition asserts that Hubal's idol was housed in the Kaaba (q.v.) prior to Muḥammad's conquest of Mecca, after which it was destroyed. See Allāt, al-ʿUzzā.

Ḥubāshah Annual market located in Tihāma (q.v.), about a six-day journey south of Mecca.

Ḥudaybiyah Located just on the northern outskirts of the sacred territory that included Mecca, it served as the site of the story of Muḥammad drawing up an armistice agreement with the Meccan Quraysh in Dhū l-Qaʿdah 6/ March 628.

Hudhayl Tribe of Northern Arabian descent that resided near Mecca and Taif (q.vv.).

Ḥunayn Valley a day's journey from Mecca on the way to Taif (q.v.) and mentioned in Q Tawbah 9:25–26 as the site of a battle fought in 8/630 soon after the Muslims' conquest of Mecca.

Hurmuzān (d. 23/644) Former leading general to the Sassanid monarch of Persia, Yazdegerd III, he was taken captive during the Islamic conquests in Persia and brought to Medina. He subsequently acted as an advisor until he was killed by ʿUbayd Allāh ibn ʿUmar (q.v.), who implicated him in the caliph ʿUmar ibn al-Khaṭṭāb's (q.v.) assassination at the hands of the Persian slave Abū Luʾluʾah (q.v.).

Ḥusayn ibn ʿAlī, al- (ibn Abī Ṭālib) Grandson of the Prophet and third imam of the Twelver Shiʿah, who was martyred by the Umayyads at Karbalāʾ on 10 Muḥarram 61/10 October 680.

Ḥuyayy ibn Akhṭab Leading chieftain of the Jewish clan al-Naḍīr in Medina, he took up residence in Khaybar with his family and many of his fellow clansmen after their expulsion from Medina. Ḥuyayy was later put to the sword by the Muslims in Medina alongside another Jewish clan, the Qurayẓah, for his role in aiding them to plot against the Muslims in ca. Shawwal 5/February–March 627. See Ṣafiyyah bint Ḥuyayy.

Ibn ʿAbbās, ʿAbd Allāh (d. ca. 68/687–88) Paternal cousin and Companion of the Prophet, a man of legendary learning to whom vast swaths of the Islamic tradition are attributed.

Ibn Abī l-Ḥuqayq See Sallām ibn Abī l-Ḥuqayq.

Ibn Abī Kabshah Meaning "descendant of Abū Kabsha," this was a derisive nickname for Muḥammad, the original significance of which is disputed. One explanation asserts that Abū Kabshah was an ancestor of Muḥammad from the tribe of Khuzāʿah who became infamous when he rejected his tribe's idolatrous religion; thus, Muḥammad's enemies called him "Ibn Abī Kabshah," because he too abandoned his tribe's religion. Other explanations assert that either his milch-mother's husband or the maternal grandfather of the prophet's own maternal grandfather, Wahb ibn ʿAbd Manāf, was known by the name "Abū Kabshah."

Ibn Abī Najīḥ (d. between 130–31/747–49) Meccan legal authority.

Ibn Abī Sarḥ, ʿAbd Allāh ibn Saʿd (d. ca. 36–37/656–8) Qurashī notable of the ʿĀmir ibn Luʾayy clan (q.v.) and notorious apostate scribe of Muḥammad, whom the Prophet later pardoned thanks to entreaties on his behalf by his milch-brother ʿUthmān ibn ʿAffān (q.v.). Ibn Abī Sarḥ subsequently distinguished himself during the conquest of Egypt under ʿAmr ibn al-ʿĀṣ (q.v.).

Ibn Abī Yaḥyā (d. 184/800) Medinese hadith-scholar and teacher of ʿAbd al-Razzāq al-Ṣanʿānī, disparaged for his inclinations toward Shiʿism (*al-tashayyuʿ*).

Ibn Abjar, Ḥayyān al-Kinānī (alive in 76/695) Progenitor of a famous family of physicians from Kūfah, reputed by some to have been a Companion.

Ibn al-Daḥdāḥah, Thābit A confederate (*ḥalīf*) of the Medinese Allies who died shortly after the treaty of Ḥudaybiyah.

Ibn al-Dughunnah (al-Ḥārith ibn Yazīd) (fl. seventh century AD) Chieftain of the Qārah clan of the Hūn tribe, who were allies with the Zuhrah clan of the Quraysh.

Ibn Kaʿb ibn Mālik See ʿAbd al-Raḥmān ibn ʿAbd Allāh ibn Kaʿb ibn Mālik.

Ibn Khaṭal (Hilāl ibn ʿAbd Allāh ibn ʿAbd Manāf al-Adramī) (d. 8/630) One of the handful of persons whose death Muḥammad ordered upon his conquest of Mecca. Ibn Khaṭal embraced Islam and undertook the Hijrah to Medina, after which the Prophet appointed him a collector of the alms-levy (*al-ṣadaqah*). He apostatized after he killed a slave in fit of fury because the slave neglected to prepare his meal. He then fled to Mecca seeking refuge, fearing that Muḥammad would execute him for his crime.

Ibn Mubārak, ʿAbd Allāh (d. ca. 181/797) Tradent and legal authority from Khurasan famed for his commitment to fighting on the frontier and for works on asceticism (*zuhd*) and jihad.

Ibn al-Nābighah Term of abuse directed against ʿAmr ibn al-ʿĀṣ (q.v.). His mother, al-Nābighah, was a slave woman whom her Qurashī master prostituted, thus casting considerable doubt on his actual paternity.

Ibn Shihāb See al-Zuhrī.

Ibn Sīrīn, Muḥammad (34–110/654–728) Basran tradent.

Ibn Ṭāwūs (d. 132/749–50) Yemeni tradent.

Ibn ʿUmar See ʿAbd Allāh ibn ʿUmar ibn al-Khaṭṭāb.

ʿIkrimah (d. 105/723–24) Slave-client (*mawlā*) of Ibn ʿAbbās (q.v.) freed by the latter's son, ʿAlī, and an oft-cited authority of traditions from his master.

ʿIkrimah ibn ʿAmmār (al-ʿIjlī al-Yamāmī) (d. 159/776) Basran tradent.

ʿIkrimah ibn Khālid (d. 105/723–24) Meccan tradent.

Ismāʿīl ibn Sharūs (Abū l-Miqdām al-Ṣanʿānī) (fl. mid-second/eighth century) Minor Yemeni tradent.

ʿIyāḍ ibn Ghanm (al-Fihrī) (d. 20/641) Companion and famed general of the Islamic conquests in Mesopotamia and Syria.

Jābir ibn ʿAbd Allāh the Ally (d. ca. 78/697) Medinese Companion from the Khazraj tribe, he became a staunch supporter of ʿAlī (q.v.) and his son later in life, and a prolific tradent.

Jābiyah, al- About eighty kilometers south of Damascus in the Jawlān (Golan Heights). ʿUmar ibn al-Khaṭṭāb traveled there as Commander of Faithful after the Muslims achieved victory over the Byzantines at the Battle of Yarmūk (q.v.) in ca. Rajab 15/August 636.

Jaʿfar ibn Abī Ṭālib (ibn ʿAbd al-Muṭṭalib) (d. 8/629) Cousin of the Prophet, elder brother of ʿAlī ibn Abī Ṭālib (q.v.), and among the earliest converts to Islam. He was known as "the angel-winged" (*dhū l-janāḥayn*) after being martyred at the Battle of Muʾtah in ca. 8/629. See Genealogical Table.

Jamīl ibn Maʿmar al-Jumaḥī (d. ca. 21/642) Companion and confidant to ʿUmar ibn al-Khaṭṭāb (q.v.) who witnessed Ḥunayn (q.v.) and the conquest of Egypt.

Jerusalem Temple (Ar. bayt al-maqdis; lit., House of the Holy) Common name for Jerusalem in early Arabic tradition, which refers to the location of the Temple Esplanade in particular.

Jesus, son of Mary (ʿĪsā ibn Maryam) Jesus of Nazareth of the Gospels, he is revered as a prophet in Islam but not regarded as the Son of God, although the Qurʾan does affirm his miracles as well as his virgin birth, and speaks of him as the Christ (Ar. *al-masīḥ*) and the Word of God (*kalimat Allāh*).

Jiʿrānah, al- Watering hole between Mecca and Taif where the spoils from the Battle of Ḥunayn were divided.

Jufaynah (d. 23/644) Christian writing tutor to the children of the Companion Saʿd ibn Abī Waqqāṣ (q.v.) murdered by ʿUbayd Allāh ibn ʿUmar (q.v.) when implicated in the murder of his father ʿUmar ibn al-Khaṭṭāb (q.v.). See Abū Luʾluʾah.

Kaaba Mecca's famous sanctuary, also known as the "House of God" (Ar. *bayt Allāh*) and "the Sacred Mosque" (*al-masjid al-ḥarām*), it is a cube-shaped structure toward which Muslims worldwide direct their prayers and to which they undertake the greater pilgrimage, the hajj (q.v.) in Dhū l-Hijjah and, in other months, a lesser pilgrimage (q.v.) called an *ʿumrah*. In pre-Islamic times, tradition asserts, the Kaaba was a cultic center of pagan idol worship patronized by the Quraysh (q.v.), although the Prophet Abraham had founded the site to serve rather as the centerpiece for a cult of monotheistic worship. It was ostensibly to its original purpose as a site of monotheist worship that Muḥammad restored the Kaaba during his mission as God's prophet.

Kaʿb ibn al-Ashraf (d. ca. Rabīʿ I 3/September–October 624) Leader of the Jewish Naḍīr clan (q.v.) assassinated by Muslim tribesmen from the Aws (q.v.) for plotting against the Muslims and for scurrilous verses he purportedly composed against the Prophet and the Muslim women of Medina. See Ibn Abī l-Ḥuqayq.

Kaʿb ibn Luʾayy Clan of the Quraysh (q.v.). See Genealogical Table.

Kaʿb ibn Malik (d. 50/670 or 53/673) Bard of the Prophet and Medinese Ally from the Khazraj clan (q.v.).

Kalb Christianized Arabian tribe of southern origin and a powerful branch of Quḍāʿah (q.v.) whose territories lay in the steppe regions between Syria and Iraq.

Kalbī, Muḥammad ibn Sāʾib al- (d. 146/763) Early historian and scholar from Kūfah.

Kathīr ibn al-ʿAbbās ibn ʿAbd al-Muṭṭalib Companion, son of the Prophet's uncle al-ʿAbbās (q.v.), and early tradent of Medina who died during the caliphate of ʿAbd al-Malik ibn Marwān (r. 685–705).

Khadījah bint Khuwaylid (d. 619) Muḥammad's first wife, the first to believe in his prophethood, and the mother of his daughters Ruqayyah, Umm Kulthūm, and Fāṭimah (q.vv.). See Genealogical Table.

Khālid ibn Saʿīd ibn al-ʿĀṣ (d. ca. Jumada I or II 13/July–August 634) Companion and Emigrant who converted to Islam after receiving a vision at age five, he was also among those to undertake the first Hijrah (q.v.) to Abyssinia. He is said to have died during the conquest of Syria, either at Marj al-Ṣuffar or Ajnadayn.

Khālid ibn al-Walīd ibn al-Mughīrah (d. 21/642) Qurashī military commander who defeated the Muslims at Uḥud but who, after his conversion in 6/627 or 8/629, distinguished himself as one of the Muslims' most skilled military strategists, for which reason tradition calls him "God's Sword" (*sayf Allāh*).

Khālid ibn al-Zubayr (fl. first/seventh century) Companion and son of al-Zubayr ibn al-ʿAwwām (q.v.), born in Abyssinia.

Khazraj See Aws and Khazraj.

Khubayb ibn ʿAdī the Ally (d. ca. Safar 4/July–August 625) Early Muslim martyr from the Aws clan.

Khuwaylid ibn Asad Father of Khadījah bint Khuwaylid (q.v.), Muḥammad's first wife, and grandfather of the Companion al-Zubayr ibn al-ʿAwwām (q.v.).

Khaybar Oasis approximately 150 kilometers from Medina, famous for the wealth of its date palms and, during Muḥammad's lifetime, its large Jewish population.

Khuzāʿah Northern Arabian tribe closely allied to the Quraysh and key to their power in Mecca.

Khuzāʿī ibn Aswad (or Aswad ibn Khuzāʿī al-Aslamī) Medinese Ally and member of the expedition to assassinate Sallām ibn Abī l-Ḥuqayq (q.v.).

Kinānah Arabian tribe whose territory lay near Mecca.

Kūfah A garrison city, like Basra (q.v.), founded in 17/638 during the Islamic conquests on the banks of the Euphrates river in the alluvial plain of Iraq. The city briefly served as ʿAlī ibn Abī Ṭālib's (q.v.) capital during his vying for the caliphate and remained a key center for Shiʿite Islam for centuries thereafter.

Layth ibn Saʿd, al- (94–175/713–91) Famed tradent and jurist of Egypt.

Lesser pilgrimage (Ar. ʿumrah) Any pilgrimage to the Kaaba (q.v.) in Mecca (q.v.) undertaken outside the month of Dhū l-Hijjah. See Hajj.

Liḥyān Clan from the Hudhayl tribe (q.v.).

Mālik ibn ʿAwf al-Naṣrī (d. ca. 92/710–11) Bedouin chieftain of the Hawāzin (q.v.) who fought against the Muslims at Ḥunayn in 8/629 but who, after his defeat, joined causes with the Muslims and participated in the early Islamic conquests.

Mālik ibn Aws ibn al-Ḥadathān al-Naṣrī (d. ca. 91–92/709–11) Late Companion.

Mālik ibn Mighwal (d. 157/774 or 159/776) Kūfan tradent.

Maʿmar (ibn Rāshid al-Azdī) (d. 153/770) Basran tradent and principle author of *The Expeditions*.

Maʿn ibn ʿAdī (al-Balawī) (fl. first/seventh century) Companion and tribal confederate (*ḥalīf*) of the Medinese Allies.

Manāṣiʿ, al- Area designated for women to relieve themselves in Medina located due east of the Prophet's mosque and north of Baqīʿ al-Gharqad.

Maʿrūr ibn Suwayd (al-Asadī) (d. ca. 82/701) Kūfan tradent who purportedly lived to be 120.

Marwān (I) ibn al-Ḥakam Companion and first caliph of the Marwānid branch of the Umayyads (r. 64–65/684–5), he was a formidable power broker among the Islamic conquest elite from the caliphate of ʿUthmān ibn ʿAffān (q.v.) onward.

Maslamah ibn Mukhallad Medinese Ally from the Khazraj tribe who was instrumental in the conquest of Egypt and later served as the region's governor from ca. 47/668 until his death on 25 Rajab 62/9 April 682.

Masʿūd ibn Sinān Medinese Ally from the Khazraj tribe who participated in the assassination of Ibn Abī l-Ḥuqayq (q.v.) and purportedly died fighting at the Battle of Yamāmah in 12/632.

Maymūnah (bint al-Ḥārith ibn Ḥazn al-Hilāliyyah) (d. 61/681) Muḥammad's last wife, whom he married in 7/629 during his lesser pilgrimage (q.v.) to Mecca prior to the city's conquest.

Mecca The cultic center of the Hejaz in pre-Islamic Arabia and of the Islamic world thereafter, Mecca was the birthplace of Muḥammad and central hub of its powerful ruling tribe, the Quraysh; it remains the holiest city of Islam and the direction of prayer (*qiblah*) for all Muslims.

Medina Known as Yathrib in pre-Islamic times and situated about 160 kilometers from the Red Sea and 350 kilometers north of Mecca, it soon became known as "the city of the Prophet" (Ar. *madīnat al-nabī*) after it became the destination of Muḥammad's Hijrah, the site of the Prophet's Mosque, and the capital for his polity and that of the first three caliphs thereafter.

Mihjaʿ (al-ʿAkkī) (d. Ramadan 2/March 624) Freedman (*mawlā*) of ʿUmar and the first Muslim martyred at the Battle of Badr.

Mikraz ibn Ḥafṣ (fl. seventh century AD) Qurashī notable of the ʿĀmir ibn Luʾayy clan (q.v.).

Minā Located in the hills east of Mecca on the road to ʿArafah, it serves as a waypoint on the course of the pilgrimage rites for the Hajj (q.v.) and was the site of one of the Meccan pilgrimage fairs before Islam. See Dhū l-Majaz; ʿUkāẓ.

Miqsam ibn Burjah (d. 101/719–20) Early Meccan tradent.

Miqyas (ibn Ḍubābah) al-Kinānī (d. ca. Ramadan 8/January 630) Apostate Muslim whom the Prophet ordered to be killed after Mecca's conquest. He purportedly converted to Islam after his brother Hāshim ibn Ḍubābah was accidently killed during the expedition of Muraysīʿ (ca. Shaʿban 5/ December 626–January 627) by a Medinese Ally, but his conversion was merely a ploy to gain access to his brother's killer, whom he murdered even though he accepted payment of the wergild.

Misṭaḥ ibn Uthāthah ibn ʿAbbād ibn al-Muṭṭalib ibn ʿAbd Manāf (d. 34/654–55 or 37/657–58) Companion and Emigrant implicated in spreading vicious rumors against ʿĀʾishah (q.v.) and who, according to some authorities, reputedly fought alongside ʿAlī ibn Abī Ṭālib at Ṣiffīn (q.vv.).

Miswar ibn Makhramah, al- (al-Zuhrī) (2–64/623–83) Companion, Qurashī notable, and maternal nephew of ʿAbd al-Raḥmān ibn ʿAwf (q.v.), he was revered as one the "scholars of Quraysh" (*ʿulamāʾ Quraysh*).

Moses (Mūsā) Israelite leader of the exodus from Egypt of biblical fame, revered as a prophet in the Qurʾan and the Islamic tradition.

Muʿādh ibn Jabal Medinese Ally from the Khazraj clan who fought at Badr (q.vv.) at age twenty-one and whom Muḥammad sent to Yemen as his representative. He died in Syria from the Emmaus plague in 18/639.

Muʿāwiyah ibn Abī Sufyān r. 40–60/660–80) Son of Muḥammad's archrival Abū Sufyān, he converted along with his father at the conquest of Mecca. After the murder of the third caliph, ʿUthmān ibn ʿAffān (q.v.), he vied with ʿAlī ibn Abī Ṭālib (q.v.) to become the undisputed Commander of the Faithful (q.v.), a goal he achieved after ʿAlī's assassination in 40/661. Muʿāwiyah was the first in Sufyānid line of Umayyad caliphs. See Genealogical Table.

Muʿāwiyah ibn Ḥudayj al-Khawlānī (d. ca. 52/672) Participant and leader in the conquests of Egypt and North Africa, he was a staunch partisan of Muʿāwiyah ibn Abī Sufyān and the Umayyads (q.vv.).

Mughīrah ibn Shuʿbah, al- (al-Thaqafī) (d. ca. 50/670) Companion and nephew of ʿUrwah ibn Masʿūd (q.v.) who, though notorious for his criminality and lax faith, earned a reputation as a cunning fox (*dāhiyah*) in the political realm, serving as governor of Kūfa, first under ʿUmar ibn al-Khaṭṭāb and later under Muʿāwiyah ibn Abī Sufyān (q.vv.).

Muḥammad ibn ʿAbd Allāh ibn ʿAbd al-Raḥmān al-Qārī (fl. second/eighth century) Medinese tradent.

Muḥammad ibn Abī Bakr al-Ṣiddīq (10–38/632–58) The son of the first caliph, and staunch supporter of ʿAlī ibn Abī Ṭālib's (q.v.) bid for the caliphate during the Civil War. He fought alongside ʿAlī against his own half sister ʿĀʾishah (q.v.) at the Battle of the Camel and served briefly as ʿAlī's governor in Egypt until killed by the supporters of Muʿāwiyah ibn Abī Sufyān and ʿAmr ibn al-ʿĀṣ (q.vv.).

Mulāʿib al-Asinnah See ʿĀmir ibn Mālik.

Mundhir ibn ʿAmr al-Sāʿidī, al- (d. ca. Ṣafar 4/July–August 625) Medinese Ally from the Khazraj tribe known as "Aʿnaqa Liyamūt" (lit., he who hastens toward death), killed at Biʾr Maʿūnah (q.v.).

Murārah ibn Rabīʿah (fl. first/seventh century) Medinese Ally from the Aws tribe whose repentance for not accompanying Muḥammad during his expedition against Tabūk was accepted.

Naḍīr, al- Major Jewish tribe in Medina alongside the Qurayẓah (q.v.), famed for their wealth garnered from date-palm farming and for their towering, fortress-like houses surrounding Medina. See Ibn Abī l-Ḥuqayq; Kaʿb ibn al-Ashraf.

Najd A name meaning "highlands," applied to the plateau region of the Arabian Peninsula east of the Hejaz.

Najrān Arabian urban center of pre-Islamic South Arabia, Christianized in the fifth century, where the Ḥimyarites martyred large numbers of Christian of the Balḥārith tribe in ca. AD 520. By Muḥammad's lifetime, the Axumite ruler of Abyssinia had constructed a martyrion there commemorating the martyrs' deaths.

Negus (Ar. al-najāshī; from Geʿez, nägâsî*)* Rulers' title in the Axumite kingdom of Abyssinia. Named for its capital city of Axum, the kingdom was founded in the first century AD and lasted until the end of the seventh century. During Muḥammad's lifetime, Axum was regarded as Christian kingdom, the process of its Christianization having begun in the mid-fourth century under King Ēzānā (r. ca. AD 320–50), and was viewed as major regional power whose influence extended to South Arabia.

Nuʿaym ibn Masʿūd al-Ashjaʿī (d. ca. 35/656) Companion involved in the massacre of the Qurayẓah (q.v.).

Pagans (mushrikūn; sg. mushrik) Literally "associators," so-named because they were deemed guilty of *shirk*: giving worship to and seeking the intercession of beings (angels, demons, gods, etc.) alongside and to the neglect of the one God. Although Muḥammad's non-Christian and non-Jewish enemies are portrayed as the primary *mushrikūn*, in the Qur'an the Jews' worship of ʿUzayr (perhaps Ezra or, more likely, Enoch) and the Christians' worship of Jesus is considered to render them guilty of *shirk* as well.

Qādisiyyah, al- Small town on the edge of the settled regions of Iraq, known for its palm groves. It was the site of a key victory of the Muslim armies over the Persians in ca. 16/637 that opened Iraq and Persia to further conquest.

Qāsim, al-, son of the Messenger of God Son of Khadījah and Muḥammad who died at two years of age and after whom Muḥammad was called by the tekonym "Abū l-Qāsim."

Qāsim ibn Muḥammad, al- (ibn Abī Bakr) (d. ca. 106/724–25) Medinese tradent numbered among the so-called seven jurists of Medina; grandson of the caliph Abū Bakr al-Ṣiddīq (q.v.).

Qatādah ibn Diʿāmah (ca. 61–117/681–735) Blind scholar of Basra revered as a tradent and Qur'an exegete.

Qays ibn Makshūḥ al-ʿAbsī (fl. first/seventh century) Chieftain of the Murād branch of the Madhḥij tribe of Yemen who converted during the caliphate of Abū Bakr al-Ṣiddīq (q.v.) and who aided the Muslims during their defeat of the Yemeni prophet al-Aswad al-ʿAnsī and, subsequently, in the conquest of Iraq and Persia.

Qays ibn Saʿd ibn ʿUbādah (d. 85/704 or earlier) Companion, Medinese Ally from the Khazraj clan, and partisan of ʿAlī ibn Abī Ṭālib (q.v.) numbered among the "cunning foxes" (*duhāh*) of the Arabs. See Saʿd ibn ʿUbādah.

Quḍāʿah Arabian tribe of southern origin whose territories lay along the trade routes between Mecca and Syria.

Qulzum Ancient town and seaport in the Suez region of Egypt valued from antiquity for its canal to the Red Sea.

Quraysh Muḥammad's tribe and the one that dominated the affairs of Mecca in his lifetime and, thereafter, the leadership of the early Islamic polity.

Qurayẓah One of the wealthy Jewish clans of Medina, along with al-Naḍīr (q.v.). The men of the Qurayẓah were massacred and its women and children sold into captivity after betraying the Muslims during the Battle of the Trench in Dhū l-Qaʿdah 5/April 627.

Qutham ibn al-ʿAbbās ibn ʿAbd al-Muṭṭalib Young cousin of Muḥammad said to resemble him, and milch-brother of al-Ḥusayn ibn ʿAlī (q.v.). He reputedly died as a martyr in Samarkand in ca. 56/676, where there is a tomb dedicated to him known as the Shāh-e Zendah.

Rajīʿ, al- Watering hole located between ʿUsfān and Mecca (q.vv.).

Rawḥāʾ, al- Wadi located fifty to sixty kilometers from Medina and a waypoint for the hajj.

Ruqayyah, daughter of the Messenger of God (d. 2/624) One of Muḥammad's daughters from his marriage to Khadījah (q.v.), she was Fāṭimah's (q.v.) elder sister and a wife of ʿUthmān ibn ʿAffān (q.v.).

Sacred House (Ar. al-bayt) See Kaaba.

Sacred Mosque (Ar. al-masjid al-ḥarām) See Kaaba.

Sacred Precincts (Ar. al-ḥaram) The environs around Mecca, especially the Kaaba, wherein sacred proscriptions, such as those against shedding blood, must be followed.

Saʿd ibn Abī Waqqāṣ (d. ca. 50/670–71 or 58/677–78) Qurashī notable of the Zuhrah clan, Companion, and Emigrant, he is credited with founding the garrison city of Kūfah during the early Islamic conquest of Iraq.

Saʿd ibn Bakr Clan of the Hawāzin tribe (q.v.).

Saʿd ibn Muʿādh Ally and chieftain of the ʿAbd al-Ashal clan of the Aws tribe of Medina who issued the sentence against the Qurayẓah clan (q.v.) and who died shortly thereafter from an arrow wound suffered at the Battle of the Trench in 5/627.

Saʿd ibn ʿUbādah (d. 16/637) Ally, chieftain of the Sāʿidah clan of the Khazraj tribe of Medina, and fierce rival to ʿAbd Allāh ibn Ubayy (q.v.). He settled in Syria during the early Islamic conquests. See Qays ibn Saʿd.

Saʿīd ibn Zayd (al-ʿAdawī) d. ca. 50–52/670–72) Emigrant, Qurashī, and one of the earliest converts to Islam. It was in his house that ʿUmar ibn al-Khaṭṭāb (q.v.) purportedly converted to Islam, and he is said to have witnessed the Battle of Yarmūk (q.v.) and the conquest of Damascus.

Ṣafiyyah bint Ḥuyayy (ibn Akhṭab) (d. 50/670 or 52/672) Eleventh wife of the Prophet from the Jewish Naḍīr clan of Medina and daughter of a bitter opponent of Muḥammad. Her marriage took place after Khaybar was captured by the Muslims in ca. Ṣafar 7/June–July 628. See Ḥuyayy ibn Akhṭab.

Ṣafwān ibn al-Muʿaṭṭal al-Sulamī al-Dhakwānī (d. 17/638 or 19/640 in Armenia) ʿĀʾishah's (q.v.) escort back to the Muslim caravan when she was accidently left behind and with whom she was accused of having had illicit relations.

Ṣafwān ibn Umayyah (ibn Khalaf al-Jumaḥī) (d. ca. 41–42/661–3) Qurashī notable who converted only after the Battle of Ḥunayn (q.v.) and whose father was an inveterate opponent of Muḥammad and the Muslims. See Umayyah ibn Khalaf.

Saʿīd ibn al-Musayyab (d. 93/712 or 94/713) Tradent of Qurashī extraction regarded as one of the seven jurists of Medina.

Salʿ Mountain situated on the outskirts of the center of Medina.

Sālim (ibn ʿAbd Allāh ibn ʿUmar) (d. ca. 106/724) Medinese tradent and jurist and son of Ibn ʿUmar (q.v.).

Sallām ibn Abī l-Ḥuqayq al-Aʿwar, Abū Rāfiʿ Jewish merchant and chieftain of the Naḍīr tribe (q.v.) assassinated in ca. 3/625 by a band of Allies from the Khazraj (q.vv.) in a night raid on Khaybar (q.v.). See Kaʿb ibn al-Ashraf.

Sharīk (ibn ʿAbd Allāh al-Nakhaʿī) (ca. 95–177/713–94) Kūfan tradent and judge.

Shawṭ of al-Jabbānah, al- Expanse of land north of Medina where the Muslim fighters mustered prior to the Battle of Uḥud.

Shaybah ibn Rabīʿah (d. 2/624) Qurashī notable of the ʿAbd Shams slain alongside his brother ʿUtbah ibn Rabīʿah (q.v.) in a contest with ʿUbaydah ibn al-Ḥārith (q.v.) at the Battle of Badr (q.v.).

Shuʿayb ibn Khālid al-Bajalī (fl. mid-eighth century) Judge (*qāḍī*) in Rayy in Iran appointed over the affairs of the non-Muslims (*ʿāla ahl al-dhimmah*).

Shura (shūrā) Literally "consulation," in the Qur'an *shūrā* means either an authority's consulation with his subordinates (Q Āl ʿImrān 3:159) or consultation between power-sharing peers (Q Shūrā 42:38). After the caliphate of ʿUmar ibn al-Khaṭṭāb (q.v.), *shūrā* comes to refer to an "elective assembly" and an institution whereby appointed leaders of the Muslim community deliberate to choose one of their number to rule over the affairs of the community.

Shuraḥbīl ibn Ḥasanah Companion, Emigrant, and leading commander in the early Islamic conquest of Syria, he died in the Emmaus Plague in 18/639.

Solomon (Sulaymān) David's son and king of Israel of biblical fame, he is revered as a prophet and ideal king in the Qur'an and Islamic tradition.

Ṣuhayb (ibn Sinān) (d. 38/358–59) Companion and Emigrant known as the "Roman" (*al-rūmī*) because the Byzantines took him into captivity as a boy, though his family originally lived in Persian territory near Ubullah along the Tigris. He came to the Hejaz after he had been purchased as a slave by a Meccan.

Suhayl ibn ʿAmr Qurashī notable from the ʿĀmir ibn Luʾayy clan (q.v.) prominent in the negotiations at al-Ḥudaybiyah who converted after the conquest of Mecca. He participated in the conquest of Syria and died in the Emmaus Plague of 18/639.

Sulaym Northern Arabian tribe of the Hejaz whose territory lay in a basalt desert known today as Ḥarrat Ruhāṭ.

Sunnah A word that literally means "a well-trodden path" but that is used figuratively to refer to normative practice, especially the practice of the Prophet Muḥammad and his Companions.

Surāqah (ibn Mālik) ibn Juʿshum al-Mudlijī Chieftain of the Kinānah tribe whose pursuit of Muḥammad during his Hijrah is miraculously thwarted. Tradition asserts that he converted after the conquest of Mecca and died during the Caliphate of ʿUthmān ibn ʿAffān (q.v.).

Syria (Ar. al-Shām) Approximately identical with the Levant in modern parlance, including modern-day Israel-Palestine, Jordan, Syria, Lebanon, and southeastern Turkey.

Tabūk Town located in northwestern Arabia and the target of an expedition of the Prophet in 9/630.

Taif Fortified town situated high in the mountains, approximately 120 kilometers southeast of Mecca, and famous for its surrounding orchards and gardens. It was dominated by the Thaqīf tribe, who served as guardians of the town's shrine.

Tamīm Large Arabian tribe of northern descent whose territories lay in central and eastern Arabia.

Taymāʾ Oasis settlement in northwestern Arabia located some four hundred kilometers north of Medina and known for its Jewish inhabitants.

Thābit (ibn Aslam) al-Bunānī (d. 123/741 or 127/745) Tradent of Basra.

Thaqīf Northern Arabian tribe that dominated Taif and major trade partner with Mecca's Quraysh, with whom they extensively intermarried. See Taif.

Thumāmah ibn ʿAbd Allāh ibn Anas (fl. early second/eighth century) Tradent, grandson of the Companion Anas ibn Mālik, and judge (*qāḍī*) of Basra.

Thawr Cave where Abū Bakr and Muḥammad hid during their Hijrah while being pursued by their Meccan enemies.

Tihāmah Coastal lowland region of the Arabian Peninsula running along the Red Sea coast from Aqabah to the Bab al-Mandeb between modern Yemen and Djibouti.

ʿUbaydah ibn al-Ḥarīth ibn al-Muṭṭalib ibn ʿAbd Manāf (d. 2/624) Qurashī notable, Companion, and Emigrant martyred at Badr.

ʿUbayd Allāh ibn al-ʿAbbās (ibn ʿAbd al-Muṭṭalib) (d. 58/677–78 or 87/706) Companion, cousin of the Prophet, and brother of ʿAbd Allāh ibn ʿAbbās (q.v.).

ʿUbayd Allāh ibn ʿAbd Allāh ibn ʿUtbah ibn Masʿūd (d. ca. 98/716) A tradent revered as one of the seven jurists of Medina, he was also an accomplished poet.

ʿUbayd Allāh ibn ʿUmar (d. 37/657 at Ṣiffīn) Son of the second caliph ʿUmar ibn al-Khaṭṭāb (q.v.), notorious for his pursuit and murder of those he suspected to be behind his father's assassination. ʿAlī ibn Abī Ṭālib (q.v.) vowed to hold him accountable for the murders, leading ʿUbayd Allāh to make a common cause with Muʿāwiyah ibn Abī Sufyān (q.v.). See Abū Luʾluʾah.

Ubayy ibn Khalaf (d. 3/625) Qurashī notable of Mecca, close friend of ʿUqbah ibn Abī Muʿayṭ (q.v.), and inveterate opponent of Muḥammad in Mecca who was later slain by the Prophet's own hand at the Battle of Uḥud (q.v.).

ʿUdhayb, al- Body of water near the site of al-Qādisiyyah (q.v.) and later a way-point on the hajj route from Kūfah to Mecca (q.vv.).

Uḥud Mountainous plateau approximately five kilometers north of Medina where a major battle between the Muslims and the Meccan Quraysh took place in Shawwāl 3/March–April 635, according to al-Zuhrī (q.v.).

ʿUkāẓ The most prominent of the pre-Islamic Meccan pilgrimage fairs, it was held in the month of Dhū l-Qaʿdah prior the pilgrimage to ʿArafah and Mecca (q.v.) and was situated southeast of Mecca between Nakhlah and al-Ṭāʾif (q.v.). See Dhū l-Majāz, Minā.

Umaymah bint Khalaf (al-Khuzāʿiyyah) (fl. seventh century AD) Companion, Emigrant, and wife of Khālid ibn Saʿīd (q.v.).

ʿUmayr ibn Saʿd Medinese Ally from the Aws clan who participated in the conquest of Syria. He settled in Ḥimṣ, where he served as governor and died during the reign of either ʿUmar ibn al-Khaṭṭāb or Muʿāwiyah ibn Abī Sufyān (q.vv.).

Umayyads Caliphs descended from the ʿAbd Shams clan of the Quraysh whose rule lasted from 40/661 to 132/750, when they were toppled by the Abbasids. The first Umayyad caliph was ʿUthmān ibn ʿAffān (q.v.), but convention recognizes Muʿāwiya ibn Abī Sufyān (q.v.) as the founder of the dynasty.

Umayyah ibn Khalaf (al-Jumaḥī) (d. 2/624) Qurashi notable, wealthy trader, and opponent of Muḥammad slain by the Muslims at Badr (q.v.). See Ṣafwān ibn Umayyah.

Umm Ayman (Barakah bint Thaʿlabah) (d. ca. 10/632) The Prophet's servant nanny, whom he fondly called his "second mother" (*ummī baʿda ummī*) and to whom he married his adopted son Zayd ibn al-Ḥārithah (q.v.).

Umm Ḥabībah (Ramlah bint Abī Sufyān) (d. 44/664–65) Wife of the Prophet and daughter of Abū Sufyān ibn Ḥarb (q.v.). She was previously married to the early Meccan convert ʿUbayd Allāh ibn Jaḥsh, but when they undertook the Hijrah to Abyssinia together, ʿUbayd Allāh converted to Christianity and abandoned Islam, causing the dissolution of the marriage. The Prophet married her after she arrived in Medina upon returning from Abyssinia in ca. 8/629.

Umm Jamīl (Fāṭimah) bint al-Khaṭṭāb (fl. first/seventh century AD) Early convert and sister of ʿUmar ibn al-Khaṭṭāb.

Umm Kulthūm, daughter of the Messenger of God (d. 9/630) One of Muḥammad's daughters from his marriage to Khadījah (q.v.), she married ʿUthmān ibn ʿAffān (q.v.) after the death of her sister Ruqayyah (q.v.).

Umm Misṭaḥ bint Abī Ruhm (fl. seventh century AD) Mother of Misṭaḥ ibn Uthāthah (q.v.) who reveals to ʿĀʾishah (q.v.) the involvement of her son in spreading rumors about ʿĀʾishah's alleged affair.

Umm Salamah (Hind) bint Abī Umaymah ibn al-Mughīrah d. ca. 59–60/678–80) Companion, Emigrant, and wife of Muḥammad. He married her in 4/626 after the death of her first husband, Abū Salamah ʿAbd Allāh ibn ʿAbd al-Asad, who died from wounds received at Uḥud (q.v.).

ʿUqbah ibn Abī Muʿayṭ (d. 2/624) One the most inveterate opponents of Muḥammad, along with Ubayy ibn Khalaf (q.v.), with whom he is said to have been friends. He is the father of al-Walīd ibn ʿUqbah (q.v.).

ʿUqbah ibn al-Ḥārīth, Abū Sarwaʿah (d. before 72/691) Qurashī notable of the Nawfal clan and reputed executioner of the martyr Khubayb ibn ʿAdī (q.v.).

ʿUrwah ibn Masʿūd al-Thaqafī (d. 9/630) Negotiator with the Prophet at al-Ḥudaybiyah on behalf of the Quraysh, he later converted to Islam but was killed by his fellow tribesmen in Taif (q.v.) during the Muslims' siege of the city.

ʿUrwah ibn al-Zubayr (ca. 23–93/643–712) Son of the the Companion al-Zubayr ibn al-ʿAwwām (q.v.) and prominent tradent, regarded as one of the seven jurists of Medina.

Usāmah ibn Zayd (d. ca. 54/674) Companion and son of Zayd ibn Ḥārithah and Umm Ayman (q.vv.) who distinguished himself in battle under the Prophet and during the caliphate of Abū Bakr al-Ṣiddīq (q.v.).

ʿUsfān Watering hole located two days' journey by caravan from Mecca to Medina (q.vv.).

ʿUtbah ibn Rabīʿah ibn ʿAbd Shams ibn ʿAbd Manāf (d. 2/624) Chieftain of the Quraysh and opponent of the Prophet slain at Badr.

ʿUthmān ibn ʿAffān Companion, Emigrant, and Qurashī notable of the ʿAbd Shams, and the third caliph of Islam (r. 23–35/643–55) known as Dhū l-Nūrayn, "Possessor of Two Lights," after having married the Prophet's two daughters, Ruqayyah and Umm Kulthūm (q.vv.). See Genealogical Table.

ʿUthmān (ibn ʿAmr ibn Sāj) al-Jazarī (fl. mid-eighth century) Tradent, preacher (*qāṣṣ*), and slave-client of the Umayyads.

ʿUwaym ibn Sāʿidah Medinese Ally from the Aws clan who died during the caliphate of ʿUmar ibn al-Khaṭṭāb.

ʿUyaynah ibn Ḥiṣn ibn Badr al-Fazārī (fl. first/seventh century) Cheiftain of the Fazārah clan of Ghaṭafān (q.v.) whose territory lay in Wādī l-Rummah in Najd, he converted to Islam just prior to the conquest of Mecca.

ʿUzzā, al- One of the three so-called "daughters of God" mentioned in Q Najm 53:19–20 said to have been worshipped by the Quraysh prior to Islam. See Allāt, Hubal.

Wādī l-Sibāʿ Valley outside Basra where al-Zubayr ibn al-ʿAwwām (q.v.) was killed after fleeing the Battle of the Camel.

Wahb ibn Munabbih (ca. 34–110/654–728) Yemeni tradent of Persian origin.

Wakīʿ ibn al-Jarrāḥ (d. 197/812) Arab tradent of Kūfah.

Walīd ibn al-Mughīrah, al- (d. ca. 1/622) Qurashī notable, powerful leader of the Makhzūm clan, and vicious persecutor of Muḥammad's followers in Mecca.

Walīd ibn ʿUqbah ibn Abī Muʿayṭ, al- (d. 61/680) Qurashī notable of the Umayyah clan who converted to Islam after the conquest of Mecca in 8/630. During the conquests, he had a notorious run as the governor of Kūfah under ʿUthmān ibn ʿAffān (q.v.), a position he lost due to his reputation as a debauched drunk.

Walīd ibn ʿUtbah ibn Rabīʿah, al- Son of ʿUtbah ibn Rabīʿah and Qurashī notable of the ʿAbd Shams clan slain in a contest with the Hāshim clan at Badr in 2/624.

Waraqah ibn Nawfal ibn Rāshid ibn ʿAbd al-ʿUzzā ibn Quṣayy Qurashī monotheist and cousin of Muḥammad's first wife, Khadījah (q.v.), who was reputedly learned in the biblical tradition.

Wāṣil al-Aḥdab (ibn Ḥayyān al-Asadī) (d. ca. 120/738) Kūfan tradent known as "the hunchback" (*al-aḥdab*).

Yaḥyā ibn al-ʿAlāʾ al-Bajalī (fl. mid-eighth century) Tradent of al-Rayy in Iran.

Yarmūk River flowing into the Jordan River nine kilometers south of Lake Tiberius and the name of the most decisive victory of the Muslims against the Byzantines during the Islamic conquest of Syria. It was fought in Rajab 15/August 636 in Syria in Wādī al-Ruqqād near the river's banks.

Yathrib See Medina.

Ẓafār Ancient capital of the South Arabian kingdom of Ḥimyar in the Yemen and the origin of the beads in ʿĀʾishah's (q.v.) prized necklace.

Zamzam Sacred well of Mecca located within its Sacred Precincts southeast of the Kaaba (q.vv.); legend claims that the well was first discovered by Abraham's (q.v.) consort Hagar and her son Ishmael and subsequently rediscovered by Muḥammad's grandfather, ʿAbd al-Muṭṭalib (q.v.).

Zayd ibn Dathinnah (d. Ṣafar 4/July–August 625) Medinese Ally and Companion taken captive alongside Khubayb ibn ʿAdī (q.v.) and later killed during the expedition of Biʾr Maʿūnah (q.v.).

Zayd ibn Ḥārihtah "The beloved of the Messenger of God" (*ḥibb rasūl allāh*), who was once considered Muḥammad's adopted son and thus known as Zayd ibn Muḥammad at the time of his conversion. He had been a freed slave of Muḥammad prior to his adoption. Zayd's adoption by Muḥammad was subsequently nullified by a revelation abolishing adoption (Q Aḥzāb 33:4–5), and he then returned to his former name, Zayd ibn al-Ḥārithah al-Kalbī. He is the only Muslim aside from Muḥammad to be mentioned by name in the Qur'an (see Q Aḥzāb 33:37). He perished on the battlefield as the commander of the expeditionary force to al-Mu'tah in ca. 8/629.

Zayd ibn al-Ḥasan (ibn ʿAlī ibn Abī Ṭālib) Great-grandson of the Prophet and sharif of the Hāshim clan charged with the management of the lands inherited from the Prophet (*al-ṣadaqāt*), he lived at least until the reign of ʿUmar II ibn ʿAbd al-ʿAzīz (r. 99–101/717–20).

Zaynab bint Jaḥsh (al-Asadiyyah) (d. 20/641) Wife of the Prophet, whom he married in 4/626 after her divorce from his freedman and adopted son Zayd ibn Ḥāritha (q.v.) in accord with divine command; cf. Q Aḥzāb 33:37.

Zaynab, daughter of the Messenger of God (d. 8/629–30) Khadījah's (q.v.) and Muḥammad's eldest daughter, who married Abū l-ʿĀṣ ibn Rabīʿ (q.v.).

Zubayr ibn al-ʿAwwām, al- Companion, Emigrant, and Qurashī notable murdered in 35/656 after he fought in the Battle of the Camel against ʿAlī ibn Abī Ṭālib (q.v.). See Genealogical Table.

Zuhrī, Ibn Shihāb al- (d. 124/742) Qurashī notable and eminent founding figure of the Islamic scholarly tradition. He was Maʿmar's (q.v.) teacher and his principal source for the narrations found in *The Expeditions*.

Genealogical Table of the Quraysh of Mecca

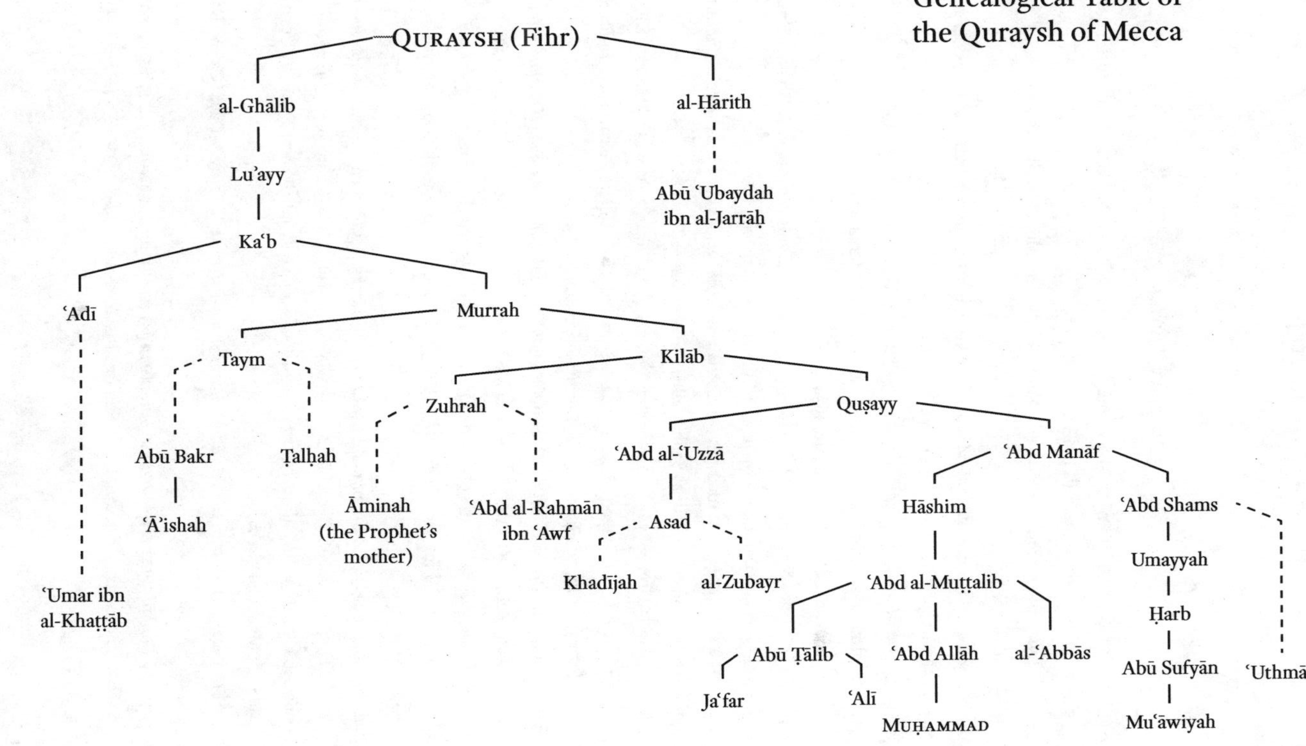

Bibliography

Primary Sources

ʿAbd al-Razzāq ibn Hammām al-Ṣanʿānī. *Al-Muṣannaf,* 11 vols., ed. Ḥabīb al-Raḥmān al-Aʿẓamī. Beirut: al-Majlis al-ʿIlmī, 1972.

———. *Tafsīr al-Qur'ān,* 3 vols., ed. Muṣṭafā Muslim Muḥammad. Riyadh: Maktabat al-Rushd, 1989.

Abū Nuʿaym al-Iṣfahānī. *Dalā'il al-nubuwwah,* 2 vols., ed. Muḥammad Rawwās al-Qalʿajī and ʿAbd al-Barr ʿAbbās. Beirut: Dār al-Nafā'is, 1986.

———. *Ḥilyat al-awliyā' wa-ṭabaqāt al-aṣifyā',* 10 vols. Beirut: Dār al-Fikr, 1967.

Abu ʿUbayd al-Qāsim ibn Salām. *Kitāb al-Amwāl,* ed. Muḥammad Ḥāmid al-Fiqī. Cairo: al-Maktabah al-Tijāriyyah al-Kubrā, 1934.

Abū Zurʿah al-Dimashqī, ʿAbd al-Raḥmān ibn ʿAmr. *Tārīkh,* 2 vols., ed. Shukr Allāh ibn Niʿmat Allāh al-Qūchānī. Damascus: Majmaʿ al-Lughah al-ʿArabiyyah, 1980.

Azraqī, Abū l-Walīd Muḥammad ibn ʿAbd Allāh al-. *Akhbār Makkah wa-mā jā'a fīhā min al-āthār,* 2 vols., ed. Rushdī al-Ṣāliḥ Malḥas. Mecca: Dār al-Thaqāfah, 1985.

Balādhurī, Aḥmad ibn Yaḥyā al-. *Ansāb al-ashrāf,* vol. 1, ed. Yūsuf al-Marʿashlī. Beirut: Klaus Schwarz, 2008; vol. 4/2, ed. ʿAbd al-ʿAzīz al-Dūrī and ʿIṣām ʿUqlah, Beirut: Das Arabische Buch, 2001; vol. 5, ed. Iḥsān ʿAbbās, Beirut: Franz Steiner, 1996.

Bayhaqī, Abū Bakr Aḥmad ibn al-Ḥusayn al-. *Dalā'il al-nubuwwah wa-maʿrifat aḥwāl ṣāḥib al-sharīʿah,* 7 vols., ed. ʿAbd al-Muʿṭī Qalʿajī. Beirut: Dār al-Kutub al-Islāmiyyah, 1985.

———. *al-Sunan al-kubrā,* 10 vols. Hyderabad: Dā'irat al-Maʿārif al-Niẓāmiyyah, 1925–37.

Bukhārī, Muḥammad ibn Ismāʿīl al-. *Al-Ṣaḥīḥ,* 3 vols. Vaduz: Jamʿiyyat al-Maknaz al-Islāmī, 2001.

Dhahabī, Shams al-Dīn Muḥammad ibn Aḥmad al-. *Tārīkh al-islām wa-wafayāt al-mashāhīr wa-l-aʿlām,* 17 vols., ed. Bashshār ʿAwwād Maʿrūf. Beirut: Dār al-Gharb al-Islāmī, 2003.

Fasawī, Abū Yūsuf al-. *Kitāb al-Maʿrifah wa-l-tārīkh,* 4 vols., ed. Akram Ḍiyā' al-ʿUmarī. Medina: Maktabat al-Dār, 1990.

Ibn ʿAbd al-Barr. *Al-Durar fī ikhtiṣār al-maghāzī wa-l-siyar,* ed. Shawqī Ḍayf. Cairo: Dār al-Taḥrīr, 1966.

———. *Al-Tamhīd li-mā fī l-Muwaṭṭa' min al-maʿānī wa-l-asānīd,* 26 vols., ed. Saʿīd Aḥmad Aʿrāb. Rabat: Wizārat al-Awqāf wa-l-Shu'ūn al-Islāmiyyah, 1974–92.

Ibn Abī Khaythamah, Abū Bakr. *Al-Tārīkh al-kabīr*, 4 vols., ed. Ṣalāḥ ibn Fatḥī Halal. Cairo: Al-Fārūq al-Ḥadīthah, 2004.

Ibn ʿAsākir, Abū l-Qāsim ʿAlī ibn al-Ḥasan. *Tārīkh madīnāt Dimashq*, 80 vols., ed. Muḥibb al-Dīn ʿUmar ibn Gharāmah al-ʿAmrawī. Beirut: Dār al-Fikr, 1995–2000.

Ibn Ḥajar al-ʿAsqalānī. *Fatḥ al-bārī fī sharḥ Ṣaḥīḥ al-Bukhārī*. 17 vols. Cairo: Maktabat Muṣṭafā al-Bābī al-Ḥalabī, 1959.

———. *Lisān al-Mīzān*, 10 vols., ed. ʿAbd al-Fattāḥ Abū Ghuddah. Beirut: Dār al-Bashā'ir al-Islāmiyyah, 2002.

Ibn Ḥanbal, Aḥmad ibn Muḥammad. *Al-Musnad*, 12 vols. Vaduz: Jamʿiyyat al-Maknaz al-Islāmī, 2009.

Ibn Hishām, ʿAbd al-Malik. *Al-Sīrah al-nabawiyyah*, 2 vols., eds. Muṣṭafā al-Saqqā, Ibrāhīm al-Abyārī, and ʿAbd al-Ḥafīẓ Shalabī. Beirut: Dār al-Fikr, n.d.

Ibn al-Jawzī, Abū l-Faraj. *Virtues of the Imam Aḥmad ibn Ḥanbal*, 2 vols., ed. and trans. Michael Cooperson. New York: New York University Press, 2013–14.

Ibn Khayr al-Ishbīlī. *Al-Fahrasah*, 2 vols., ed. Ibrāhīm al-Abyārī. Cairo: Dār al-Kitāb, 1989.

Khalīfah ibn Khayyāṭ. *Kitāb al-Ṭabaqāt*, ed. Suhayl Zakkār. Beirut: Dār al-Fikr, 1993.

Lālakā'ī, Ḥibat Allāh ibn al-Ḥasan al-. *Sharḥ uṣūl iʿtiqād ahl al-sunnah wa-l-jamāʿah*, ed. Aḥmad ibn Saʿd ibn Ḥamdān al-Ghāmidī. Riyadh: Dār al-Ṭībah, 1994.

Ibn Saʿd al-Zuhrī. *Kitāb al-Ṭabaqāt al-kubrā*, 9 vols., ed. Eduard Sachau. Leiden: Brill, 1905–40.

Mizzī, Jamāl al-Dīn al-. *Tahdhīb al-Kamāl fī asmā' al-rijāl*, 35 vols. Bashshār ʿAwwād Maʿrūf. Beirut: Mu'assasat al-Risālah, 1983–92.

Samhūdī, ʿAlī ibn ʿAbd Allāh al-. *Wafā' al-Wafā bi-akhbār dār al-Muṣṭafā*, 5 vols., ed. Qasim al-Samarrai. London: al-Furqān, 2001.

Ṭabarānī, Sulaymān ibn Aḥmad al-. *Al-Muʿjam al-kabīr*, 25 vols., ed. Ḥamdī ʿAbd al-Majīd al-Salafī. Cairo: Maktabat Ibn Taymiyyah, 1983.

Ṭabarī, Abū Jaʿfar Muḥammad ibn Jarīr al-. *Tārīkh al-rusul wa-l-mulūk*, ser. I–III, eds. M. J. de Goeje et al. Leiden: Brill, 1879–1901.

ʿUṭāridī, Aḥmad ibn ʿAbd al-Jabbār al-. *Kitāb al-Siyar wa'l-maghāzī*, ed. Suhayl Zakkār. Beirut: Dār al-Fikr, 1978.

Wallace-Hadrill, J. M., ed. and trans. *The Fourth Book of the Chronicle of Fredegar*. London: Thomas Nelson, 1960.

Yāqūt al-Rūmī al-Ḥamawī. *Muʿjam al-buldān*, 8 vols. Beirut: Dār Ṣādir, 2010.

Zubayr ibn Bakkār, al-. *Al-Akhbār al-muwaffaqayyāt*, ed. Sāmī al-ʿĀnī. Baghdad: Maṭbaʿat al-ʿĀnī, 1972.

———. *Al-Muntakhab min Kitāb azwāj al-nabī*, ed. Sukaynah Shihābī. Beirut: Mu'assasat al-Risālah, 1983.

Secondary Literature

Abbott, Nabia. *Studies in Arabic Literary Papyri*, 3 vols. Chicago: University of Chicago Press, 1957–72.

Anthony, Sean W. "The Domestic Origins of Imprisonment: An Inquiry into an Early Islamic Institution," *JAOS* 129 (2009): 571–96.

———. "Dionysius of Tell Maḥrē's Syriac Account of the Assassination of ʿUmar b. al-Khaṭṭāb," *JNES* 69 (2010): 209–24.

———. *The Caliph and the Heretic: Ibn Saba' and the Origins of Shīʿism*. Leiden: Brill, 2012.

———. *Crucifixion and Death as Spectacle: Umayyad Crucifixion in Its Late Antique Context*. New Haven, CT: American Oriental Society, 2014.

———. "Muḥammad, the Keys to Paradise, and the *Doctrina Iacobi*: A Late Antique Puzzle," *Der Islam* 91 (forthcoming 2014).

ʿAthamina, Khalil. "The Appointment and Dismissal of Khālid ibn al-Walīd from the Supreme Command: A Study of the Political Strategy of the Early Muslim Caliphs in Syira," *Arabica* 41 (1994): 253–72.

ʿAwwājī, Muḥammad ibn Muḥammad al-. *Marwiyyāt al-Zuhrī fī l-maghāzī*, 2 vols. Medina: Al-Jāmiʿah al-Islāmiyyah, 2004.

Bashear, Suliman. *Arabs and Others in Early Islam*. SLAEI 8. Princeton: Darwin, 1997.

Beaucamp, Joëlle, Françoise Briquel-Chatonnet, and Christian Julien Robin, eds. *Juifs et chrétiens en Arabie aux Ve et VIe siècles: Regards croisés sur les sources*. Paris: Centre de reserche d'histoire et civilization de Byzance, 2010.

Beeston, A. F. L. "The Martyrdom of Azqir." *Proceedings of the Seminar for Arabian Studies* 15 (1985): 5–10.

Bitan, Uri. "Asmā' *Dhāt al-Niṭāqayn* and the Politics of Mythical Motherhood." *JSAI* 35 (2008): 141–66.

Boekhoff-van der Voort, Nicolet. "The *Kitāb al-maghāzī* of ʿAbd al-Razzāq ibn Hammām al-Ṣanʿānī: Searching for Earlier Source Material." In *The Transmission and Dynamics of the Textual Sources of Islam: Essays in Honour of Harald Motzki*, edited by Nicolet Boekhoff-van der Voort, Kees Versteegh, and Joas Wagemakers, 25–47. Leiden: Brill, 2011.

Brown. Jonathan A. C. *Ḥadīth: Muḥammad's Legacy in the Medieval and Modern World*. Oxford: Oneworld, 2009.

Burns, Dylan Michael. "The Apocalypse of Zostrianos and Iolaos: A Platonic Reminiscence of the Heracleidae at NHC VIII, 1.4." *Le Muséon* 126 (2013), 29–43.

Busse, Heribert. "The Destruction of the Temple and Its Reconstruction in the Light of Muslim Exegesis of Sūra 17:2–8." *JSAI* 20 (1996): 1–17.

Chabbi, Jacquelin. "Histoire et tradition sacrée: la biographie impossible de Mahomet." *Arabica* 43 (1996): 189–205.

Chelhod, J. "La *baraka* chez les Arabes." *RHR* 148 (1955): 68–88.

Comerro, Viviane. *Les traditions sur la constitution du muṣḥaf de 'Uthmān*. Beirut: Ergon, 2012.

Conrad, Lawrence I. "Recovering Lost Texts: Some Methodological Issues." *JAOS* 113 (1993): 258–63.

———. "Heraclius in Early Islamic Kerygma." in *The Reign of Heraclius (610–641): Crisis and Confrontation*, 95–112. Edited by Gerrit J. Reinink and Bernhard H. Stolte. Leuven: Peeters, 2002.

Cook, D. "The *Aṣḥāb al-Ukhdūd*: History and *Ḥadīth* in a Martyrological Sequence." *JSAI* 34 (2008): 125–48.

Cook, Michael. "The Opponents of the Writing of Tradition in Early Islam." *Arabica* 44 (1997): 437–530.

Crone, Patricia. "Angels versus Humans as Messengers of God: The View of the Qur'ānic Pagans." in *Revelation, Literature, and Community in Late Antiquity*, 315–36. Edited by Philippa Townsend and Moulie Vidas. TSAJ 146. Tübingen: Mohr Siebeck, 2011.

———. "The Religion of Qur'ānic Pagans: God and the Lesser Deities." *Arabica* 57 (2010): 151–200.

———. "*Shūrā* as an Elective Institution." *Quaderni di Studi Arabi* 19 (2001): 3–39.

Crone, Patricia, and Adam Silverstein. "The Ancient Near East and Islam: The Case of Lot-Casting." *Journal of Semitic Studies* 55 (2010): 423–50.

de Blois, François. "The 'Sabians' (Ṣābi'ūn) in Pre-Islamic Arabia." *Acta Orientalia* 56 (1995): 39–61.

de Prémare, Alfred-Louis. "'Il voulut détruire le temple.' L'attaque de la Ka'ba par les rois yéménites avant l'Islam: *Aḫbār* et Histoire." *Journal Asiatique* 288 (2000): 261–367.

Déroche, François. *Qur'ans of the Umayyads: A First Overview*. Leiden: Brill, 2013.

Diem, Werner, and Marco Shöller. *The Living and the Dead in Islam: Studies in Arabic Epitaphs*, 3 vols. Wiesbaden: Harrossowitz, 2004.

Djaït, Hichem. *Le vie de Muḥammad*, tr. Hichem Abdessamad. Paris: Fayard, 2007–12.

Donner, Fred M. *The Early Islamic Conquests*. Princeton: Princeton University Press, 1981.

———. *Narratives of Islamic Origins: The Beginning of Islamic Historical Writing*. Princeton: Darwin, 1998.

———. *Muḥammad and the Believers: At the Origins of Islam*. Cambridge, Mass.: Harvard University Press, 2012.

Ebstein, Michael. "*Shurṭa* Chiefs in Baṣra in the Umayyad Period: A Prosopographical Study." *Al-Qanṭara* 31 (2010): 103–47.

Elad, Amikam. "The Beginning of Historical Writing by the Arabs: The Earliest Syrian Writers on the Arab Conquests." *JSAI* 28 (2003): 65–152.

EI2 *Encyclopædia of Islam*, 2nd edition. Edited by P. Bearman, Th. Bianquis, C. E. Bosworth, E. von Donzol, and W. P. Heinrichs. Leiden: Brill, 1960–2002.

EI3 *Encyclopædia of Islam*, 3rd edition. Edited by Gudrun Krämer, Denis Matringe, John Nawas, and Everett Rowson. Leiden: Brill, 2007.

EQ *Encyclopædia of the Qur'ān*. Edited by Jane Damen McAuliffe et al. Leiden: Brill, 2001–06.

Esders, Stefan. "Herakleios, Dagobert und die 'beschnittenen Völker,'" in *Jenseits der Grenzen: Beiträge zur spätantiken und frühmittelalterlichen Geschichtsschreibung*, 239–312. Edited by Andreas Goltz, Hartmut Leppin, and Heinrich Schlange-Schöningen. Millennium-Studien 25. Berlin: W. de Gruyter, 2009.

Gacek, Adam. *Arabic Manuscripts: A Vademecum for Readers*. Leiden: Brill, 2009.

Giladi, A. "Some Notes on *Taḥnīk* in Medieval Islam." *JNES* 3 (1988): 175–79.

———. *Infants, Parents, and Wetnurses: Medieval Islamic Views on Breastfeeding and Their Social Implications*. Leiden: Brill, 1999.

Gilliot, Claude. "Les 'informateurs' juifs et chrétiens de Muḥammad." *JSAI* 22 (1998): 84–126.

———. "Poète ou prophète? Les traditions concernant la poésie et les poètes attribuées au prophète de l'islam et aux premières generations musulmanes." In *Paroles, signes, mythes: Mélanges offerts à Jamal Eddine Bencheikh*, 331–96. Edited by F. Sanagustin. Damascus: Institut Français d'Études Arabes, 2001.

Goitein, S. D. *Studies in Islamic History and Institutions*. Leiden: Brill, 1966.

Goldfeld, Isaiah. "The Illiterate Prophet (*al-nabī al-ummī*): An Inquiry into the Development of a Dogma in Islamic Tradition." *Der Islam* 57 (1980): 58–67.

Goldziher, Ignaz. *Muslim Studies*, tr. C. R. Barber and S. M. Stern. London: George Allen & Unwin, 1971.

Görke, Andreas. "The Relationship between *Maghāzī* and *Ḥadīth* in Early Islamic Scholarship." *BSOAS* 74 (2011): 171–85.

———. "Prospect and Limits in the Study of the Historical Muḥammad." In *The Transmission and Dynamics of the Textual Sources of Islam: Essays in Honour of Harald Motzki*, 137–51. Edited by Nicolet Boekhoff-van der Voort, Kees Versteegh, and Joas Wagemakers. IHC 89. Leiden: Brill, 2011.

Görke, Andreas and Gregor Schoeler. *Die ältesten Berichte über das Leben Muḥammads: Das Korpus 'Urwa ibn az-Zubair*. SLAEI 24. Princeton: Darwin, 2008.

Görke, Andreas, Harald Motzki, and Gregor Schoeler. "First Century Sources for the Life of Muḥammad? A Debate." *Der Islam* 89 (2012): 2–59.

Griffith, Sidney H. "The Gospel in Arabic: An Inquiry into Its Appearance in the First Abbasid Century." *Oriens Christianus* 69 (1985): 126–67.

———. "Christian Lore and the Arabic Qur'ān: The 'Companions of the Cave' in Sūrat al-Kahf and Syriac Christian Tradition." In *The Qur'ān in Its Historical Context*, 109–38. Edited by Gabriel Said Reynolds. London: Routledge, 2007.

———. *The Bible in Arabic: The Scriptures of the "People of the Book" in the Language of Islam*. Princeton: Princeton University Press, 2013.

Guidetti, Mattia. "The Contiguity between Churches and Mosques in Early Islamic Bilād al-Shām." *BSOAS* 76 (2013): 229–58.

Günther, Sebastian. "New Results in the Theory of Source-Criticism in Medieval Arabic Literature." *Al-Abḥāth* 42 (1994): 3–15.

Hagan, Gottfried. "The Imagined and the Historical Muḥammad." *JAOS* 129 (2009): 97–111.

Haider, Najam. "Contesting Intoxication: Early Juristic Debates over the Lawfulness of Alcoholic Beverages." *ILS* 20 (2013): 48–89.

Halm, Heinz. "Der *Masğid* des Propheten." *Der Islam* 83 (2008): 258–76.

Halevi, Leor. *Muhammad's Grave: Death Rites and the Making of Islamic Society*. New York: Columbia University Press, 2007.

Hamdan, Omar. "The Second *Maṣāḥif* Project: A Step towards the Canonization of the Qur'ānic Text." In *The Qur'ān in Context: Historical and Literary Investigations into the Qur'ānic Milieu*, 795–835. Edited by Angelika Neuwrith, Nicolai Sinai, and Michael Marx. Leiden: Brill, 2010.

Hamori, Andras. *The Composition of Mutanabbī's Panegyrics to Sayf al-Dawla*. Leiden: Brill, 1992.

Hinds, Martin. "The Ṣiffīn Arbitration Agreement." *JSS* 17 (1972): 93–129.

Horovitz, Josef. *The Earliest Biographies of the Prophet and Their Authors*, ed. Lawrence I. Conrad. SLAEI 11. Princeton: Darwin, 2002.

Hoyland, Robert G. "The Earliest Christian Writings on Muḥammad: An Appraisal." In *The Biography of Muḥammad: The Issue of the Sources*, 276–97. Edited by Harald Motzki. Leiden: Brill, 2000.

———. "Writing the Biography of the Prophet Muhammad: Problems and Solutions." *History Compass* 5 (2007), 1–22.

———. "The Jews of the Hijaz in the Qur'ān and in Their Inscriptions," in *New Perspectives on the Qur'ān: The Qur'ān in Its Historical Context* 2, 91–116. Edited by Gabriel Said Reynolds. London: Routledge, 2011.

Jarrar, Maher. *Die Prophetenbiographie im islamischen Spanien: Ein Beitrag zur Überlieferungs- und Redaktionsgeschichte*. Frankfurt am Main: Peter Lang, 1989.

———. "'*Sīrat Ahl al-Kisā*": Early Shī'ī Sources on the Biography of the Prophet." In *The Biography of Muhammad: The Issue of the Sources*, 98–155. Edited by Harald Motzki. Leiden: Brill, 2000.

Jones, J. M. B. "The Chronology of the 'Maghāzī'—A Textual Survey." *BSOAS* 19 (1957): 245–80.

Juynboll, Gautier H. A. *Encyclopedia of Canonical Ḥadīth*. Leiden: Brill, 2007.

Kennedy, Hugh. *The Armies of the Caliphs: Military and Society in the Early Islamic State*. Routledge: London, 2001.

Khoury, Raïf Georges. *Wahb b. Munabbih*. Wiesbaden: Harrassowitz, 1972.

Kister, M. J. "Notes on the Papyrus Text about Muḥammad's Campaign against the Banū al-Naḍīr." *Archiv Orientální* 32 (1964): 233.

———. "'God Will Never Disgrace Thee': An Interpretation of an Early Ḥadīth." *Journal of the Royal Asiatic Society* (1965), 27–32.

———. "*Al-Taḥannuth*: An Enquiry into the Meaning of a Term." *BSOAS* 31 (1968): 223–36.

———. "On the Papyrus of Wahb ibn Munabbih." *BSOAS* 37 (1974): 545–71.

———. "The Massacre of the Banū Qurayẓa: A Re-Examination of a Tradition." *JSAI* 8 (1986): 61–96.

———. ". . . And He Was Born Circumcised . . .: Some Notes on Circumcision in Ḥadīth." *Oriens* 34 (1994): 10–30.

———. ". . . *Lā taqra'ū l-qur'āna 'ala al-muṣḥafiyyīn wa-lā taḥmilū l-'ilm 'ani l-ṣaḥafiyyīn* . . .: Some Notes on the Transmission of Ḥadīth." *JSAI* 22 (1998): 127–62.

Klar. M. O. "*And We cast upon his throne a mere body*: A Historiographical Reading of Q. 38:34." *Journal of Qur'anic Studies* 6 (2004): 103–26.

Kohlberg, Etan, and Mohammad Ali Amir-Moezzi. *Revelation and Falsification: The Kitāb al-qirā'āt of Aḥmad b. Muḥammad al-Sayyārī*. Leiden: Brill, 2009.

Lecker, Michael. "Biographical Notes on Ibn Shihāb al-Zuhrī." *JSS* 41 (1996): 21–63.

Lowin, Shari. *The Making of a Forefather: Abraham in Islamic and Jewish Exegetical Literature*. IHC 65. Brill: Leiden, 2006.

Madelung, Wilferd. *The Succession to Muḥammad: A Study of the Early Caliphate*. Cambridge: Cambridge University Press, 1997.

Maghen, Ze'ev. "Davidic Motifs in the Biography of Muḥammad." *JSAI* 35 (2008): 91–139.

Mashūkhī, 'Ābid Sulaymān al-. *Anmāṭ al-tawthīq fī l-makhṭūṭ al-'arabī fī l-qarn al-tāsi' al-hijrī*. Riyadh: Maktabat al-Malik Fahd al-Waṭaniyyah, 1994.

Melchert, Christopher. "The Concluding Salutation in Islamic Ritual Prayer." *Le Muséon* 114 (2001): 389–406.

Millar, Fergus. "Hagar, Ishmael, Josephus, and the Origins of Islam." *Journal of Jewish Studies* 44 (1993): 23–45.

Modarressi, Hossein. *Tradition and Survival: A Bibliographic Survey of Early Shīʿite Literature.* Oxford: Oneworld, 2003.

Motzki, Harald. "The Murder of Ibn Abī l-Ḥuqayq: On the Origin and Reliability of Some *Maghāzī* Reports." In *The Biography of Muhammad: The Issue of the Sources*, 170–239. Edited by Harald Motzki. Leiden: Brill, 2000.

———. "The Author and His Work in the Islamic Literature of the First Centuries: The Case of ʿAbd al-Razzāq's *Muṣannaf*." *JSAI* 28 (2003): 171–97.

Müller-Kessler, Christa, and Michael Sokoloff. *A Corpus of Christian Palestinian Aramaic, vols. IIa-b: The Christian Aramaic New Testament Version from the Early Period.* STYX Publications: Groningen, 1998.

Nagel, Tilman. *Mohammed: Leben und Legende.* Munich: Oldenbourg, 2008.

———. *Allahs Liebling: Ursprung und Erscheinungsformen des Mohammedglaubens.* Munich: Oldenbourg, 2008.

Nöldeke, Theodor, Friedrich Schwally, Gotthelf Begsträβer, and Otto Pretzl. *The History of the Qur'ān*, ed. and trans. Wolfgang H. Behn. Leiden: Brill, 2013.

Noth, Albrecht, with Lawrence I. Conrad. *The Early Arabic Historical Tradition: A Source-Critical Study*, 2nd ed., trans. Michael Bonner. SLAEI 3. Princeton: Darwin, 1994.

Neuwirth, Angelika. *Der Koran als Text der Spätantike: Ein europäischer Zugang.* Berlin: Verlag der Weltreligionen, 2010.

———. *Der Koran I: Frühmekkanische Suren.* Berlin: Verlag der Weltreligionen, 2011.

Powers, D. S. *Muḥammad Is Not the Father of Any of Your Men: The Making of the Last Prophet.* Philadelphia, PA: University of Pennsylvania Press, 2009.

Qāḍī, Wadād al-. "How 'Sacred' Is the Text of an Arabic Medieval Manuscript? The Complex Choices of the Editor-Scholar." In *Theoretical Approaches to the Transmission and Edition of Oriental Manuscripts*, 13–53. Edited by Judith Pfeiffer and Manfred Kropp. Beirut: Ergon, 2007.

Reinhart, A. Kevin. "Juynbolliana, Gradualism, the Big Bang, and *Ḥadīth* Study in the Twenty-First Century." *JAOS* 130 (2010): 413–44.

Reynolds, Gabriel Said. *The Qur'ān and Its Biblical Subtext.* London: Routledge, 2010.

Robin, Christian Julien. "Arabia and Ethiopia." In *The Oxford Handbook of Late Antiquity*, 247–332. Edited by Scott Fitzgerald Johnson. Oxford: Oxford University Press, 2012.

———. "Abraha et la Reconquête de l'Arabie déserte: un réexamen de l'inscription Ryckmans 506 = Murayghan 1." *JSAI* 39 (2012): 1–93.

Robinson, Chase. *Islamic Historiography.* Cambirdge: Cambridge University Press, 2003.

———. “The Violence of the Abbasid Revolution.” In *Living Islamic History: Studies in Honour of Professor Carole Hillenbrand*, 225–56. Edited by Yasir Suleiman. Edinburgh: Edinburgh University Press, 2010.

Rubin, Uri. “Morning and Evening Prayers in Early Islam.” *JSAI* 8 (1987): 40–64.

———. “Muḥammad’s Curse of Muḍar and the Blockade of Mecca.” *JESHO* 31 (1998): 249–64.

———. “The Assassination of Kaʿb b. al-Ashraf.” *Oriens* 32 (1990): 65–71.

———. “*Iqrāʾ bi-ismi rabbika . . . !* Some Notes on the Interpretation of *Sūrat al-ʿalaq* (vs. 1–5).” *Israel Oriental Studies* 13 (1993): 213–30.

———. “The Shrouded Messenger: On the Interpretation of *al-Muzzammil* and *al-Muddaththir*.” *Jerusalem Studies in Arabic and Islam* 16 (1993): 96–110.

———. *The Eye of the Beholder: The Life of Muḥammad as Viewed by the Early Muslims*. Princeton: Darwin, 1995.

———. *Between Bible and Qurʾān: The Children of Israel and the Islamic Self-Image*. Princeton: Darwin, 1999.

———. “The Life of Muḥammad and the Qurʾān: The Case of Muḥammad’s *Hijra*.” *JSAI* 28 (2003): 40–64.

———. “On the Arabian Origins of the Qurʾān: The Case of al-Furqān.” *JSS* 54 (2009): 421–33.

Sadeghi, Behnam, and Mohsen Goudarzi. “Ṣanʿāʾ 1 and the Origins of the Qurʾān.” *Der Islam* 87 (2012): 1–129.

Saleh, Walid A. “A Piecemeal Qurʾān: Furqān and Its Meaning in Classical Islam and Modern Qurʾanic Studies.” *JSAI* (forthcoming).

Sanders, E. P. *The Historical Figure of Jesus*. Penguin: New York, 1996.

Schäfer, Peter. *The Jewish Jesus: How Judaism and Christianity Shaped Each Other*. Princeton University Press: Princeton, 2012.

Schoeler, Gregor. *The Oral and Written in Early Islam*, trans. Uwe Vagelpohl and ed. James E. Montgomery. Routledge: London, 2006.

———. *The Biography of Muḥammad: Nature and Authenticity*, trans. Uwe Vagelpohl and ed. James E. Montgomery. Routledge: London, 2011.

———. “Grundsätzliches zu Tilman Nagels Monographie *Mohammaed, Leben und Legende*.” *Asiatische Studien* 65 (2011): 193–209.

Sellheim, Rudolf. “Prophet, Chalif und Geschichte: Die Muhammad-Biographie des Ibn Isḥāq.” *Oriens* 18–19 (1965–66): 33–91.

Sezgin, Fuat. *Geschichte des arabischen Schrifttums*. Leiden: Brill, 1967–2010.

Shoemaker, Stephen J. "In Search of 'Urwa's *Sīra*: Methodological Issues in the Quest for the Historical Muḥammad." *Der Islam* 85 (2011): 257–341.

———. *The Death of a Prophet: The End of Muḥammad's Life and the Beginnings of Islam.* Philadelphia, PA: University of Pennsylvania Press, 2011.

Silverstein, Adam. "On the Original Meaning of the Qur'anic Term *al-shayṭān al-rajīm*," *JAOS* 133 (2013): 21–33.

Sinai, Nicolai. "Hisham Djait über die 'Geschichtlichkeit der Verkündigung Muḥammads.'" *Der Islam* 86 (2011): 30–43.

Sizgorich, Thomas. "'Become infidels or we will throw you into the fire': The Martyrs of Najran in Early Muslim Historiography, Hagiography, and Qur'anic Exegesis." In *Writing "True Stories": Historians and Hagiographers in the Late-Antique and Medieval Near East*, 125–47. Edited by M. Debié, H. Kennedy, and A. Papaconstantinou. Turnhout: Brepols, 2009.

Stillman, Yedida Kalfon, and Norman A. Stillman. *Arab Dress: A Short History from the Dawn of Islam to Modern Times.* Leiden: Brill, 2003.

Szilágyi, K. "A Prophet Like Jesus? Christians and Muslims Debating Muḥammad's Death." *JSAI* 36 (2009): 131–72.

Torijano, Pablo A. *Solomon, the Esoteric King: From King to Magus, the Development of a Tradition.* JSJS 73. Leiden: Brill, 2002.

Tottoli, Roberto. "Muslim Attitudes towards Prostration (*sujūd*), I. Arabs and Prostration at the Beginning of Islam and in the Qur'ān." *Studia Islamica* 88 (1998): 5–34.

Ullmann, Manfred. *Wörterbuch der klassischen arabischen Sprache.* Berlin: Harrassowitz, 1957–2008.

van Gelder, Geert Jan. *Classical Arabic Literature: A Library of Arabic Literature Anthology.* New York: New York University Press, 2012.

Wansbrough, John. "Gentilics and Appellatives: Notes on Aḥābīš Qurayš." *BSOAS* 49 (1986): 203–10.

Wensinck, A. J. et al. *Concordances et indices de la tradition musulmane.* Leiden: Brill, 1936–88.

Yuval, Israel J. "The Myth of the Jewish Exile from the Land of Israel: A Demonstration of Irenic Scholarship." *Common Knowledge* 12 (2006): 16–33.

Further Reading

Studies on the Biography of Muḥammad

Recent, modern biographies of Muḥammad by English-speaking scholars who can read the Arabic sources (and hopefully other relevant languages as well) are surprisingly scarce. Nonetheless, three short and highly readable introductory books by such scholars can be enthusiastically recommended:

Brown, Jonathan A. C. *Muḥammad: A Very Short Introduction.* Oxford: Oxford University Press, 2011.

Cook, Michael. *Muhammad.* Oxford: Oxford University Press, 1983.

Donner, Fred McGraw. *Muḥammad and the Believers: At the Origins of Islam.* Cambridge, Mass.: Harvard University Press, 2012.

Fortunately for English-speaking readers, the historical study of the evolution of the biographical traditions about Muḥammad, and especially the hadith, have made a more robust showing. Essential readings are:

Brown. Jonathan A. C. *Ḥadīth: Muḥammad's Legacy in the Medieval and Modern World.* Oxford: Oneworld, 2009. (An introductory work that is head and shoulders above any of its predecessors.)

Crone, Patricia. *Meccan Trade and the Rise of Islam.* Princeton: Princeton University Press, 1987.

Horovitz, Josef. *The Earliest Biographies of the Prophet and Their Authors,* ed. Lawrence I. Conrad. SLAEI 11. Princeton: Darwin, 2002.

Juynboll, Gautier H. A. *Encyclopedia of Canonical Ḥadīth.* Leiden: Brill, 2007.

Motzki, Harald, ed. *The Biography of Muhammad: The Issue of the Sources.* Leiden: Brill, 2000.

Motzki, Harald, with Nicolet Boekhoff-van der Voort and Sean W. Anthony. *Analysing Muslim Traditions: Studies in Legal, Exegetical and Maghāzī Ḥadīth.* Leiden: Brill, 2010.

Powers, D. S. *Muḥammad Is Not the Father of Any of Your Men: The Making of the Last Prophet.* Philadelphia, PA: University of Pennsylvania Press, 2009.

Rubin, Uri. *The Eye of the Beholder: The Life of Muḥammad as Viewed by the Early Muslims.* SLAEI 5. Princeton: Darwin, 1995.

Schoeler, Gregor. *The Oral and Written in Early Islam.* Trans. Uwe Vagelpohl and ed. James E. Montgomery. Routledge: London, 2006.

———. *The Biography of Muḥammad: Nature and Authenticity*. Trans. Uwe Vagelpohl and ed. James E. Montgomery. Routledge: London, 2011.

Shoemaker, Stephen J. *The Death of a Prophet: The End of Muḥammad's Life and the Beginnings of Islam*. Philadelphia, PA: University of Pennsylvania Press, 2011.

Biographies of Muḥammad Translated into English

Several scholarly translations of prophetic biographies can be found, but most readers (and indeed many scholars) find the idea of reading them quite daunting inasmuch as they offer translations of massive, multivolumed Arabic compositions. Nevertheless, comparing the accounts and the approaches of the various author-compilers can be illuminating. Below I list the best translations of the biographies of Ibn Isḥāq (d. 150/767), al-Wāqidī (207/822), and Ibn Kathīr (774/1373).

Alfred Guillaume, trans. *The Life of Muḥammad: A Translation of Ibn Isḥāq's Sīrat Rasūl Allāh*. Karachi: Oxford University Press, 1978. (Guillaumes's translation attempts to reconstruct Ibn Isḥāq's work by inserting the portions missing from Ibn Hishām's recension from that preserved by the historian al-Ṭabarī (d. 310/923). The recension of al-Ṭabarī was subsequently retranslated when his massive universal history was translated into English as *The History of al-Ṭabarī*, general editor Ehsan Yarshater (Albany, NY: SUNY Press, 1985–2007). For the relevant volumes, *see* vol. 6, *Muḥammad at Mecca*, trans. W. Montgomery Watt and M. V. MacDonald (1987); vol. 7, *The Foundation of the Community*, trans. M. V. McDonald and W. Montgomery Watt (1987); vol. 8, *The Victory of Islam*, trans. Michael Fishbein (1997); and vol. 9, *The Last Years of the Prophet*, trans. Ismail K. Poonawala, (1990).

Rizwi Faizer, Amal Ismail, and Abdulkader Tayob, trans. *The Life of Muḥammad: al-Wāqidī's Kitāb al-Maghāzī*. New York: Routledge, 2011.

'Imād al-Dīn Ibn Kathīr. *The Life of the Prophet Muḥammad*, 4 vols. Trans. Trevor Le Gassick. Reading, UK: Garnet, 1998–2000.

Recommended in addition to the above is Tarif Khalidi's *Images of Muhammad: Narratives of the Prophet in Islam Across the Centuries* (New York: Doubleday, 2009), which collects samples of the prophetic biographies from diverse genres and traditions across the centuries.

Index

About the NYU Abu Dhabi Institute

The Library of Arabic Literature is supported by a grant from the NYU Abu Dhabi Institute, a major hub of intellectual and creative activity and advanced research. The Institute hosts academic conferences, workshops, lectures, film series, performances, and other public programs directed both to audiences within the UAE and to the worldwide academic and research community. It is a center of the scholarly community for Abu Dhabi, bringing together faculty and researchers from institutions of higher learning throughout the region.

NYU Abu Dhabi, through the NYU Abu Dhabi Institute, is a world-class center of cutting-edge research, scholarship, and cultural activity. The Institute creates singular opportunities for leading researchers from across the arts, humanities, social sciences, sciences, engineering, and the professions to carry out creative scholarship and conduct research on issues of major disciplinary, multidisciplinary, and global significance.

About the Typefaces

The Arabic body text is set in DecoType Naskh, designed by Thomas Milo and Mirjam Somers, based on an analysis of five centuries of Ottoman manuscript practice. The exceptionally legible result is the first and only typeface in a style that fully implements the principles of script grammar (*qawāʿid al-khaṭṭ*).

The Arabic footnote text is set in DecoType Emiri, drawn by Mirjam Somers, based on the metal typeface in the naskh style that was cut for the 1924 Cairo edition of the Qur'an.

Both Arabic typefaces in this series are controlled by a dedicated font layout engine. ACE, the Arabic Calligraphic Engine, invented by Peter Somers, Thomas Milo, and Mirjam Somers of DecoType, first operational in 1985, pioneered the principle followed by later smart font layout technologies such as OpenType, which is used for all other typefaces in this series.

The Arabic text was set with WinSoft Tasmeem, a sophisticated user interface for DecoType ACE inside Adobe InDesign. Tasmeem was conceived and created by Thomas Milo (DecoType) and Pascal Rubini (WinSoft) in 2005.

The English text is set in Adobe Text, a new and versatile text typeface family designed by Robert Slimbach for Western (Latin, Greek, Cyrillic) typesetting. Its workhorse qualities make it perfect for a wide variety of applications, especially for longer passages of text where legibility and economy are important. Adobe Text bridges the gap between calligraphic Renaissance types of the 15th and 16th centuries and high-contrast Modern styles of the 18th century, taking many of its design cues from early post-Renaissance Baroque transitional types cut by designers such as Christoffel van Dijck, Nicolaus Kis, and William Caslon. While grounded in classical form, Adobe Text is also a statement of contemporary utilitarian design, well suited to a wide variety of print and on-screen applications.

About the Editor-Translator

Sean W. Anthony (Ph.D., University of Chicago, 2009) is Assistant Professor of Islamic History in the Department of History at the University of Oregon. His research interests include the history of the late antique Near East, early Islam and the historical Muḥammad, and the formation of the canonical literatures of Islam. He is also the author of *The Caliph and the Heretic* (2012), a study of changing portraits of Islam's earliest and most notorious heretic, Ibn Saba', and their uses in sectarian polemics; and *Crucifixion and Death as Spectacle* (2014), a study of the changes the institution of crucifixion underwent in the Near East during the sixth to eighth centuries AD. He has also published numerous articles on the Qur'an and Hadith, early Shiʿism, late antique apocalypticism, and the historiography of early Islam.